Revolutionary Traveller:
Freeze-Frames from a Life

REVOLUTIONARY TRAVELLER

Freeze-Frames from a Life

John S. Saul

ARBEITER RING PUBLISHING • WINNIPEG

Arbeiter Ring Publishing
201E-121 Osborne Street
Winnipeg, Manitoba
Canada R3L 1Y4
www.arbeiterring.com

Printed in Canada by Transcontinental Printing
Cover by Robyn Taylor
Design by Relish Design Studio

MANITOBA ARTS COUNCIL CONSEIL DES ARTS DU MANITOBA 40 YEARS/ANS Canada Council for the Arts Conseil des Arts du Canada Canadian Heritage Patrimoine canadien

With assistance of the Manitoba Arts Council/Conseil des Arts du Manitoba.

We acknowledge the support of the Canada Council for our publishing program.

ARP acknowledges the financial support to our publishing activities of the Manitoba Arts Council/Conseil des Arts du Manitoba, Manitoba Culture, Heritage and Tourism, and the Government of Canada through the Book Publishing Industry Development Program (BPIDP).

Printed on 100% recycled paper.

Library and Archives Canada Cataloguing in Publication

Saul, John S., 1938-

Revolutionary traveller : freeze frames from a life / John S. Saul.

Includes bibliographical references and index.
ISBN 978-1-894037-37-2

1. Saul, John S., 1938-. 2. Apartheid--South Africa. 3. Liberty. 4. Equality. 5. Social justice. 6. Capitalism. 7. Political activists-- Canada--Biography. 8. Authors, Canadian (English)--20th century-- Biography. 9. Editors--Canada--Biography. I. Title.

JC571.S29 2009 323.092 C2008-906938-2

Published in South Africa by STE Publishers
2nd floor, The Mills 66 Carr Street Newtown
Johannesburg, South Africa

ISBN 978-1-920222-41-3

South African Association of Canadian Studies

This book received financial support from the South African Association of Canadian Studies, www.canadianstudies.co.za

OTHER BOOKS BY JOHN SAUL

Socialism in Tanzania: Politics and Policies, co-edited with Lionel Cliffe, 2 vols. (1972-3)

Essays on the Political Economy of Africa, with Giovanni Arrighi (1973)

Socialism and Participation: Tanzania's 1970 National Election, co-edited with the Electoral Studies Committee, University of Dar es Salaam (1974)

Canada and Mozambique (1974)

Rural Cooperation in Tanzania, co-edited with Lionel Cliffe and others (1975)

Words and Deeds: Canada, Portugal and Africa, with the Toronto Committee for the Liberation of Southern Africa (1976)

The State and Revolution in Eastern Africa (1979)

The Crisis in South Africa, co-authored with Stephen Gelb (1981, rev. ed. 1986)

O Marxismo-Leninismo no Contexto Moçambicano (1983)

A Difficult Road: The Transition to Socialism in Mozambique (1985)

Socialist Ideology and the Struggle for Southern Africa (1990)

Recolonization and Resistance: Southern Africa in the 1990s (1994)

Namibia's Liberation Struggle: The Two-Edged Sword, with Colin Leys, & others (1995)

Millennial Africa: Capitalism, Socialism, Democracy (2001)

The Next Liberation Struggle: Capitalism, Socialism and Democracy in Southern Africa (2005)

Development after Globalization: Theory and Practice for the Embattled South in a New Imperial Age (2006)

Decolonization and Empire: Contesting the Rhetoric and Reality of Resubordination in Southern Africa and Beyond (2007)

for EPS,
fellow-traveller

INTRODUCTION

Reflections of a Revolutionary Traveller

Occasionally, both in the global South and in northern countries like Canada, one hears the sneer, directed at those who choose to move around the globe as a way of making contact with, and contributing to, the cause of people struggling for more humane and equitable social outcomes, that he or she is nothing but a *revolutionary tourist*. There's sometimes something in the charge, of course. Certain people do like to revel in a range of exotica, including the hardships and struggles of those in the global South, as they toodle about, yet often the same people can never quite get around to engaging in very much struggle when back, surrounded by the comforts of home.

Still, those whom I've known who seek to play such an itinerant revolutionary role do so with a much more profound sense of commitment to those in struggle to transform the public weal, nationally or globally, than this. In fact, sticking with the same basic conceit, I'd choose to call them revolutionary travellers, not revolutionary tourists, and this book is, in aspiration at least, an account by one such would-be "traveller" of his own attempt to link up with such struggles and to bring them back home in order to demonstrate the ties between them... at both ends of the connection, one might say. In short, the book seeks to register the fact of solidarity as many, including myself, have attempted to live it—something that is, of course, easier to do when one becomes convinced that struggles around the world, in both southern Africa and Canada for example, are linked together by their focus upon a common enemy: capitalism, both local and global.

Better perhaps to state this latter premise baldly here, although some readers may now be tempted to merely throw up their hands in disgust at such "left-wing rant." It doesn't seem to me to be "rant" though, having arrived at my understanding of the ways of the world not merely through direct experience (as a "traveller," as it were) but also through the most rigorous kind of scholarly/scientific analysis, a few recent samples of which are included here.

I might also add here that I have, after the main lines of the present book were established, come across, and quite by chance, the invocation of a similar trope—the distinction between "tourist" and "traveller"—in another recent book also published by my present publisher Arbeiter Ring (in 2007): an exemplary study of photography by Susan Close entitled *Framing Identity*. Citing cultural critics like Jonathan Culler and Daniel Boorstin, she highlights the distinction they make, in Culler's case, between "the traveller [as] someone who has journeyed to another location for work as opposed to the tourist who travels for recreation" and, in Boorstin's, between "the traveller [who] was working at something [and] the tourist [who] was a pleasure seeker." But this is actually a usage somewhat oblique to my own main intent in also invoking such a distinction. For my use of the distinction contrasts the tourist who gawks to the traveller, the "revolutionary traveller," who seeks, as I have suggested, to act in solidarity with those engaged in struggle against a common global adversary: capitalist-driven imperialism.

WHAT ABOUT THE MEMOIR, more specifically, of a *revolutionary* traveller? Of course, one can write a memoir from any perspective one chooses, from an angle of vision chosen as idiosyncratically as one likes. But what if one is inclined to take seriously—and not merely to breeze by—the tense dialectic that must inevitably exist between personal voice and experience on the one hand and the broader patterns of social and economic structures that frame, and even up to a point shape, personal voice and experience on the other. For, once taken seriously, one finds that one can no longer fall back on the trope of mere "narrative" to defend the supposed idiosyncrasies of one's story. One must begin, as well, to discuss those structures—social patterns that have solidified into structures with some real determining effect—that the individual biography comes up against. In short, how we see such structures, how we analyze and evaluate them, inevitably becomes part of our story.

But how should we choose what structures to grant analytical weight to? I'll make no claims to a higher wisdom on this, but, once having asserted the above, my own story (sited as I feel it must be on the terrain of the structure-individual dialectic) cannot be simply an idiosyncratic and personalized narrative, or even a record of one person's existential choices, real as these so often have been. It becomes necessary, instead, to face up to the analytical challenges involved in reflecting upon the necessary *simultaneity* of narratives, private and public. And here I come back, beyond the existential, to my own sense, empirically grounded and much reflected upon, that the structure of economic production and distribution, of economic hierarchy and economic power, is amongst the most important of such structures. If this makes me a "Marxist" so be it, although it does not force me to imagine that some kind of crude economic reductionism is inherent in that label.

Certainly I would not assume even for a minute that the realities of political inequality and possible authoritarianism are not also shaping us, shaping our world, in very real and crucial ways—in ways linked to the world of social and economic inequality but certainly not reducible to them. I have recently argued[1] the pressing need to give due weight to both considerations of "political science" and "political economy" in any consideration of real-world situations. For example, practising democrats (in Africa and elsewhere) emphasize, accurately enough, the importance of "establishing democratic institutions in order both to discipline would-be autocrats and to help preempt the authoritarian tendencies" that tend so readily to become a (regrettable) attribute of political life, not least in Africa.

This is an approach I also seek to exemplify in the chapters that follow—and is something as true for the study of southern Africa as it is more generally. After all, the reckless course of a Robert Mugabe, so destructive of his own country and in defiance of the legitimate hopes and demands of Zimbabwe's people, is presently much more reflective of the drive for power and privilege by a demented dictator and other deeply implicated fellow members of his own country's ruling class than it is of any imperatives arising from the Empire of Capital. True, the arrogant drive to power of Mugabe and his vicious cohort is not without material foundations—but it is fuelled by its own grim "logic of power" too. It is also true that some of Mugabe's overseas critics—in the circles of power in the US, the UK, Canada—do stand poised to recolonize Zimbabwe for the Empire of Capital (as they have already succeeded in doing in nearby South Africa) when opportunity should permit—even if, in the interim, they don the plausible (though quite misleading) advocacy of democratic principles to attack Mugabe and company. So, no: a pox on both their houses. Zimbabweans must work for a better future than either Mugabe or "the West" can offer them.

Secondly, both practitioners and theorists also stress the potential importance of democratic institutions "to the reconciliation of 'differences'—especially those that are 'communally defined' by ethnicity, by religion and by race"—and to the facilitating of "order" and of "nation-building." In short the same need for care, balance, and circumspection as we give to the real weight and meaning of the "political" realm *per se* (as NOT being merely reducible to the "economic" realm) must also be given to various structures that define "difference": to racial hierarchies and discriminations, for example, but also, crucially, to modes of gender-based (read: male) dominance.

Of course, I have written extensively elsewhere[2] of the crucial importance of giving such an appropriate degree of analytical resonance not only to gender and racial but also to religious and ethnic variables within any viably Marxist approach to social reality. Nonetheless, the overall point should be clear: for me Marxism has nothing whatsoever to do with "economic reductionism"!

In fact, I have spent much of my writing life working on the troubled cusp of these various competing determinacies, their interactions, their contradictions, their mutual reinforcements. I am also aware that there are other structures besides, whether these lie deep in the inner psyche or out there in our vastly troubled ecosphere. Nonetheless, the fact remains that I find the economic structure to be pretty damned central and important—

so important, in fact, that any memoirist who take the dialectic between individual and social structure at all seriously cannot really remain neutral, either in their writing or in their lives as they choose to live them, with reference to the alternatives that seem available in that sphere. To live is to choose. And most central here is a choice, unavoidable for anyone who chooses to live in the real world (and yes, to paraphrase Dr. Johnson's famous retort to Bishop Berkeley regarding "reality", the world's structures, and not least its dominant economic structures, are very, very *real*: kick them and see, especially if you are amongst the poorest of the poor of the global South).

Moreover, the choice, as regards the economic structure that can and must frame our lives, seems straightforward: for capitalism or against it! *Hier stehe ich*: I can do no other. No other, but to choose, as any good Marxist would, against capitalism (though also for gender equality, for meaningful democracy, and against racism). For capitalism is a socioeconomic system that has meant, both historically and contemporaneously, the highlighting of an all too often unsavoury "possessive individualism;"[3] the spawning of extreme socioeconomic inequalities especially on a global scale (see chapter 7, below); the embracing, for the human species, of the primacy of personal and social aggression above all else; the negating of any real democracy in favour of the power of money (and the monied); and the jeopardizing, increasingly, of the human habitat in which we find ourselves. Of course, I am well aware that many, indeed most, in my own society—Canada being among the more affluent countries in the malignant global hierarchy we presently know—"choose" to take such a system for granted, either tacitly as the commonsense of their daily lives or more actively as a self-conscious and positively embraced ideological choice. Nonetheless, many of us have instead chosen to opt *against* capitalism and the global hierarchy it fosters, and *for* a vision of a more just, equitable and productive social order and the range of concrete struggles necessary to realize such a vision.

I think, to anticipate my case in this book, socialism embodies this vision and this kind of a meaningful hope. But this is not to say that the practice of realizing an alternative to capitalism can be an easy one: the twentieth century was a graveyard of any too simple a hope for a socialist alternative. Indeed, as the new century dawned we have seen, principally, the squaring-off of the self-righteous advocates of capitalist global assertion against the advocates of equally self-righteous and diverse particularisms (ethnic, religious and the like). In short, the centre, the socialist centre, has not held. Nonetheless the choice remains open to humanity as to how better to live, how to live at one with our fellows and with our grievously threatened environment, what to live for, and why? It ain't over 'til it's over, after all.

BUT DON'T LET ME TURN YOU OFF with too much Marxism, too much socialism, right off the top. After all, you may still want to know what the memoir of a *revolutionary traveller* is actually going to look like, especially if it is to be about—as of course it must be—"solidarity." At minimum, such an emphasis tends to shift the book's centre of gravity away from any too exclusive focus upon the author himself and instead onto other actors and situations—onto those, in fact, with whom a relationship of solidarity is being established. It is this story, their story, that I try principally to tell here, drawing in my observation of and participation with those in struggle over the past five decades.

What then, specifically, has the choice for "solidarity," for the role of "revolutionary traveller," actually meant in my life? As the following pages will document, I have sought to make real my identification with those whom Frantz Fanon once termed "the wretched of the earth" and, in particular, with the people in struggle in southern Africa. The link that identification has sought to concretize has been one forged, to begin with, during seven years spent teaching in Tanzania in the 1960s and early 1970s. There I met and talked not only with Tanzanians and other East Africans but also with many cadres from all of the movements struggling for liberation from a particularly intransigent brand of white minority rule further south. The sensibility and commitment I developed there also deepened back home when, upon my return in the 1970s, I was able to work with others, in Toronto and elsewhere in the global North, to act, through our newly formed (1972) Committee for the Liberation of Portugal's African

Colonies/TCLPAC, soon the Toronto Committee for the Liberation of Southern Africa/TCLSAC, to forge positive and mutually satisfactory links with the liberation struggles in southern Africa.

Note, however, that our solidarity with those struggles cut both ways, including deep into Canada itself: my comrades in Canada, like myself, were determined not to be tourists in our own country! From the very beginning we sought to explore Canada's own far from savoury role (via our mining companies, for example, and our own government's two-faced economic, diplomatic and NATO-defined role in support of Portugal, Rhodesia and South Africa in that part of the world), and to link to Canadians negatively affected by the same companies and by our government's own shabby and capitalist-defined policies at home. This is the way in which we defined our remit, then, and it also became a defining principle of *Southern Africa Report*, when TCLSAC ultimately launched that magazine in the 1980s.

But it was a principle I also learned through other kinds of involvements, notably with *This Magazine* throughout the 1970s. Previously entitled by its founders *This Magazine is About Schools*, the magazine sustained its leftward bent even as it broadened its scope in the 1970s. I was pleased to be asked to join its editorial team shortly after my return to Canada from Tanzania. I seized upon the opportunity since, in such a setting, I could hope to sustain my own quest for solidarity through a closer connection to admirably engaged Canadian-based writers and activists than I might have been easily able to find otherwise. Indeed, I was asked, long years later (in 2006), to write, for a special fortieth anniversary issue, my thoughts on any concept that spoke to my time on the editorial board and also to the continuing history of the magazine itself. I chose the word "solidarity," writing of it as follows:

> Just back from almost a decade in Africa, I spent every Friday afternoon for the next ten years (including most of the 1970s) huddled around Rick Salutin's kitchen table, hatching *This Magazine*s with my one-time prof Mel Watkins and John and Lorraine and Rosemary and the rest, advocating left nationalism and contributing occasional bits of whimsical writing. But basically I stuck to my last as a convinced supporter of liberation struggle in southern Africa and beyond, while also underscoring, pen in hand, the all too

> comfortable role that an only mildly beleaguered— by American imperialism—"official Canada" (and Canadian capital) played on the wrong side of the various fights for freedom that we at the magazine cared about. Myself deeply involved in the anti-apartheid movement at the time, I was pleased to see how genuinely the others, activists and writers on diverse fronts, cared about such issues and the response from readers was gratifying too. "One struggle, many fronts"— the very idea of "solidarity"— was as true then as it is now and I also learned to make the connection to real issues here and to real Canadians in the course of my time with the mag. No small flag for *This* to have kept flying, of course, and no less needed now, in these dark Harperesque times of brutal aggression and smug global self-righteousness.

In short, I learned a great deal about the meaning of the struggle for justice and equality in Canada from my decade with *This Magazine* and from my fellow editors. Moreover, I became even more convinced by the *This Magazine* experience of a need, one that we had already felt in TCLPAC from the outset, to work to also embed our solidarity initiatives in Canadian struggles, and to always question the entire range of Canada's "official" links, many of them quite exploitative, to southern Africa. What was being forged here, we increasingly felt, was not just an identification with and support for those at the receiving end of white-faced oppression in southern Africa—for this was something that could all too easily become merely "charitable" and therefore rather patronizing if we let it. No, we were increasingly seeking, as suggested, genuine *solidarity* with the people of southern Africa, comradeship with them in a shared struggle against oppressive structures both world-wide and local.

It is not surprising, then, that when I eventually left the editorial fold of *This Magazine* after ten years it was to help bring a more magazine-like weight to our new *Southern Africa Report*. Perhaps, with SAR, I would myself be able to call on some of the lessons I'd learned through ten years with *This Magazine*. But we had already had a somewhat more modest but eminently presentable cyclostyled magazine, *TCLSAC Reports*, for some years to build on. Moreover, there was a shifting cast of hard-working comrades who now were to meet virtually every week for the next fifteen years, not least Joe Vise whose technical know-how converted our texts, rounded up from writers across the southern African region and elsewhere (including in Canada), into a crisp and authoritative magazine four or five times a year, and Margie Adam who imagined the covers that gave our magazine its distinctive stamp. In fact, it was difficult not to be pleased, many years later (in early 2008), when we received from one of the editors of the excellent new South African magazine *Amandla!* a note stating that "the last issue of the *Southern Africa Report* was a sad day for some of us and an important inspiration behind the launch of *Amandla!*"

As I note below, the entire first section of this "memoir" is really one man's running account of the struggle for southern Africa. In order to convey that changing reality, I draw principally on my own writings of the time in both *SAR* and in *This Magazine*, as well as in the New York-based *Monthly Review* (at whose press I was simultaneously publishing a number of my book-length contributions to an understanding of Africa as well). "Freeze-frames" I've called them: that moment in film when the motion in the motion picture stops, when the storyline, at a particularly salient point, freezes in the frame. Salient, yes, but the story continues, as does one's life, as does the struggle itself.

Such moments, such "freeze-frames," do not exhaust my own writings on the developments of the forty years they cover, of course.[4] Nonetheless, the various articles (especially those included in this book's first five chapters), published as they were in diverse magazines over forty years and composed in the heat of various moments of ongoing political struggle, are not random in import. Taken together and linked here by means of an ongoing narrative, they form the beginnings of a history both of the struggle for a liberated southern Africa—but also, with respect to our own country's global involvements as epitomized by our southern African policies, of a struggle for a more just Canada as well.

An autobiography too? Not quite. For I do not in this book reflect at any great length on the process that moved me, from a placid home in North Toronto, to embrace a more revolutionary vision of the world. Nor do I seek to probe why such a person as me came to work, albeit not perhaps in the most appropriate ways or with any very staggering success, both to help rein capitalism in and to also face down the smug sense of western/white racial and cultural superiority that has accompanied (not least in Canada) capitalism's present global triumphs. Nor do I devote much time to the path that led me from Toronto, via the US and the UK, to Tanzania where my heterodox view of the workings of the world was first most pointedly formed. Indeed, I will say little enough even about that Tanzanian experience (although I emphasize my years there in chapter 1), formative though it certainly was in so many ways. Such experiences would perhaps provide the stuff of an alternative, more self-conscious "autobiography." Here though, and as stated, the main focus is on the kind of solidarity I came to forge with those struggling against global capitalism, principally in southern Africa, and on the dramatic nature of those struggles themselves.

Of course, even while so engaged, I continued to reflect upon and to teach and write about the broader global conditions that have framed the struggles that most preoccupied me, both in their victories and in their setbacks. These are well recorded in published form elsewhere. Below—in Part 3 (Section 1)—I merely include some of my most recent reflections on those conditions, these being, in their own right, "freeze-frames" of an ongoing intellectual journey: "freeze-frames" of imperialism and of the novel "Empire of Capital" that now wages war, both economic and otherwise, upon the global South; of the renewed "recolonization" imposed by that Empire, especially on the African continent; and of the resistance that emerges to confront the new imperial enemy, sometimes still in broadly socialist and gender emancipatory terms although sometimes in the much narrower terms of religious and ethnic fundamentalism.

Then, in Part 3 (Section 2), I turn inward, not away from the struggle, but with the intention of relating my political and left-intellectual commitments to other dimensions of the life I have tried to live. Again, I will attempt to convey some of this broader sense of life—my life, at any rate—lived through relevant texts that I have produced along the way. For these texts reflect, in effect, my own continuing effort to not allow a commitment to "the struggle" and to the radical transformation of global political and economic structures to deaden my sensitivity to the "human"—a reality that I also sought to access through my reading and writing, my listening and my playing. I hope some of my thoughts on these varied fronts may be of interest; certainly they have helped define whoever it is that I have become. Even more important, as I add in a final brief "Conclusion" (an essential grace note to such a text), have been friends and family. I begin that note with some brief reflections on mortality, thoughts occasioned by my near fatal accident several years ago. For friends and family were crucially important to my recovery.

But, needless to say, they have been important to my life more generally. To the various comrades whose presence is either mentioned or implied in the subsequent chapters of this book, I owe a great debt of gratitude. I owe a great deal too to those who, quite concretely, have made this book happen both in Canada and in South Africa. First off, my thanks on that score to John Samson and his team at Winnipeg's Arbeiter Ring Publishing who from the first grasped what I had in mind for the book, liked the sound of it and vigorously encouraged me throughout the process of bringing it to market in finished form. I feel there is a particular appropriateness to this Winnipeg link as well; after all, my father was born in Winnipeg, my grandfather and grandmother were both graduates of the University of Manitoba in the late nineteenth century (my grandmother one of the first woman to so graduate apparently), and my great-grandfather Saul was one of the best damn Irish stone-cutters that the city has ever seen. (My mother, a Shannon from Sault Ste. Marie, was, like the Sauls, descended, in the male line, from refugees to Canada from the Irish Famine of the 1840s and '50s). In South Africa, Reedwaan Vally at STE was equally enthusiastic to see the book published in that country and in the southern African region of the continent (a possibility I myself deeply cherished). Moreover, he was able to do so in part through the assistance of the well-known poet Ingrid de Kok Fiske of the University of Cape Town—and of the South African Association of Canadian Studies of which she is currently the chair; the Association invited me to give several lectures in South Africa early in 2009, and later also helped with the book's publication.

Finally, though, the book is dedicated to my wife, Pat Saul, who has accompanied me, as a fellow "revolutionary traveller," on our joint journey of almost fifty years' duration, shared with me the joy of our children, their spouses, and our four grand-children, supported me firmly during my own hard times—while also forging an impressive career of her own. Thank you, EPS: to you I dedicate this book.

---

1. John. S. Saul, *The Next Liberation Struggle: Capitalism, Socialism and Democracy in Southern Africa* (Toronto, Durban, New York and London: Between the Lines, University of KwaZulu-Natal Press, Monthly Review Press and The Merlin Press, 2005).
2. See chapter 3, "Identifying Class, Classifying Difference," of my *Development After Globalization* (Delhi, London and Durban: Three Essays Collective, Zed Press and University of KwaZulu/Natal Press).
3. To quote the title, and evoke the content, of a fine old book by my erstwhile professor at the University of Toronto, Brough Macpherson, *The Political Theory of Possessive Individualism* (Oxford: Clarendon Press, 1962). As I shall again note below, one of the highlights of my graduate studies at the University of Toronto was to take a course in political theory from Macpherson in which the then draft chapters of this crucial book were amongst our essential seminar reading assignments.
4. For these an interested reader might refer my contributions to many volumes in the exemplary annual series of volumes, the *Socialist Register*, as well as to my various books, over the years, of more scholarly hue. For the latter, see my list of previously published works in the opening pages of this book.

Part One
The Struggle

PREFACE

The Struggle

On Southern Africa ... and Canada

I'd already been on the move before I plugged into the struggles for liberation from white minority rule in southern Africa — from a B.A. and M.A. in Toronto to the further study of political Science (and, increasingly, "African Studies") in Princeton, New Jersey and in London, England for starters, still a "tourist" and with the goal of professional qualification still principally in mind. But perhaps I was, if only very gradually, becoming a more revolutionary one, thanks, not least, to radical teachers and friends like H. H. Wilson at Princeton and Ralph Miliband in London and also to some agreeable and challenging fellow students.

And to various instructive experiences along the way: serving my time (my social-democratic moment) as election-day organizer for a failed campaign in the York South constituency by the NDP's David Lewis and under the tutelage of my friend (and the campaign's head) Gerry Caplan; helping to organize at Princeton a counter-rally and large demonstration, drawn from activists from New York and right across New Jersey, to protest the invited presence, by the University's Whig-Clio Society, of Mississippi governor and radical racist Ross Barnett when he came to speak on campus; picketing in Nassau Square in downtown Princeton, with a handful of others and to the jeers of a mass of posh undergrads, Kennedy's actions during the Cuban Missile Crisis; fleeing charging horses in the environs of London's American Embassy while demonstrating against America's growing role in Vietnam; and even, a little later, being present in Paris during the May of 1968. But it wasn't until my wife and I moved on from London to Tanzania that I could really begin to think of myself more as a "traveller," in the sense indicated in my introduction, than as a tourist.

We were lucky in our timing, of course. Pat and I came to Tanzania in 1965 for the period of six months to a year to gather materials for my presumed doctoral thesis on rural development in that country. But, given the drama of the moment in that country, we ended up staying for the next seven years. Exciting years too and perhaps any memoir of mine should properly start with those. They were years of family growth to begin with: our two children, Nick and Jo, were both born in Dar, at the Aga Khan Hospital, Pat's room overlooking the sunrise and the Indian Ocean. They were years of our personal growth, too. But these were also, as luck would have it, the Arusha Declaration years, years of African assertion and self-confidence that, if ultimately less than the full success we all hoped them to be, were indeed notable times, for Tanzanians and expatriates alike. To our years there I will turn in my first chapter.

In 1972, however, we returned to Canada, fresh from the Tanzania years, but also, in my case, coming directly out of the bush of northern Mozambique's Tete Province where I had accompanied a group of Frelimo guerrillas into the semi-liberated areas of their country (see chapter 2, below). The echo of the words of Frelimo's President, Samora Machel, in my back garden immediately upon my return from Tete and on the eve of my departure with my family to come back to Toronto still rang in my ears: "The knowledge of our country's struggles is, in your own country, still this much" (and he held up his thumb and forefinger positioned merely a millimeter apart). "You must go and help us to do something about that." It was not "an order" exactly but it was very difficult to ignore—and, in any case, it fit well with my own evolving thoughts on the matter.

Of course, I could not do it alone, and besides there were others in Toronto and elsewhere in Canada who were already engaged with liberation support and anti-apartheid activities. There were also a lot of fresh recruits to such a struggle, some returned from assignments with CUSO and other Canadian NGOs in Africa, and some younger people whose concern for the situation in southern Africa was, perhaps, a bit more vicarious, but no less real and deeply felt for that fact. One comrade I found my way to quickly was Murray MacInness, who was not too long back from Angola from which, as a United Church missionary, he had been expelled by the Portuguese for his strong opinions and tireless activities with and on behalf of the Angolans themselves. Together, along with a growing group of others—my brother, Bill, and my friends Jonathan and Nancy Barker, all three just back themselves from stints in Tanzania, Judith Marshall and Kae Elgie, Joe and Mary Vise, Kim Jarvi, Doug Sider (an undergraduate at Victoria College in the U of T who actually decided during TCLPAC's very early meetings that he should switch to medical school, so that, upon graduation, he would have something real and tangible to offer the Mozambicans and then did precisely that!)—we started the Toronto Committee for the Liberation of Portugal's African Colonies/TCLPAC (subsequently, with the fall of Portuguese colonialism, renamed as the Toronto Committee for the Liberation of Southern Africa/TCLSAC).

Over the next several decades these comrades and many others lobbied and campaigned in support of the liberation movements in the region, and, through writings, meetings and more dramatic kinds of action, against the involvements of the Canadian government and Canadian corporations on "the wrong side" in southern Africa. We sponsored a process of community awareness by a myriad of events, notably our Cinema of Solidarity series, showing films about various progressive struggles in Canada and elsewhere around the world to packed-house audiences at the Medical Sciences Auditorium at the University of Toronto.

Indeed, our events were becoming so salient as to attract reprisals as on the occasion of our presenting to Frelimo's North American representative, Shafrudine Khan, the funds that we had raised to purchase a truck to assist Frelimo in its armed struggle and its humanitarian activities in and along the borders of its liberated zones in northern Mozambique. With most of us settled in the hall, the Western Guard, a racist and right-wing Toronto group (shouting "White Power! This Meeting is Over!"), struck against those left in the lobby at various ticket-taking, book and information tables (including my own eight-year-old son.) The TCLPAC members, my brother included, beat the intruders back, but not before some of our own blood was shed, and the Western Guard had accomplished considerable destruction, of our various tables still in the lobby and of one huge window at the end of the lobby through which they hurled a chair. But then the meeting continued, Shafrudine Khan himself merely noting "that we (Frelimo) are quite used to this kind of thing." It was a good meeting, too.

As noted above, this kind of activity was consolidated by another experience, my invitation, not long after return, to join the editorial collective of *This Magazine*. Indeed, I have already suggested that many of the articles, the "freeze-frames" that help form the substance of the first two sections of the present book—comprising as they do a kind of intermittent chronicle, broken down by decades, of the southern African struggle over almost forty years—were originally written for a range of outlets, not least *This Magazine, Southern Africa Report* and *Monthly Review*.

Indeed, it strikes me forcibly as I scan the old copies of *SAR*, that a companion volume which collected the editorials we wrote in each issue over the fifteen years of our existence would also comprise a useful parallel "Baedeker" to the struggle in southern Africa and in Canada over the number of years that Section 1 seeks to knit together from my own pieces. In any case, as the various articles and extracts—these "freeze-frames," moments frozen in time as part of an on-going struggle and, more personally, of an on-going memoir—collected here will evidence, I continued to follow events in southern Africa directly: I frequently travelled there and I was also to teach there again—in Mozambique and in South Africa. Yet this all began with another trip, in 1972, that was fateful (for me, in terms of my own autobiography certainly!): the visit to the liberated areas of Mozambique described, subsequently, at the outset of chapter 2 in this section.

CHAPTER ONE

The 1960s

Tanzania[1]

Insofar as this book has any autobiographical intent it would, as I have said, actually have to start its account quite early on. And by this I don't just mean, say, with my transition from diapers to short pants or from high school to university. More important for purposes of the present chapter it would require a much more detailed account than I can hope to offer here of my early and formative experience in Tanzania (and in the liberated areas of Mozambique) when my lifelong commitment to Africa, and particularly to the southern portion of that continent, was shaped.

Thus my African travels began in Tanzania where my wife and I arrived at an especially exciting time. It was clear that President Julius Nyerere, whatever the strengths and weaknesses of his various presuppositions and practices, was, on a continental and world scale, a figure of enormous importance and consequence. And he was about to carry his people and his country significantly to the left in many ways, if not all, that were extremely promising. I wrote a lot about the country and its experiments in what Nyerere liked to call "African Socialism" then and I have also done so since. I will not repeat that material at length here, except to quote two paragraphs, reflecting my own mixed assessment of what Nyerere and his colleagues accomplished during the Arusha Declaration years, drawn from my most recent attempt to think through the meaning of the Tanzanian experience during that period. On the one hand,

> ... it is important to underscore the correctness of the basic premise from which Nyerere's policies flowed: the global capitalist system did not then, does not now, serve Africa well. Here, in Nyerere's words [as I quoted some of his post-retirement intervention criticizing the IMF and other global actors] was ... a spirit of proto-socialist critique that makes Nyerere's writing so important a resource for a new generation of Africans as they reactivate their struggle for social, political and economic transformation along, dare I predict it, socialist lines.

Yet, as I also wrote, certain more negative lessons of the failed Tanzanian experiment were equally clear:

> Speaking personally, however, [the lesson] has been a painful and difficult one to learn over the years. Indeed, I learned it perhaps even more as a fellow traveller of Frelimo's post-liberation, left-developmental socialist project in Mozambique [see chapters 2-4, below] than I did in Tanzania. A socialist aspiration of some kind—a challenge to the illogic of actually existing capitalism, both globally and as it works its malign purposes on the African continent itself—must be at the core of any meaningful response that Africa is eventually to make to the crisis in which it finds itself. We learn that positive lesson from, amongst others but not least, Julius Nyerere. But, as that aspiration reemerges politically, it must be a far more democratic project than anything Africa has witnessed in the name of socialism heretofore. In the end ... we learn that negative lesson, too, from, amongst others but not least, Julius Nyerere.[2]

Thus, while praising his attacks upon domestic class formation and ethnic divisiveness, and his support of southern African liberation, I was negatively struck by such occurrences as the high-handed assistance that Nyerere afforded to Sam Nujoma of Namibia when the latter was under fire from many within his own movement, protecting Nujoma from such criticisms by conniving in the arbitrary jailing of democratic claimants in SWAPO-in-exile. In addition, there were such moments as the smashing of progressive strikes at the Mount Carmel Rubber Factory and elsewhere, and as, most dramatically, TANU's crushing of the Ruvuma Development Association, an exemplary rural initiative and one apparently fully dedicated to the realization of Nyerere's own goal of "rural socialism."[3]

It was in this complex setting, then, that my own deepening understanding of Tanzania and of Africa was crystallized and not least through my own political practice. And the main focus of that practice was, for the seven years I was employed at the University in Dar es Salaam, both my own teaching as well as closely related university-focused struggles across a broad front. For such work was taking place within an environment that made teaching, like everything else in that country at the time, profoundly political.

Indeed everything in Tanzania seemed to be in movement just then—and this had become all the more true by the time (1966) I was asked to sign on there to teach at the University (though it was, until 1970 when it obtained its complete autonomy as the University of Dar es Salaam, formally a "University College" within the University of East Africa). Indeed, I was to spend seven formative years, on a contract at first arranged by the university through Canada's External Aid—even as the changes in the air took concrete form in the Arusha Declaration, the document that signalled a dramatic shift to the left for the country. This is not the place to debate the merits of the precise leftward steps the country was prepared to take under Nyerere's leadership; I have done that myself, as I've suggested, and so have many others. Of more immediate significance for me was that the winds of change spawned by that Declaration were soon to be felt dramatically at the new University where I now taught.

And the growing sense there was that the institution, though recently launched, had been crafted, under Nyerere's own guidance and with the advice and assistance of various well-intentioned but entirely orthodox advisors (like Cranford Pratt of the University of Toronto who became the University College's first Principal), in far too conventionally liberal and western a manner: their work, "creative" enough in a narrow sense if you like, but terribly unimaginative with respect to the requirements of the time and of the place. The University now needed, it seemed to many, to be significantly altered to articulate more clearly a Tanzanian ethos and a socialist aspiration. This overall sense was palpably Tanzanian in origin and general thrust. Nonetheless, the ironic fact was that there were still relatively few Tanzanians actually on the faculty at the university. As a result, a larger responsibility than might otherwise have been the case fell, necessarily, upon the expatriate faculty to take a more significant role in defining the changes that a recast

Tanzanian university might now require within the country's new orientation.

A basic rethinking of the university was triggered by two significant events. One of these was a large student protest (1966) against their being expected to enter National Service for two years after graduation. Nyerere and others were enraged by what they saw to be the effrontery of this apparently selfish action and immediately had the students who massed in protest on the State House lawn rounded up, returned to the campus to collect their belongings, and immediately dispatched by busses to their home villages (only to return to the campus after many months if the local population were to confirm their worthiness to return). Those employed at the university were encouraged to see these elitist attitudes (as they were interpreted, correctly, by the government) that so scarred the bulk of university students as evidence of the fact that the university had failed to serve any developmental purpose very useful to Tanzania itself.

Secondly, the student crisis of 1966 was taken by Nyerere himself as one among a number of significant indications that his own developmental plans, as well as those of the country as a whole, were markedly askew (the students, after all, were not entirely out of step with the prevailing attitudes of the elite as a whole). In fact, the university's own crisis was amongst the crucial events that moved Tanzania to articulate, through its new Arusha Declaration (and other related statements of novel intent), a much more explicit socialist ideology as guide to its ongoing development efforts. This broader initiative merely intensified further the pressure on the university to recast itself to serve the new, more clearly specified, goals of the country more effectively.

ONE IMMEDIATE RESULT was a well-attended working conference on redefining and recasting the University in which I, like so many others, was actively involved—in my case, as a member of a group of nine faculty members who put forward a particularly radical reading of the problem and of possible steps that might be taken. I had already been involved in one initiative, taken in the wake of the first confrontation at the university (the "sending down" of large numbers of students referred to above), when I joined with

Dennis Phombeah, a then senior Tanzanian civil servant whom I had known in London during his time with the Tanzanian High Commission there, and Roger Murray (who would become a life-long friend) then working with the ruling political party, TANU, to prepare and submit a memo to Nyerere arguing the case for some dramatic remedial action at the University.[4]

Now, for the conference on the university and in the context of the newly minted Arusha Declaration, the proposals of our larger group of university-sited faculty members invoked, among other things, a sharp critique of the intellectual methods of work being followed at the university, especially the division of departments and fields into sharply distinguished subject matters that, we argued, thereby robbed students of the opportunity to earn the kind of totalizing perspective on social reality that could really provide the intellectual basis for a socialist understanding. The document that we prepared—included here in one summary version, with a covering letter written, once again, by Phombeah, that was sent directly to the President—became, in a longer, much more detailed, and also more widely circulated, version, a focus of considerable debate at the Conference itself.[5] Though many academics, both expatriates and western-trained Tanzanians, were sharply critical of our attack upon their presumed monopoly of highly specialized expertise we were successful to the extent that our document became one core focus of the discussion at the conference.

A. Dennis Phombeah's covering letter addressed to both the President of Tanzania (Nyerere) and to the 2nd Vice-President (Rashidi Kawawa)

THIS PROPOSAL WHICH I AM FORWARDING is the work of a small study group, most of whose members are teachers at the University College [the names follow].

The recommendations for radical change both in organization and curriculum of the so called "Common course" is based upon a political analysis of the existing education offered at the University college. Despite the youth of the University College, these inherited educational patterns and values ["inherited" from prevailing Western models, needless to say] have already sunk quite deep roots and themselves now present a major obstacle to the development of a socialist culture and intelligentsia in Tanzania. Our thinking about education is heavily influenced by these ideas. If we think over a long term, the argument for daring and creative innovation which will make our university a motor force rather than a rearguard or passive spectator in our socialist development should be taken very seriously.

The important part of the memorandum is the attempt to devise a way of changing the way our students think about society and culture and development. The intention here is obviously a socialist one, but one that goes beyond the external grafting of a few hours weekly of "political education" or "orientation" lectures by political and national leaders to bring the university into closer lines with political trends. If this could be done from within, by some such proposal as this, it would relieve us of a great deal of worry and work regarding the university.

The syllabus offered clearly needs more work, and would meet with a lot of objections from existing departments. Committed socialists at the University College are rather few, and will always be put in a minority in Faculty and Council meetings, or at the forthcoming University Conference. I think the Government and Party will have to give a lead as to the depth and direction of internal change we would like to see on the Hill. This means that we must ask ourselves whether the various small changes and gestures of goodwill which have recently come out of the university will be enough. The main fear of members of this group I have talked with seems to be that such partial proposals do not go to the root of the problem, which is contained in the intellectual assumptions and values of "western education"—which still exercises domination over the University College, Dar es Salaam, as over all similar post-colonial universities.

Dennis Phombeah (signed)

B. The document itself as submitted to President Nyerere by the "Group of nine lecturers"

THE ARUSHA DECLARATION HAS BROUGHT INTO SHARPER FOCUS the whole question of the nature and role of our educational institutions. Tanzania is now firmly committed to the course of self reliance and socialism; yet the implementation of this option for the organization and curricula of our schools and colleges has scarcely begun to be examined.

The position of the University College, the apex of the educational pyramid and agency for the production of leading administrative and technical personnel, is of critical importance in the whole strategy of Tanzanian socialism and development. A disjunction between the assumptions and practices of this institution and the values and goals of the society as a whole has very alarming consequences. The dangers inherent in this situation are given some prominence in the [aforementioned] paper "An Approach to the University College Problems"[6] and this argument and proposal are intended to find some solution to the problems identified in that earlier memorandum.

Our starting point is that the University can and should play an important role in the development of socialism in Tanzania. It has the obligation and possibility to produce committed intellectuals, men and women who share a distinctive and unified world outlook, a particular way of perceiving, comprehending and understanding man's social universe. In short, the University must produce people who think and act as socialists.

At present, however, the University is doing no such thing. The formation which students receive has so far resulted in the conspicuous production of non-socialist modes of thought. There are of course many reasons for this. But the most fundamental is the actual intellectual organization of the University along lines inherited from Western models the basic assumptions of which have remained exempt from theoretical criticism and practical transformation. In particular it is the *fragmentation* of perspectives entailed by separate academic disciplines which provides the main obstacle to the development of an integral and coherent vision of man in history and society. Instead, these divisions—*if they are not subsumed and contained within a wider framework of understanding*—operate to produce technicians and technocrats with highly specialized knowledge but little or no comprehension of social development as a unitary process.

The increasing specialization of knowledge, and the constitution of these "specialties" into self-sufficient academic disciplines each with their own "laws," theory and techniques, can be related to the historical development of capitalism. Each area or realm of knowledge becomes more intensive and monopolistic of energy and intellect, thus rendering more and more difficult any *comprehensive* understanding or questioning of capitalist economy, society and culture as a system. In capitalist countries, this fragmentation has certainly facilitated the production of uncritical and conformist intellectual practitioners, though the fragmented disciplines themselves may attain a high degree of sophistication and elaboration in their own terms.

It may be argued that the long-term tendency of this type of education leads to the impoverishment of "intellectuals" themselves and of collective culture in general, and is thus wasteful and detrimental even in a developed society. But there can be no doubt that an underdeveloped society, and especially one such as Tanzania that is committed to socialism, simply cannot afford to waste its educated and intellectual resources in this way.

The sheer loss of potential involved is already amply demonstrated. Students formed in this sort of intellectual environment are almost inevitably elitist, technocratic, devoid of socialist perspective or creativity. The students rusticated following their demonstration against the White Paper on National Service cannot be returned to the University with any confidence of a "change of heart"—that is, of intellectual and moral conviction—so long as the present orientation and assumptions remain unchallenged. An illustration of the degree of alienation built into this system can be found in the response of our academic economists to the question of nationalization in Tanzania. Most characterized it as a "political" move, to which they were prepared to give their support, while yet criticizing it as "economically" unsound. In reality, the nationalization programme can very well provide Tanzanians with the discipline and self-determination that are an indispensable prerequisite for breaking through the imprisoning circle of poverty and underdevelopment. But the arbitrary rupture between what is "economic" and what is "political" prevents professional economists from grasping an elementary process of this nature.

A reevaluation of the inherited disciplinary organization and structure is a normal part of the overall process of decolonization of education. It is doubly necessary when the national society is seriously engaged upon a difficult struggle to break with capitalist institutions and values and to create an original socialism.

If it is accepted that disciplinary fragmentation functions to inhibit the development of a coherent socialist vision, it would appear that come countervailing organizational and intellectual programme is an indispensable element of the "re-education" of our students. How could this be conceived?

Very broadly, the alternatives that suggest themselves are these:

a. Importing more socialist teachers within existing disciplines.
b. Giving more socialist "content " to existing disciplines.
c. Creation of an Inter-Disciplinary Committee supervising some hours weekly of "Common Instruction."
d. Creation of an autonomous new Department.

In our view, it would not be enough simply to insert additional socialist staff into existing departments or further "socialist" content into the existing syllabus. The present divisions are too deeply entrenched, both organizationally and intellectually, for such dissipated attack. Again, a refurbished "Common Course" that is merely an aggregate of these disciplines loosely coordinated by an interdepartmental committee would certainly not be sufficient to overcome fragmented perspectives or foster a serious and unified approach to social and historical reality. The kind of approach that is needed is one which would enable the student to conceptualize the various analytically fragmented fields of man's activity—"economic," "social," "political," "legal," "artistic," "scientific," "religious" and so on—as in reality dynamically interrelated. The shattered and abstracted "parts" must be reconstituted into their real totality, in terms of which they will be analyzed and made meaningful. The object of developing this kind of synthetic awareness of the forces and structures constituting a social totality would be precisely to make possible a new way of thinking about Tanzanian (or East African?) realities and problems in all their concreteness and specificity. This new type of refection, and of allied research, would in turn transform the content and meaning of the specialized or technical knowledge at present imparted through discrete disciplines. The organizational precondition for the elaboration of this alternative and rigorous mode of thought is a framework within which a *new methodology* can be developed.

It seems to us that a completely revolutionized conception of the Common Course might provide the key. This should be sited in an autonomous Department of Social Analysis. The Head of this Department might initially draw upon selected staff from other departments; but in the long run he must develop his own departmental staff. Recruitment should be carefully filtered to obtain teachers oriented towards, and creative in, this kind of pioneering work. The course offered would be integral and coherent. It would aim to evolve a theoretical framework, a scientific approach, and an accumulating body of empirical research. The course would be compulsory, and should occupy not less than 1/3 of the student's time in each of the three years. Originally, this suggestion may have different organizational implications for different faculties, and may involve an increase in the number of years required for the degree or a lengthening of the academic year. The organizational problems should not be insuperable.

The advantages of this radical proposal seem to be two-fold. In the first place, existing, specialized or technical knowledge—which at present constitutes the student's "education"—will be situated within and framed by an orienting framework. The graduate who will have gone through this course in Social Analysis will subsequently approach his technical or administrative work from a much more than narrowly "specialist" standpoint. The technical work of the existing "Departments" will be enriched for the student while he is at the college, and, after graduation, he will systematically relate his special area of operation—whether it be concerned with Settlement Programmes, Codification of Laws, a Literacy Project or Cultural Policy, or Cooperatives—to a general understanding of social formation and social dynamics. The second gain will be that technical or administrative "experts" will be better able to situate themselves and their responsibilities within the total context of social needs and problems. This is an essential step in the breaking down of complacent elitism.

The elaboration of the teaching and research work of such a Department is to a considerable extent a product of practice and experiment. It is impossible to produce a blueprint for something novel and untried. The course will be a creative and exciting exercise for both teachers and students. The syllabus, which is appended, is clearly tentative. But it does demonstrate, we believe, that such a syllabus is viable, can maintain a high level of intellectual rigour, and can, by the third year, produce students who are equipped to confront the theoretical, practical and strategic problems of Tanzanian socialism in a positive and creative spirit, as socialist intellectuals.

There then follows a draft outline of a possible "Common Core Course in Social Analysis for University College, Dar Es Salaam" specifying a proposed syllabus for each year of the three year degree programme. And the document concluded with the following final paragraph:

To sum up, we propose the creation of an autonomous Department of Social Analysis under its own Head. It will offer a course compulsory for all Tanzanian students (though perhaps voluntary for Kenyans and Ugandans). This course will possess a considerable weight in overall curriculum—not less than 1/3 the total time in the three years. We believe that this Department would provide the best opportunity for overcoming the negative features of the present disciplinary divisions and for producing a coherent vigorous socialist orientation toward comprehension of the process and problems of development in Tanzania, in East Africa and in Africa.

Dr. G. Arrighi, Department of Economics
Miss C. Hoskyns, Institute of Public Administration
G. Kamenju, Department of Literature
Miss F. Livingstone, Faculty of Law
Dr. J. Mellen, Department of Political Science
S. Picciotto, Faculty of Law
Dr. W. Rodney, Department of History
J. Saul, Department of Political Science
H. Shore, Literature and Drama

(signed by all: the version of the document prepared for the President was also signed by R. Murray of TANU Research who helped both to frame it and to lay the foundation for the longer, somewhat parallel, document submitted to the University Conference)[7]

OF COURSE, WE WERE NOT SO NAÏVE as to think that we could ensure "socialism in one syllabus," as we joked at the time, or simply substitute pedagogy for politics and political economy. The struggle at the university was merely to be one front of a much larger attempt to chart new ways forward for Tanzania. Although neither the broader struggle for socialist transformation in Tanzania nor the narrower one for university transformation along progressive lines would ultimately be terribly successful, the contestation at the university did provide a privileged setting for societal and personal learning during the years I was there. In consequence, both I and a number of others sought to elaborate upon the lessons we thought might be learned in seeking to quite self-consciously transform the intellectual infrastructure of the university to more readily serve socialist purposes and help to foster progressive premises of knowledge very different from the western and capitalist style "commonsense" that intellectual activities at the university were otherwise stumbling into.

Thus, in much additional writing, both by members of the "Group of Nine" and by others, there was an attempt to clarify further what all the fuss was about. My colleague Idrian Resnick, for example, put together a book (in 1968), with multiple contributors, entitled *Tanzania: Revolution by Education,* that placed the whole field of educational policy under a microscope—

a book that included, as an essential point of reference, President Nyerere's own crucial position paper of the time "Education for Self-Reliance." Alongside pieces that, among other things, reflected on the University College debates I was asked to prepare an essay on some of the broader implications of these debates. I entitled my extended piece "High Level Manpower for Socialism,"[8] from which I excerpt some key paragraphs here, beginning with the following introduction to the theme.

SYSTEMATIC PLANNING TO MEET THE NEEDS for high level manpower must be a hard-nosed business, including the manipulation in a conscious manner of a number of factors to achieve a desired distribution of career patterns designed to fit both long and short-term national goals. Small wonder that manpower planners have little patience with academic critics who "have never met a payroll" and are far too prone, it is felt, to ignore the exigencies of economy, plant and personnel that must be the daily concern of the planner. This mistrust of carping criticism is perhaps doubly justified in Tanzania where, as far as I can make out, a manpower plan far more sophisticated than those of most other countries in the world, and particularly those in Africa, has been developed in the years since independence. Nonetheless, there are real limitations to the techniques that have been brought to bear to confront the challenges of equipping Tanzania with local personnel who have the varied talents necessary to meet the challenges of development—and these limitations become the more striking as Tanzania increasingly articulates its chief development goal: a genuinely socialist society...There was little enough justification in the past for ignoring the real problems that this poses for the educational sector; there is none since the promulgation of the Arusha Declaration. ...In consequence, my argument here will be a simple one, an attempt to set out a number of premises and assumptions that should be central to any discussion of the role and training of high level manpower, especially in a socialist Tanzania.

I then clarified a number of general premises that in Tanzania could begin to provide a framework within which planning for the recruitment and training of high-level manpower might more positively proceed. I noted, first, that:

...one of the most commonly articulated themes of existing technical personnel in a wide range of fields is that certain issues are merely "ideological," or "political" (sometimes even "emotional") and therefore beyond their scope of interest. Yet such a usage of the term "ideological" has become a pernicious abuse of the rhetorical art, particularly as it tends to be directed against the raising of important questions—those relating to the pattern of class formation in a given society, for example, or the quality of life available to that society's members. Generally, these are areas of inquiry that are subject to less precise measurement than questions of, say, the increase in the national product and the like. But it would be a brave person who would insist categorically that the gross national product is somehow markedly more determinative of the essential pattern of life for the citizenry than the pattern of that national product's distribution and the class structure that exists. And differential opportunity, lack of national economic independence, even exploitation, are, in any case, readily visible in many of their manifestations, even if not so easily measurable. Similarly, the policy questions raised by such issues are no less "technical" in their demands upon rational and planned response than are other policy challenges. It is no doubt unfortunate that in order for such issues to be adequately represented at the highest level of power there cannot be, say, a Ministry for the Avoidance or Mitigation of Class Formation, yet this difficulty is inherent in the issue itself. For class formation is the product of a number of processes—cultural, economic, social and political—and cannot be readily compartmentalized; it is thus the problem of all ministries. The danger is, of course, that the responsibility of all becomes the task of none and this has tended to be the case in more than one "socialist" country.

Here too I commented on the persistent "failure of the technocratically inclined to view society as a totality," and the related failure to recognize that extremely determinative choices continue to be made in the very course of "not choosing." And I also questioned several prevalent "myths" at play in the situation at hand, a first myth that sought to evoke, erroneously, the figure of the "non-political" civil servant as giving only "purely technical" advice, and a second that tended to assume a gap between any given "policy decision" (deemed to be "political"!) and its implementation, the latter being seen again as purely "technical" exercise. But the truth, I argued, is quite different: all policy decisions "demand a constant creativity on the part of those officials charged with working them out in practice; this is especially true for bills with a socialist edge, which often go to the heart of complex and ticklish social issues. It is not necessary to raise the spectre of the kind of full-scale sabotage that has met the attempts of other socialist governments to work with entrenched bureaucracies in more developed countries. The point is merely that many policies will demand sympathy and subtlety in their implementation, and a sense of the broader ramifications of day-to-day 'decision-making.'" And I carefully analyzed two examples: the first an April 1967 conference of agricultural economists and planners from the three East African countries held in Dar es Salaam to discuss sectoral planning for agriculture, and the second the important *Cooperative Report of 1966*. Both offered striking examples of the kinds of limitations on the perception of "technical" advisers that I was speaking of.

I then identified a second inhibiting factor upon informed creativity as lying in "the fragmented vision that tends to characterize people trained, all too specifically, for professional careers" and then reviewed, precisely, the debate at the conference on the role of the university and the argument, presented (as included above) by our group of nine lecturers, reiterating that

> the narrowness of the perspective imparted by the specialized discipline comes, in turn, to characterize the specialized work of the "technocrat" after his/her graduation. The argument so presented has particular cogency for the social sciences but it should be evident that the work of practitioners in all fields—law, education, engineering, architecture, even the pure sciences—has ramifications for the society as a whole, impinging upon it in various ways; a "real" awareness of such aspects of their work is essential to creative performance in any specialized role. The incompatibility, already demonstrated, between "somnambulists"[9] and socialism should, therefore, be a matter of grave concern to those charged with the genesis and training of the high level manpower team.

Finally, I noted some of the fears that were voiced by our critics and it was in thinking these through that I drew the essay to a close:

The first was that any such innovation would cut against the pressing need for the training of "specialists." This entire essay will, I hope, have helped undermine the faulty logic of such a retort. Obviously, technical skills of a very high order are in short supply and a major chore of the university must be to provide them. But it would be a "false economy" to think that this can be done at the expense of the kind of broad insight and understanding that alone makes their use wholly relevant to contemporary Tanzania. A second fear was that such a course would be designed merely for preaching a set of values. This is precisely the opposite of being the case. In fact, such a course has been articulated in part to counter the glib argument that the need for "political education" could be met exclusively by a series of speeches from political leaders involving, no doubt, a fair degree of exhortation. However interesting and undoubtedly useful these might be, it should be clear by now that they will also be inadequate. It is impossible to force people to make value judgments in any dicated direction, though you may induce tacit conformity. What you can hope to do, on the other hand, is enable them to perceive the full implications of their actions, awaken them to a more complete consciousness, as it were, and leave to them the task of squaring their consciences with reality, as now freshly seen.

A positive value judgment as to the merits of socialist endeavour is an essential aspect of any creative socialist commitment, of course. Moreover, it may be usefully repeated here that the making of such a value judgment is susceptible to influence from the whole pattern and trajectory of the broader society and culture. But such a Common Course as we are here discussing can also be important, for it begins to exemplify the parameters of *a socialist mode of thinking* and analysis that must both supplement and help situate such values.

The reasons for this should by now be clear and will not require extended repetition. Put briefly, however, the saliency of historical movement that such an approach underscores helps to undermine the sanctity of the status quo, thereby imparting a sense of *potentiality* to one's vision of society and of mankind. In addition, the saliency of "totality" underscores the multidimensionality of obstacles, such as entrenched power, penetrating into various spheres of life, that block the road to progress, and helps to reveal the innumerable and related social fronts on which changes must accumulate to build a new society, these together imparting an intellectually *revolutionary* dimension to one's concerns. Only when this kind of perception becomes possible can a student be expected to know the world as a socialist, and later, as a practitioner, adopt the creative style of work of one. Finally, it is possible that some more direct inroad can be made into complacent elitism by this route: technical "experts" may be brought to see their own roles as small, if also important, contributions made within a much more complex social universe.

Perhaps, I concluded, our suggestion of the "Common Course," designed for the University College, would also be suitable for adaptation and use elsewhere in the educational system and the society. One thing, I felt, was clear, however. For here was an issue that educationists and manpower planners had been slow to confront:

Yet engage with it they must, for the whole question of such training demands a subtle balance of technical assessment and broad sensitivity. Thus the introduction of this kind of orienting framework into the educational programme carries costs; perhaps in certain fields its implementation might even dictate the extension of the number of years required to earn a degree. And it does not affect those "experts" and "technicians" already at their desks and in the field; some profound consideration of policy will be necessary on this front as well. It is my own conviction that many of the costs involved in tackling such issues will prove marginal when measured against the payoffs that are possible. One thing is certain: it must be an essential task of those concerned with high level manpower—and with socialism—in the years ahead to present the leadership with options and arguments that evidence an awareness of these crucial dimensions.

THE STRUGGLE OVER SYLLABUS AT THE CAMPUS was to have a powerful effect on the various participants in it, of course. This was true not least in my own case for it premised a lifelong attempt to develop a firmly non-disciplinary and radical approach to my own writing and teaching in later years. It was no accident that I would eventually find my way into a Social Science department at York University's Atkinson College in Toronto, a department that reveled in its escape from the conventional North American academic parameters of disciplinary rigidity. There I was able to develop an approach firmly rooted in a political economy perspective (of Marxist provenance) while never losing sight of my firm commitment to the kind of political understanding that I felt political science, at its best, could sometimes deliver.[10]

Arrighi too (of whom more below) found his way from a narrow, if highly sophisticated, background in a very technocratic brand of economics to a home in several Sociology Departments in the United States where he could pursue his valuable enquiries into the political economy of global capitalism. The work of several others in our original Group of Nine (and beyond it) proved to be similarly expansive, especially when, as was often the case, we found ourselves back in "Northern" educational institutions where, quite frankly, learning was "more and more about less and less." Needless to say the overwhelming weight of such "education" seldom, if ever, made the slightest reference to anything like the "Common Course" sensibility evoked above that could have encouraged interrogation of the "commonsense" premises of a firmly capitalist-bound education. Nor was it terribly easy for students, otherwise sited firmly within the cocoon of such "commonsense," to readily develop an understanding that would radically question established wisdom and established power.

But, of course, we are still, in this chapter, in Africa, more specifically in Tanzania, and in the early 1970s. For me, at the time, the personal fall-out of this moment of reassessment at the University was particularly eye opening. I was, to make a long story short, very soon informed that my pending Canadian-financed External Aid contract would not be renewed for another contract period. Personal interviews (to use a polite word for the testy exchanges involved) with the Canadian ambassador in Tanzania, Mr. Alan McGill, as well as extended correspondence (in part facilitated by my calling upon Ed Broadbent, then NDP leader, for intercession) with both Mitchell Sharp, the then Secretary of state for External Affairs, and his advisor Maurice Strong found them all being mealy-mouthed but unapologetic, seeking to palm much of the "blame" for my sacking on Tanzanian criticisms of my role to which they were merely responding. Ironically, then, I was almost at once rehired at the university on a local contract, without any criticism whatsoever of my active involvement in the University debate (though on terms that, inevitably, represented a 70% reduction of my relatively lofty Canadian Aid salary!) My days of active engagement in the struggle in Tanzania were, as we shall see, far from over, whatever may have been the intentions of the Canadian government in severing my employment.

BUT BEFORE PROCEEDING WITH THAT TALE allow me to emphasize that while in Tanzania and even when engaged in the range of campus struggles alluded to here, I did manage to get on with other scholarly work as well. Indeed, the campus was an intellectual hothouse on any number of fronts and, to an extraordinary degree, a perpetual stimulus to thought and action. Thus, I myself continued with the rural development work I had first begun in order to write my thesis for Princeton, a project that now took on even greater weight and meaning and substance in situ; I studied closely the country's political and administrative systems; and I examined a host of other issues. I was fortunate to collaborate as co-author on various pieces with a range of colleagues—Lionel Cliffe, Jonathan Barker, John Loxley, Roger Woods—and also to co-edit a number of books on the country.[11]

Of somewhat broader scope, however, was my collaboration with the above-mentioned Giovanni Arrighi, who came to Dar after his own detention and near arrest for very practical and applied liberation-support related work in (then) Rhodesia. It was Arrighi who encouraged me to join with him in pushing out from the Tanzanian case to examine the continental and global implications of what we had both begun to discover in East and Central Africa. Ultimately, our various papers from these years found published form in our Monthly Review Press volume *Essays on the Political Economy of Africa*.[12] A briefer version of the essential argument underlying our joint project was published in *Monthly Review* in May 1969, and I include that shorter article here as a kind of stage-setter for my continuing work on such issues over the next forty years (work exemplified briefly in chapter 6, below).[13]

A SOPHISTICATED SOCIALIST POSITION in contemporary Africa must fuse a concern for an increased rate of economic development with a perception of the role played in the development process by the existence and emergence of classes and groups with divergent interests and differential access to benefits. Only if these factors are taken into account can one understand the extent to which the productive potential of African societies, and therefore their development and structural transformation, are constrained by the present pattern of world and domestic economy and society. The available surplus is being drained away, for example, as the repatriated profits of overseas firms; or it is consumed by self-indulgent domestic elites. As a consequence, the generation of a larger surplus from an aroused and mobilized peasantry is discouraged. It is, in brief, the pattern of inequality that tends to hamper a rise in productivity.

In this situation a viable socialist strategy will have to face dilemmas of choice in three closely related policy spheres. On the international level, it will confront the specter of international capitalism and a grave inequality of financial power— realities which place major constraints on general development. On the domestic scene, it will face the problem of the relationship between "town," the centre of administration and of such industrialization as takes place, and "country"—a relationship from which real development could spring but which all too often defines a split between unequal and unconnected spheres of a society falling short of genuine transformation. Finally, such a socialist strategy will have the problem of agricultural development itself in a rural sphere where inequalities can and do begin to emerge, although, at least in the short run, these have a rather more ambiguous impact on the pace of development than the other inequalities already alluded to. We will attempt briefly to analyze the nature of the contemporary African situation in order to provide a backdrop against which any serious debate on revolutionary strategy in independent Africa must, in the future, be set.

I

The vast majority of the population of tropical Africa consists of independent producers who, except in marginal ways, do not depend on wage employment for their subsistence. In order to promote the productivity of these producers, two problems have to be faced: (a) the problem of creating incentives to bring idle land and labor into production and (b) the problem of using the surplus actually produced by the peasantry in such a way as to promote the steady growth of labor productivity. The first problem is related to the ability of the modern sector to create incentives to increased productivity in the traditional sector; while the second problem is related to the types of organization of production and socioeconomic institutions in the traditional sector which are most likely to evoke desired responses to stimuli generated in the modern sector. Most traditional sectors of African economies still have some surplus productive capacity since population pressure on the land, though growing, is generally not yet severe. For this reason the first of these two problems must be given a central position in any discussion of African economic development.

There are three main forms of surplus absorption in the modern sectors of present-day African economies: the export of profits and investment income in general; the discretionary consumption of a small "labor aristocracy"; and productive investment, embodying capital-intensive techniques, mainly concentrated in sectors other than those producing capital goods.

To take the last point first: the use of capital-intensive techniques of production in Africa is not only the result of technological factors. In addition, the investment policies of the modern international corporations in underdeveloped economies and the wage and salary policies of the independent African governments (which, in turn, depend upon the character of their power base) are equally relevant.[14] With regard to the former, the fact that methods of management, organization, and control have evolved in the metropolitan centres and cannot be easily adapted to the conditions obtaining in underdeveloped areas has meant that labor-intensive techniques are often not even taken into consideration by the corporations. More important still, the corporations apply to all their branches technical methods corresponding to their financial position, and this implies capital-intensive techniques irrespective of the situation in the territories where the investment takes place.

But capital-intensity has also been favored by the salary and wage policy of independent African governments. Salary structures were inherited from previous colonial regimes; and, as Africans gradually entered the civil service and took over managerial positions in large foreign concerns, they received the basic salaries already attached to the posts. A huge gap between the incomes of the elites and sub-elites in bureaucratic employment on the one hand and the mass of wage workers on the other thus appeared, bringing the whole level of labor incomes into question. Given the political influence of urban workers on African governments, which are the major employers of labor, a steady rise in wages ensued. This steady rise is of course favored by, and tends to strengthen, the capital-intensity bias of investment. Capital-intensity means that labor is a lower proportion of costs, so that the individual concern is more willing to concede wage increases (especially foreign oligopolies which can pass on cost increases to the consumer). And this in turn reinforces the tendency toward capital-intensive growth, and so on in an upward spiral.

With regard to the distribution of productive investment between sectors, there seem to be two main reasons, besides obvious technological factors, for the observed underinvestment in the capital goods industries of tropical Africa. In the first place, the very bias in favor of capital-intensive techniques discussed above tends to promote the use of highly specialized machinery and consequently restrains the growth of demand for capital goods that could be produced locally. Secondly, in non-industrialized economies the market for capital goods is small, and if such goods are to be produced at all there must be good reasons to believe that the whole economy will develop rapidly and in such a way as to nourish a market for capital goods. The great calculating rationality, care, and circumspection in approaching new developments that characterize modern corporations prevent the repetition of the process, typical of the nineteenth century, whereby competitive entrepreneurs and financial groups often undertook investments which were actually "unjustified" by market conditions but which nonetheless fostered the industrialization of less-developed economies. In short, in Africa, the lack of development of the capital goods sector restrains the expansion of productive capacity and of the internal market, perpetuating the dependence of the tropical African economies on the growth of demand for their primary products in the industrial centres. It is not surprising therefore that these economies have been unable to grow faster than their exports.

In fact, in the period 1960-1965, per capita real product increased at an average rate of 2.0 percent per annum. This relatively low rate of growth, combined with the effects of the "wage-mechanization" spiral discussed above, has resulted in a decrease in the proportion of the labor force in wage employment in most countries, and has been accompanied by a widening gap between urban and rural incomes. Not all categories of urban workers have benefited from this widening gap. A large proportion of them consists of semi-proletarianized peasants who periodically engage in wage employment. This migrant labor force is not "stabilized" and in general does not acquire the degree of specialization required in industrial enterprises that use capital-intensive techniques. These laborers as a class cannot gain from the "wage-mechanization" spiral since higher individual incomes are matched by a reduction in their wage-employment opportunities.

The higher wages and salaries, however, induce the better-paid section of the labor force to sever their ties with the traditional societies. Their consequent stabilization in the wage economy promotes specialization, greater bargaining power, and further increases in their incomes, which tend to become three or more times higher than those of unskilled workers. The standards of living of this tiny section of the working class approximate and often surpass those of the lower strata of the elites in bureaucratic employment in the civil service and international corporations. It must therefore be included with the latter in what may be called, somewhat inappropriately, the labor aristocracy of tropical Africa. It is the discretionary, and indeed conspicuous, consumption of this "aristocracy" which absorbs a significant proportion of the surplus produced in the money economy.

The third significant form of surplus absorption is the profits, interest, dividends, fees, etc., transferred abroad by the international corporations. Foreign private investment in underdeveloped economies has been, in the recent past, an efficient device for transferring surplus generated abroad to the advanced capitalist countries. Insofar as tropical Africa is concerned, this transfer of surplus is bound to increase in the future for obvious reasons. It seems in fact that returns of the order of 15-20 percent on capital, usually on the basis of an investment maturing in about three years, are required to attract foreign capital in tropical Africa. It follows that, in order to offset the outflow of profits, foreign investment in the area must steadily grow at a rate of 11-14 percent per year, which can hardly be expected in economies growing at a rate of 4-5 percent. Thus, while the transfer of surplus has been somewhat contained during the present phase of easy import substitution, the outflow can only become more serious in the years ahead as that phase comes to an end.

The development potential of this pattern of surplus absorption is remarkably poor. The slow growth of the money economy and the concurrent high rate of mechanization and automation hold back the growth of wage employment opportunities for the peasantry. More important still, the absorption of a considerable share of the surplus by the discretionary consumption of the labor aristocracy (which directly and/or indirectly creates demand in the industrial centres), and by the transfer of investment incomes abroad, restrains the growth of internal demand for peasant produce. As a consequence the creation of stimuli to increase productivity in the rural areas is left to the sluggish expansion of foreign demand for African produce. The stagnation of peasant incomes and productivity has in turn a negative impact on the growth potential of the modern sector itself, since it further hampers the expansion of the internal market. In the light of these considerations, the current economic growth of tropical Africa may properly be characterized, in Ignacy Sachs's terminology, as "perverse growth," i.e., growth that undermines rather than enhances the potentialities of the economy for long-term development.[15]

The foregoing analysis suggests the advisability of a policy of disengagement from international capitalism. It also suggests, however, that such disengagement is not a sufficient condition for development. The labor aristocracy can in fact be expected to continue to use its power in the state-controlled modern sector in order to appropriate a considerable share of the surplus in the form of increasing discretionary consumption. Under these conditions "perverse growth" would persist, notwithstanding state ownership of the means of production. In order to achieve "real" long-term development, disengagement from international capitalism will have to be accompanied by a change in the power base of African governments.

II

In contemporary tropical Africa many striking ambiguities are readily identifiable on the ideological plane. Ideas about "development" and "equality" are not systematically linked, and "socialist" strategies emerge which leave much to be desired. And it is well to note that these ambiguities have tended to characterize the discussion of policy even in those African states which have professed themselves to be the most radical.

There has, for example, been little grasp, within the doctrine of "African socialism," of the nature of the inequalities discussed above. There has been a failure to face up to the necessity for policies which would divert a good proportion of the surplus from urban consumptionism (with an import and luxury bias) to rural incentives and capital formation. To be sure, occasional attacks upon trade unions and trading groups (generally those of non-African origin) are justified as a redressing of inequalities that hinder socially beneficial capital accumulation, but such a line of analysis is seldom rigorously applied to the society as a whole. (In the case of trade unions, the attacks, despite the rhetoric, have generally involved a politically motivated exercise of institutional control rather than a concerted effort to institute wage restraint.)

Thus perceived inequalities get very easily swallowed up and analytically blurred within the framework provided by the continent's distinctive "socialist" ideology. Here we refer to that strand of the ideology that has been characterized by Peter Worsley as "populism."[16] In Africa this has involved the claim, by almost all leaders, that African societies are, even now, classless. The foundations for pervasive social solidarity are supposed to be found in traditional society and to exclude any socioeconomically meaningful stratification.

Just as the populist strand in "African socialism" obscures the realities of class formation, so it is important, if somewhat paradoxical, to observe that much of the criticism of "neocolonialism" in Africa has served to obscure the realities of international capitalism's involvement on the continent. For again, despite the rhetoric, all states have felt it necessary to deal with "the enemy." At the same time they have seldom felt compelled to undertake a serious analysis of the impact on their own economies and societies of investment by an increasingly monopolistic brand of international capitalism in terms of the choice of techniques, the absorption of labor, the reinvestment of profits, and the generation of internal demand. For example, the possibility that many, if not most, forms of imported capital may be worse than none at all, despite the subsequent existence of plant on the ground and a handful of indigenous employees, is seldom brought to debate. Policy statements thus oscillate rather erratically between the abstract slogans of "neo-colonialism," a useful instrument with which to forge national unity behind the leaders, and a "forced" acceptance of the "necessity" to encourage foreign investment in order to obtain skills and equipment.

More than mere intellectual confusion is at stake here, of course: these ideological strands must be situated in relation to the social structure of contemporary African societies. In colonial and economically underdeveloped Africa an indigenous dominant class with power grounded in the process of production had, by and large, not developed (though the emergence of an indigenous trading class, particularly in West Africa, cannot be wholly ignored and has played an important role in determining the course of some "socialist" experiments). As a consequence the political and bureaucratic groups which did rise to prominence were characterized by what Roger Murray has called a greater "relative social autonomy and plasticity."[17] After independence, when past education, political record, and current bureaucratic position came to be the chief determinants of privilege in the new society, a rather narrow vested interest in the system and a growing consciousness of a differential position Vis-à-vis the mass became dominant features of the new elites—*une bourgeoisie plus proche d'un mandarinat,* as Dia has called them.

It is within this context that one must place trends to an increased centralization of power and ideological myth-making for popular consumption which can be seen to express a clear institutional and, behind that, class interest. And within this framework much state intervention, only marginally related to a generalized socialist development strategy, can be at least partly explained as the conscious proliferation of jobs for incoming recruits to the dominant group. At the very least, given the nature of the bureaucratic elite, any glib identification, by leaders or observers, of socialism in Africa with *etatisme* and policies of economic centralization must be viewed with suspicion. And of course a sustained stand against the blandishments of foreign capitalism, or even a critical scrutiny of its potential contributions, cannot be expected from such a group.

Much evidence is available to demonstrate the importance of these patterns even in such states as Guinea, Mali, and Nkrumah's Ghana; there too the burden of the expensive administrative structure and of urban consumptionism pressed upon the surplus.[18] Insofar as real attempts were made to escape from the irrationalities involved, as in Ghana, the absence of a mass social and political base rendered them half-hearted and self-defeating. Moreover, in their relationship with international capitalism, Ghana and Guinea were not so different from less militant regimes, and equally shortsighted. Thus it has been strongly argued that Nkrumah's policies in this sphere, as epitomized by the Volta River Project, merely resulted in a marginal redefinition of "the politics of mediation," in the suggestive phrase of Fitch and Oppenheimer.[19]

This is not surprising: any serious attempt to face up to international capitalism would presuppose a growing awareness of the centrality of the pattern of surplus absorption and utilization to development strategy, and some readiness to correct existing irrationalities. The inevitable corollary, however, would have to be a parallel attack on the privileges of those very classes that constitute the power base of most African governments. Any strategy directed toward socialist construction in Africa must therefore face up to the full complexities involved in creating a state power dedicated to the task, and in generating or tapping social forces capable of underpinning such a state.

It is perhaps possible that such a novel power base could be found by combining elements of a mobilized peasantry and a transformed urban and rural proletariat, thereby producing a genuine "workers and peasants" state. Tanzania is the country in contemporary Africa where socialist aspirations figure most prominently in the development equation and most powerfully affect the policies that are being pursued. For the President, Julius K. Nyerere, has increasingly displayed, in a series of important policy documents, a sophisticated awareness of many of the patterns of African change which we have discussed: the importance of the rural/urban dichotomy, the relative lack of socialist direction provided by a mere "attitude of mind," some of the ambiguities of foreign economic involvement in the domestic economy, and the realities of rural stratification. This has led, among other things, to the "Arusha Declaration," which embodies an attempt to enact a self-denying ordinance against many kinds of economic aggrandizement by the elite (especially as regards the ownership of property); to the nationalization of banks, insurance companies, export-import houses, and certain processing and manufacturing concerns, with some eye to relating their investment and other decisions more directly to the interests of national development; and even to the introduction into the policy debate of the theme of socialist modes of production for the rural sector.

Yet the ruling Tanzanian party has remained relatively untransformed and ineffective for mobilizing peasants and workers behind such programs in any coherent way, and a systematic industrialization strategy along the lines articulated above is still lacking. These weaknesses could well undermine Nyerere's attempt to channel the efforts of political and bureaucratic elites in a direction likely to ensure genuine development. Finally, it must be said that even if the Tanzanian effort is one which deserves support, however qualified, from all socialists, it remains a relatively isolated experiment. In most African countries the incumbent leadership is much more compromised, and the quality of the political parties ostensibly working toward "socialist" goals leaves much to be desired. Even more ominously, the character of intra-elite competition in contemporary Africa, and in particular the rise of the military to a position of special prominence, show the strength of forces driving the situation in a counterrevolutionary direction.[20]

Ultimately the playing out of Tanzania's project was not, as suggested above, to be successful for reasons that I and many others have discussed at length elsewhere. Yet I have found the general analysis that underlay this article to be a sound one and, while I hope I have learned a thing or two in subsequent years, I find, as also noted above, that much of it still serves to anchor my analysis some forty years later.

TO RETURN, HOWEVER, TO MY REMAINING YEARS on "the Hill" (as the university, on a rise that was then on the outskirts of Dar es Salaam, was colloquially known) the fact is that, beyond my sacking by the Canadian government, there followed a period of some five additional years in which the drama of the seminal university conference discussed above continued to play itself out. The curriculum did not come to articulate the vision we had proposed, although a certain number of modifications along such lines were embarked upon. A first step was the launching of a "common course" based curriculum, especially in the first year, that was indeed designed to situate, even to critique, established disciplinary departments and specializations.

Moreover, such activities intersected with the growing radicalism of at least one group of students, an activist group that chose to take the Arusha Declaration quite seriously (I commented on this development in at least one article of the time, one entitled "Radicalism and the Hill"—first published in 1970 in the *East Africa Journal).*[21] There were also hot intellectual debates, forged not least by the aforementioned cadre of radical students, notably by Issa Shivji whose seminal text "The Silent Class Struggle" was to launch for him upon a long, honourable and still-continuing career as lawyer, social critic and community activist in his native Tanzania. But Shivji's text also gave rise immediately to a strong and valuable exchange on the nature of contemporary Tanzania and about the realities of class, socialism and struggle there.

I myself was privileged, along with several others on the campus, to be invited by the students to contribute to a forum in the student's exemplary publication, *Maji-Maji,* in its very first issue, dated January, 1971 (this replacing the now banned magazine of similar political thrust, *Cheche*), and thus be part of the dialogue. Other invited contributors were Tamas Szentes, a Hungarian who was the University's Professor of Economics, and Walter Rodney the University's noted historian from Guyana. The debate as a whole was published in a separate volume by the Tanzanian Publishing House and also included in the aforementioned two volume *Socialism in Tanzania* that my friend and colleague Lionel Cliffe and I edited to encompass a selection from the mass of material on the topic being produced by Tanzanians and others at the time.[22] In my own contribution, for example, I criticized Shivji for his possibly underestimation of the degree of "class struggle from below" that might still become a factor in defining progressive outcomes for Tanzania, looking to the emergent ujamaa village programme and various verbal commitments to "worker's power" of the time as possible harbingers of such possibilities—somewhat naively as soon proved to be the case.[23]

There were intellectual sparks being struck then, and they would continue to be visible in the ongoing work, over a number of decades, of Shivji and others. But with the expulsion of student union president Simon Akivaga (see below) and the crushing of various immediate demands the student radicalism that had grown since the first days of the crisis would continue only with increasingly less practical effect. True, there was also to be contestation throughout the rest of the 1970s over the nature of the university, including a student protest march to town in 1978 (that was, however, brutally repressed). Though at least for a time some kind of struggle did continue, much of such activism as continued came now to represent more the all too predictable internecine posturings of a marginalized left than indications of a more vibrant struggle—paralleling in this way the overall drift of Tanzania more generally away from the high point reached during the first Arusha Declaration years.

Indeed, any struggle over the fate and nature of the University itself was now to be waged less as framed by either students or faculty as by the increasingly negative preoccupations of the Tanzanian elite itself (including Nyerere!). For the ebullience on the campus had made that elite quite uneasy. The final straw came in 1972. TANU, the ruling party, had issued a new set of guidelines, *Mwongozo*, designed, ostensibly, to encourage active criticisms and initiative from below. There was the distinct possibility, though, that this document was more rhetorical than really very profoundly democratic in its thrust. Soon the students found just how accurate their scepticism regarding the actual democratic import of *Mwongozo* was actually to prove to be: some sharp divisions between students and administration followed and culminated in a particularly dramatic incident—one that also evidenced broader contradictions already visible within the overall Tanzanian socialist project. Indeed, as I have written elsewhere, any too romantic a picture of Tanzania in those days would be found to have "something missing" if one allows, even briefly,

> the cold wind of reality to blow through it. I have personal memories, after all, of the invasion of the campus of the University of Dar es Salaam by the field Force Unit in 1970—the time when, before my eyes, my student Akivaga, the Kenyan leader of the University Student Council, was dragged at gunpoint down the cement stairs of the central administration building, then tossed like a sack of old clothes into an army vehicle and sped away to expulsion both from the university and from the country. Nor can I forget other firsthand accounts [alluded to above]...of protesting students being savagely beaten by security forces as they marched down the Morogoro Road to town in 1978.

Tanzanian faculty members who tended to side with the students, were also severely disciplined, as in the case of Arnold Temu, who, "thrown out of Parliament for questioning the regime's handling of university matters and later sacked from the university itself, [was] sent effectively into exile as an itinerant academic." As I recently wrote, in adding an illuminating footnote to Temu's story:

> As it happens, Temu's case also produced one of the most poignant moments in a research trip I took to Dar es Salaam in the summer of 2001. Sitting at the bar in the New Africa Hotel, I glanced to my right and eventually recognized, under the shared disguise of age, Arnold Temu himself. As it turned out he had just returned to Dar to take up a job at the new Open university there. Further discussion brought, unsolicited, a startling statement from him: he had sworn to himself not to return to live in Tanzania as long as Nyerere was alive. He thus offered a perspective on "Mwalimu" and his "democratic sensibility" that is, at the very least, worth recording.[24]

In short, slowly but surely progressive voices were being stilled. In addition, the contracts of many expatriate faculty members were merely allowed to lapse, and this time there was no further court of appeal. Indeed, in the course of this housecleaning, I was to be fired again.

I was learning other things too, not least from my growing awareness of Nyerere's rather constrained "democratic sensibility" although some of the lessons took a while to sink in. For even though my growing confidence in the strength of the case for a socialist alternative to Africa's underdevelopment was reinforced by the realities of both Tanzania and Mozambique, I was slower to grasp the very real limitations of the chosen one-party route towards such a goal. It was a lesson I would also learn from the practice of Frelimo (the Front for the Liberation of Mozambique) as I discuss in subsequent chapters. Taking off from the Temu case, I suggested in a recent retrospective reflection[25] on the broader meaning of the Tanzanian experience, that such dubious developments

... WERE AT LEAST AS EXEMPLARY OF THE TRUE MEANING of "one-party democracy" for many ordinary Tanzanians as were the "democratic one-party elections" they were being encouraged to participate in—and that they actually gave the lie to certain of Nyerere's more general democratic pronunciamentos as well as to some of his claims to be empowering ordinary people in their struggle against nascent class formation in the country. Here I would reaffirm my judgment that Cranford Pratt [author of *The Critical Phase in Tanzania, 1945-1968: Nyerere and the Emergence of a Socialist Strategy* and with whose views I has often sparred over the years] was mistaken not to have taken these moments, and the underlying contradictions within Nyerere's own project that they revealed, much more seriously than he did at the time. Here, too, I would offer the hypothesis that Pratt was willing to shelve temporarily his liberal-democratic misgivings and give Nyerere's project of guided democracy too much the benefit of the doubt because of his own great confidence in, and respect for, Nyerere the man —but also because he took the potential challenges of "nation-building" much more seriously than he ever took the imperatives of class struggle and socialist construction in Tanzania!

But what, then, of my own analysis? I still think that I saw the negative significance of these latter dimensions (Mount Carmel, the RDA, the university) of Tanzanian reality on Nyerere's watch more clearly than did Pratt and that I was correct to state as much. And yet, that said, my own view that the one party state could be genuinely democratized from within—albeit not so much by means of the intra-party competitive elections emphasized by Pratt as by the empowerment of workers, peasants, women and students through their own self-organization within the one-party system and within the polity as a whole—was no less mistaken in its way than was Pratt's view.

Of course, developments at Mount Carmel, at the university, at the RDA (twinned as this latter move would quickly become with a more generalized pattern of enforced villagization in the rural sphere) all suggested, soon enough, that a democratic transformation from below of the one-party state was not going to be allowed to happen in Tanzania. Still, slow to learn, I was to make a similar mistake with reference to the emerging situation in Mozambique, this time embracing (with, if anything, even more enthusiasm) the claim to "democratic substitutionism" made by the Frelimo leadership there—even while awaiting, once again in vain, for the empowerment from below that one hoped would provide the necessary popular complement to drive and sustain the initial revolutionary gestures and quasi-socialist breakthroughs being made from above by that leadership.

In consequence of these mistakes in judgment, I have since come to think self-organization for popular democracy requires, as a necessary (although decidedly not sufficient) conditions, institutionalized guarantees of open debate, freedom of political and social organization (including independent trade unions, women's organizations, peasant associations, as well as opposition political parties) and unfettered ventilation by the media of any and all issues. These alone can provide the terrain upon which popular forces may hope to group and sustain the fight for their rights and the satisfaction of their needs. Is this a call for a greater degree of "liberalism" in Africa? It can be put that way if you like. I myself see it as reflecting a clear acknowledgment of just what is necessary, in Africa and elsewhere, in the way of democratic guarantees in order to give democratic forms the potential to be real and meaningful (i.e., to release revolutionary energies and to advance class and other popular struggles) for those who need them most.

True, as Karim Hirji has suggested in a recent article, under some circumstances the introduction of a multi-party system can carry a society even further away from a practice of the empowerment of ordinary citizens than was the case under its prior one-party system. Perhaps this has even been the case, thus far, in Tanzania where many citizens may have had their interests more effectively represented within Nyerere's so-called one-party democracy than through the current multi-party system. Indeed, as political scientist Paul Kaiser has eloquently argued, the move towards a multi-party system has facilitated in Tanzania a deepening pattern of elite corruption and opportunism and of wasting inter-ethnic and religious rivalry of precisely the sort Nyerere may have feared. Certainly, a litany of comments about such negative developments was the chief stuff of dinner table conversation with Tanzanian comrades on my visit there in 2001.

Yet even this denouement does not strengthen the claim that one-party states work well to empower ordinary people and to advance their interests, even in the short-run. While we should not understate the importance of leadership to realizing processes of political change on the one hand, nor romanticize the spontaneous militancy of "the masses" on the other, perhaps we have learned enough from the African experience, (including that of Nyerere's Tanzania) to realize that the real, not notional, democratic accountability of leaders to their presumptive popular constituency must be a crucial part of the African development agenda.

MEANWHILE, THERE WERE OTHER EVENTS THAT OCCURRED during my last remaining months on the campus that apparently hastened my enforced departure and that of many others. There were, for example, key incidents that manifested the playing out of the struggles around issues and possibilities raised, several years earlier, at the University Conference itself. Thus, on campus and beyond the Akivaga/Temu imbroglios, it was becoming ever clearer that resistance to progressive change had significantly crystallized amongst the less radical of the expatriate faculty, their ranks now reinforced by growing numbers of returning (from overseas training) Tanzanian academics—many of whom were prepared to see, in ongoing attempts to change the terms of university-level education, a real challenge to the very foundations of their own hard-earned expertise. In consequence, their conservative notions meshed easily with the mouldy views of various of the expatriate faculty. Such a group stuck quite firmly to their disciplinary guns and against the thrust of faculty reorganization—something that was, as it happened, just then being planned for by an official (and, on balance, quite radical) planning committee of which, with others (both expatriate and Tanzanian), I was a member.

Specifically, what was now at stake was our continuing effort to change the academic infrastructure, through faculty reorganization, of the university itself. We already had, for example, managed to begin a process of "revolution through education" by launching a quite imaginative common course, for all students, and designed, along lines suggested above, to integrate the understandings of different levels of society in a potentially radical manner. But realizing any more sweeping alteration to the departmental and syllabus structure was to prove an extremely difficult task, with resistance this time springing, as suggested, from within the professoriate itself. Nonetheless, there were a number of us, Tanzanians and expatriates alike, who continued to fight for an ongoing process of retooling along more progressive and less conventionally western lines. The climax? Amidst growing tension, our efforts were, at one extremely tempestuous faculty meeting, at last rejected (a meeting in which, for the very first time in seven years in Tanzania, I heard a very opportunist and highly rhetorical brand of black-nationalist racism directed against some of us rather than any substantive argument). This and other events of the time indicated clearly that my days, as well as those of others like me, were numbered: it was now to be only a matter of weeks before a number of us, Tanzanian and expatriate, black and white alike, were sacked and more or less forced to leave the country.

With the result that, in 1972, I came to teach out my last days in Dar. As I did so, I reflected quite specifically on the likes of Frantz Fanon and other Africans who were warning of "false decolonization" under continuing western dominance, of the potential abuse of power by indigenous members of the petty-bourgeoisie, and of the possibility that remained within Africa for something much better to yet emerge.[26] Indeed, working along similar lines, I was engaged in teaching the first offering of a new East African Society and Environment course (EASE), a core course for all first year students that we had hoped to see as one of the key building blocks for the transformed university; with any luck, we thought, it could begin to have the transforming impact upon our students that we had had in mind since the University conference a few years earlier.

The course, a further iteration of the Development Studies course that had initially exemplified such an attempt, marked, in and of itself, a good start, I thought. But time was clearly against us. Of course, the student radicalism that had grown since the first days of the crisis would continue—but, truth be told, after the expulsion of Akivaga and the crushing of immediate demands, it tended to continue to increasingly less practical effect: as noted above, there would be various sparks throughout the rest of the 1970s but too often these became merely sparks struck between various left factions over matters of doctrinal purity rather than indications of any genuine and principled struggle. As for the shifting balance within the faculty, I have already commented on the degree to which class and professional interest, often masquerading as academic concern with standards and the like, had begun to frame outcomes as the initial impetus of the Arusha Declaration started to fade.

It was in such a still charged atmosphere on the campus that, in March 1972, our EASE course, one that had begun amidst very high hopes some nine months before, drew to a close. It fell to me to give the final lecture of the year, the notes for which lecture I still have and here merely set out more coherently as a text. A kind of personal valedictory for a period which I had deeply enjoyed and learned a great deal from, I summarized, in that lecture, something both of the EASE experience itself, and of my own sojourn in Tanzania—a period during which, I now feel, I had begun to learn to be a "revolutionary traveler," rather than a mere tourist. I resurrect some of what I had to say then from those lecture notes of the time:

AFTER SO MANY LECTURES, seminars and assignments prepared and presented over seven years it would be nice to conclude this particular course, my last, with something so spectacular that it might even catch the attention of those fellows up there in the far corners of room who are always sneaking a look at the newspaper. But I can't think of anything that might accomplish that, except possibly writing the final examination questions on the blackboard or actually presenting Akivaga to the class again and in person. Since both of these things are against the rules, however, I'll have to settle for something a little less dramatic.

To begin with: after a year of such intensive work as we have undertaken in this course it would be nice to end up with a spectacular conclusion, some definitive set of propositions about, and solutions to, the development problems in East Africa. But we have seen that there is no such set of easily packaged answers to the challenges that confront East African societies. Moreover, even to pretend to summarize a course like the present one—one that represents already a synthesis of a wide range of materials and perspectives—would be far too grandiose an aspiration. However, it may at least be possible in the hour we have to remind ourselves of some of the main lines that have emerged from our analysis and attempt, finally, to draw some of those lines together. And we might even attempt to follow those lines right into this very lecture hall.

1. By way of conclusion, therefore, let us start at the broadest possible level and then gradually bring the focus nearer and nearer to home. At the very outset we noted that we would adopt two main methodological premises:

a. the importance of non-disciplinary analysis, the argument being that it is impossible to interpret meaningfully the economic, political, social, cultural and even the environmental dimensions of East African reality without systematically interrelating the consideration of each of these dimensions with *all* of the others, and
b. the importance of viewing the present—the contemporary structure, current strategies and policies—in historical perspective, the present as history, as it were.

At the beginning the argument for such a non-disciplinary, totalizing, methodology may have sounded excessively abstract to you, even when spelled out carefully, as in Arrighi's important article, "Revolution for the Social Sciences." Now, however, we have exemplified, over many weeks, this methodology in practice and you are now in a position to judge for yourself whether such an approach illuminates the "development problem" more effectively and realistically than any very likely alternative methodology (e.g. via the primacy granted to discrete disciplines). I would hope, however, that enough of the strength of such a perspective has been proven to encourage you to hold onto it as a reference-point when, in subsequent years, you go on to more specialized, more "technocratic," pursuits—a pattern of training that is necessary, perhaps, but that carries with it real dangers of distortion unless continually situated within a larger, more comprehensive framework such as we have been developing.

2. Most important for our purposes has been the specific application of the method, its use in tracing a *specific historical process*—namely, the rise of capitalism in Western Europe and North America and of capitalist-driven imperialism throughout the rest of the world (including, of course, in North America itself in the first instance); the emergence of a socialist alternative articulated on a worldwide scale; and the placing of a "Third World" within such an evolving context.

The advantages of beginning with such a global approach to East Africa should now be apparent. At the most straightforward level a number of examples, both positive and negative, can be evaluated, comparatively, for their possible relevance to the solution of East African problems. More important (i) it is only in this way that one can fully grasp the forces that have actually shaped the present structure of East Africa's economy and society; and (ii) it is only in this way that one can identify those aspects of the context—the hegemony of global capitalist imperialism and the reality of dependence, the centrality of domestic class-structures and class forces, the potential of worldwide progressive forces—that can be most relevant to the selection of development strategies and policies in the future.

In this way you begin to be empowered to see the problem of development, not as an abstract model but as a lived historical reality. Of course the various models we have looked at—Seidman's "dual economies," Frank's "development of underdevelopment," concepts of "growth without development" and "perverse growth" (apparent economic growth that actually makes the structural transformation necessary for genuine development more difficult, a reality only comprehensible using an historical and non-disciplinary perspective)—are all useful to developing a perspective within which the relative merits and true developmental potential of systems like socialism and capitalism becomes apparent, not as merely moralistic or utopian alternatives but in scientific terms and as being about development.

In fact, Ehrensaft[27] in one of your readings for today puts the basic point quite strongly:

> Semi-industrialization occurs in Third World capitalist regimes rather than full industrialization. [The argument can be] organized around the following central proposition: a [fundamentally dependent and subordinate] capitalist structure of production in Third World political economies blocks the emergence of a national bourgeoisie which (i) would find it in its interest during a given historical period to act in ways that lead to a societal acquisition of the organizational and cognitive capabilities to utilize the most potent productive techniques available and (ii) has the power to mobilize society in pursuit of this interest.

In short, one begins to sense the need for an alternative to capitalism to break through this logjam at the levels of both global circumstances and national class realities.

3. It is these last remarks that bring us directly to East Africa itself. Again, Ehrensaft summarizes the main point:

> The principle substantive implication of the structures of domination approach for Sub-Saharan Africa is that regional and continental integration within a structure of global capitalist domination will result, at best, in semi-industrialization rather than full growth. Examination of large economic units such as Brazil and India shows that size alone is not sufficient to overcome the inherent tendencies of peripheral capitalism toward early oligopolization and consequent restriction of production. If Africa is to move beyond [what is at best] semi-industrialization, it must change not boundaries but regimes and must create a viable non-capitalist order.

This is, in effect, what we have been doing: developing a serviceable history of East Africa using what is, in effect, a "structures of domination" approach and placing Tanzania's own strategies and policies firmly in that context.[28] This is not entirely easy because, as Ehrensaft says, such an analysis is not yet done very often (something that puts you on an important frontier in doing your own essays, of course). In this way it has become clear, I hope, that peripheral capitalism, the highpoint of whose aspiration can only be a kind of "semi-industrialization, is the norm in East Africa—even though, as we have seen, Kenya is said by some analysts to be an exception to this view as to capitalism's non-developmental prospects.

4. Ehrensaft takes his point further, of course, noting both the drive toward East African unity and, especially, Tanzania's own attempt to break this pattern. He also suggests that

> a great deal of historical research is required in order to trace the historical evolution of historical capitalism in Africa since 1500. The works of Furtado or Ferrer on Latin America or Wertheim on Indonesia are good methodological guides for the type of historical research which is needed. Synthesizing structural-historical studies of individual African national societies are required as well as more limited studies that analyze narrower ranges of phenomena within the context of national and international power structures.

"Limited studies that analyze narrower ranges of society": this is merely one more reason, beyond the pressing and practical imperatives for so doing in a post-Arusha context, for our having concluded this course with detailed case studies of specific Tanzanian policies (always set within the broader context we have been exploring, of course).

True, it is better to divide the Tanzanian totality into such "pieces" as "industrial strategy," "rural development," "education," and so on than into the abstract pigeon-holes of "economics," "political science," "geography," "literature" and "sociology." But there are some dangers in this way of proceeding too: it cannot be emphasized too often that we must be careful to put the pieces back together again and to understand all these various policy fronts as being very closely inter-related indeed. How to do this? Should one kind of consideration come first in order to situate the others? Do some fronts of policy warrant more attention than others? These were issues that we, as the teachers of the course, agonized over a great deal.

For not only do these overlap with important questions as to strategic choices, the allocation of scarce resources, and the like, but they are also all related to the broader issues as to the nature of the overall Tanzanian social system that we were looking at before we even launched into our case studies:

a. Clearly we must continue to consider ideology, especially in the way it enunciates the very values and priorities that shape the conceptualization of the development problem, both generally and quite specifically.
b. We must also consider the popular base of such policies, not least the way in which they can and should be meeting the real needs of the people—and the extent to which "the people" (both workers and peasants) actually is empowered to press their own needs and choices upon decision-makers.
c. And there is, of course, the question of those decision-makers themselves, which is, self-evidently, a potential elite with its own possible class and bureaucratic self-interest in ensuring narrow policy outcomes that actually sustain the overall system of underdevelopment. This is a potential conflict between technical skill and policy-makers own interests and ideologies that we have seen illuminated especially clearly in the writings of Malcolm Segall on Tanzania's health system. But it is a point, a challenge, that has come up many times in our various seminars.

5. Moreover, we can bring this kind of focus to bear on this very university itself. Whatever our differences, we all share many of the same attributes and many of the same temptations. For we are all on the way to becoming part of the "elite," for whom our education is a potential key to power, privilege and bureaucratic arrogance. What, in short, of the University? Fortunately there is an observer, the Ugandan Okot p'Bitek, arguably East Africa's leading contemporary poet, who has recently put the relevant point here far more eloquently than I could hope to do and I will quote him[29] to you here:

> I believe that most of our social ills are indigenous, that the primary sources of our problems are native. They are rooted in the social setup, and the most effective solutions cannot be imported. But must be the result of deliberate reorganization of the resources for tackling specific issues...
>
> The most striking and frightening characteristic of all African governments is this, that without an exception, all of them are dictatorships, and practice such ruthless discriminations as make the South Africa apartheid look tame. African socialism [for example] may be defined as the government of the educated, for the educated. You cannot become a member of *their* parliament unless you speak English of French or Kiswahili. You may be the greatest oral historian but the will never allow you anywhere near *their* University.
>
> This is not discrimination by white settlers against Africans, but discrimination of Africans by Africans, discrimination by the "black suit" town tribesmen, discrimination by the educated men in power against their fellow men—their brothers and sisters, mothers and fathers, against their own folk left in the villages.
>
> I feel like shouting a revolutionary slogan:
>
> "The uneducated of Uganda unite
> You have nothing to lose but your chains."
>
> The students in our University are not revolutionary. They are committed and conservative. They have vested interests. They look forward to graduation, the circumcision ceremony before joining the "big car" tribesmen. Our university and schools are nests in which black exploiters are hatched and bred, at the expense of taxpayers, or perhaps heartpayers.
>
> And when they have fallen into things
> They eat the meat from the chest of bulls
> And their wives grow large buttocks
> And their skins shine with health,
> They throw themselves into soft beds
> But the hip-bones of the voters
> Grow painful sleeping on the same earth
> They slept before Uhuru[30]

> I leave it to political scientists to explore and analyse this strange situation whereby Independence means the replacement of foreign rule by native dictatorship. What does equality mean in newly independent African states?

There is no doubt, in light of this formulation, that we, you and I, are potentially an important part of the *problem* of underdevelopment.

6. We can even narrow our focus further by looking at the course, East African Society and Environment, in which we are presently engaged. For, whether you realize it or not, EASE is a dangerous course. In certain important ways it grew out of the student crisis of 1966 right here on this campus. There was much talk at the time about the necessity of having political education to transform you, the students, into potential political leaders of the construction of socialism. One catch though: you can't really effectively force people to be creative socialists which is what you really need to ensure the genuine construction of socialism.

It was nonetheless felt by many of us, however, that one thing the university should be discouraged from doing was to stand in the way of students developing an understanding of what socialism is all about. Yet that is what the university, we felt, was actually doing at the time—and is still, to a very large extent, doing. As suggested in Arrighi's article (mentioned earlier), one we read at the very outset of this course, a major way in which the conventional university does this is by dividing up reality into diverse foci of disciplinary specialization and presenting mystifying, ahistorical models that obscure the real problems of development and help to hide the realities of ideology, power and capitalist economic structure.

In sharp contrast, EASE is the latest in a series of attempts, many of them resisted vigorously by conservative forces both within the University and without, to overcome these and other barriers in the way of a socialist understanding—by means of exemplifying better scientific work and seeing society as a coherent whole. In fact our approach can be seen to be important: because it is the only way in which you can hope to actually see enough of reality to really know what is going on.

But it cannot—and I repeat, cannot—make you into a socialist. In fact, this is precisely where and why EASE is so dangerous. For such a course may merely make you more self-conscious and knowledgeable exploiters: if you come to see even more clearly where you, as prospective elites, fit into the picture, you may merely be better armed of defend your own interests as they could be most narrowly defined (in terms of the privileges attendant upon your elevation to membership of a dominant class and/or in terms of personal selfishness). It is a danger that any progressive lecturer presenting such material must live with uneasily. But, of course, there are other options as to how you might come to use the knowledge you acquire here too. We live in hope.

7. This last point brings the focus, finally, right down to you and me: where we take our stand, what choices we make. And this kind of personal, existential choice is, I repeat, something the course can't say anything very much about. So I won't, except to quote Amilcar Cabral, who, as you know, is one of my favourite points of reference. The quote itself exemplifies one of his most important emphases. And perhaps in the present context—in which you as fledgling members of the petty bourgeoisie must consider what future choices you will yourselves make—his statement has special resonance:

> What attitude [he asks] can the petty bourgeoisie adopt? Obviously people on the left will call for the revolution, the right will call for the "no-revolution," i.e., a capitalist road or something like that. The petty bourgeoisie can either ally itself with imperialism and the reactionary strata in its own country to try and preserve itself as a petty bourgeoisie or ally itself with the workers and peasants who must themselves take or control to make the revolution. We can be very clear what we are asking the petty bourgeoisie to do. Are we asking it to commit suicide? Because if there is a revolution, then, the petty bourgeoisie will have to abandon power to the workers and peasants and cease to exist *qua* petty bourgeoisie.
>
> ...I think this helps to clarify the character of the revolutionary petty-bourgeoisie. If I may put it this way, I think one thing that can be said is this: the revolutionary petty bourgeoisie is honest; I.e., in spite of all hostile conditions, it remains identified with the fundamental interests of the popular masses. To do this it may have to commit suicide but it will not lose: by sacrificing itself it can reincarnate itself, but in the condition of workers and peasants. In speaking of honesty I am not trying to establish moral criteria for judging the role of the petty bourgeoisie when it is in power; what I mean by honesty, in a political context, is total commitment and total identification with the toiling masses.[31]

Commit suicide? Yes, it can be done in Tanzania too. [I then briefly reviewed several case studies we had done in the course, concluding that] in the short-run, until the mass of the Tanzanian population finds the way and will to push us even harder than they have, we—you and I—do have some leeway (probably too much) to make our choice: are we to be part of the problem or part of the solution?

Speaking for myself, the powers-that-be here don't seem to want me around anymore. So, I'll return to Canada in a month or so and try, if I have the courage and character to do so, to "commit suicide" as a member of the North American middle-class in the interests of a worldwide revolution: socialism is nothing if it is not international in scope, after all. You, you get to stay here, and to decide, as potential new recruits to the Tanzanian petty-bourgeoisie, what to do with yourselves. I can merely hope that this course will have made this decision more challenging and more complicated for you than it might otherwise have been. In making such decisions, as well in the examinations, I will conclude then by saying: "*Nawatakia heri. Asanteni, jamaa*" (Good luck, and thanks, comrades).

There were ideas here, still in embryo, that I would adopt, with various considered modifications over the years, as I came, eventually, to build a university teaching career in Canada (I've just this year [Spring, 2008] given my final "post-retirement" class at Toronto's York University, from where I actually retired as a full-time faculty member several years ago—after more than three decades in the ranks). I would teach and write under such an umbrella over the many years—but I was also sustaining my link to Africa even more actively than that, as the next four chapters will testify.

I RETURNED TO CANADA FROM TANZANIA, then, before the end of the year, 1972. My intention was to write the story of my Tanzania years, to flesh out the substance of the differences that drove the above-mentioned conference and its momentary redirection of the university, and to detail the Akivaga crisis that gave a clear signal as to just how unlikely it was going to be to see any very substantial remoulding of Tanzania actually realized. However, I was soon, as I will shortly discuss, caught up in the struggle for liberation to the south of Tanzania, in Mozambique and elsewhere in southern Africa. Moreover, I was by now even more conscious of a need to ground my theory in a practice that I was not now to be allowed to continue with in Tanzania in any case.

I would therefore seek to so ground it either in Canada or southern Africa (or, as it turned out, in some combination of both fronts of struggle). Thus I would, with others, seek to expand liberation support work to also embrace a politics of resistance to those aspects of Canadian reality that had helped to move Canada to the wrong side of that escalating struggle in southern Africa. Not that I took the attempts to create a new society—and, among other things, a new university—back in Tanzania any less seriously than I had done up to that point. Indeed, one thing I brought back with me, when I shipped my belongings home to Canada, was an extraordinary cache of materials—faculty board minutes, reports and documents, my own notes—that recorded the struggle at the university in very great detail. It was my intention, upon my return to Canada to write a careful and, I hoped, illuminating account of that whole process—from which Tanzanians, as well as others, seeking to overcome the lingering force of western cultural imperialism in such institutions as universities, might learn useful lessons.

As it happened I was so quickly drawn forward into the liberation support/anti-apartheid struggle, and to writing more and more about southern Africa itself, that I never did launch my study of Tanzania's university (although I was, subsequently, to experience at first hand related university-centred struggles in Canada, Mozambique and South Africa!). Enter, a few years ago, Michelle Borbonniere, a Queens graduate then just enrolled in a Master's programme in African history at Dalhousie University, and eager to write on the "crisis" at the University of Dar es Salaam during the Arusha Declaration years. At a stroke I passed from being, in my own self-definition, an historical protagonist to being an historical source! I was, of course, interviewed. But I had more to give: that historical archive still mouldering away, more than thirty years later, in my basement. This I gladly passed on to Michelle who wrote a formidable Master's thesis on the basis of these and other materials and interviews she was able to collect. Moreover, she is now at Stanford pursuing a PhD, her thesis to be focused on more or less the same topic. Only this time she plans to get to Tanzania and interview local people on the ground. Me, I can't wait to see the result.

AND SO I HAVE HAPPILY CEDED THE TASK of writing up the saga of the University of Dar es Salaam's early years to the likes of Michelle Borbonniere and other younger and committed historians. But why hadn't I done the job—the writing of an account of the struggle at the university in the context of a then highly charged Tanzanian political scene—myself? Here, as I've hinted above, the vagaries, personal and political, of life interceded. First off, my wife and I agreed that, with no employment and now with two small children, we should return to Canada—although neither of us had a job in hand there either. Nonetheless, Pat, though she had managed to complete her Master's degree in History at the University in Dar and done some teaching, was anxious to get home and relaunch a career in teaching in Canada that she had begun before our marriage and our subsequent travels from New Jersey to London to Tanzania. I, too, felt that this would be a good plan and agreed to shoulder the role of "house-husband"—minding our two very young children, for starters—until something of my own turned up. This was a role I came to play, pretty exclusively, for the next three years, once back in Toronto, until a teaching job did turn up for me at York University's Atkinson College, then an admirable home of part-time night school students and numerous worthy, and slightly bent (leftward!), colleagues.

In those first years, I did find time to write up my research on rural Tanzania into a doctoral dissertation that I finally presented (unsuccessfully) at Princeton (see "Preface" to Section C). Still, I doubt that my relocation back to Canada (and to the domestic realm) would alone have been sufficient to deflect me from becoming an historian of the developments on "the Hill" (as we have seen the university referred to, above) in Tanzania. No, the fact is that, as we packed and planned to leave Dar, I also received an invitation, to visit, with Frelimo[32] soldiers, the liberated areas of Tete Province in northern Mozambique, one front in their struggle against the Portuguese oppressors of their native country. It was a trip that would alter my life in crucial ways. I will turn to it in the next chapter.

CHAPTER TWO

The 1970s

Southern Africa and Canada

As noted above, my biography as "political traveller" (if I may continue to be so bold as to think of my life in these terms) should probably start with my Tanzania years, for the reasons already alluded to. Yet I would increasingly come to think of myself as a kind of lifelong broker between unfolding happenings in Africa and my native Canada to which I returned in 1972 and the Tanzania link was more about actively participating on the ground in real struggles there. I did not lose a strong emotional tie to Tanzania but, upon returning home to Canada, I was increasingly being carried away from it emotionally towards the fresh struggles for liberation against entrenched white racism and imperial domination further south—and ultimately to links with it that also stretched back into Canada and the imperial North more generally.

Of course, Tanzania was on the very cusp of that struggle, both geographically and in terms of continental political commitments. And it bordered directly on Mozambique, with Dar es Salaam becoming the actual cutting-edge of events unfolding further south. In fact, it was for this reason that the shift in my priorities and commitments had already begun in the latter stages of my Dar es Salaam sojourn—as I deepened my range of contact with people in the various southern African liberation movements. This was particularly true as regards Mozambique and its Front for the Liberation of Mozambique (FRELIMO) movement, many of whose militants I had begun to know as I learned from them of their struggle against Portuguese colonialism. I did some volunteer work with them as well, helping with the movement's English-language publication, *Mozambique Revolution*, among other things.

In fact, when my contract was not renewed at the University in Dar (1972) and I was slated to return to Canada, I was approached by two Frelimo comrades—Samora Machel, by now the President of the movement, and Jorge Rebelo, Frelimo's "responsavel" for information with whom I had worked most closely on *Mozambique Revolution*. They offered me an opportunity to travel to the liberated areas of Tete Province in Mozambique with a group of armed Frelimo guerrillas in order to see the struggle that I had been helping to write about with my own eyes and to report back.[33] I immediately began walking extended distances up and down Dar's coastal road to get in some kind of shape for the long marches that would inevitably be part of such an arduous journey—on foot, although in the company of an armed column of guerrillas!—from the Zambian border about two-thirds of the way to the Zambezi and back. The following account, written upon my return, captures something of the drama—for me!—of such an adventure, one that was to shape so much of my subsequent life.

I began the original article that contained an account of my trip by examining the broad parameters of the Portuguese struggle and its international implications. The second half, however, contained an account of my trip and it is from this that I draw here:

WE HAD SPENT SIXTEEN DAYS with Jose Moyane, Frelimo Chief of Defense (and Acting Regional Secretary) for Tete Province and had marched with him over 70 miles into the interior of Mozambique—across the main Fingoe-Zumbo Road, by then abandoned by the Portuguese, and two thirds of the way to the Zambezi. Now, as our stay drew to a close, we met with him for the last time. He began by summarizing, for more than an hour, the current state of the struggle in Tete and in Mozambique as a whole, helping us to pull together our myriad impressions from the trip. He explored with us, as well, the implications of Frelimo's military advance into the crucial province of Manica and Sofala, an advance which had only just been confirmed by reports reaching our column (this was in August-September, 1972) but which can now be seen, as noted above, to have become the major determinant of the recent overthrow of the Portuguese government itself.[34] The clarity of analysis and the impressive dedication that we had come to recognize as being typical of Frelimo "responsibles" were again apparent as we talked with him. But it was when we turned to more personal matters that we reached what I now see to have been an even deeper level of understanding of the meaning of the Mozambique revolution.

We had asked almost all of the many Mozambicans we interviewed inside the liberated areas to supplement their analysis of the current situation with some autobiographical remarks. We did so more reluctantly in Moyane's case, given his position and the many claims upon his time. But once asked he warmed to the theme, and in sketching at length his autobiography he gave us a particularly vivid picture of the realities of southern Africa and of the grisly nature of Portuguese oppression. Older (at 36) than most of the other cadres we met during our stay, he had also experienced at first hand even more than they the day-to-day humiliation and brutalities of the Portuguese presence. He was able therefore to trace in detail the many menial jobs he been forced to take (including one in the South African mines, where his father, working there before him, had died), the discrimination and abuse which he had experienced, and his hard struggle over the years to piece together the rudiments of a primary education. He also spoke of his slowly growing political consciousness, sparked in part by events elsewhere—Nkrumah in Ghana, Nyerere in Tanzania, the fight against the Federation, Congolese independence, the outbreak of fighting in Angola—and by the dramatic visit of Eduardo Mondlane to Mozambique (at a time when the latter was still with the United Nations) in 1961. Moyane began to see the way out of his isolation; in 1963 he escaped from Mozambique to Tanzania and, in his own words, then "entered into the collective life of Frelimo." With this phrase he abruptly brought the account of his "autobiography" to a close. Quite unconsciously, it seemed, he was thus making the point that his history was now the history of Frelimo and of the Mozambican people as a whole.

The key to the future of Mozambique can be discerned in this anecdote. For Moyane's conclusion reflects a spirit—difficult to present in terms other than those which sound cliched and romanticized—which is nonetheless discernible everywhere in the liberated areas. I was continually meeting cadres, very often in their early twenties, at various levels of the Frelimo structure who astonished me with their sure grasp of the essentials of the struggle and their obvious dedication. I was tempted to contrast them, perhaps unfairly, with too many of the conservative students (of the same age group) I had known well during seven years at the University of Dar es Salaam. After drawing such a comparison, the fields of practice and of struggle appeared even more obviously to be the ideal terrain for leadership training—better, certainly, than most of the formal education system which has been inherited from colonialism elsewhere in Africa.

There were some closely related aspects of life in free Mozambique that also struck me. Travelling with armed combatants and occasionally staying at military bases deep inside Mozambique, it was impossible not to consider the dangers of militarism—all the more so in light of the past decade of continental developments. Significantly, Frelimo seemed equally preoccupied with such problems, and with any future danger to the nature of post-liberation Mozambican society that might arise from this quarter. Sebastião Mabote, Frelimo's Chief of Military Operations with whom we also travelled throughout our stay in the liberated areas, raised the question on a number of occasions, discussing frankly both the Algerian case and the grotesque situation in much of army-dominated black Africa. Too often elsewhere, he felt, "they don't explain to the soldiers why they have these arms"; in contrast, "politics commands the army in our case."

Thus all militants, including those most clearly assigned to administrative posts, had military training and, as we saw for ourselves, ordinary villagers were everywhere actively engaged in local militia units. Moreover, those involved directly in military work were constantly reminded of, and instructed in, the basically political nature of the overall struggle for Mozambican independence of which they form a part;[35] we were even fortunate enough to meet several of the political commissars who were undertaking precisely this kind of educational work within the army and at the movement's "Centres of Preparation." After obtaining independence, Mabote assured us, the campaign will continue against the establishment of any form of caste system premised on what he dismissively termed "military professionalism." Many of the military personnel we interviewed echoed, in one form or another, Mabote's statement that "we are making a revolution, not a war of conquest."

The latter statement is particularly crucial. For, ultimately, the main check upon militarism and other forms of bureaucratic involution of the liberation struggle in Mozambique was seen, by Mabote and others, to be the existence of an active popular base for that struggle. Equally important, the existence of such a base is also the key to the military success that has thus far been achieved against the Portuguese; in Mabote's words, "the atomic bomb in this war is the people's consciousness." There is of course a strong popular sentiment upon which to build in Mozambique; the Portuguese have seen to that. At a large public gathering which we attended inside the country, the appropriate mood was established at the outset by requesting an indication from the crowd of all those who had been abused or stolen from by the Portuguese, all those pressed into labour on the roads or in the South African mines, all those who had carried a white man's sedan chair (as several of the very old men evidently had done in their time), and the like. Yet spontaneity has not been the whole story either. Beyond this, we witnessed the importance of the institutions that give a new form to the hostility felt by peasants towards the Portuguese, and of the methods of political work which provide that vague sentiment with a new content, revitalizing and further radicalizing it.[36]

Thus, in institutional terms, we found an ongoing political system, spawned by Frelimo, which reached right up from the village level and we learned, from those involved, of the active political life at village, circle, district, and regional levels where the work of elected representatives meshed remarkably smoothly with that of Frelimo-appointed officials. Obviously there are possible contradictions here, but all the evidence indicated that these were being effectively resolved. Certainly, the most important guarantee of this was that the point was constantly being made to Frelimo cadres in all the movement forums in which we participated that they take great pains to premise their political activity and mobilizational responsibilities upon respect for and confidence in the people. Nor was it at all unusual to find even ordinary soldiers saying, as one did in the course of our interviews, that "without the people we cannot do anything."

One incident in particular suggests itself to me as a measure of this reality. In visiting a village of about 300 people at a few hours' march from the district headquarters where we were staying, we were accompanied by a group of 40 or more armed men and women. Yet when we arrived in the village we were warmly welcomed; more importantly, the soldiers mixed freely with the villagers, helping with chores or sitting casually with old women by the fire as the latter cooked supper. There are not many countries in the world where the arrival of a group of soldiers (or even a single policeman!) could be the signal for life to continue normally. Yet in liberated Mozambique this is the order of the day.

At one level, the immediate advantages of using methods of work that can produce this kind of link between guerrilla and peasant are self-evident. We saw, for example, the extent to which the active involvement of ordinary villagers in the transportation of war material and other essentials is basic to the ongoing confrontation with the Portuguese; and we learned of the importance of agricultural supplies provided by villagers to Frelimo forces. The existence of such a milieu also guarantees greater security for Frelimo movements and the more ready recruitment of new full-time militants. And the long-term implications are no less important: the discouragement of any drift towards elitist preconceptions and/or self-defeating authoritarian methods on the part of the cadres certainly, but equally impressive the growing self-confidence of the villagers themselves. This was evidenced for us by their active participation in public meetings and in the quality of their discussions with us at the village level. But perhaps it was epitomized most pointedly by one of a village's elected officials who, in an exchange with the Frelimo district commissar travelling with us, stated that he and his fellow villagers now felt Frelimo to be really concerned to serve the interests of the people. But what if things didn't change basically after independence? Then we would have to think again, and act accordingly, he said. A firm basis, one might suspect, for the sustaining of Frelimo's revolutionary trajectory!

"Revolution" was a word we heard often inside Mozambique. In fact, one of the first points which Comrade Mabote made to us as we set out from the Zambian border for the interior was that the imperatives of mobilizing against a recalcitrant colonialism like that of Portugal gave Mozambicans a chance most other African states had missed. Here nationalist self-assertion could not remain a surface phenomenon, but inevitably involved a basic re-ordering of social relationships inherited from traditional society and from colonialism—in short it meant, in Mabote's words, "the opportunity to have a revolution." For Mabote, "it is not sufficient merely to defeat the enemy; we must also be prepared to remake things afterwards. We conquer, but this is not the main point. Rather, we are 'conquering' the consciousness of the people with the concept of a society worked out by the people." And he specifically echoed an idea I had first heard expressed by Eduardo Mondlane himself shortly before his assassination: that it would be almost a pity if Mozambicans were to defeat the Portuguese too quickly since so much is being learned in the course of the struggle. In so arguing, it is evident that both Mondlane and Mabote were only half-joking.

The checks upon elitism and the stimulus to the people's own self-confidence, discussed above, are examples of the lessons being learned, as are the strenuous efforts devoted in the liberated areas to developing educational and health systems tailored to the people's needs. We saw clear evidence of the latter accomplishments when we visited schools and clinics—profoundly impressive, however under-equipped they might be—in a part of Fingoe district where such facilities had been unknown throughout the long years of Portuguese control.

Other evidence was the conscious concern to transform the substance of women's roles in the new Mozambique. This will be a long process which has only just begun, but it could be measured, modestly, in the statement of one very young woman cadre in Frelimo who told us that the biggest change which the movement had brought to her life was that now when she spoke men listened to her. Certainly, Frelimo's concern with this issue was most apparent. At one public meeting we attended, much the largest proportion of the discussion was devoted to exploring with the villagers the importance of affirming women's basic equality. And, significantly, three recent deserters from the Portuguese side spontaneously pinpointed the treatment of women as comrades within the movement as the most striking of many differences that they had noted since joining FRELIMO. It was this, one said, which had suggested to them most forcefully that "something new is being created." Moreover, the challenge to pre-existing orthodoxies regarding the question of women was merely one part of a much broader cultural revolution. Just as impressive were the efforts, described by a young teacher (and exemplified for us by the students at his school), to play subtly upon the prevailing art forms of the area, encouraging the local people to rework their songs and dances so that, without denaturing them, they could be given a political or social shading relevant to contemporary imperatives. Indeed, something of the breadth of the revolutionary concept that was at work in free Mozambique could be glimpsed in another of Mabote's half-joking remarks when he insisted good-humoredly to a gathering of Frelimo militants that "not to sing well is a political error."

Finally and centrally, there were changes to be seen in the economic life of the liberated areas. "We know that the basis of the struggle is economic," Mabote observed, "that there are two classes: the exploited and the exploiters. Colonialism and capitalism develop from this point." Frelimo's emphasis is to be a different one: "Our population produces individually, but we are working towards collective production—that is the general goal." One example of this collective emphasis was provided by the two hard-working "responsibles" from Frelimo's Department of Production and Commerce who accompanied us on our trip and whose current task was the establishment of a number of "people's stores" in that part of Tete Province which we were visiting. But it was the changing relations of production in one of the villages that particularly caught my attention—perhaps because of my own studies of efforts at collective rural development in neighboring Tanzania.

In this particular village, to quote a previously cited article, "I discovered a division of labor which incorporated a significant proportion of collective farmed fields, work on these being recorded in a log-book against eventual distribution of the proceeds. I found metal-workers and basket-makers, who had originally worked as mini-entrepreneurs in the village, now working as part of this collective division of labor, their time spent also being recorded in the village book." The community spirit thus engendered seemed also to make it easier for the village to shoulder those broader responsibilities noted above—helping to feed the fighting forces by providing produce and joining periodically in the carrying of vital materials from the frontier. In short this was an experiment that compared favorably with most of the "ujamaa villages" one knew in Tanzania. Here, too, the evidence begins to suggest "that in such a peasantry, increasingly well organized and now working self-consciously against various forms of exploitation, there can be seen some guarantee of the continued forward momentum of the Mozambican revolution, even after independence has been won."[37]

Slowly, then, during our stay inside the liberated areas a picture of the new Mozambique took shape for us, a picture of a revolutionary society in the making. It remained true that the achievements visible on the ground had not yet been formulated into a fully coherent ideology. In fact, the thrust of Frelimo's accomplishment remains profoundly populist in some respects, and certainly Mabote himself, in our conversations, eschewed the use of an unambiguously socialist vocabulary. Yet the direction of development emerged clearly enough in the movement's practice, and it is this very process of radicalization which is increasingly being codified by Frelimo responsibles, and increasingly being grasped by ordinary Mozambicans.[38] Discussion of the dangers of "exploitation" and of elitism and entrepreneurship, continual emphasis upon the need for the most basic sorts of democratization, knowing comparisons between the various development choices made by Russia, Korea, China,

Scandinavia—such topics were the stuff of our dinner-table conversation inside Mozambique. To be sure, some left sectarians—secure within the cocoons of their own theoretical abstractions—will recoil from the loose ends that a real revolution thus evidences. Nonetheless, we may be certain that the guardians of the status quo in southern Africa were well aware that such a process has all too great a promise, that from their point of view it presents all too pressing a threat.

It is important to note, therefore, that about the latter—those guardians of the status quo—Frelimo has no illusions, for the most theoretical developed aspect of the movement's ideology is undoubtedly its anti-imperialism. How often we heard it reiterated inside Mozambique that the enemy is not the Portuguese people but the Portuguese state and its colonial apparatus, not the white race but the imperialist system. Opportunist brands of racism and "ultra-nationalism" were constantly being condemned and the dangers of neocolonialism widely discussed. The reverse side of this coin was also much in evidence—a profound and deeply moving internationalism. The welcome afforded us throughout the liberated areas was proof of this, of course. It was gratifying for me, as a white and a Canadian, to be warmly accepted as a comrade by such people, despite the graphic realities on a world scale of racial oppression and North American imperialism. But such a reception also heightened my own awareness of how much more progressives in the metropolitan countries must do about southern Africa in order to be worthy of such trust and friendship.

My trip to Tete took place in 1972. I returned to Dar and from there I left almost immediately to return to Canada with my family. But not before I had the brief final meeting, that I mentioned earlier, with Samora Machel in the garden of the house where my wife and I were staying in Dar.

VERY SOON, BACK IN TORONTO, we were able to become part of a strong group of people prepared for action in that city in support of Frelimo and of the struggles against Portuguese colonialism. Not that there weren't already principled Canadians, alert to the issue of southern Africa and to the enormities of white minority rule there prior to 1972. Thus, when I first arrived home (in 1972) the work of stitching together such a group of Canadians concerned with and about southern Africa had already begun, but much remained to be done. Moreover, those of us who came together in Toronto to form a new "Toronto Committee for the Liberation of Portugal's African Colonies/TCLPAC" were also determined to not become merely vicarious cheerleaders for Frelimo and other such movements. From the very beginning we sought to underscore Canada's official links to the wrong side of the struggles in southern Africa. As it happened I was invited to make my own first foray into this issue when I was invited, shortly after my arrival back home, by friends associated with the Canadian magazine, *Canadian Forum*, to write an editorial on the subject for their March, 1973, issue, one I entitled, advisedly, "Both Sides of the Street."

CANADA'S POLICY TOWARD SOUTHERN AFRICA HAS BEEN, over the years, a fundamentally dishonest one. Government spokesmen have found it very easy to be self-righteous about the situation there, characterized as it is by a vicious and blatant combination of racial oppression, economic exploitation and anachronistic colonialism. But expressions of pious distaste for what the white regimes are doing in South Africa, Zimbabwe/Rhodesia, Namibia/South-West Africa, Angola and Mozambique invariably have been combined with a practice of "business as usual" which more than cancels out the piety.

Why raise this issue again when a small handful of Canadians have been raising similar points for years (in "The Black Paper," September 1970, *Canadian Forum*, for example) with little effect. Quite simply because the contradiction that lies at the heart of Canadian policy will be a much more difficult one to straddle in the future than it has been in the past. Unfortunately for all those who would thus seek to work both sides of the street in southern Africa, the situation has begun to change rapidly; the tempo of the Africans' own challenge to white hegemony has picked up, and as the struggle has escalated, so too an increased polarization between the various protagonists has taken place. Policy-making about southern Africa now ceases to be a matter of mere moralizing about a static, if "regrettable," situation; the whole question has now been placed firmly on the political agenda, with the result that even a refusal to act will be much more clearly revealed as a choice of sides. In short, the 1970's are witnessing developments in Southern Africa that separate the rhetoric from the reality of Canadian foreign policy in a particularly graphic manner.

Escalation? Certainly the progress achieved by Africa's liberation forces is a fact that even the most conventional news media have had more and more to recognize. This despite the equally obvious fact that the struggle of the African masses against the powerful forces which oppress them will continue to be a long and difficult one. But the dramatic events in Durban, South Africa, earlier this year echoed similar events in Namibia a year earlier. Recent months have also brought the first wholly convincing evidence that the black liberation forces of Zimbabwe—at last operating under a united military front—can mount a viable military challenge to the Smith regime. Most significant of all there is the onward march of the guerrillas who oppose Portuguese colonialism in Mozambique, in Angola and, further north, in Guinea-Bissau. Even the white press in Southern Africa no longer attempts to hide the scope of that advance.

On the contrary, the most dire kind of warnings are now being sounded as the Movement for the Liberation of Mozambique (Frelimo) has ringed the area of the Cabora Bassa dam and harasses all communications in Tete Province, and it has carried the war into Manica and Sofala, home of the vital port of Beira and of the main road and rail that link Rhodesia to the sea. Moreover, not only does the tide of liberation run strong, it also runs deep. When, for example, I had the opportunity to accompany Frelimo guerrillas into the liberated areas of Tete Province in August of last year I saw not only an impressive military apparatus in action but also, well inside the country, a whole network of political institutions, social services and economic activities in full swing under the leadership of Frelimo. I found the Portuguese presence reduced to a merely occasional harassment (crop destruction and the like) by plane and helicopter. And, most significantly, I discovered at public meetings and through visits to villages inside Mozambique a level of popular enthusiasm and involvement in the struggle far higher than I had dared to expect and of a kind that has underwritten the cumulative success of guerrilla struggle elsewhere.

Inevitably such successes have evoked even more determined resistance from those who oppose the cause of African freedom. Though certain contradictions do exist among the various White regimes in southern Africa, these are becoming marginal considerations as the boundaries that divide the territories from one another are seen, increasingly, to be irrelevant to the imperatives of sub-continental defence. Thus Rhodesians are fighting in Mozambique, and some South African forces are already active in Rhodesia, in Angola and in Mozambique (where they help to man the perimeter of the Cabora Bassa dam). Clearly this escalation is bound to accelerate; the most sober of commentators from South Africa can now report that "the likelihood is increasing that a task force, drawn from the South African and Rhodesian defence forces will be sent to Mozambique to help the Portuguese blunt the mounting black-guerrilla onslaught" (*The Christian Science Monitor*). Even more ominous, perhaps, is the opinion of South Africa's military commander, Admiral Bierman, who expresses great trepidation about the pattern of guerrilla success in Portugal's African colonies and who recently concluded an article in *Paratus*, the journal of the South African armed forces, with the argument that

> A regional treaty or alliance is an excellent goal, and should be pursued with vigour, but in the long term this can only serve as an intermediate alternative to the final aim... It is imperative that a super-power be involved in the strategy for the southern hemisphere... We must persuade the West that Communist penetration into the southern hemisphere is a direct threat to Western Europe and the rest of the free world.

Unfortunately, one "superpower" seems already to have cast itself for the role. While France, West Germany and the United Kingdom—through NATO and also more directly—are all implicated in the defense of the white redoubts, it is the deepening commitment of the United States in the prolongation of the status quo in the area that has most recently been highlighted: by the authorization of the sale of aircraft and helicopters to South Africa, for example, and by the violation of UN sanctions against Rhodesia, by a loan/aid package of $436 million to Portugal, a sum crucial to that country's economy and its war effort, as part of the Azores Agreement of 1971, and by the apparent consolidation of many more subterranean linkages. As Richard Barnet has concluded in a recent survey of American policy in southern Africa for the *New York Review of Books*: "... the United States (under the rhetoric of containing violence and preventing war) now appears ready to step up its assistance to the minority racist and colonial governments in beating back challenges to their rule." Recently the *Toronto Star* provided a feature article with the headline "Mozambique: another Vietnam," and suggested that Portugal's unwinnable war in that colony evokes such an analogy. But only a failure of imagination could have encouraged the paper's staff writer to phrase the point so narrowly. For it is all too likely that Mozambique (and, beyond that, all of southern Africa) will become "another Vietnam" not just for the Portuguese, but also for the South Africans—and for the United States itself.

How has Canada reacted to these new realities? Sad to relate, only with further hypocrisy. True, this country has avoided the worst, and most obvious, forms of complicity. We scrupulously back the flow of Canadian arms to Portugal and have observed the United Nations sponsored sanctions against Rhodesia; we have done just enough, in effect, to retain some small measure of credibility in the rest of black Africa. Yet beyond these narrow limits, and even when compared with many other western countries, our copy-book is badly blotted. Thus Portugal could not carry on her colonial wars without the military assistance that her participation in NATO makes available; however, even as countries like Norway, Denmark and Iceland have begun, *within* NATO *itself*, to question vigorously such a state of affairs, Canada has remained virtually a silent partner in this kind of complicity with colonialism. There are signs that the above-mentioned countries will press this point further within NATO in the near future; there are no signs that Canada will join them.

To take another example, Canada is now a major trade partner of Angola (or, phrased more precisely, of the Portuguese who are in possession of Angola). The marketing of Angola oil, heavily taxed at source, has become a crucial economic crop for Portuguese hegemony. Meanwhile, Gulf Oil, which nervously avoids introducing large quantities of oil from Cabinda (in Angola) into the United States, has with impunity turned Canada into the world's largest consumer of this product. Canada's peculiar brand of branch-plant imperialism has few more clear-cut expressions. And American-based multinational corporations have also seen to it that Canada is one of the world's leading consumers of Angolan coffee—a product wrung from Angola Africans under conditions of virtual slave labour. Here too a comparison may be illuminating. Popular outrage in Holland recently forced both Angolan coffee and Angolan oil out of the Dutch market and Dutch protests had a similar deterrent effect upon Gulf Oil there. Nor should the issue of Alcan's participation in the Cabora Bassa project be conveniently forgotten; it is, after all, the Swedish and Italian governments themselves who finally helped to scotch the involvements of their national firms in that infamous scheme, something the Canadian government seems never to have contemplated despite some highly vocal complaints by Canadians against this sorry state of affairs.

These instances represent merely the tip of the iceberg in any case. For we have seen that the struggle against Portuguese colonialism *inevitably* becomes a struggle for the liberation of *all* of southern Africa. Yet, as spelled out in *The Black Paper,* Canadian-based firms are active throughout the area—not least in the mining sector. Here one particularly striking case can serve to reveal the characteristic texture of Canada's approach to the economic exploitation of the sub-continent; even at a time when the American government was recently restraining American mining firms from new investments in Namibia/South Africa because of the doubtful legal status of South Africa's hold upon that territory, the Canadian government has sought at no time to question the growing involvement of Falconbridge mines there. But the fact of official Canadian indifference to the obvious political implications of supposedly "neutral" patterns of trade and investment is now sufficiently well-known. The fact does suggest, however, that as the liberation struggle spreads across southern Africa and deeper into the real heartland (in South Africa) of Canadian investment in the area, a government so motivated may find its "interests" drawing it ever more strongly into overt support for the status quo.

Then there is the question of the liberation movements themselves. Canada's constant emphasis upon the need for non-violent solutions in southern Africa (a particularly grating feature of Mitchell Sharp's African tour in 1971) has also helped us to gloss over the very nature of South African apartheid and Portuguese colonialism; our chosen emphasis is all the more obviously an anachronism at this advanced stage of the struggle. Surely it must be recognized for what it is, a fig leaf designed merely to cover an unwillingness to contemplate the replacement of established powers in the region. While Canada procrastinates in this fashion the struggle, literally, continues and once again other governments, not merely from the East but also Sweden, Holland, Denmark, Norway (not to mention the World Council of Churches), have moved to give virtual recognition—and considerable aid—directly to such movements as Frelimo and the Popular Movement for the Liberation of Angola (MPLA). One might also expect from such countries a sympathetic response to claims for recognition as an independent country made by the freedom fighters of Guinea-Bissau when the latter, now in control of the land area of their country, follow through on their promise to establish such a state later this year. Can one expect such an enlightened adjustment to the realities of the situation from Canada? The most recent round in Canada's double game is hardly encouraging.

Thus at the end of last year (1972) the United Nations General Assembly passed one of its most strongly worded resolutions about the situation in Portuguese Africa, calling for negotiations where possible, but also affirming

> that the national liberation movements of Angola, Guinea (Bissau) and Cap Verde and Mozambique are the authentic representatives of the true aspirations of the peoples of these territories and, pending their accession to independence, recommends that all governments ... when dealing with matters pertaining to the territories, should ensure, in consultation with the Organization of African Unity, the representation in an appropriate capacity of the territories by the liberation movements concerned (Para. 2).

The resolution also requested

> all governments, the specialized agencies and other organizations within the U.N. system and non-governmental organizations to render to the peoples of Angola, Guinea (Bissau) and Cap Verde and Mozambique, in particular the populations in the liberated areas of those territories, all the moral and material assistance necessary to continue their struggle for the achievement of the inalienable right to self-determination and independence (Para. 4).

And it called

> upon all states to take forthwith all possible measures to put an end to all activities that help to exploit the territories under Portuguese domination and the peoples therein and to discourage their nationals and bodies corporate under their jurisdiction from entering into any transactions or arrangements that contribute to Portugal's domination over, and impede the implementation of the declaration with respect to, these territories (Para. 6).

Canada voted, with ninety-seven other countries, *for this resolution*.

Yet when the Canadian delegate subsequently rose to address the General Assembly in order to explain Canada's vote, it was Canada's other face, the face of her complicity in southern African oppression, that he turned to the world. Canada was in favour of negotiations, of course—that is why it had supported the resolution—but "in supporting the right of people of these territories to choose their own representatives we cannot agree with the provisions of operative para. 2 which would have the United Nations make this designation on their behalf [!]" Moreover, "my delegation also wished to express once more its reservations about violent solutions to these problems and to references in this resolution which imply support for such activities." Certainly no liberation movement could draw any assurance from such statements. "As for operative para. 6 we continue to oppose attempts to interfere with trade in peaceful goods with Portugal and *her territories*" (my emphasis). So much for restraining Canada's "bodies corporate"—Gulf, General Foods, Alcan. So much, indeed, for Canada's vote in support of the resolution. For qualified in this way Canada's vote really lay with those six countries—South Africa, Portugal, the United States, Brazil, Spain and the United Kingdom—who recorded a negative vote. There we were, still working both sides of the street.

In fact, Canada's role has changed hardly at all from that correctly described and condemned by the authors of *The Black Paper* several years ago. Socialists would probably want to take the argument of that document further and to stress that such a pattern of policy is not due to any mere lack of information or sympathy on the part of Canadian decision-makers. Rather it is the inevitable by-product of the structure of Canada's economy and society, the country's own colonial status and capitalist imperatives virtually determining subservience to imperial demands within NATO and the worship of established trade and investment patterns at the expense of any discernible principle. Indeed, it could be argued very convincingly that the primary contribution of Canadians to the African cause would be to carry out our own "liberation struggle" at home.

At the same time, the realization of the latter goal is obviously a very long-term proposition: the nature of the southern African situation is such as to dictate that both socialist and concerned "liberals" also seek ways to minimize the damage Canada can do to the Africans' cause in the short run, bearing in mind that for this country to continue to stand pat and to seek some non-existent middle road of compromise is, more than ever, to find ourselves on the wrong side. There may be more room than one suspects for modification of Canada's policies towards southern Africa, even within the established structures. It will certainly be worth some considerable effort to work for such a modification in any case. The alternative—an ever more obvious complicity in the white backlash in Southern Africa—is too grisly to contemplate with equanimity.

I sought to reinforce this point in the conclusion to the brief book of the time, *Canada and Mozambique*, which had reproduced, as a first chapter, the *Canadian Forum* article included above. For, as Marcelino dos Santos, the Vice-President of Frelimo, had recently replied (1973), when questioned on a CBC radio programme, as to whether his movement was receiving any help from Canada:

> Really, Canada has made many statements but... I must say frankly that knowing what Canada (has) said several times... but knowing that Canada is doing nothing real to help the liberations movements, one should at least ask: is... the Government of Canada sincere? We don't believe it, and we hope that Canada will try to show us that it is really sincere.

To what would dos Santos attribute "this ambiguity in the attitude of Canada" then? "I'm forced to accept," he continued, "that Canada continues to think it preferable to have relationships with colonialist and fascist regimes than with people who are fighting for their freedom and their dignity." As we then noted, "the facts bear out unequivocally Mr. dos Santos' accusation. Throughout the pre-coup period, while Portugal stood four-square against African advancement, Canada's complicity in Portuguese colonialism was all too apparent." In the "Conclusion" to *Canada and Mozambique* I then proceeded to set out the details of Canada's links to Portuguese activities in Africa: these existed on the three fronts, the economic, the military and the political, and I reproduce that section of the text here.

Economic: Canada's most crucial tie to Portugal in Africa has been the economic one. The obvious importance to colonialist Portugal of Western economic linkages—those of trade and investment—need not be proven here. The extent of Canada's participation in this deadly exchange is less well known. Most important has been our standing as the world's fourth of fifth leading customer for Angolan coffee and *the world's number one importer of Angolan oil*. But our purchases of Mozambican tea (rising from 50,000 pounds in 1961 to 1,700,000 pounds in 1972) have also been significant. There can be no doubt that revenues earned from the sale of these products—the sky-rocketing amounts made available in payments and royalties by Gulf Oil for its Cabinda concession, for example—were critical for a time to Portugal's ability to retain its shaky grip in Africa. One might also mention again the Alcan case. The firm's participation in the notorious Cabora Bassa Dam project in Mozambique (a deal that helped Canada's aluminum exports to Portugal and Mozambique soar from $300,000 worth in 1969 to over four and a half million worth in 1972) was never queried by the Canadian government, despite a number of public protests at home and the aforementioned precedents of the

Swedish and Italian governments stopping their own national firms from getting involved.

Once again, Mitchell Sharp, then Secretary of State for External Affairs had arguments (if one can grace them with that term). Asked in 1973 whether the Canadian government hoped to increase its trade with "Portuguese Africa," he replied blandly: "In peaceful goods, yes. I think it is a very good idea. We believe in the Canadian government that trade helps to bring about contacts that do in fact influence policy"! The appointment that same year of Michael Chapman as commercial Representative for Canada in Luanda, the Portuguese capital of Angola, could therefore come as no surprise. At "a pleasant lunch (the account is from *Provincia da Angola*, February 22, 1973)... in a room of the Hotel Tropico, attended by a number of people related to the commercial and industrial sectors of Angola, the Provincial Secretary of Education, the Director-General of Angolan Security [!], and the Head of the Canadian Commercial Delegation in Johannesburg, Mr. R. Parlour...," Mr. Chapman put the relevant point clearly at the time of his appointment: "Canada has every interest in increasing its commercial transactions with Angola... My function will be precisely to increase commercial and industrial relations which are necessary for both parties."

Military: In line with United Nations resolutions, Canada has been reasonably careful to avoid supplying arms directly to Portugal, although given Canada's entanglements with NATO-related defense production this country's hands may be far from clean even in this respect. Thus, Richard Lobban, when visiting the liberated areas of Guinea-Bissau a year or two ago, found Canadian components amidst the wreckage of one of the Fiat G-91 airplanes supplied by West Germany and shot down by the PAIGC. But the main charge against Canada on this front refers to its silent complicity, throughout the long years of Portugal's African aggressions, in NATO's crucial links with Portugal. Theoretically, arms that became available to Portugal under NATO arrangements were not to be used in Africa; it is well known that Portugal violated these regulations flagrantly and also profited in vital ways from NATO training, spending and research work. Yet when Norway did make a public statement denouncing Portugal at the NATO ministerial meeting in Lisbon in 1971 Canada continued its silence. Nor had we ever criticized those NATO members who did directly service the Portuguese war effort.

Mitchell Sharp had an answer here too. As he replied last year to concerned Africans who pressed him on this point: "I have frequently taken advantage of NATO ministerial meetings to raise the question of Portuguese colonial policy on a bilateral basis with the Portuguese foreign minister. However, I do not think it would be either appropriate or productive to raise the issue in the NATO Council"! Even if one were (probably unwisely) to believe Mr. Sharp, it would still be an inadequate response. For it seems clear that NATO is, in any case, more than a mere European defense network. It is much better understood as being one link in a broader western chain of defense against *any* challenge to the global *status quo* of international capitalism. It would also appear that, in this chain, southern Africa, including until recently Portugal's African colonies, has become a valued link to be stoutly defended. In effect, Canada's subservience to the intention of the United States and other members of NATO vis-à-vis Portugal may merely have reflected this country's embracing of such a broader policy of counter-revolution.

It is true, of course, that NATO has now to yield to the logic of the Portuguese coup (the coup being basically reformist in any case, seeking the liberalization of an outmoded fascism rather than a socialist revolution) and the decision to decolonize in Guinea-Bissau and in Mozambique. Nevertheless, the precedent of Canada's record of silence within NATO remains disturbing, not only with regard to the possible developments in Angola (where the question of Portuguese colonialism and western presence is still very far from being settled) but even more with regard to South Africa and to the future. For in South Africa the western stake is particularly high, NATO's involvement growing, and our subservient position within capitalism's global defense network even more likely to link us to the wrong side in an escalating situation.

Political: Here the main point is that Canada has systematically undermined the credibility of the liberation movements, at the U.N. and elsewhere, by prating disingenuously about the need for "peaceful" and "non-violent" solutions in southern Africa (where, unfortunately for our case, institutionalized violence is already the defining characteristic of the regimes of white domination), rather than supporting unequivocally the struggles of the African people. This is apparent from the United Nations debate quoted above. Willfully ignoring the violence inherent in the very practice of Portuguese colonial oppression and the fact that wars of national liberation were already more than ten years old in Portugal's African colonies (now only to be won or lost, not ignored or denied!) Mitchell Sharp, up to the very last minute, reiterated tired nostrums like: "The Canadian government is opposed to giving aid to violence. It's part of our principles." Small wonder that on his notorious African tour in 1971 Sharp, while often repeating this theme, also used press interviews to openly flirt with the misleading notion of a possible "dialogue" with South Africa, a propaganda line then being pushed throughout independent Africa by the South African regime itself.

It must be noted, however, that even before the Portuguese coup there was something of a shift of position. In August, 1973, at the time of the of the Commonwealth Conference in Ottawa, Prime Minister Trudeau did hint at the possibility of Canada's providing some assistance to the liberation movements in step with that Conference's final communiqué and along the lines, presumably, of the "humanitarian" aid already given by the governments of Sweden, Denmark, Norway and Holland and by the World Council of Churches. Early in 1974 certain concrete steps were taken. It was announced that CIDA would provide aid to southern African liberation movements—not directly mind you, but by matching funds for projects put forward by various non-governmental charitable organizations (OXFAM and the like).

This seemed a promising precedent, although in subsequent debate it became clear that Mr. Sharp was intent upon blunting the edges of the policy. The government's public rationale ranged from a belittling suggestion that we were merely covering our bets vis-à-vis the liberation movements (who, after all, might someday assume power) to a strenuous playing down of the amounts involved (which are, in fact, quite small). Needless to say, there was no parallel suggestion that we were prepared to question those far more important economic and military links that lend support to the other side in the southern African contestation. Most importantly, our single-minded (and ultimately quite demagogic) commitment of "peaceful solutions" remained untransformed in Sharp's presentation of the issue, and the opportunity to educate Canadians as to the real nature of the conflict in southern Africa was not seized upon. It is, of course, possible that some progressive elements in CIDA may have helped to facilitate Canada's broaching this initiative (an initiative that is, in any case, now in limbo because of an intervening election). But in light of the facts adduced above it seems likely that a less savoury logic lay at its core. In a context of isolation it had become increasingly difficult to work "both sides of the street" in southern Africa by offering merely the same tired rhetoric to balance our vital ties to the white redoubts. Aid to the liberation movements, suitably qualified, must have seemed a tempting posture to strike—adding a dash of substance to our rhetoric, and raising our credibility with important constituencies in the Commonwealth and in Black Africa—all without committing ourselves to any very strenuous (or costly) opposition to our southern African allies in Portugal and South Africa!

Such skepticism regarding the government's motives seemed further justified when we note the fact of our extreme reluctance, throughout this same period, to recognize the newly independent state of Guinea-Bissau (where independence had been declared on September 24, 1973); Canada's calculated inaction on this issue has demonstrated much more clearly our true position. Although Sharp had said early in 1973 that dealing with the liberation movements in Portuguese Africa would be possible "only if they established an independent government and they established what is necessary to have diplomatic relations," now, when such conditions presented themselves in Guinea-Bissau, he back-tracked in Parliament:

> We are watching developments in Guinea-Bissau with great interest. So far we have not been able to establish that the so-called independent Government is effectively in control.

Yet by that time 74 countries (eight more than recognize Israel, for example) had recognized Guinea-Bissau. And when a resolution at the United Nations was presented in November condemning "the illegal occupation by Portuguese military forces of certain sectors of the Republic of Guinea-Bissau and acts of aggression committed by them against the people of the Republic" it was decisively passed by a vote of 93-7. Predictably, Canada abstained. But not merely abstained. After further pieties from Canada's delegate "deploring" the situation in Portugal's African colonies, the Canadian delegate (Mme. Begin) noted that the resolution seemed to assume the recognition of Guinea-Bissau:

> We cannot, moreover, conceal the sense of resentment we feel over the fact that through such a draft resolution a majority wishes to impose upon a minority an act of recognition which should, according to the rules of international law, be a free and sovereign act and, consequently, taken without compulsion.

Resentment! Even as rhetoric this was a much stronger word than "official Canada" had ever used to describe its reaction to the imposition of a comprehensive system of colonial oppression by a *minority* upon a majority in Portugal's African colonies.

Nor was this the only recent example of foot-dragging at the United Nations. As if to add insult to injury, Canada actually voted against a resolution of even more general significance in December 1973, a resolution that directly challenged Portugal's claim to represent Mozambique, Angola and Guinea Bissau at the United Nations. Four of the twenty-two members of Portugal's delegation were listed as coming from Portugal's "African territories," a totally unacceptable formula to most of the other delegations. The latter then pressed the issue in the plenary session of the General Assembly and introduced a motion to exclude these members from the Portuguese contingent. They reaffirmed the obvious but crucial point, that neither the Portuguese-dominated colonies of Angola and Mozambique, nor independent Guinea-Bissau could be considered a part of Portugal. And the vote, when it was taken, was impressive; 94 to 14 against (including, regrettably, Canada), with 21 abstentions. Not surprisingly, the subsequent comment on Canada's vote (a comment appearing in a lead editorial entitled "Sorting our friends from our enemies") in *Mozambique Revolution*, Frelimo's official English language publication, was particularly crisp:

> ... what are we to make of the revelation that both the Netherlands and Canada rejected a resolution stating so clearly and simply that Portugal cannot, at the United Nations, pretend to represent the people of Mozambique, Angola and Guiné. Surely this is the most basic and elementary of premises from which support for our cause must spring.
>
> After such actions have been taken by Holland and Canada, can any meaning be given to pious pronouncements by these governments—to the effect that "the Dutch government is going to give support to the liberation movements because it wants to speed up the process of decolonization in the territories occupied by Portugal," for example, or that the Canadian delegation "deplores the fact that the principle of self-determination as conceived by the United Nations is still being denied to the peoples of the territories under Portuguese administration.
>
> Thus, the escalation of our struggle is having the effect of sorting our friends from our enemies and clarifying the lines of battle. Obviously, this is not because we choose our friends and enemies on any a priori grounds. We welcome the support of any government which is prepared to link itself honestly and straightforwardly to our cause. Rather it is the actions of various countries which enables us to learn their true positions. In this way, the events at the United Nations have been instructive.

The tortured nature of Sharp's and Begin's formulations, cited above, is readily apparent. Time was running faster in Portuguese Africa than "official Canada" could easily keep pace with. In fact, it seemed possible that the coup in Portugal and the beginnings of a defusing of the situation in the colonies facilitated some significant face-saving for the Canadian government. As a result and at long last—in August, 1974, after Portugal has concede independence to Guinea-Bissau and the latter country was poised to enter the United Nations—Canada could finally recognize the independent state. In time, though presumably once a gain at the very last minute, Canada may be moved to grant its blessing to a Frelimo government in Mozambique.

I noted one especially menacing bit of foreshadowing inherent in our foot-dragging vis-à-vis Portugal in Africa, for as a *Globe and Mail* editorial of the time opined, regarding the pending downfall of Portugal's power in Africa: "The odds against Rhodesia and South African grow longer." As I continued:

In short, the demise of Portugal in Africa has, more clearly than ever, placed in question the fact of white domination in the whole of southern Africa. Yet official Canada is unlikely to respond to this reality in such a way as would align us with those forces in Rhodesia/Zimbabwe, in South-West Africa/Namibia and in South Africa which are, like their counterparts in Mozambique and Angola, further developing the capacity to take up arms against the established structures of privilege and white terrorism in their native lands.

Moreover, with reference to South Africa in particular, there is unlikely to be the *deus ex machina* of a coup to cut short the prospect of further escalation in the white dominated territories—and thereby take Canada off the hook. We have seen that it is not hard to strike a balance concerning the policies of official Canada towards Portugal's African colonies. In August, 1973, various Canadian groups organized a "counter-conference" (a "People's Forum on Southern Africa and the Commonwealth") in Ottawa at the time of the Commonwealth Conference itself in order to focus attention on the issues of southern Africa. In addition to representatives of the region's various liberation movements, Mr. John Malecela, Tanzania's Foreign Minister was a featured speaker and he addressed himself specifically to the question of the role of outside countries. Even if you cannot aid our cause of liberation, he said, at least *do not help our enemies*. Canada failed this simple test *via-a-vis* Portugal in Africa. Unfortunately, there is every reason to think that we will do so again in the case of the rest of southern

Africa—where Canada's stake in the *status quo* of white supremacy may appear to be even greater in the eyes of the powers-that-be.

Also emphasized here was the fact that Canadians were involved in a number of concrete actions, against the grain of those exemplified by our government's own policies, "to provide material aid to the liberation movements, to educate Canadians concerning the situation in southern Africa, and to bring pressure to bear upon Canadian governments and corporations." Here I cited the material aid activities of the Liberation Support Movement in British Columbia and the African Relief Services Committee; the vigorous exposé of Alcan at its own general meeting by Project Mozambique; the African Information Group's important work in mounting a boycott against firms importing Angolan coffee beans; Vancouver's Southern African Action Coalition's boycott of South African wine and liquor that moved even the British Columbian government to begin to move in a similar direction; TCLSAC's own fundraising on behalf of Frelimo. I then concluded my survey by further discussing our own campaign against Gulf Oil Canada Limited and Canada's link to Portuguese Africa as specifically concretized in the Gulf case.

Indeed, interestingly enough, our Gulf campaign earned us Gulf-Canada's attempt to infiltrate a hired undercover informant into our own TCLPAC organization—an attempt that we were only able to foil through the skilled work of a private detective of our own. Moreover, as described in the introduction to this section (A), our activities earned us attention of another, equally unsavoury, kind: from those right-wing racists who physically attacked one of our Cinema of Solidarity meetings in Toronto. More generally, however, activities like that of both exposing and opposing Gulf Canada's links to colonial oppression in Angola also enabled us in link up with the "growing number of Canadians coast-to-coast [who] are becoming uneasy about our country's own colonial status and the subservience to the United States of our own domestically dominant classes." As I then wrote:

It is true that even such concerned Canadians are less likely to be aware of the sub-imperial role for which this socioeconomic structure has also cast us—a role that arises from the fact that multi-national corporations operating in Canada and significant segments of our own privileged classes have developed a vested interest in fostering Canada's exploitative relations with the less developed areas of the world. It is for this very reason that the effort to forge a link between African struggles and political developments in Canada can serve both as an educative device and a focus for mobilization—to the benefit of the struggle on both fronts. In Quebec (itself twice colonized: by English Canada and by international capitalism) this is obvious and the recent coffee campaign there has explicitly emphasized this parallel in dramatic posters" "Quebec-Angola: Zones å Liberer." But for Canada more generally the point is also relevant.

When, for example, members of the Toronto Committee for the Liberation of Portugal's African Colonies (TCLPAC) first began to confront Gulf Canada on the Angola question we found that Canada's imports of Angolan oil were primarily transshipments, the crude being brought to Canada to be cleaned before being sent on to the United States. Further investigation revealed the negative implications of this kind of "development" for Canada's Maritime Provinces where this processing is taking place. And this, in turn, led to the following conclusion (in TCLPAC's "Larceny by Proxy: Gulf Oil Canada Ltd. and Angola," *This Magazine*, January, 1974):

> The pattern that Gulf and others are helping to produce in the Maritimes is not a new one. Evidence from Canso (where the Gulf Oil refinery has been constructed) suggests a lesson beginning to be learned by more far-sighted Third World countries but not yet learned by Canadians: that "development" brought by the multi-nationals means the uncontrolled dislocation of existing socioeconomic patterns, the uncritical adoption of capital-intensive technology and the mere addition of fragmented parts of more complex industrial process—these parts, in themselves, having little capacity to produce spread effects.
>
> Indeed, marginal industrialization, whether it occurred at the site of the resource supply itself (Angola) or at a transit point en route (Canada) has similar effects. Neither Angola nor Canada move towards becoming a self-sustaining, integrated political economy relaying on their own material or human resources for development and basically oriented to realizing the hopes and aspirations of their own peoples. Instead, both are relegated, albeit at dramatically different material levels, to dependent roles within the hierarchies of imperialism. Of course, in Angola this pattern has the further disadvantage of helping to prop up a gross and archaic structure of direct colonial domination that must be removed

> before Angolans can even begin to think about optimal use of their own resources. But it is ironic that Canada may actually be paying heavily for the dubious privilege of contributing to the continued colonial oppression in Portugal's African colonies.

Thus, in confronting Gulf in Angola, Canadians were also being forced to raise further questions about our own society and about the combination of imperial dictate from the United States and of imperatives derived from Canada's own domestic capitalist structure that define this and other kinds of complicity in colonialism for Canada. Related lessons can be learned in Mozambique and elsewhere in southern Africa. Under such circumstances it become clear that progressive Canadians can (in the words of the TCLPAC article just cited) take up support for freedom fighters in Mozambique and other territories "not as mere humanitarians, patronizing, however subtly, their cause, but as comrades, engaged in common struggle against worldwide structures that oppress us all."

AS WILL BE APPARENT FROM THE ABOVE, and well beyond any writing of my own on such subjects, I had been fortunate to be able, upon returning to Canada, to join with others to launch the Toronto Committee for the Liberation of Portugal's African Colonies/TCLPAC. And, as seen, we were soon involved in a variety of campaigns and protests in the Toronto area and beyond.[39] Among other things, we were busy together researching, writing and publishing materials on Canada's role in supporting Portugal in Africa. Indeed, by 1974, TCLSAC was ready to produce a volume pulling together a number of the well-received articles we had published in the past few years on Portugal in Africa, and on Canada's role. As it happens, the book itself, entitled *Words and Deeds: Canada, Portugal and Africa*, was ready to come off the press at almost exactly the same moment as the historic 1974 coup in Portugal foreshadowed the end of Portugal's cruel role in Africa.[40] True, we were soon left with boxes of unsold copies—but it was a price we were well prepared to pay to be a part of history now moving forward with seven league boots. It was also true, of course, that the struggle for freedom in "Portuguese Africa," not to speak of elsewhere in southern Africa, was by no means over. To the kind of development that the coup did represent, I will turn in a moment. However, before that coup happened I had the chance to return briefly to Tanzania where I again met Samora Machel; I commented on this meeting in an article of the time (albeit one written a few months later and in the immediate wake of the coup in Portugal itself).

IN JANUARY OF THIS YEAR (1974) I was in Tanzania, and had the opportunity to speak with Samora Machel, the President of Frelimo, who was passing through on his way back to the liberated areas of Mozambique after a successful visit to Somalia. I knew of the dramatic military advances which had been made in the sixteen months since my own visit to Mozambique—advances such as the successful attacks on critical communications arteries linking Rhodesia, through Manica and Sofala, to the sea—which were now being widely reported in the South African press, and which had already sown the seeds of the subsequent coup in Portugal. I expected Samora to speak primarily of these developments and was surprised when he chose instead to emphasize the continuing social and political consolidation of free Mozambique.

Thus, throughout 1973, a number of conferences of Frelimo personnel had been held, devoted to exploring crucial questions of national reconstruction—education, health, production, the question of women (the latter conference being attended by some 80 women cadres of Frelimo). Samora Machel also spoke of an August meeting in Cabo Delgado where key militants from all over the country had assembled to assist the movement in a broader effort at "ideological clarification." There, in particular, methods of political work had been a key theme, and Samora concluded his description of that meeting to me by stressing the three key phrases which had come to summarize the deliberations there: "popularize the political line, democratize the methods of work, collectivize the leadership." Clearly, the practices that I had observed in 1972 were now being even more clearly theorized and generalized by Frelimo.

There was no reason to be surprised at such an ordering of priorities of course. As argued above, one of the great strengths of Frelimo has been the fact that, quite literally, politics is in command; central to the movement's success remains the realization that popular involvement and responsive and committed leadership go hand in hand and that these, in turn, premise military accomplishment. Moreover, this reality continues to make Frelimo the formidable protagonist it is—a movement now playing from strength in its bargaining with the Portuguese. Nor is it surprising that Mozambicans beyond the bounds of the liberated areas are responding so unequivocally to the movement's promise of a genuine revolution in their country.

These are the positive signs, though are other factors that dictate caution in predicting the short-run ramifications for Africa of the Portuguese coup. Indeed, in such an unresolved situation, it is obvious that the need to sustain the struggle against Portuguese colonialism continues to be a pressing one. Furthermore, the various aspects of the broader southern African picture that are ominously reminiscent of the build-up of the Vietnam conflagration make the urgency of a growing concern on the Left for the struggles there especially clear. Here it remains only to reaffirm one main point: that amidst all the uncertainties of the southern African situation we can at least be certain of our responsibility to support Frelimo in its exemplary and genuinely revolutionary efforts.

AS IT HAPPENED, ONLY A FEW MONTHS LATER IN 1974, we were hosting in Toronto a delegation to Canada from the principal Angolan liberation movement, MPLA, a delegation led by its President Agostino Neto, when the news of the coup in Portugal came. In fact, Neto and his comrades had just sat down for formal luncheon at our committee's headquarters in St. Paul's United Church with a number of other Canadian liberation support activists when a phone-call came for Neto himself to share the news that such a dramatic event had just occurred—even if the full implications of this happening were still unpredictable. Nonetheless, the jubilation of the Angolan delegation—and of the Canadians assembled at St. Paul's for lunch—was very real. The delegation itself almost immediately broke off their Canadian tour to return as quickly as they possibly could to Europe and to Africa to embark upon the next stage of their struggle.

Like them, we in TCLPAC sensed that this was, indeed, the beginning of the end for Portugal in Africa—if not, as events would soon show, of Angola's own travails. As I noted in an article for *Monthly Review* (September, 1974): "Bourgeois commentators have taken to writing smugly of 'the myth of the guerrilla.'"[41] Yet guerrillas in

Mozambique (together with their counterparts in Angola and the independent Republic of Guinea-Bissau) have now brought down the Portuguese government." And I quoted Zambia's President Kenneth Kaunda who welcomed Samora Machel, President of the Front for the Liberation of Mozambique (Frelimo), to Zambia (where the latter had come in June to commence talks with Mario Soares, the new Portuguese Foreign Minister) by stating: "Without the Frelimo fighters led by Comrade Samora on this continent, Portugal herself would still be under a dictatorship. Freedom fighters on this continent have also freed the people of Portugal."

As was apparent the struggle against Portugal's imperial presence was not now merely concluded. There was a complicated political situation within post-coup Portugal itself and within the entire Western camp to be unraveled—as well as complexities on the side of the liberation movements in the colonies and of their own allies. But it was impossible to ignore the positive implications of the coup for the entire Portuguese colonial empire as it then existed in Africa, placing Angola and Guinea-Bissau alongside Mozambique for a piece I then wrote for *This Magazine* (8, 4, Nov.-Dec., 1974) and entitled "Portugal in Africa: The Beginning of the End." For the mood was increasingly upbeat and with good reason. As I wrote:

TIME WAS RUNNING FASTER in "Portuguese Africa" than "official Canada" could easily keep pace with [I here again cited Mitchell Sharp in this regard[42]]. On April 25th [1974], a coup in Portugal qualitatively changed the situation and, after some further infighting in Portugal, paved the way for the beginning of a serious effort at decolonization. Yet [as noted above, by Kenneth Kaunda] this coup was first and foremost the achievement of the liberation movements in Guinea-Bissau, Mozambique and Angola...

For it was precisely the fact that the Portuguese were facing defeat in Africa—a fact first stated publicly in General Antoine de Spinola's own book *Portugal and the Future* early this year—that eventually turned the army against the fascist regime in Portugal and released those popular energies so much in evidence in that country today. Then, in turn, the coup and its aftermath fed back into the African situation and served to change things there in a dramatic fashion. Not that the struggle for independence in Guinea-Bissau, Mozambique and Angola is now neatly concluded. This is far from being the case. Nevertheless, crucial advances have been made—advances that no search for a "peaceful solution" would ever have brought to the African people.

Even these advances were not immediately certain, however. In the wake of the coup in Portugal there was a fierce struggle for power between right-of-centre elements grouped around Spinola (now the new President) and left-of-centre elements grouped around the most active members of the Armed Forces Movement that had actually engineered the original coup. Both wings of the junta sought a "liberalization" of the out-moded Salazarist system, but differed sharply over the extent of liberalization and democratization that should occur. In July, this struggle was resolved, at least temporarily, in favour of those to the left-of-centre.

Independent Guinea-Bissau Confirmed

The way was not clear for more straightforward negotiations with the African Party for the Independence of Guinea and Cape Verde (PAIGC) than has been possible in the immediate post-coup period. Guinea-Bissau had declared its independence a year earlier, on September 24, 1973, and was already recognized by over 80 countries. Now at last, the Portuguese too were prepared to acknowledge this independence and dissolve all further claims upon the territory. They set September 10 as the date of "independence" and on that date facilitated the final transfer of power. The Guineans chose not to invest that date with any great significance, however; for them independence had been grasped on a different date—and a full year earlier!

But now, of course, Guinea-Bissau has been admitted into the United Nations and even the Canadian government, at the very last moment, has recognized the new government...[43]

Frelimo Takes Over

Dramatic strides towards independence have also been taken in Mozambique, the second of the colonies that Portugal has traditionally held in Africa. Here, too, it was difficult to be confident that the coup had changed the situation in any fundamental way. But the military strength of Frelimo and the wide-ranging public support that it enjoyed not only in the liberated areas but also throughout the country meant that any neo-colonial solution for Mozambique had been virtually preempted by Frelimo. Thus, when the more progressive of the Portuguese military officers, together with their allies in the Socialist and Communist parties, finally consolidated their power, it was clear to them that they must now bargain on Frelimo's own terms.

It was under these new conditions that, in early September, a Frelimo delegation led by the movement's President, Samora Machel, met with an official Portuguese delegation again in Lusaka. As a result, an agreement was concluded that would bring Mozambique its independence within a year. Almost immediately a provisional government was established with Frelimo clearly in command. It occupies two-thirds of the positions thus created and Joaquim Chissano, a senior Frelimo official, is serving as Premier. The provisional government in turn is to provide the core of the of the government that will ultimately assume full power in Mozambique—on June 25, 1975, when Samora Machel will, in all probability, become the first President of the country. The Portuguese had retreated from their insistence that there be an election or a referendum prior to the granting of independence. Any elections would now take place only after independence, and be organized by the Mozambicans themselves. The Portuguese had been forced, in the end, to recognize the reality of the Mozambique revolution and the legitimacy of Frelimo's claim to represent the Mozambican people.

Frelimo in turn might seem to have compromised—accepting the necessity of a process of transition towards independence and accepting the prospect of an interim period of virtual dual power during which the Portuguese military will still be formally in charge of defense and internal affairs. In fact, this is merely a well-calculated risk for Frelimo—a gamble upon the good intentions of the Armed Forces Movement (although it is, in any case, a gamble further guaranteed by the continuing military strength of Frelimo and its wide-spread popular support). Moreover, the "gamble" has paid immediate dividends, for when hostile white settlers reacted violently to the news of the Lusaka agreement—actually seizing the airport and a radio station in Lourenço Marques and going on the rampage in Beira—the Portuguese army ultimately moved to quell the uprising by its own people and to reaffirm, in the strongest possible manner, the agreement itself.

Of course, many of the dissident whites remain (though the entire white population numbers only a couple of hundred thousand in a population of 8 million) and there is news of mercenaries like Mike Hoare (once active in the Congo) gathering, mysteriously funded, in the vicinity of Mozambique. Predictably, too, Uriah Simango—arch-priest of such co-opted and counter-revolutionary elements as exist—surfaced in Lourenço Marques on the side of the white terrorists during the week of troubles in September. Thanks to such right-wing elements and with South Africa hovering nervously just across the border, there might still be further bloodshed during the transitional period. Moreover, as noted, there is always the risk that the delicate balance in Portugal that for the moment has provided a left-of-centre orientation to the regime there could be upset. Any such reversal of direction in Portugal could find Frelimo, in the transitional period, sharing power with a very different and much more menacing "ally" than is the case at present. Nonetheless, whatever may be the continuing dangers, it will be difficult to reverse a process that has shifted the situation so dramatically in the direction of a free and Frelimo-led Mozambique. Odds are that June 25, 1975, will in fact witness the realization of that goal.

Angola's continuing struggle

The situation in Angola, the third of Portugal's historic colonies, is much more complicated—and much less promising. For Angola is by far the richest of the three, with its oil, iron, diamonds, coffee and the like. This in itself would be enough to strengthen the hand of conservative factions within the Portuguese state during the struggle there to define a strategy of decolonization. Even if prepared to accept the revolutionary solutions PAIGC and Frelimo in their respective territories, Portugal may work towards a far more muted and ambiguous result in Angola, a possibility that is strengthened by the stake of a number of powerful multinational corporations (like Gulf Oil and Krupp) in Angola. Moreover, the white settler community there is larger, better organized and more ruthless and vociferous than its counterpart in Mozambique.

This on the colonial side. As for the African side, it is, for a variety of complex reasons, deeply divided. There are three movements: MPLA, UNITA, and FNLA. [Although notably less successful in such terms than their counterparts in PAIGC and Frelimo] Africans in Angola have nonetheless managed to wage a strong fight against the Portuguese for 13 years. Nonetheless, the infighting has certainly hurt them. Such dissension could be further exploited by their enemies either to delay independence or to reduce its meaning to a "false decolonization" favourable in the extreme to western interests.

Indeed, there has been little progress made towards establishing a timetable for independence in Angola—although the Portuguese have spoke vaguely of a two year process which would culminate in that end. Certainly the range of possible scenarios is a wide one. For those who would support the African struggle there the vigilance recommended earlier is, of course, especially appropriate. On the one hand we must hope that an even stronger and more determined African initiative will emerge from the current period of reconciliation. On the other hand, we must be prepared to expose any machinations arising from the side of the western establishment that would further complicate matters and seek to forestall the African revolution. Certainly the activities of "official" Canada—corporate (e.g., Gulf Oil Canada Ltd.) and governmental—vis-à-vis Angola in the pre-coup period leave little room for optimism that we will find ourselves readily playing a positive role in the area. In Angola, particularly, *a luta continua*—the struggle continues.

Indeed, Angola's future would prove extremely fraught even though it did come to independence "on schedule" in 1975 and under MPLA leadership. But it was greeted, almost immediately, by an invasion from South Africa, repulsed only with the essential and ongoing assistance of the Cubans. There was also the marked and aggressive hostility of the United States and the wrecker's role, supported for many years from outside by apartheid South Africa and the US, played by the ambitious and high-handed Jonas Savimbi and his UNITA movement. Crucially, too, there were the seductions, on government and opposition alike, of resource hungry oil and diamonds-centred corporations. The "opportunities" for personal enrichment certainly fired the MPLA's own arrogant and authoritarian tendencies. Indeed, the greed and power-mongering of the two strongest movements, MPLA and UNITA, would produce a wasting war and domestic socioeconomic devastation for the vast majority of the country's population for another thirty years. Nonetheless, it was difficult not to hail "the end of the beginning" in "Portuguese Africa," and to look beyond the victories there to the future of the rest of the region:

There is one final lesson to be derived from developments in "Portugal's African colonies. For the success of the struggles in Guinea-Bissau, in Mozambique, and in Angola has also significantly advanced the struggle in the rest of southern Africa in Namibia, in Zimbabwe and in South Africa itself—and placed the white minority regimes in those countries in much greater jeopardy. Even Toronto's *Globe and Mail* has noted this fact, arguing in an August editorial devoted to developments in

Mozambique that "the odds against Rhodesia and South Africa grow longer." Escalation of the confrontation in so strategic a centre for the operations of international capitalism as South Africa is obviously of even greater global significance than any shift in Portuguese Africa; here the makings of a Vietnam for the seventies and eighties are all too apparent. Moreover, Canada's stake in the status quo of white supremacy in the rest of southern Africa no doubt will appear to be especially great in the eyes of our Canadian powers-that-be; Canada's response to such escalation is likely, therefore, to be even less savoury than it has been with respect to Guinea-Bissau, Mozambique and Angola. Only one thing is certain: further escalation is inevitable. The tide of liberation now washes at the very borders of South Africa, and inside the country the rumblings of the black working-class are increasingly difficult to wish away. For Portugal in Africa it is the beginning of the end, for South Africa merely the end of the beginning.

OBVIOUSLY, ANGOLA WAS A CRUCIAL PART of the Portuguese equation in southern Africa. Nonetheless, even before the surfacing of the additional complexities of the situation alluded to above, it had long posed something of a dilemma for those of us in the support movement abroad. Although the most progressive of the liberation movements there, the MPLA was, in our experience, a far more thorny movement to link ourselves with than was Frelimo in Mozambique. Indeed, so brittle, defensive and uncommunicative was the MPLA in our experience that it is difficult now not to see this as an index of something much more important: a closed, top-down politics that would eventually turn very sour indeed, in particular for the mass of the Angolan population. At the same time, nothing defined the MPLA for us so clearly as the nature of the enemies it earned: the morally bankrupt FNLA and the gruesomely opportunist UNITA and their two most prominent backers, the apartheid South African government and the unapologetically counter-revolutionary American one. It is difficult to feel that we were wrong in backing the MPLA as strongly as we did, for the cynical destabilization of the country from both inside and outside (by both South Africa and the United States) that continued for decades must be emphasized. But the siege of Angola exposed weaknesses of the MPLA that were themselves disappointing, and full of negative future portent (as time would also clearly reveal).

Similarly, during this period, we were attempting to take the measure of the Zimbabwean liberation struggle, also singularly complex, and about which I have written at length elsewhere. Thus, even in the 1970s it was clear that Robert Mugabe and his confidants were a very suspect team of liberators indeed. I myself then being moved to see in the Zimbabwe Peoples' Army (ZIPA) the emergence of a third force, beyond the two movements ZANU and ZAPU, that had more promise than either of those two.[44] With the victory of Mugabe and ZANU in that struggle for pre-eminence within the forces of liberation, it was difficult not to view Zimbabwe's independence at the end of the 1970s as being, in the form that it took and under the leadership of Mugabe and his cronies, very much a mixed blessing for the mass of the Zimbabwean population.[45] It was essential, of course, to applaud the departure of Ian Smith and his particularly crude and exploitative brand of white-minority rule. But Mugabe's brand of "independence" was to prove to be, in its own right, a very evil outcome indeed, one from which the mass of the Zimbabwean population suffers to this day.[46] Several of the texts identified in the footnotes may help the inquisitive reader, and there is beyond them a rich body of literature to be explored as well (even if it does not make for heartening reading).

Most immediately, however, I felt compelled, in various fora, to expand upon my analysis of the Angola situation, noting that it had been "widely misinterpreted (often quite willfully, it would seem) in conventional, liberal/conservative circles in Canada, but also in some radical ones. Rather surprisingly, the essence of such misinterpretations has been similar. It stems from a temptation to ignore the concrete history of the struggle in Angola and the specific social and political characteristics of the territory itself. The result is the reduction of the full complexity of the situation there to a mere manifestation of 'great-power politics.'" I will not repeat that analysis here (see, however, my "Angola and After" in *Monthly Review*, May, 1976, and in *This Magazine*, April-May, 1976) beyond noting that it argued vigorously the claims of MPLA, even as it noted with some unease the auguries of a troubled future for

Angola (and the bulk of the Angolan population) that the then-present situation foreshadowed. However, the Angolan situation also provided a further opportunity to underscore the dispiriting flaws in Canada's own approach to southern Africa, something I emphasized in concluding the essay on Angola just cited:

EVEN "OFFICIAL CANADA" NOW HAS BEEN FORCED to keep pace with events. To be sure, for many months delegations requesting that Canada recognize the People's Republic of Angola met a stone wall in Ottawa, the government's refusal sometimes phrased in ironic counterpoint to its earlier and parallel refusal to recognize Guinea-Bissau for long months after that country's winning of independence. Then one of the Canadian government's primary arguments was that PAIGC did not hold the capital city, Bissau. In the Angola case, MPLA's holding of Luanda was seen as being unimportant. Plus ça change... Similarly, Prime Minister Trudeau, far from using the opportunity of a recent official visit to Cuba to enlighten Canadian opinion about Angola, chose to further mystify it. For the Canadian government merely adopted a position on the issue worthy of Henry Kissinger and—tacitly accepting the latter's "threat to NATO," "red menace" frame of reference—tacitly sanctioned South Africa bluster. Nonetheless, by the end of February, Canada had followed other Western countries—though not yet the United States—in recognizing the People's Republic of Angola as that country's legitimate government.

That much seems settled. The fact remains that the continuing confusion over what really happened in Angola—the victory of the popular forces—has obscured the broader significance of the confrontation there. The reference here is to the overt involvement of South Africa in the Angolan struggle, its defeat by a combined MPLA-Cuban force, and the ramifications of this involvement and defeat. What is evident is that the question of South Africa itself has now been placed on the historical agenda more forcefully than at any previous time, and the myth of the white laager's invincibility tarnished, perhaps irrevocably. Revolutionary forces within South Africa can only be the beneficiaries.

Of course South Africa has used the opportunity of military action in "the North" to buttress itself in Namibia.[47] But internally, African advances in Mozambique already have had their impact, as the trial of the SASO Nine in Pretoria for last year's pro-FRELIMO demonstrations is currently demonstrating. Now not only have Vorster's catastrophic Angolan adventures thrown the South African white community off its stride, but they have also made a further contribution to growing black militancy, as seen, for example, in the fourth annual Congress of the Black People's Convention, meeting amidst war hysteria in South Africa in December, that came out in direct support of MPLA. Internationally, the Republic's illegal hammerlock on Namibia must be even more open to question, and SWAPO will now have its Angolan base, as MPLA has promised. In addition the military situation in Zimbabwe has begun to heat up again, with African action resting this time on a much firmer foundation. There are also hopeful signs that the Soviet Union, having reaped propaganda gains in Africa from its assistance for MPLA, will seek similar gains by more effectively backing liberation groups elsewhere. Perhaps China too will have learned something from its disastrous Angolan policies and begin again to play the positive role in supporting genuine popular forces in other southern African locales that it once did in Mozambique. In short, it is a heady time in southern Africa...

A HEADY TIME, INDEED. For we would soon see—the following year, in fact—the complete collapse of Portugal in Africa, TCLPAC being invited to participate in the Independence Day celebrations in Mozambique. We also moved to change our name from TCLPAC to the Toronto Committee for the Liberation of Southern Africa/TCLSAC. For we were well aware that the struggle for a liberated southern Africa was far from over—as long as a white minority remained in control of Zimbabwe, South-West Africa and, especially, South Africa. Indeed, the costs to Mozambique and Angola of having won their independence well before the people elsewhere in the region had done so would prove to be very high, as apartheid South Africa's continuing siege (supported by the United States) of both Mozambique and Angola would soon demonstrate. To that story we will have to return.

Meanwhile, however, Mozambique was free and I returned in 1975 for the very moment of independence, and the moving celebration it inspired. I recounted that visit under the title "Invitation to a Celebration," in the pages of *This Magazine*, in the November-December issue of 1975 and in *Monthly Review* (as "Free Mozambique") also in December, 1975; I reproduce that text here.

JUNE 24, 1975. On the main road to Machava Stadium, Lourenço Marques [very soon to be renamed Maputo], Mozambique. Soon to be free Mozambique: the People's Republic of Mozambique. But now, a driving rainstorm, heavy traffic. Will we make it by midnight to see the Portuguese flag come down and the new Mozambican flag replace it? Out of our minibus and a wild dash for the stadium, joined by hundreds of others caught up in the spirit and drama of the occasion, afraid, amidst the mounting excitement, to miss even a moment of the events.

Just in time. Samora Machel, President of the Front for the Liberation of Mozambique (Frelimo), and soon to be the first President of Mozambique, has also been delayed by traffic. Now, in the early minutes of June 25th, the flag-raising ceremony proceeds, the vast crowd cheering as Comrade Samora, briefly but eloquently, proclaims the country's independence. We're together, representatives of various Western support groups, and we embrace one another enthusiastically. Embrace, too, Mozambicans, strangers and old friends. I greet Janet Mondlane, wife of Eduardo, Frelimo's first President, assassinated by the Portuguese in 1969, greet Felisberto, a Frelimo comrade from the days when the movement's headquarters was a dingy office on Nkrumah Street in Dar es Salaam, greet two militants with whom I travelled to the liberated areas of Tete Province in 1972. Was that really only three years ago? Enthusiastic guerrillas fill the sky with tracer bullets. Too much like the real thing for my taste, but who can blame them? Independence Day.

I. A Celebration

No one knows better than the Frelimo leadership that the changing of a flag marks merely the beginning of a new phase of their struggle. Nonetheless, Mozambicans weren't about to underestimate the significance of their accomplishment—the military defeat of a ruthless colonial power, one with full imperialist backing—nor deny themselves the opportunity of celebrating their victory. And the first ten days I spent in Lourenço Marques were just that, a celebration—a celebration in which the ceremony at Machava Stadium was merely one highlight among so many others.

It began for us the Friday John Saxby and I—the "Canadian delegation"—reached Lourenço Marques by plane from Lusaka. On the flight was Oliver Tambo, President of the African National Congress of South Africa, and the airport was packed to overflowing with cheering people for his arrival—here, in Lourenço Marques, less than 100 miles from the South African border! Of course the crowd was even larger and more enthusiastic a few days later when Samora himself arrived in the city for the first time in well over a decade of self-imposed and active exile. Then even the streets—already festooned with innumerable banners, signs, and window displays—were lined with people every inch of the way along the route of his entry into the city, and we joined with thousands of others in welcoming him.

There followed the flag-raising, and early the next morning (after only a couple of hours' sleep) the formal investiture of Samora Machel as President. It took place in a small room in the City Hall, but I was fortunate enough to be invited— sitting, as it happened, in the same row as Alvaro Cunhal and Mario Scares, come from Portugal. Here, at close range, I experienced most fully the meaning that these days must have held for the direct participants in them. Marcelino dos Santos, Vice President of FRELIMO and one of the first militants enlisted to the cause of Mozambique's national liberation, read a brief statement, proclaiming the choice of Samora Machel as President, and Machel made an even briefer statement of acceptance. They then turned to each other and embraced—a conventional enough gesture among Mozambicans. But this was an embrace with a difference—slow, measured, deeply felt, as they looked at each other, their eyes filming over with tears. Two comrades of long years in the struggle, firmly united in their pride and in their accomplishment.

Words fail me here—I have never been so moved. I watched as the new President next went onto the balcony, and proceeded to address the huge crowd gathered in the civic square. Characteristically, his speech, one of the most important ever delivered by an African leader,[48] now dealt not so much with what had been accomplished as with what remains to be done. For Frelimo, and for Mozambique, the struggle, as they have affirmed so often, continues.

But the celebrations continued, too. That afternoon, an amazing parade—floats dramatizing, often with high good humor, the evils of colonialism, the realities of the struggle, and the possible areas of future social and economic advance. And thousands upon thousands of people marching past under the banners of workers' groups, the women's organization, the military. Afterwards, the chanting crowd surging around the reviewing stand to greet the President, who mixed with the people freely. But how would he ever get away? Joaquim Chissano, Frelimo's Prime Minister during the transitional government period, took the mike. "Comrades, the President is not visiting among you, he has come to stay. But now he must go. Please clear a way." Little response.

Then: "Comrades, are we an organized people?" A huge roar: "We are." Chissano: "Then organize yourselves. You don't need police to do it for you. You are your own police. Please let the President through." And slowly, but surely, they did!

The next day, an impressive youth festival at the stadium, and at night, a banquet for all the guests. Speeches by Said Barre of Somalia, Chairman of the Organization of African Unity, and by President Samora, who made a point of singling out for thanks those support committees who, he said, had worked "on the difficult front of the Western countries." A frank and friendly exchange of speeches between Samora and Vasco Gonçalves, then Prime Minister of Portugal. Yet another chance to see old friends and make new ones, Frelimo militants from all levels of the organization and comrades from around the world. That night, for example, we ate dinner with Shafrudine Khan, Frelimo's New York representative for many years and guest of honor at a 1974 session of TCLPAC's "Cinema of Solidarity" in Toronto which was attacked by White Power thugs [described in the introduction to this section (A)]. And the next evening a brief meeting with the President himself. At a reception for the various delegations he received with enthusiasm the greetings we conveyed from the many Canadians who had gathered in Toronto on June 25th to celebrate Mozambican independence. "International solidarity," "proletarian internationalism," call it what you will—such phrases inevitably seemed less abstract for me, more real and urgent, in such a setting.

Nor was this all. Throughout these ten days, woven around the various formal ceremonies, there was also a rich array of cultural events—plays, singing, dancing, poetry readings, marionettes—taking place throughout the city (and, as I later learned, throughout the country). The cultural sphere has always been an arena of major Frelimo accomplishment—something that I had seen for myself in the liberated areas in 1972—and so it proved to be again in Lourenço Marques. Two plays in particular stood out: one on the history of Mozambican women from traditional society through colonialism to the revolutionary present; another on the broader development of the liberation struggle itself, with its many deep-seated contradictions and its impressive resolutions of those contradictions. As John Saxby has written of one of these plays:

> In a dramatic sense it was splendid stuff: warmth, humor, passion, and dignity, as well as political sophistication; first-rate acting, with subtlety of expression and manner and obvious enjoyment on the part of the actors; and the language itself a delight to hear, musical lilts and great

rolling phrases all intermixed. One can usually excuse a bit of amateurishness for good intentions and political awareness, but this gave away nothing to anyone.[49]

Once again, a phrase from the revolutionary chapbook was leaping off the page. "Liberation as the release of creative popular energies": the real thing was all around me.

II. Staying On

The celebrations over, I stayed on in Mozambique to look behind the scenes—talking with leaders in the capital about their plans and visiting Zambezia Province in the agricultural heartland of the country in order to see Frelimo at work closer to the ground. The experience was instructive, reinforcing impressions already gleaned during the celebration period. For if the coming of formal independence has not altered substantially anything in many other African territories, this is unlikely to be the case in Mozambique. Here was a movement come to power with a clear sense of purpose, a firm popular base, and a cadre of leaders of the very highest caliber.[50] In consequence, a process of profound and revolutionary change, already underway in the liberated areas well before independence, seems certain to continue, despite the greater problems that Mozambique now faces.

Such problems are, needless to say, the main legacy of Portugal's 500-year colonial record in Mozambique. Though finally defeated militarily by Frelimo, the Portuguese left behind the devastation caused by their brutal military tactics and, even more importantly, the structure of an economy warped to service the needs of Western commodity markets, of South Africa, and of Portugal itself, rather than the needs of the African population. It will require considerable skill to reconstruct the economy along alternative, more self-reliant, and productive lines.

It was too early, at the time of my trip, to confirm what this would mean substantively in every sector. But it was immediately clear from talks with Marcelino dos Santos (the Vice President who was appointed Minister of Development and Economic Planning in the first days after independence) that existing links with multinational companies and agribusiness conglomerates will be severely scrutinized, with nationalizations sure to follow. Moreover, some of the crucial keys to control already lie with the new government. The Banco National Ultramarino (the Overseas National Bank) played a ubiquitous role in the private sector of the economy in both pre-coup Portugal and Mozambique.

Nationalized by Lisbon in 1974, the bank now passes to FRELIMO as part of the independence settlement. And this appears to be only the beginning. There can be little doubt that a full-fledged socialist solution to the problem of Mozambique's underdevelopment is on the agenda.

Ultimately, this will also involve a complete economic break with South Africa, although the extreme dependence of the Mozambican economy on that country means that it will not come precipitously or at the expense of the wholesale disruption of the economy. For example, dos Santos confirmed that in the short run workers will continue to go to South Africa—though Mozambique will press for better conditions and wages. Meanwhile, the new government will work as rapidly as possible to restructure the economy along self-reliant lines so that these workers can soon be absorbed at home. The same strategy will hold for creating alternatives to dependence on earnings from South Africa's traffic through Mozambican ports and its use of Cabora Bassa hydro-electric power.[51] There are clearly dangers in such a strategy of phased disengagement, but I found that no one understands this better than Frelimo's own leaders. There are good reasons to have confidence in their skills and commitment during this difficult transitional period.

Of course Frelimo's idea of the proper terrain for national reconstruction is a broad one, and in the service sector, where the opportunities for significant transformation are most readily available, the substance of change has been even more immediately apparent. Talks with Helder Martens, the Minister of Health, with Graça Simbine, the Minister of Education, or with Fernando Ganhao, new Rector of the University, documented the dramatic shift of priorities in an egalitarian, rural-oriented, direction. Not merely talk, but action. Within the first few weeks, private medical and legal practice and private funeral services were nationalized. It was made clear that in free Mozambique no one was to make a profit from the personal discomfiture of his/her compatriots. Private schools met a similar fate. And positive efforts to forge a new educational format and a nationwide program of cultural revitalization, efforts which had given rise to important conferences and planning sessions even before independence, are to be reinforced. Hard to miss the fact that the future seemed vibrantly open-ended in so many spheres. Hard not to feel, somewhat enviously, how exciting it must be to be a teacher or a culture worker in such a setting.

As always with Frelimo, the underlying basis of success is political. Here continuity is crucial. I had first witnessed the impressive methods of political work—the building of grassroots participation and village-level democracy which has been so important to the movement's success—when I visited the liberated areas with FRELIMO guerrillas. Now, in independent Mozambique, I found an impressive attempt to generalize these methods to the rest of the country, to places where only clandestine political work had been possible prior to liberation. In fact, this task was Frelimo's central preoccupation during the period of the Transitional Government (those months from September 1974 to June 25th, during which Frelimo shared power with the Portuguese). Now the coming of independence can only serve to intensify such an effort.

In the sprawling city of Lourenço Marques, as in Zambezia Province, the key has been the *grupos dynamizadores* (dynamization groups). Frelimo's most impressive peacetime innovation, these grupos are committees established in every sector of the society—in school and workplace, in urban neighborhood and rural village—which, from my observation, are now providing Mozambicans with impressive new opportunities for self-government and political education.

We had seen the *grupos* at work in Lourenço Marques, but it was on the trip to Zambezia Province that I felt able fully to grasp their vitality. We visited a number of them, including the regular weekly meeting of the chairpersons of the area's grupos, and were as excited to hear of their work— literacy training, the facilitation of women's participation, construction of schools and local community centres, political struggle sessions, and the like—as we were moved by the warm reception for the "comrades from abroad" which we received everywhere. Of particular interest was a visit to a "pre-cooperative," a large collective rice farm which represented the joint activity of three or four different grupos in the area. Here, in embryo, was Frelimo's long-run plan for the rural areas, a move toward collectivization, the establishment of rural "communes," premised on an avoidance of the bureaucratization and coercion all too characteristic of neighboring Tanzania's related attempts at ujamaa-villagization. And the safeguard against any such denouement is to be precisely the political self-management of a self-conscious peasantry, acting through agencies like the *grupos dynamizadores*.

Leadership is also crucial to this process, and it was therefore encouraging to meet the full range of Frelimo cadres at the provincial and district levels in Zambezia. I was able to confirm, in particular, that a high caliber of personnel is not merely a feature of the very top of the organization. To be sure, recruitment of skilled cadres remains important and Frelimo has made the establishment of a party training school an urgent priority. But many outstanding people have begun to come out of the ranks of the guerrilla movement, adapting to the new tasks at hand. Fortunately so, for the need is great. A visit to the British-owned Sena Sugar Estate and a morning spent with the European manager—a man of predictable views and demeanor—touring the locations which housed the migrant workers in desperate conditions confirmed that much. That same afternoon, a long talk with the recently arrived, Frelimo-appointed political commissar on the Estate provided a sharp contrast in viewpoint and a sense of the work already begun (even prior to any nationalization which might eventually be forthcoming) in mobilizing the workers on the new economic battlefront.[52]

Politicization is an equally pressing priority in the urban areas, especially in a city as large and as corrupt as Lourenço Marques. Seeing it for the first time I could not but feel some sympathy with the Cambodians in their haste to evacuate their own capital after liberation! Still, it is here that the working class is to be found, a potential pillar of the revolution despite the fact that an effective urban police network had made clandestine political work tremendously difficult in the cities under the Portuguese. Now the integration of the workers into the Frelimo scheme of things presents some real challenges. Nonetheless, *grupos* in the workplace are providing a stepping stone—to all appearances an effective and democratic one—toward the new trade unions which are coming into being; indeed, in several cases they have even become the nucleus of real workers' self-management (in a cashew-processing factory abandoned by its Portuguese owners, for example).

Even at the university—most hierarchical and deeply colonized of inherited institutions—the *grupos* initiative was in train, throwing up, in addition, a new kind of structure for the faculty boards. From now on the latter are to be constituted by three representatives from the teaching faculty, three from the students, and three from the staff (typists, cleaners, etc.)—the dean to be chosen, in turn, from that number. Seven years spent teaching in an African university helped me to realize how startling a beginning this was.[53]

There was one final question that preoccupied me during my visit, and that concerned the links of a free Mozambique with the ongoing struggle for the liberation of the rest of Southern Africa. In this regard, the reception accorded Oliver Tambo was a significant event. And a similar reception greeted Agostinho Neto, President of Angola's MPLA, when he arrived in Lourenço Marques. The latter movement is engaged in a life-or-death struggle against two other movements with unequivocally neocolonial credentials; indeed, one of them, Holden Roberto's FNLA, has the firm and aggressive backing of Zaire's sinister General Mobutu and the Americans (as well as, for no good reason, the Chinese). Frelimo's several strong statements on MPLA's behalf during the week of ceremonies could be seen as serving notice on the rest of Africa—and on the very large Chinese delegation in attendance—as to where their true responsibilities lie in Angola. It was evident that the liberation of Mozambique has added a strong, fresh, and progressive voice to African councils.

Of even more direct concern is Rhodesia-Zimbabwe, now exposed along an extended frontier to a fully liberated Mozambique. Frelimo has said it will shoulder the burden of sanctions against Rhodesia despite the dislocations in Mozambique's domestic economy that are sure to follow. At the same time there is probably some despair at the reluctance of Zimbabwean Africans to break off their internecine struggles long enough to focus their armed attention on the Smith gang, still in power. Here, backing the African National Council is deemed the best bet: a vehicle for at least the preliminary merging of Zimbabwe's factions, and a possible forum within which a process of renewal and radicalization might eventually emerge. In the meantime, though they don't talk about it, it is likely that well-trained Frelimo personnel will be at work to pass on some of their expertise to ANC forces regrouping along the Zimbabwean border.

Diplomatic pressure on South Africa over the Zimbabwe question will also continue. Indeed, something of a domino theory seems to be at play: to up the ante for South Africa in its involvements beyond its borders—in Zimbabwe and Namibia—sufficiently to peel off these territories from the white laager, with the much tougher nut of the Republic itself waiting to be cracked at a later stage. Obviously, this broad struggle will not be an easy one. But in talks with Marcellino dos Santos, Jorge Rebelo (Minister of Information), and others, there was little doubt that free Mozambique has enlisted for the duration in the battle for Southern Africa.

Coolheaded and committed appraisals of their economic and social problems prevail, as they do of the challenges of continuing political mobilization and of the broader Southern African context in which they find themselves. And, increasingly, there is firm action springing from such appraisals. This is what I found in Mozambique during the first weeks of freedom. Perhaps Joaquim Chissano, now Mozambique's Minister of Foreign Affairs, put it best. When we met for the first time in several years and joyfully embraced at a reception early in the week of celebrations he said, quite simply, "So, we did it... Let us continue."[54]

III. Home Thoughts

For Canadians there was an additional message in the ceremonies that marked Mozambique's celebrations of the winning of independence, a graphic significance in the fact that FRELIMO, quite consciously, had chosen not to invite the Canadian government to participate. This was in spite of Canadian representations to Frelimo requesting such an invitation, and, as one senior Zambian official in attendance in Lourenço Marques explained to me, in spite of our attempts to persuade Zambia to intervene with Frelimo on official Canada's behalf.

Instead, the "Canadian delegation" consisted of myself and John Saxby, a fellow member of TCLSAC. We were invited, we were informed in Mozambique, to represent the many people in Canada whom Frelimo knew to have been sympathetic to its cause during the ten long years of war. In contrast, the Canadian government was seen as having lent its firmest support to the side of continuing Portuguese colonial hegemony.[55]

Frelimo was quick to point out that reluctance to invite the Canadian government should not be seen to prejudice future diplomatic relations between the two countries. It was meant primarily to underscore the fact that the celebrations were a gathering of friends, of those who had supported the Mozambican people's lengthy struggle. On that basis Canada was not invited, although the guest list ranged all the way from the representatives of many Western churches, through officials of a number of the Scandinavian countries, to a delegation from the People's Republic of China.

One should not underestimate the importance of this action by Frelimo. Those of us who have, over the years, argued the case that Canada's economic, military, and diplomatic support for the white-minority regimes of Southern Africa far outweighs the formal lip-service that we sometimes pay to the cause of African freedom, have been met by the charge that this is an intemperate view, that Africans see these things quite differently, that they recognize the "positive role" which this country plays. [I here quoted Vice-President Marcellino dos Santos' CBC interview, also quoted above, regarding Canada's unsavoury role. As I then noted: "The Vice President was equally frank when I spoke with him in Lourenço Marques."]

To be sure, we need have no illusions that significant change in Canadian policy is in the offing merely as a result of our government's failure to be invited to Mozambique. Canada's stance in Southern Africa is not some arbitrary jeu d'esprit, but reflects instead deeper imperatives which are built into the very structure of our society and economy. Nonetheless, Frelimo's rebuff is a hard and undeniable fact, one which helps refute the government's publicly stated case for its policies. Perhaps, in consequence, official Canada will be somewhat less prone in future to fob off its domestic critics with shallow arguments.

For many Canadians, however, this is pretty small solace. To us, it is as obvious as it is to Frelimo that Canada, acting in its official capacity within the international state system, presents itself at virtually every opportunity as the firm ally of imperialism. Of course, it is equally obvious that dos Santos' "explanation," quoted above, of the roots of Canadian policy does not represent anything like a fully theorized statement concerning Canada's external role. Indeed, it is doubtful whether Frelimo has had either the time or the occasion to address itself to a careful appraisal of Canadian political economy. Clearly, we are the ones who must do more of the spadework which is required: to specify the extent to which our acting in concert with imperial designs is merely the external expression of our dependent subordination to the United States, to reveal the important domestic classes and interests which have a stake in our playing this role.

In this, we will not be wasting our time. For there is no reason to think that resistance to our negative role abroad will be any less important than resistance to other manifestations of the contradictions within our society in building, over a broad front, an effective movement of the Left in Canada. Enough, in this regard, that FRELIMO has made a firm and absolutely crucial distinction between the Canadian state on the one hand and the Canadian people on the other. Especially since, in doing so, the movement has provided us with something else of importance: an opportunity to exemplify, on the occasion of Mozambique's independence, a genuine internationalism, this being an opportunity which is generally denied to Canadians by the actions and intercessions of our official spokespersons in the international arena!

Home thoughts from abroad. Triggered, perhaps, by a remark of Comrade Chauke when he introduced Polly Gaster (of the U.K. Solidarity Committee) and myself to a meeting of the chairpersons of the *grupos dynamizadores* in the town of Quelimane, Zambezia Province. We had told the meeting something of our own countries and of the conditions under which we had been carrying out our support work. Chauke then reminded the audience of the ways in which Tanzania and Zambia had, in years past, provided Frelimo with a base area from which to launch its successful struggle. Turning to us, he told the others: "Mozambique is now their base."

It was a *bon mot,* of course, obviously more metaphor than reality. Even as a metaphor, however, it did have resonance, at least for me. It is important, no doubt, to avoid the temptation of merely getting off on other people's revolutions, thereby evading the more difficult task of bringing about necessary changes in one's own society. Yet it would be equally mistaken to forget that progressives in Canada are participants in a worldwide struggle or to downplay the significance of the kind of unofficial "people's diplomacy" in which we engaged in Mozambique. To be in Mozambique this summer was certainly to sense more deeply than ever before the rewards of genuine freedom, the drama of a people making its own history. But it was also to feel, tangibly, the importance of our reinforcing each other, around the world, in our efforts to attain such goals.

MEANWHILE, LINKS TO CANADA AND CANADIAN STRUGGLES also came calling, ones sited well beyond the question of Canada's unsavoury links to the wrong side in southern Africa, although clearly related to it. For example, I was invited in 1976 to present a brief on behalf of both the Indian Brotherhood of the Northwest Territories and the Métis Association of the Northwest Territories to the Mackenzie Valley Pipeline Inquiry then taking place, under the chairpersonship of Justice Thomas C. Berger, in Yellowknife, NWT. As explained to me by my one-time professor and good friend Professor Mel Watkins, then on leave from the University of Toronto and working with the Dene Nation, I was not, needless to say, being asked to pretend that I was expert on the specificity of native claims in Canada nor on the merits of the Dene position itself. Rather, I was invited to draw directly on my own experience and to reflect on the question of "Nation and Nationalism in the Third World." This was seen to provide a useful reference point for the overall case that the Dene were mounting for justice in the

Far North and I was pleased to make a presentation to the Berger Inquiry in April of that same year, offering the following brief:

MY TESTIMONY WILL DISCUSS CERTAIN FEATURES of the realities of "nation" and "nationalism" in the Third world. No attempt will be made to apply my findings directly to the case of the Dene Nation, since any such undertaking would fall outside the range of my own knowledge and expertise. Nonetheless, this evidence would not be presented unless I were confident that there are lessons to be learned from a comparative approach which can help illuminate and legitimate the Dene claim.

I. The Nation

There has been much debate in the scientific literature about what, precisely, constitutes a nation. A variety of criteria have been suggested, most prominently the existence of a common history, territory, culture and language. Yet there has been a great variation in the applicability of these criteria to the people who have successfully asserted their claim to "nationhood" in the past fifty years. This has been particularly true for people who have lived, until well into this century under colonial or semi-colonial conditions, and who have economies both poor and under developed—the peoples of the so-called "Third World." Some such people have a centuries old experience of commonality (e.g., China and certain other Asian countries), some only a very limited common experience arising from their initial inclusion as "tribes" within the arbitrary boundaries established by European colonialism (e.g. most parts of Africa). For the latter, their nationalism is as much a matter of *aspiration* as it is one of established fact. But this does not make it any less real or important. Indeed, in much of Africa the very process of asserting "nationhood" has often been a crucial process in deepening the awareness of the mass of the population concerned as to their participation in the nation and as to the new opportunities that such participation offers them.

Therefore, the first point suggested by Third world experience is that any exercise in semantics designed to define the "essence" of a nation or designed to measure any given people against such a criterion is beside the point. The nation is, quite simply, any group that demands to be treated as such. Of course, a common history, territory, culture and/or language are very important, as is a shared experience of oppression and exploitation. These common features can help give focus, meaning and strength to the efforts of the peoples involved. The presence of such attributes can also help to convince outsiders to accept the claim to nationhood being made. But, in the Third World, it has been the demand itself that has been of primary importance, and the success of previously subjugated peoples to have their demand accepted. In consequence, what the remainder of this testimony will focus upon is, firstly, the very good reasons why the demand to be treated as a nation has been made by Third World peoples and, secondly, some of the results and implications of that demand having been made.

II. Nationalism

> Enough of these massacres
> I have suffered for five hundred years
> I can bear it no longer
> This forced labour
> I suffered on the railways
> In the fields of cotton
> In the timber mills and on the sisal plantations
> I can bear it no longer
> I can bear it no longer
> This was the cry of the people
> Of those who have suffered
> Since the first day of the invasion
> The people say: Enough
>
> D. S. Maguni, a nationalist poet in Mozambique

The period since the Second World War has seen the dramatic rise of nationalism in the Third World. The reason is simple: the concept of the nation and the political reality of nationalism have proven to be the most *effective* tools for resisting continued European hegemony in colonial and semi-colonial areas of the world and for winning independence. Other methods have been tried. When European imperialists first began to arrive in Africa, for example, there ensued in virtually every territory so assaulted a period of "primary resistance" on the part of peoples about to be colonized. After such initial resistance had been crushed by the military might of Europe, the indigenous population was either marginalized or forced into playing a subordinate role within the overarching imperial economy and society. In the words of Amilcar Cabral of Guinea-Bissau (Africa's outstanding nationalist activist and theoretician, until the time of his assassination by Portuguese agents in 1973), what was happening to the "dominated people" was, quite simply, "the negation of its historical process!"

Indigenous populations continued to try various means of regaining a measure of autonomy and independence; for example, there was a pattern of sporadic (and usually much too isolated) acts of resistance, both violent and non-violent, and there were attempts at assimilation, with the consequent but limited advancement of a few of the *indigenes* within the alien system. Yet isolated acts of resistance proved futile. And attempted assimilation failed in any significant way to alter the broader structures of exploitation and oppression that the population as a whole faced in each territory. It also involved too much of the past of the peoples concerned to be acceptable to them. In the twilight years of colonialism, Third World peoples were showing themselves prepared to build for the future in "modern" ways, but only in terms recognizable to them and which they defined for themselves. To a new generation of leaders, and ultimately to the broader population as well, the nation seemed to provide a framework both large enough and focused enough within which they could finally realize their goals. As Cabral put the point in the article previously cited:

> ... national liberation is the phenomenon in which a given socioeconomic whole rejects the negation of its historical process. In other words, the national liberation of a people is the regaining of the historical personality of that people, its return to history through the destruction of the imperialist domination to which it was subjected.

Of course, the choice of "the nation" by Third World peoples as a primary instrument in their drive for liberation and self-realization was partly a result of the way in which the outside world was structured. Even where the nation as such was a relatively alien, European, concept, its construction seemed a necessary achievement in order to deal effectively with a generally hostile and aggressive external environment—an environment that was, of course, organized into nations. As Basil Davidson, one of the most sensitive contemporary writers on African history, has observed, this lesson began to be learned by some quite early in the colonial epoch:

> *Become nations: or you cannot become free*. In some such imperative as this the European message reached African ears, decade after decade, through a multitude of more or less skeptical exhortations. A people without nationalism was said to be a people without history, and a people without history could have no identity, and therefore no real claim on that

> dignity and self-respect which even the poorest European peoples had successfully acquired for themselves. The lesson was to be well learned.

In this way, the achievement of national status was seen to have become, in a world of nations, a *sine qua non* for having one's grievances and aspirations taken seriously.

The decision to act on this latter assumption has proven to be quite correct tactically; of that there can be little doubt. Nevertheless, there has been a great deal more to Third World nationalism than merely tactical considerations. As Davidson goes on to affirm of the African situation:

> The case is clear: nationalism in Africa today is primarily a claim for equality of status and of rights, for personal dignity, self-respect, full participation in the things of the material world as well as in the things of the spirit: a consistent effort to rescue Africans from their condition of acquired inferiority to which they have been relegated through the years. And this is everywhere true.

This quotation is a useful evocation of the *positive* attributes of successful nationalism. It touched on the three spheres in which the promise of nationalism's making a substantive contribution to the betterment of Third World peoples can be seen to lie: the political, the cultural and the economic.

The potential *political* contribution of nationalism is the most obvious. A successful nationalism means the establishment of a political entity with a significant new degree of self-determination. Can there be any disagreement with the argument that self-determination is better than subjugation to imperial dictate for the peoples of formerly colonial or semi-colonial countries? The assertion of the demand for independence may also have the effect of releasing the creative energies of increasing numbers of people in the nation concerned. To be sure, this has not always happened, but the independent nation has provided at least the potential forum for increased democratization that, by definition, a continued imperial framework could never provide. Moreover, even the very political process involved in staking the new nation's claim to recognition has tended to have a profoundly democratizing effect, as many new people are drawn, for the first time, into an active involvement in shaping their own destinies. This is something that I witnessed for myself when I visited the liberated areas of Mozambique in 1972 during that country's struggle for freedom against the Portuguese colonial power. There, too, I witnessed the manner in which "nationhood" can also help to transcend the most parochial of tribal loyalties, the latter often focussing attention on units too isolated and narrowly traditional to facilitate a full effective political mobilization against the external agents of oppression.

The cultural contribution of nationalism can also be great. The cultural and psychic depredations of conquest and imperial control have been well documented by writers such as Cesaire, Memmi, James, Cabral and Fanon, those who have themselves sprung from colonial backgrounds and who have been able to reflect profoundly upon such themes. Significantly, the outstanding African nationalist leader, Samora Machel of Mozambique, echoed precisely these writers' themes in a speech presented on the occasion of his inauguration as President of the new People's Republic of Mozambique in June 1975 (Mozambique having become independent after more than ten years of struggle against Portuguese colonialism):

> It was in order to keep our people subjected to its domination that colonialism tried—in some cases, particularly in the urban areas, with some success—to destroy our personality, sow division, and created a slave mentality towards the foreigner. Assimilation was not merely the fascist caprice of a senile dictator (Salazar), but was in fact mental enslavement to the foreigner in its purest form, a deliberate process of negating all the culture, history and traditions of our people. A man thus spiritually destroyed became a living corpse, a docile receptacle for the colonizer's way of thinking, acting and living...This is the heritage we are reaping today.

With "our traditions humiliated, our civilization negated," a situation was created in which alcoholism [was] made widespread and prostitution and the disintegration of the family" and the like. Terrible problems, but ones with which a free Mozambique can at least begin to deal.

The practical response of Samora Machel and his colleagues in Mozambique to many of these problems has been the same as that suggested by Frantz Fanon in his well-known book, *The Wretched of the Earth*: to provide the stimulus for the rebirth of a *national culture*. Such a culture could hope to blend the best and most relevant of traditional values with a concern for contemporary reality and contemporary problems—in fact, just such a humane blend as is rejected by definition by the architects of assimilation. As Fanon enjoined his fellow Third World intellectuals, tempted by the individual rewards attendant upon their assimilation:

> We must work and fight with the same rhythm as the people to construct the future and to prepare the ground where vigorous shoots are already springing up. A national culture is not a folklore, nor an abstract populism

> that believes it can discover the people's true nature...A national culture is the whole body of efforts made by a people in the sphere of thought to describe, justify and praise the actions through which that people has created itself in existence. A national culture in underdeveloped countries should therefore take its place at the very heart of the struggle for freedom which these countries are carrying on.

Nor is the evocation of such a possibility in any way a speculative one. Among the most extraordinary things that I witnessed for myself in revisiting Mozambique in June 1975 for that country's independence celebrations was the extraordinary display of creative energies released in the cultural sphere—in all sectors of the population and, literally, in all the art forms that one could imagine—by the fact of freedom. For previously defeated and disoriented people, the pride of accomplishment and sense of possibility that a successful nationalism engenders has often been such as to set them again on the road to significant accomplishment in every sphere.

What, finally, of the potential economic contributions of nationalism? Julius Nyerere, President of Tanzania and one of the most innovative of Africa's postwar nationalists has put one important point particularly clearly in his essay "Economic Nationalism":

> Surely, if it is reasonable or understandable that Britain, Canada and France should protect their strong economies against domination by the even stronger American economy, it is also reasonable that Africa should be concerned about these matters? The fact that our national economies are weak does not alter things. On the contrary, the fact that we are underdeveloped makes such industry as does exist the more vital to our future. It becomes more essential, not less, that our major means of production should be under the control of the people, and that the people's representatives should determine the policies followed.
>
> As I have said, this economic nationalism has nothing to do with the ideologies of socialism, capitalism or communism. The time, and the method, of securing such control where it does not already exist will vary. But it would be absurd to expect Africa to accept that the well-being of its people should be indefinitely controlled from outside. Whatever economic system the peoples of different African countries eventually adopt, it is quite certain that the key positions of their economy are in the hands of their own citizens.

Nor is this merely a question of control for its own sake. The argument must be placed in the context of a virtual flood of recent studies that have proven, at least to my satisfaction, that the unalloyed economic impact of advanced capitalist economies upon the economically "backward" parts of the world has had (and continues to have) disastrous consequences. Quite simply, there is no "invisible hand" that dictates equitable distribution and evenness of development in the world economy. The evidence is incontrovertible: them as has—those at the centre of the system who are rich in capital, technology and power—gets (For a further argument to this effect see, among other sources, my own book, written with Giovanni Arrighi, and entitled *Essays on the Political Economy of Africa*.)

It is perfectly true that in such an imbalanced world not all of the new nation-states—perhaps not even the majority—have managed to defend their people against the kind of economic polarization between centre and periphery, metropole and hinterland, which characterizes, empirically, the functioning of capitalism on a world scale. Obviously, under such circumstances, national control only makes a contribution if it goes beyond being merely formal and nominal. Nonetheless, what is equally clear is that, without a national focus and a national presence, Third World peoples would be entirely defenseless against imperial dictate and subordination, as defenseless as they were under colonialism. Crystallization as a nation has proven to be a necessary—though not sufficient—condition for economic development in the modern world.

III. Liberation?

This last point warrants further discussion. As a growing body of writers have argued in recent years, a nationalist assertion can also manifest some severe weaknesses when measured against what is actually necessary to do in order to deal with the problems of underdevelopment. Thus, the most eloquent chapter in the book by Frantz Fanon cited above—one that precedes his stirring chapter on the (potential) virtues of "national culture"—is entitled, precisely, "The Pitfalls of National Consciousness." Here Fanon points out very clearly that concrete nationalisms have been unduly preoccupied with merely the winning of formal political independence and that such a narrow preoccupation can have a number of negative consequences.

It can, for example, give such an *appearance* of achievement that other pressing questions concerning cultural integrity and indigenous economic control will tend to be overlooked. Indeed President Nyerere of Tanzania has gone so far as to argue that "it is comparatively easy to get independence from a colonial power—especially one which claims to base its national morality on the principles of freedom and democracy. Everyone want to be free, and the task of the nationalist is simply to rouse the people to a confidence in their own power of protest." But to build "real freedom" is quite another matter, and Nyerere observes that unless the goals of the nationalist movement are broadened and deepened "the anti-colonial struggle will almost certainly have intensified the difficulties of realizing such 'real freedom'."

Related to this, nationalism leading to "independence" has often had the concrete result, in the Third World, of bringing into formal positions of power and authority indigenous elites who remain culturally and economically identified with the *status quo* and the imperial system. Such a "false decolonization" can involve merely an Africanization (or Asianization or the like) of the prevailing local power structure, with little alteration in the lot and prospects of the ordinary people of the society flowing from such a transformation. It is not surprising that in 1967 Nyerere "warned that the people should not allow their freedom to be pawned as most of the leaders were purchasable. He warned further that in running the affairs of the nation the people should not look on their leaders as saints or prophets." The President stated that the attainment of freedom in many cases resulted merely in the change of colours, white faces to black faces without ending exploitation and injustices, and above all without the betterment of the masses." Fanon, in emphasizing a parallel dimension of this reality, has been equally eloquent:

> The national middle class discovers its historic mission: that of intermediary. Seen through its eyes, its mission has nothing to do with transforming the nation; it consists, prosaically, with being the transmission line between the nation and a capitalism, rampant though camouflaged, which today puts on the masque of neo-colonialism.

The economic channels of the young state sink back inevitably into neo-colonialist lines. The national economy ... is literally controlled. The budget is balanced through loans and gifts, while every three or four months the chief ministers themselves or else their governmental delegations come to the erstwhile mother countries or elsewhere, fishing for capital.

In short, newly independent nations that have been structured on this kind of basis have become prey both to stronger economic centres and to the aggrandizement of indigenous elites. On the one hand, this has meant leadership much more closely aligned with its international partners than with its own people and, in consequence, an increasingly authoritarian direction for many new nations. On the other hand, as hinted above, it has meant that multinational corporations which dominate the international economy have had great success in bending such nations—and, in particular, such elites—to their will. And the results have been predictable. We might cite here another source to reinforce the picture sketched in the previous section. Thus, in a series of articles in so un-radical a forum as the *New Yorker* (and subsequently published as a widely read book, *Global Reach*) Richard Barnet and Steven Muller noted unequivocally that

> The negative impact of global corporations on living standards, employment rates and economic justice has occurred despite the fact that many corporate officials would like it to be otherwise and believe that it can be. The unfortunate role of the multinational business in maintaining and increasing worldwide poverty results primarily from the dismal reality that global corporations and poor countries have different—indeed, conflicting—interests, priorities and needs. The primary interest of corporation is profit maximization, and this means it is often advantageous for the balance sheet if income is diverted from poor countries. Eager as they are to be good corporate citizens, the managers owe their primary allegiance to company shareholders. Their businesses, they like to say, are neither charities nor welfare organizations, although some do devote modest resources to good works. The claims of the global corporations rest instead on the theory of the marketplace, which says, in effect, that by enriching themselves they enrich the whole world. This, unfortunately, has not been the reality.

The new nation seriously interested in development must be one that can articulate firmly its different "interests, priorities and needs"—and make them stick.

It becomes clear, then, that the possession of formal political independence by a "people" is no guarantee of economic progress. This is why the more sophisticated and dedicated nationalists in the Third World—writers and activists like Fanon and Nyerere committed to the goal of "nationhood" in Africa and elsewhere (however critical they may be of various practices carried out in its name)—have begun to lay more and more emphasis on cultural and economic dimensions of the struggle, and on the need for internal democratization. I revert once more to my own experience with the nationalist movement in Mozambique: precisely this kind of emphasis there has enabled Marcelino dos Santos, Vice-President of the country, to distinguish what he terms "primitive nationalism" from the much more relevant and radical kind of nationalism that has gradually taken shape in his country and that has begun to face up to the kind of challenges we have been discussing. To be sure, such nationalists as dos Santos have also sought a very high degree of political autonomy. Nonetheless, the point stands that the formalities of "independence" are increasingly seen to be much less important than the *actual substance* of autonomy, control and self-realization.

IV. Conclusion

As noted at the outset, an attempt to apply the lessons of Third World experience in any kind of systematic way to the case of the Dene would involve a great deal of speculation on my part. In conclusion, I would merely advance the following observations:

1. The apparent coherence—in terms of history, territory, culture and language—of the Dene as a nation is important, but in any case merely strengthens a claim by the native people to guarantee their self-defense *via* a nationhood that is solid on other grounds.
2. These other grounds are immediately evident from a comparative analysis of Third World nationalism. This analysis suggests that for peoples like the Dene who have been defeated and colonized the claim to nationhood has become a *necessary*—though not sufficient—condition to their reclaiming the political, cultural and economic autonomy they require in order to achieve development.
3. In light of Third world experience of the weaknesses as well as the strengths of nationalism, the refusal of the Dene to fetishize formal independence or "separatism" (as some hostile critics have attempted to portray their position) and instead to concentrate their attention upon the winning (and institutionalizing) of sufficient autonomy to guarantee cultural integrity, economic power and the basis for genuinely democratic control over their own lives by the people concerned is completely logical—and fully justified.

BUT, OF COURSE, IN MOZAMBIQUE independence had been an option and indeed, as expected, it proved to be the necessary option for Mozambicans at long last to avail themselves of in 1975. Moreover, we in TCLSAC continued to have a strong link with that country, a number of our own committee's members being among the first wave of international "cooperants" who flocked to Mozambique to lend their skills to the efforts of national and socialist construction taking place there (something my wife and I would also do in the early 1980s). Indeed, we were also helping, working with CUSO, to recruit such people from beyond our ranks, while also keeping our direct links with the country alive—as the next article, published in *This Magazine* in 1979 under the title "Mozambique: The Next Phase" will testify.

Re-reading the piece, however, I am struck by my own acceptance of, even enthusiasm for, the vanguard, single-party political model that Frelimo had brought to a new Mozambique. In the previous chapter I reflected on the fact that despite "my growing (and continuing) confidence in the strength of the case for a socialist alternative to Africa's underdevelopment," I was rather "slower to grasp the very real limitations of the chosen one-party route towards such a goal." I suggested that this latter was "a lesson I would also learn from the practice of Frelimo" and it was a theme I would continue to reflect upon in much subsequent writing. Despite this weakness, however, I continue to believe that the essay I now include captured much that was very real and exciting about the process of transformation as both imagined and in part realized by Frelimo in the early years of Mozambique's independence. This remains true even if, as I now can see more clearly in hindsight, my enthusiasm for the truly admirable qualities of the Frelimo leadership in those early days did tend to blind me to some of the possible, perhaps inevitable, costs of the framework of political leadership and participation that they chose to adopt.

LIVING IN TANZANIA, initial base of the Mozambican struggle for independence, I had the opportunity more than a decade ago to witness at close quarters the dramatic developments which were forging, in Frelimo, a strong and exemplary revolutionary organization. A trip to the liberated areas in 1972 enabled me to see on the ground the extent to which such developments were also foreshadowing the construction of a new, independent, and socialist Mozambique. Then, in June 1975, I returned as a guest at the country's independence celebrations to observe the initial phases of the effort to generalize the lessons of the liberation struggle to the entire country and to carry forward these lessons as policy in the many novel spheres that now lay open to Frelimo action. Small wonder that a trip back to Mozambique this year (1978) seemed an important one to make, offering as it did the chance to see how three years of the sobering realities of state power had affected the thrust of those previous initiatives.

The circumstances of the trip were also important. I travelled as a member of a delegation of Canadians, many from the Toronto Committee for the Liberation of Southern Africa (TCLSAC) of which I am a member. This delegation—more than a dozen of us—had been invited by Frelimo and the Mozambique government to undertake a study tour of the country, and we were warmly received throughout the four southern provinces in which we travelled. Some of my most vivid memories of the trip are of the greetings of welcome—as Canadians and as comrades—proffered to us by peasants and workers in the communal villages, state farms, and factories which we visited, as well as by state and party activists. As I once again experienced Frelimo's impressive spirit of humane and non-rhetorical internationalism, I realized that this was just another of the many achievements of Mozambique's earlier struggles which has been carried over intact into the country's new phase.

I. Sobering Realities

Yet I speak of "sobering realities." These there are, and in abundance. In consequence, the mood in Mozambique was different from the euphoric one I had encountered during the first weeks of independence in 1975. When I asked Marcelino dos Santos, Minister of the Plan, which was the more difficult, the current efforts at socialist reconstruction or the liberation struggle itself, the reply was immediate: unquestionably, the current phase! As many others expressed it, the terrain for action is now so much more vast, the obstacles to progress so much more subtle, the gains so much less tangible. Not that Frelimo has forgotten its motto ("The Struggle Continues"), but one was now struck by the clear awareness among Mozambicans—so familiar from the early days of the armed struggle when I first met Frelimo militants in the dingy little offices on Nkrumah Street in Dar es Salaam—that they have once again enlisted for a long haul.

In what ways, then, is the context for Mozambique's socialist project a hostile one? First and foremost, the visitor is conscious of entering a war zone. Coverage by the Western media had simply not prepared us for the savagery of the war which Rhodesia is waging against Mozambique. There were constant first-hand reports of damaging air attacks all along the border and well inside the country during the six weeks we were there, and on one occasion a bomb of apparent Rhodesian provenance exploded in a restaurant in Maputo itself.[56] The costs to Mozambique have been high, not only in human lives and in the destruction of expensive infrastructure, but also in the necessity to tie up in military roles many more trained cadres than would otherwise have been the case; the consequent cost to current mobilization efforts of the loss of the often highly developed political skills of such people has been important.

Important, too, have been disjunctions caused by Mozambique's implementation of sanctions against Rhodesia. Thus the port of Beira, which we visited, has been reduced to a mere echo of its former activity (though all the dock workers, even if underemployed, have been kept on the job) and crucial revenues lost. And migrant labour to Rhodesia, an erstwhile backbone of the dependent economy along the border, was cut off precipitously, well in advance of the planned rural transformation in Mozambique that might have begun to absorb those workers productively at home. When to all this is added the expense of fielding vast numbers of refugees in Mozambique, an expense which, like other related ones, has never been met to the extent originally promised by the international community (e.g., the Commonwealth), one understands why many Mozambicans were quick to say that the main contribution supporters outside could make to their development efforts would be to force the Smith gang out of power in Zimbabwe once and for all.

Mention of the erstwhile movement of migrant labor to Rhodesia points toward another crucial dimension of Mozambique's precarious situation. No country in Africa has inherited from colonialism an economy so viciously distorted, though its warping by the Portuguese to service South African needs was much more dramatic than any subordination to Rhodesia. In order to keep such an economy afloat at all in the short-run, the country has had to yield something to the logic of this dependency looking to continued revenues from southern Mozambicans migrating to work in South Africa, for example, and to port and transport earnings from goods shipped via Maputo from the Transvaal. Moreover, South Africa provides a crucial link for the modern sector of the economy; at the steel mill in Maputo I found that fully 95 percent of the inputs—iron ingots, wood and coal, machine parts—came from there, and at present much, much more cheaply than from any conceivable alternative source.

The Frelimo government is thus faced with the prospect of attempting to do two potentially contradictory things simultaneously: sustaining something of its inherited structure in order to avoid economic collapse, while beginning to search out openings toward an economy very differently structured. Nor does time stand still while this attempt unfolds: in the past few years the South African mines themselves have moved well ahead of Mozambique's own schedule for disengagement from South Africa, with a resultant disastrous curtailment of the number of Mozambicans working in the mines and severe consequences for both the country's balance of payments and unemployment figures in the south. Paradoxically, the opportunity thus afforded for restructuring the economy merely puts much greater pressure at the moment on a government already under severe strain.

The same paradox characterizes other sectors. For colonial Mozambique was also firmly mired in the classic posture of supplier of raw materials—cotton, cashews, sugar, copra, tea—to Portugal and the West, a structure topped off by a narrow industrial sector directed toward servicing the rather specialized needs of the privileged white population. Yet here again Mozambique has not been afforded the luxury of time, both to sustain something of the productive contribution of these activities while also working to transform them. Instead, collapse of production in crucial spheres has threatened to whisk away many of these activities all too precipitously, the key here being the dramatic pull-out, across the board, of the Portuguese (of 250,000 present at independence, only 15 to 20 thousand remain). Not that this pullout was ever willed by the government; indeed, every attempt has been made to safeguard the non-racial character of the regime. But the majority of Portuguese have responded negatively to the reality of their obvious loss of special privileges and to the implications for their class position of the nationalization of buildings, various professional activities, (law, medicine, etc.) and the like.

Attended by a considerable amount of economic sabotage —often of a merely spiteful kind—this departure left gaping holes in the social services (including a fall from about 600 doctors—for a population of 6 million!—to 50 within six months) and in productive spheres. In agriculture a number of large estates (producing copra, sugar, and tea) were left under the (supervised) control of big foreign companies and have continued to operate, but the wholesale abandonment of settler farms, particularly in the south, posed a very serious threat to food production, an undertaking on which most of them concentrated. Equally important was the collapse of the network of commercialization in the rural areas (affecting both the retailing of consumer goods and the purchasing of produce, as well as transport), with the marketing of cash crops by peasants of the north—and so also the balance of payments—being severely affected. And, of course, in the industrial sector there was also the threat of disaster in many spheres as entire complements of owners, managers, and technical staff often abandoned their enterprises. Small wonder that many Mozambicans were tempted to feel that merely weathering such a storm must be the order of the day.

Covering all these technical fronts while also advancing the work of mobilization necessary to draw people outside the formerly liberated areas firmly into the network of Frelimo-sponsored institutions meant that trained and trusted cadres were soon spread thin on the ground. As we shall see, the release of popular energies which the defeat of the Portuguese and Frelimo's accession to power facilitated has been important in filling this gap, but considerable reliance has had to be placed not just on technical personnel carried over from colonial days—some of whom are ill-adapted to the tasks of socialist reconstruction—but also on large numbers of *cooperantes*. The latter input, like other kinds of external aid, has its virtues; many skilled and dedicated people—including a number of Canadians—are now able to make an active contribution to Mozambican socialism, for example. But there are dangers, too, dangers which arise from the ideological overtones inherent in even the most technical-sounding of aid schemes, and this is not merely a threat from the subliminal liberal-cum-social democratic influence introduced by, say, Dutch or Scandinavian assistance.

The latter kind of influence loomed particularly large in the heyday of Tanzania's ultimately abortive socialist efforts, but Mozambique places itself much more firmly in the so-called "socialist camp" than Tanzania ever did, and thus the problem is posed somewhat differently there. Of course, no serious observer could deny the positive role that the Soviet Union has played, past and present, in supporting liberation movements in Southern Africa, and Eastern bloc assistance continues to be important to Mozambique (both substantively in the present phase, but also potentially, as a possible "last resort" if white-regime-sponsored incursions were to escalate even further). But it is difficult to be entirely sanguine about the ideological ramifications and possible impact upon policies of this kind of "socialist" assistance: its technical dimensions are often ensnared, abroad as at home, in the most technocratic and authoritarian definitions of preferred social relations of production and methods of political work, and the whole package is decked out with a particularly lifeless and demobilizing patina of official

"Marxism-Leninism." It will become apparent as this article proceeds that a substantial and sanguinary inoculation against too great a spill-over of such negative influences has been provided by the continuing vitality of Mozambique's own revolutionary tradition. But what has been said does underscore the importance of the present process of defining more sharply Mozambique's own ideology, a process given fresh impetus at Frelimo's Third Congress in 1977 when, for the first time, the movement (now to become a party) explicitly proclaimed Marxism-Leninism as its chosen framework.

II. A Luta Continua

Such difficulties have not preempted creative policies. We had every chance to sound these out, not only in the ministries responsible, but also on the ground in rural and industrial settings, in schools, clinics, and the like. Not surprisingly, in a country in which 95 percent of the population lives in the rural areas, agricultural transformation takes centre-stage. Moreover, there are precedents for progressive developments in this sphere. The emergence of collective production was already an important reality in the liberated areas, as I had observed for myself in 1972, and independence provided the opportunity for parallel initiatives throughout the rest of the country.

Unfortunately, this seems to have been, at first, an instance of almost too much "politics in command." The necessary technical underpinnings of such a program did not keep pace, and failures led to some retrenchment. Moreover, the focus of post-independence attention in the agricultural sphere was almost immediately wrenched away from such undertakings by the retreat of the Portuguese. As noted above, the collapse of settler farming in the south jeopardized food supplies to the cities, and a quick response to the emergency so created was imperative. The decision: to convert these already abandoned agricultural enterprises into state farms and, of necessity, to devote a considerable proportion of scarce energies and resources to keeping their often highly mechanized activities in operation.

Despite problems, this move was a success, but it also involved certain risks, most importantly the risk of, in effect, making too much of a virtue out of necessity. To see in elaborate mechanization a solution to rural problems is a temptation for all underdeveloped countries and to overvalue quasi-industrialized agriculture—the state-farm—is perhaps a particular temptation for such of those countries as are in receipt of substantial Eastern European aid. The question of whether Mozambique had succumbed too uncritically to such temptations was one which was being hotly debated while we were in the country, and it was instructive to learn later that, shortly after our departure, the Minister of Agriculture, a senior Frelimo cadre, had been replaced. The reason: "He had repeatedly shown that his conception of development was wrong and in contradiction to the process of advancing to socialism. He refused to implement the priority defined by the leading bodies in relation to communal villages. In essence, he does not place trust in the people, he does not consider people to be the determining element of development."

In fact, such "communal villages"—*aldeais communais*—are already the framework for peasant-based, peasant-led, collectivization; and we could see in the countryside this brand of rural transformation being exemplified. True, many such villages reflect their origins in the response to those natural disasters which hounded independent Mozambique's first years: terrifying floods in the Limpopo and Zambezi river valleys provided the initial incentive to group peasants from the valleys in villages on higher ground. And in the north the need to settle returning refugees and to place on a new footing erstwhile "strategic hamlets" created by the Portuguese was a pressing stimulus. Most often, the fact of living together, the better to receive essential services, is still the most prominent feature of such villages. But the seed of collective production has also been planted, and the new Commission on Communal Villages, created within the President's Office in 1978 even before the sacking of the Agriculture Minister, gives promise of encouraging its growth both in existing villages and in crucial, peasant-based provinces like Nampula, where the move towards collectivization has been in relative abeyance. Though initiatives in this sphere will be equally dependent upon parallel efforts to reestablish rural networks of commercialization and transportation, it was hard to escape the feeling that, in the current revitalization of grassroots rural transformation, one was witnessing a crucial moment in the Mozambican revolution.

In the industrial sphere, too, policy tended to move in fits and starts, adapting to the paradoxical demands, noted above, of a collapsing, yet profoundly warped, industrial sector. Which of these two to tackle first—the collapse or the distortion—remained a dilemma. Party and government have moved quite soberly here, making "best utilization of installed capacity" the watchword, with any much more dramatic structural transformation a goal for the future. But not the indefinite future: it was reassuring to learn in various interviews how conscious planners were of the dangers inherent in even the most unavoidable compromises with their economic inheritance.

Moreover, the Frelimo government, despite its relative caution, had begun quite early on to arm itself with the means for a different sort of planning, through nationalization of crucial sectors: not merely such preserves of local privilege as the private professions (medicine, law) and ownership of buildings, but also all banking, insurance, and oil installations, as well as that wide range of manufacturing firms of various sizes which had fallen into the hands of workers and the state following the departure of the Portuguese. In addition, even those large multinational firms which continue to operate—they are particularly important in estate agriculture (copra, tea, etc.)—do so under quite firm government scrutiny, a scrutiny so real that when one private firm, operating the coal mine at Moatize, chose to flout government guidelines on worker safety it too was immediately nationalized.

Not that Mozambique has assumed the mere act of nationalization to have established socialism or to have guaranteed the existence of a "self-centred" and autonomous economy. A much more important clue to the future has been the clarity of aspiration and intention manifested this year (1978) in such settings as the country's first National Conference of Planning (itself forced into being by the more systematic affirmation of the socialist goal at Frelimo's Third Congress [1977]). Thus it has been firmly enunciated that agriculture, though still seen as a major earner of foreign exchange, must come first to service local food requirements and industrial development, and that industry is to become the "dynamizing factor" which will slowly wrest the economy from its neocolonial format.

In fact, the "essential needs" of the bulk of the population are now much more consciously front and centre as targets for production, a promising source of direction both for the reconversion of existing industries and for the establishment of such new ones as are to be planned for the future.[57] Indeed, one senses that the next few years will be almost as full of crucial decisions for Mozambique in the industrial sector—and in the overall planning process—as in agriculture. Yet for our delegation the main promise lay in the fact that, as socialists, we were able to ask few, if any, questions in these spheres which Mozambicans were not already asking themselves. We came away with the clear sense that such constraints as the country's links to South Africa and its subordination to the global division of labour were seen as precisely that—constraints, not opportunities, to be bent and ultimately broken.

Things were somewhat more straightforward in the service sector. Intentions, at least, could be quite clear, even if the legacy of several centuries of Portuguese colonialism has been staggering needs and far from adequate means at the new government's disposal. Health is a case in point, with the priority of a rural-based, prevention-oriented, people's health program, already well established in the liberated areas, continuing to underpin current practice. As one expatriate doctor who had also worked in Tanzania put the point to me: "The socialist premises which some people were struggling, often unsuccessfully, to establish in Tanzania arc virtually taken for granted here. The real struggle, difficult enough but representing a much more advanced stage, is to implement them."

The most dramatic initial advance in this respect has been the extraordinary vaccination campaign. This program, in which over 95 percent of the population have been given basic innoculations, was deemed unprecedented in their own experience by World Health Organization officials who participated in it; it also provided ample testimony to the efficacy of those Frelimo political networks responsible for mobilizing popular participation in the program. Equally encouraging has been the ongoing attempt to attack professional hierarchies and democratize the medical workplace in the interests of releasing human energies. Here the vast Maputo Central Hospital, where several senior officials (including the President) intervened to facilitate the process, provided an impressive example. But, in any case, this merely represented a pattern that was at work much more broadly in Mozambique.

In fact, the efforts made to facilitate democratization of profoundly exclusivist, sexist, and hierarchical institutions were also apparent in the various educational institutions which we visited (the colonial school having had no equal with respect to the above shortcomings). We found faculty, support staff, and students beginning to pin down ways of actively participating in the definition and implementation of their own programs at all levels. But equally impressive was the root-and-branch approach to educational change that was the substance of policy. No doubt the risks entailed by possible error are somewhat less dramatic in education than in more directly productive spheres. In consequence, educationists told us of quite coolly and self-consciously scrapping most of the pre-existing syllabuses and teaching materials, then allowing the hard work and creativity of education workers to wrest from the ensuing "crisis" courses, texts, and classroom practices which are both much more profoundly Mozambican and, of course, more socialist in content. The method seemed to be working, and in such an environment it became all the more difficult to imagine parallel revolutionary aspirations being lost to view even in the most difficult realms of agricultural and industrial policy.

III. Vitoria e Certa?

Thus, even more striking for us than the harsh constraints which confront Mozambique in its new phase was the way in which the long-term goals of Mozambique's radical transformation kept rising to the surface—to premise policy-making and, indeed, to revitalize it. Contrast this with other African countries where such goals, even if enunciated, are drowned in the "pragmatic" and commonsensical calculations of the "short-run"; there, structural transformation is merely indefinitely postponed and hence rendered rhetorical. But if, despite the necessity for very real compromises, radical advance does remain firmly on the agenda in post-colonial Mozambique, what is the precise source of such promise for the revolution there? The answer, it seemed to me as I toured the country, was already firmly rooted in the experience of the liberated areas and, in its current manifestation, is threefold: it lies in the politicization of the development process, in the democratization of the political process, and in the concretization of Marxism with reference to the realities of Mozambique's own history and current circumstances. Obviously it is difficult to disentangle these threads that are tightly interwoven, but it is important to try to do so.

First, just as guerrilla warfare has come to be seen not as mere militarism but rather as a political process grounded in the clear statement of long-term goals of societal transformation and in the active, self-conscious participation of the people themselves, so too development is understood as being much more than a technical exercise. True, the often rather baroque structures of the Portuguese colonial state are far from having been completely dismantled. Moreover, bureaucratic "operators" and narrow technocrats—indigenous and expatriate, and, in each category, those of both "Eastern" and "Western" provenance—are not absent from Mozambique. Yet everywhere such elements seemed to be coming under some kind of positive political pressure. General political education is stressed—much of each Saturday morning in each ministry is given over to group study of a weekly text published in the newspaper, for example—but a central key is, increasingly, the party.

Indeed, the past year has seen the beginning of the "structuring" (as the phrase goes in Mozambique) of the new party out of the old, more amorphous movement. This involves the creation of party cells in every sector of the society—in ministries, factories, farms, schools, hospitals, neighbourhoods—and these cells are already working further to underwrite an ongoing debate about fundamentals, a debate which helps to keep long-term socialist priorities, including the priority of socialist methods of political work, front and centre in every institution. Nor, in such a context, is party membership something to be lightly undertaken. Complementing our discussions of policy with a number of long, semi-autobiographical talks with young party cadres (and would-be cadres) we were able to see how high the standards are, how much is expected from such people in the way of hard work and commitment, and how impressive is the response of many of the younger generation to the opportunities for revolutionary activity provided by Frelimo.[58]

Such attributes of "vanguardism" are important: the radical premises of progress are visibly alive in Mozambican offices and factories and farms—they are the very real currency of discourse—in ways that I had never seen them to be alive in Tanzania, for example. But all this would be much less promising were it not wedded to a second feature, the democratization of the various structures in question. For democracy is quite tangible in Mozambique. Just as real and active popular participation had been a necessary ingredient of guerrilla success in the liberated areas and war zones of pre-independence Mozambique, so now we observed it to be at work not only in the hospitals and schools mentioned above but in all the other kinds of production centres which we visited. Formerly the *grupos dinamizadores* (literally, the "dynamizing groups"), established throughout the country by Frelimo as a matter of top priority during the transition period leading up to independence, had provided the framework for such popular involvement [as discussed above]. But these, although extraordinarily important in the short run, represented a still somewhat unclear blending of political movement and mass organization. In consequence, as the *grupos* began to be displaced by party cells whose functions and membership are more clearly and exclusively defined, so too there had also to emerge a parallel network of mass organizations with much sharper identity.

There have been, during the past year, elections of representatives to the newly established People's Assemblies at local, district, regional, and national levels, as well as lively mass meetings held in every sector to evaluate publicly the qualifications of people hoping to become members of the new political party. With specific reference to the factories and state farms, the pertinent organization of mass action is to be the elected "production council." This institution was often described to us as the "trade union in embryo," but it is already providing for a much more active workers' role in the production process than this term might seem to imply. We had enough talks with factory workers and "responsibles" to see that in most cases the councils, and the ubiquitous meetings of workers attendant upon their operations, have had a quite dramatic impact upon decision-making, levels of output, and improvement of working conditions. The same sense of active involvement was visible in the communal villages we visited, here as elsewhere (including ministerial offices, generally the most hierarchical of undertakings) the *reuniao*, or general meeting, providing the centre stage for lively political drama. Of course, the strength of the process has varied with the nature of the historical experience of the village in question and with the quality of political leadership in the area. But the democratic ethos seems always to be real, often extremely moving and impressive, especially in a country where, until only three years ago, any active role whatsoever was denied the vast majority of the population.

Indeed, it is more than impressive. It is true that the party plays a crucial part, itself screening candidates, for example, and, in the case of the selection of party members, taking the role of popular scrutiny as being merely advisory. The parameters of participation continue to be defined, in part, from the top down, this reality representing, in the eyes of Frelimo leaders, precisely the measure of leadership and guidance of the development process necessitated by the present situation. In this sense too—in asserting its role in raising the level of consciousness of workers and peasants and facilitating their full emergence as historical actors—Frelimo makes no apologies for being a vanguard party. At the same time, we heard enough first-hand testimony to realize that the various meetings and elections mentioned above are scarcely formalities: inputs at the base are vital; they do reach the top; and, as so many activists themselves testified, they create a situation in which party and administrative functionaries must become cadres capable of realizing their goals by political and educational means rather than administrative fiat, or be seen to fail. Indeed, a stage seems already to have been reached where the assertions of workers and peasants that these structures have actively elicited can be ignored only at the regime's peril.

Not that there was any sense of the regime's proposing to ignore them. Quite the contrary. No one seems more aware than the Mozambicans with whom I talked of how often "socialisms" elsewhere have collapsed into bureaucratized enterprises serving primarily the interests of newly formed elites. There is also much writing in the press of such dangers very close to home, in Mozambique itself. Small wonder that the popular term in the political equation is taken so seriously: as Frelimo argues, ultimately only the workers and peasants themselves can build socialism. Of course history has also demonstrated that it is notoriously difficult to strike the kind of balance between leadership and mass action that is required for a genuine transition to socialism. The effort to avoid authoritarianism will be equally complex in Mozambique.

Nonetheless, there is substantial commitment, genuine institutional creativity, and much political subtlety: it is hard to escape the feeling that the possibility exists for a fully democratic denouement to this familiar political dilemma. Moreover, even as this effort unfolds, one cannot deny what is quite visible on the ground: the fact that so many Mozambicans actually do feel that they are engaged in making their own history in novel and unmediated ways. Surely this is one very good definition of democracy. The attendant release of energies is also socialism's basic promise for the realization of development in Mozambique, the human essence of the liberation struggle which Carvalho, the former Minister of Agriculture, had forgotten to honour in the new phase.[59]

Finally, it was important for our delegation to observe the manner in which such advances were being consolidated ideologically: as noted earlier, Frelimo has now more formally proclaimed its ideology to be that of "Marxism-Leninism." True, there have been Marxists in Frelimo from an early date and, in any case, the movement's practice came, increasingly, to coincide with Marxist perspectives as it transformed itself during the armed struggle. But the further, self-conscious systematization of the party's position within the Marxist tradition is now expected to make that practice much more coherent and accessible for purposes of political education and more capable of generalization as a framework for policy-making in novel spheres.

This is a correct perception. A Marxist approach does have the distinct promise of yielding sharper definitions, both of the complex nature of contemporary imperialism and of the class struggle which must continue within the development process, than Frelimo's own experience—left untheorized—can provide. But one had some reason to fear that such an ideological option might have its costs as well. After all, as argued earlier, Marxism-Leninism has all too often become a hollow and ultimately quite demagogic rationalization for the kinds of bureaucratization of the socialist impulse referred to above. Coupled with Frelimo's strong ties of aid and inclination to the "socialist countries," this reality brings us to repeat our earlier question: Does such an apparent ideological advance merely foreshadow a similar fate?

Long talks with Frelimo personnel convinced me that this was not the case; as President Samora Machel himself put the point to me, "Africans must use Marxism, but Marxism must not be allowed to use Africans!" "Some people," he added, "seem to think that the development of Marxism ended in October 1917." In a closely related manner, it was striking to observe how often we heard not only the President but Mozambicans at all levels hark back to the liberation struggle itself in setting the stage for the discussion of current policies. Indeed, by the end of our stay our Canadian delegation almost felt we had heard the same refrain once too often. But it was not difficult to remind ourselves that these were different people we were talking to on each occasion, and that they did not, in any case, evoke the experience of the liberated areas liturgically. Rather, they were almost invariably drawing the correct lessons—precisely the lessons of politicization and democratization—and then applying them concretely to their own circumstances.

The extent to which this experience will continue to be blended into Frelimo's Marxism (and into its Leninism!) is not predetermined, of course. I would say that the question of the nature of the country's Marxism—its depth and its openness—is now a crucial terrain for struggle in Mozambique.[60] Nonetheless, the balance of class forces is such as to give promise of vitality rather than sterility in the ideological realm. If this is indeed the case, the movement's ideology will help continue to underwrite progressive policies, including a reinforcement of the country's ability to winnow the wheat from the chaff of Eastern—as well as Western—aid. There is even the possibility, in light of what has been said above, that Mozambique will find itself making its own distinctive contribution to the historical experience of Marxism. It is, after all, a tradition much in need of revitalization in the Third World.

Clearly, it is late in the historical day to be naive about the claims to socialist advance that are made by manifestly underdeveloped and dependent agricultural countries in the hostile global environment of rampant and competing imperialisms. Too often their promise has turned to dust in the absence of global transformations that could help to ease their burden and to clear their path. But it would be equally naive for analysts to err in the opposite direction and replace the crucial dialectic that invariably exists between will and circumstance with a model premised on the sterile determinism of "objective conditions." Nothing is certain in Mozambique, but what, ultimately, is impressive there is the fact that, under trying conditions, popular classes — peasants and workers — are in motion, and that a leadership is in place which has begun to raise self-consciously all of the questions about a transition to socialism that the most intelligent and/or jaundiced left observer from the West could think of. It was instructive to see some of the answers to these questions taking shape in Mozambique this past summer, and it will be even more instructive to watch the process unfold in the future. Equally valuable was the reminder, as I returned to the North American late-seventies' political doldrums and to our own often apparently "hostile environment," that the struggle can continue.

THOSE OF US WHO HAD BEEN ACTIVE IN TCLPAC were prepared to take our victories where we could find them and to celebrate accordingly. But in the cases of Zimbabwe, Namibia and South Africa the indications were that Africans were in for an even longer and more arduous struggle against white-minority rule than in Lusophone Africa. It was a continuing struggle in which many of us felt compelled to enlist under the banner of our now rebranded committee TCLSAC. And I, personally, felt the need to widen my own solidarity efforts to embrace ever more actively the rest of Southern Africa. Thus we now recast our work at TCLSAC to resist ever more assertively the grim reality of apartheid South Africa — a country deaf to any claim to political voice made on the part of the over eighty percent of its own population that was not white but also willfully destructive, as part of its defensive posture, of its neighbouring states in the region.

We began to mount campaigns against apartheid in all its enormities, a theme I will return to in the following chapter in discussing the growing prominence within our work of resistance to the substantial loans being made by international banks — including several Canadian banks—to South Africa. Such activities would continue throughout the 1980s but by 1976, we were already embroiled in action against, amongst other things, the attempt by certain South Africans (led by Harry Oppenheimer's son, Nicky) to challenge the growing anti-apartheid sports' boycott — at the very time it was about to be effected against South Africa at the Montreal Olympics—by bringing a cricket team from SA to tour Canada.[61]

As the *Globe and Mail* headlined a front page article on the occasion when the tour hit Toronto: "31 charged in protest against South African cricket team," then beginning its piece with the statement that "Thirty one people were charged with trespassing Saturday after demonstrators tried to stop a cricket match between a Canadian team and a team from South Africa at the Toronto Cricket, Skating and Curling Club." The group, the article continued, "picketed the club and on three occasions stormed a police barricade and lay down on the field." My own claim to fame? Being part of the third wave of protesters I didn't even make it far enough to lie down between the wickets. Instead, I was tackled fiercely from behind by one of Toronto's plain-clothed "finest" who then twisted my arm behind me and planted himself on me, grinding my face into the grass, until I could be forced away to a waiting paddy-wagon. The kicker: this was precisely the picture of the event—me on the ground with the cop on top of me—that the *Globe* chose to run on its front page, much to my mother's shock and awe the next morning when she picked up her paper. Still, it remains the only time I've ever made it to the front page, and that, together with the rest of the day in jail, a subsequent court appearance, and a small fine, are the things I have to remember that particular event by.[62]

I also sought to concretize this expansion of our focus in a different way: through a trip of my own—my first—to South Africa itself, a trip I wrote of in an article for *This Magazine* (November-December, 1979) entitled, appropriately, "In the Belly of the Beast," and included here. Of course, I was forced throughout this period to pay proper attention to the growth on the ground of a movement of mass resistance, especially in the urban areas and well beyond the auspices of the ANC, that the strikes in Durban and the events in Soweto had already signalled. True, I was perhaps still somewhat too prone to assign primacy to the military exploits, planned and mounted from exile, of the ANC and to the promise of "guerrilla warfare" more generally. Yet, ultimately, South Africa was to see a victory over white-minority rule that would come about in a way different than that exemplified by the wars elsewhere in the region. In the latter settings, armed liberation movements made the principal running, whereas in South Africa mass popular action would play a much more central role. Of course, the ANC (and both the person and the image of Nelson Mandela in prison during all these long years) did earn special prominence in the South African people's consciousness and this, in turn, would legitimate its centrality to the transition that was to come. But this centrality was to occur, to a significant degree, at the expense of the populace whose popular energies actually drove the struggle in the townships and workplaces of South Africa in the 1980s. Indeed, it could be argued that the ANC's victory took place without facilitating any real meeting of the long-term needs and interests of the mass of South Africa's populace. To that story, obviously, we will have eventually to return in subsequent chapters.

AREN'T EVEN "MEN (AND WOMEN) OF GOODWILL," in Canada and elsewhere, just a little bored with the subject of South Africa? True, not a great deal can be said in that country's defense. It remains a racial oligarchy of particularly sordid kind;[63] moreover, the oppressive racist system, even liberals must admit, has much to do with guaranteeing a plentiful supply of cheap black labour and hence substantial profits for those enterprises, multinational and local, which thrive there. Unattractive, certainly. But then again, apartheid has been with us for such a long time; ugly it may be, but isn't it (albeit regrettably) more or less inalterable, with a state so strong and opposition so weak. Let's talk about something else. Or, if you must persist, can it really be quite as bad as all that (take Uganda for example)? And besides, aren't things improving, slowly (needless to say), but surely?

One thing a trip to South Africa (which I recently made) can do for you is to make you much less sanguine about such sanguinity. It's not only mistaken, it's dangerous. To begin with, things in South Africa are as bad as all that. And far from improving, they're getting worse. But change for the worse within the established structures is not the only kind of change that's apparent. The dramatic strikes in Durban in 1972-3 and the eighteen months of upheaval triggered throughout South Africa by the Soweto students in June 1976 were some indication of this fact, even if these confrontations didn't come close to overthrowing the system. Moreover, the commitment and energies that such confrontations revealed are still there, and they are beginning to find more effective point and focus. Of course, this in turn promises an escalation of violent confrontation with the apartheid state, a necessary cure some liberals may find to be worse than the disease.

Far easier to be bored, perhaps. But boredom with things South African is a luxury that will not be afforded us much longer. Durban and Soweto have placed revolution in South Africa much more firmly on the historical agenda than ever, and it seems clear that the oppressed people of South Africa intend to keep it there.

So Bad It's Worse

But is it really as bad as all that? What can I say to Canadians that isn't already revealed, much more dramatically than I can hope to phrase it, in such films as "Last Grave at Dimbaza" or "Six Days of Soweto,' or in a book like Cosmas Desmond's *The Discarded People*. After studying South Africa off and on for almost twenty years I saw little that I didn't expect to see. Yet how much more real—and chilling. To reread Desmond's book, found on a friend's shelf when I finally arrived in Maputo from inside South Africa, was now to see much more clearly in my mind's eye the horrors of the "dumping grounds" of the Kwazulu Bantustan in the making, a rural slum that also includes the African working-class ghettoes ringing Durban—and of the Bophutatswana, a Bantustan in actual realization, the "independent" labour reserve for Transvaal industry. Overcrowded, depressed, yet man-made—made by the architects of apartheid, by that less than twenty percent of the population (white) who control eighty-seven percent of the land, and so much else.

It was to relive the afternoon spent with the women in Crossroads as they planned some show of resistance to the government's announced destruction of their so-called "shantytown" on the outskirts of Cape Town. Crossroads: illegal in the eyes of the government; slated to be smashed by the same bull-dozers that had already demolished such neighbouring communities as Unibell and Modderadum; its inhabitants, particularly the women, the children, the aged and infirm, to be driven back to their so-called "homeland" in the Transkei, an impoverished pseudo-independent wasteland that many of them scarcely knew; their efforts to wrench a modicum of normal family life from the hell of the government enforced and strictly supervised "migrant labour" system quite literally to be pulled down around their ears.

To reread Desmond's and other printed account was to drive again through Cape Town's District Six, many battered shells still standing of the former houses of the city's "coloured" population, that group now exiled out onto the desolate "flats" outside the city, and to see, here and there, going up, the chic new townhouses and boutiques for whites that will replace them. It was to see the teeming multiracial daytime streets of Johannesburg literally lose their colour with the coming of the night as the black population, their labour no longer required, their presence in the city now unwelcome, hurry to the trains that will—must—take them home to Soweto. And it was to hear again, from virtually every black person with whom one talked (and from many whites as well), of beatings, bannings and almost perpetual police harassment.

Getting worse? The backlash to the Soweto events, which escalated most dramatically with the October 1977 smashing of the organizational infrastructure and personnel (Biko!) of the Black Consciousness Movement, still sets the tone. Even many of those church-sponsored initiatives that represented the last remaining expressions of liberal activism have been a target of this continuing crackdown; thus most people I talked with took it as merely a normal occurrence when one day during my stay another eighteen Catholic youth workers were arrested. Of course, there was also much talk of reform: thus some of the most egregious examples of "petty apartheid" are being modified (there are some integrated sport teams, for example); marginal adjustments that promise to provide lease-hold (though not ownership) opportunities for some urban-dwelling blacks are in the wind; *some* of the restrictions placed upon the jobs that blacks are allowed to hold are being lifted, where such restrictions impinge too grossly on management requirements for more skilled and semi-skilled labour. There are even signs of some limited—very limited—official recognition of black trade union rights, for only such rights as can be safely tucked within the framework of already established, and highly compromised, trade union structures.

Yet these are very far from touching the essentials of South Africa's exploitative reality. In the townships the scope of arbitrary administrative power over the lives of urban Africans can be seen to grow broader every day, while the government is quite explicit about the fact that any apparent reforms are an alternative to, not a step towards, majority rule. Meanwhile, at the most fundamental level, the government forges ahead with its Bantustan policy, attempting by means of the arbitrary creation of "independent" black states to formalize the existing extreme mal-distribution of land between population groups. Of course, at one level this ploy is so grossly dishonest that no state within the international community has had the nerve to recognize such illegitimate offspring of apartheid as the Transkei or Bophutatswana. For the process of unilaterally stripping millions of South Africans of their right to citizenship in their own country continues unabated. Indeed, the massive forced resettlement of black populations into these "dumping grounds" has merely speeded up. And "influx controls," which serve simultaneously to pump out such migrants from the reserves as are deemed "necessary," has been rendered more efficient by means of computerization of the notorious pass system, massive finger-printing of the black population, and the like.[64]

The implications of these realities bear emphasizing: in such a context the coming of majority rule would indeed have revolutionary implications. For it will be accompanied by unavoidable (and legitimate) demand to redress these stark inequalities—in land, labour and socio-economic power—that apartheid and capitalism have ground so deeply into the South African system. Small wonder that the superficial openness to thinking about the unthinkable that at first seemed so surprising as I read (certain selected) English-language newspapers, began to evaporate on second reading. For between the lines there was the uneasy sense that meaningful reform is, quite literally, impossible. Indeed, the chief source of strength of the Nationalist government in power is its quite explicit recognition that, with so much steam in the kettle, it cannot be let out slowly!

Thus, while an Andrew Young may bluster of optimistic false parallels between South Africa and Selma, Alabama,[65] the whites (with honourable exceptions to be sure) continue to rally ever more firmly behind the government in defense of their privileges. In consequence, even such perennial divisions within the white polity as that between English and Afrikaner have all but lost any significance they once may have had. True, more important tactical differences do exist between various fractions of capital about precisely just how much and just what kind of "reform" is in order, and divisions also surface between capital and white labour as to who should bear the costs of any easing of the job reservation system. Economic difficulties and political scandal (the recent Ministry of Information exposé, for example) also serve to fray the political consensus around the edges somewhat, while many whites who have no stomach for a fight do continue to leave the country. Yet it is quite clear that white unity is the name of the game. The encircling war—in Mozambique, Angola, Namibia and Zimbabwe—evokes the mentality of the beleagured fortress, not that of agonizing reappraisal; in reinforcement of this theme were the radio and newspaper accounts that I was constantly fielding there, full of evocative tales of the gallant "boys on the border," the South African soldiers at war in Namibia as the frontline creeps closer.

A meeting I attended at the University of Witwatersrand in Johannesburg provided a further example. White Rhodesian yahoos hurled insults at a black speaker from that country (he was to be banned from speaking the next day in Cape Town) and in the rowdy atmosphere a sympathetic questioner was punched to the ground from behind by a right-wing student. Nothing so very dramatic compared to much else in South Africa but, I was told, an unusual happening in the relatively liberal confines of Wits. As "the boys on the border" continue to return, there undoubtedly will be more of this kind of thing and vigilante activity designed to complement the police in rooting out "traitors" in the white community will also continue to grow. (The murder a year or two ago of a progressive university lecturer, Rick Turner, already provides a particularly gruesome case in point.) For some time to come, then, such a closed community seems likely to sustain the ruthless and powerful state that has thrown up a structure as prepared for lynch-mob "justice" being meted out against neighbouring black countries (the several missions into Angola, including the massacre at Cassinga, for example) as it is for unprecedented repression at home. So bad its worse, indeed.

The harder they fall

Fortunately, it is not within the white community that one looks for the main promise of change. Viewed from the bottom up rather than the top down, South Africa is not nearly so unshakable as tired pundits sometimes seem compelled to assume. We might note, first, one important, underlying factor: an economic system based on apartheid no longer works as it once did, this being a recurring theme in the newspapers I read there. Gold's international role still provides an important safety net against any too precipitous decline. But South Africa, for all its dramatic growth, remains a semi-industrialized economy, and the limitations upon its external and internal markets (the blacks low purchasing power being the negative side of the cheap labour coin, of course) have begun to weigh heavily upon it. Add rising fuel and military costs, a somewhat less buoyant investment climate in the post-Soweto period, and you have crisis—and the massive unemployment that has helped to stoke the fires of resistance. Only huge loans from Canadian and other banks keep the economic situation, and the apartheid state's ability to bolster itself up, from being worse than it is.

Yet "economic crisis" in and of itself is no guarantee of change. Even more important is the mood of resistance within the black community, obvious in the Soweto events but readily apparent to a visitor who can (in spite of the severe limitations upon access to any meeting with spokespersons from that community) step a bit off the beaten track. What I did manage to hear at first hand confirmed what one senses to be the case from outside: post-Soweto South Africa is not post-Sharpeville South Africa. The cruel wave of repression that followed the Sharpeville massacre of 1960 brought a substantial victory for apartheid. The ante was raised so quickly and dramatically by the state that the political movements in opposition—and the people as a whole—were stunned and demobilized, defeated as much psychologically as physically.

This has not been the aftermath of Soweto, despite the repression. The students of Soweto, of Cape Town, and of many other places in South Africa had, if anything, an awareness more clear than was that of their predecessors within the resistance movement of the odds against them as they embarked on their endeavours. Yet they were prepared to die. Of course, this is not to say that sheer will and courage are guarantees of victory, any more than is the fact of economic crisis. There was indeed something of the suicidal in certain of the actions that made the wave of nation-wide protest we now encapsulate in the term "Soweto"; moreover, such protest ultimately did lack the focus and the clout to really endanger the state in a fundamental way. Nonetheless, the fact remains that the existence of such a mood as was exemplified in Soweto and elsewhere is a necessary prerequisite for a revolutionary strategy and that mood has not been scotched.

It is a mood that has been reinforced by a new sense of possibilities in the region as a whole. What worries most whites inspires most blacks: Mozambique, Zimbabwe, Namibia, Angola, with the turning-back of the South African army's invasion of the latter country having been particularly important in weakening the myth of invincibility that has helped to reinforce the apartheid state. It is also a mood which determines that resistance continues to second-rate "Bantu education" (the original target of the students in 1976), while a place like Soweto remains extremely difficult for the South African state to govern. Yet, as hinted, strategy and tactics are required that take the struggle beyond the African locations, the latter being too easy to cut off (as in 1976) and surround. It was no accident that, quite early in their undertakings, students attempted to bring pressure, then persuasion, to bear on their parents (as well as upon migrant workers in the hostels) to boycott their work places. One could debate whether the stay-at-home was the best means for workers to make themselves heard but what bears noting here is my sense that, in political work in the townships, such an emphasis upon developing class consciousness has continued to grow. The rather vague, if powerful, ideological ethos of Black Power and Black Consciousness begins to give way to a more careful class analysis of the South African system.

Nothing could be more important, for black workers do have tremendous potential power. The complex industrial structure of South Africa has produced a proletariat unlike anything seen in the nationalist assertions elsewhere in Africa, and it is a proletariat upon which the delicately balanced South African economy is vitally dependent. No doubt rural-based guerrilla movements will be a dimension of the South African struggle, but are they likely to loom as large in the revolutionary equation as they did in Mozambique and Zimbabwe? Such, at any rate, was the query that struck me as I walked the skyscraper-lined streets of Johannesburg, drove past the mine compounds on the Reef, and toured the industrial areas of Durban (where the workers' actions of the early '70s have probably already given some foretaste of things to come.) If the writings of General Giap and Che Guevara provided an initial theoretical foundation for understanding happenings elsewhere in southern Africa, here one might do better to begin with a reading of Rosa Luxemburg on the Mass Strike!

For South Africans, of course, the consideration of such matters is very far from being an academic exercise and I was to hear these and other issues discussed many times. In particular, there was some criticism of the major organized actors on the African side, the liberation movements, and especially of the African National Congress (ANC), focused upon because it is far and away the most important of such movements. Some, in hindsight, would now criticize the ANC guerrillas for adventurism, for jeopardizing, through their single-minded focus on armed struggle, more seemingly modest efforts such as the organization, to better effect, of an African trade-union presence. Was the ANC relying too exclusively on the guerrilla warfare model borrowed from other African settings and underestimating the importance of the strategic economic weapon that the workers possess. And others would argue that a revolution on such sociologically complex terrain as that of South Africa would have to be multilayered and geographically uneven, will often take place under diverse local leaderships and organizational auspices, and will be a somewhat unpredictable mix of planned activity and of spontaneous outbursts. It will take deft revolutionaries indeed to keep abreast of such a process and these critics wonder aloud whether the ANC may prove too exclusive in its claims to revolutionary primacy to allow such a diversity of revolutionary energies to find full expression.

There may be an element of truth in some of these criticisms, particularly the latter one. Yet it is the case that a successful revolution needs focus and ultimately some centralization of leadership. Nor, the ANC insists, has it ignored underground activity in the urban areas, having, in addition, a substantial following among important sectors of the working class. At the same time, it would be a mistake to overlook the presence of revolutionary tinder in the rural areas, an important front since, whatever other contradictions may develop and be acted upon, military pressure must be brought to bear upon apartheid under South African conditions; it is difficult to see how this can be done other than by guerrilla warfare.

So speaks the ANC, a movement that thus continues to be at the centre of the discussion about African resistance. The latter fact is no accident. The ANC has been central since its founding in 1912 and for many years subsequently in which it tried every possible peaceful means to slow the juggernaut of white power. Only in the 1960s, beaten and banned, did it turn to a guerrilla strategy and even then, still at some distance geographically and psychologically from the struggle, it moved only slowly to engage the powerful apartheid state. Still, it retained considerable popular respect inside the country and also managed to maintain itself outside as a major vector of both concrete and moral support from both Eastern and Western sources for the struggle of South Africa's people. Its militants are thus poised to grow more active and effective as the front-line in southern Africa moves further south and as tensions grow ever more unmanageable within their country.

Indeed, it would not be surprising if the ANC proves to be the chief inheritor of the spirit of Soweto. Discussion with ANC personnel during my trip (but outside South Africa) suggested that the wind of change that has recently blown like a hurricane against the South African state has been like a breath of fresh air for the liberation movements. Thus, many of the "graduates of Soweto" have become in exile new recruits to the ANC. And new energies have been accompanied by new ideas. Certainly the movement, though active within the country and not entirely absent from the events themselves, makes no claim to have organized "Soweto"; indeed it may well have been astonished at the swift pace of developments there. Of course, it remains as before apparently strongly committed to the radical transformation of South Africa and aware that history has left it no alternative but head-on confrontation with apartheid. But I also sensed that something new was now afoot, as our discussion ranged from a subtle evaluation of the likely impact of the Bantustan policy in South Africa upon popular consciousness to an assessment of—precisely—the possible balances to be struck between urban and rural actions and economic and military tactics. An awareness of fresh possibilities has brought a concreteness to the movement's activities and an openness to its analyses that I had not always felt to be present in, say, the ANC offices in Dar es Salaam during the dog-days of the 1960s.

Moreover, the results on the ground already indicate the way forward. Certainly the great upsurge of security trials in South Africa suggests the growing presence of liberation movement militants, engaged in political mobilization and sabotage, while South Africa's Security Minister Jimmy Kruger's many warnings as to the renewed ANC threat testify to the same reality. In the past year military confrontations between the ANC and the South African state forces have taken place well inside the country at such places as Rustenburg, Zeerust and Thabazimbi. Undoubtedly, questions remain: how much more effective can such actions become (and how quickly); how will the ANC define its own strategic options over time; how will that movement interact with other centres of resistance within the society. Indeed, the endless shuffling of such variables into a whole string of possible scenarios has become a favourite pastime of South African watchers. And when one adds the range of roles open to external actors—the United States, Britain, the Soviet Union, Cuba, Nigeria—the scenario game grows even more ragged.

In addition, it would be foolhardy to underestimate the strength and self-evident resolve of the South African state and the possible range of its responses to challenge, (no one expects it to be quickly blown away like the Shah's police-state in Iran though it my be relevant to remind ourselves that the latter development would itself have been unlikely a mere twelve months ago.) In short, the situation is complicated and you will find no glib scenarios here. Merely the conclusion that the past three years have seen the struggle in South Africa joined at an entirely new level and that the tide has begun to flow against the cause of white supremacy. One does not need to have been in South Africa—though it helps—to realize that violence must be—will be—the midwife of history there. I have met few people who rejoiced in such a prospect, and, never, in twenty years, a member of a Southern African liberation movement who did so. Yet for anyone who takes the evils of apartheid seriously, the realization that it will be so is a thing of hope, not of despair

Back home where it belongs

It would be nice to imagine most Canadians rallying to the side of the majority as they fight for their freedom in South Africa. After all, apartheid is not merely playing out its deadly logic some 7000 miles away. By now it must seem almost a cliché to note that apartheid is no further away than the boardrooms of the numerous Canadian-based banks and corporations in on the action in South Africa. Yet perhaps it is a cliché that is easier to take for granted here in Canada than when, inside SA, one sees at first hand the not-so-hidden costs of our profits.

Of course, not all Canadians are indifferent to these costs, as the actions of church groups and others against such corporate activities continue to bear witness. Even Trudeau, in one of his rare moments of candour, once remarked [as quoted previously] of our South African policy that "It's not consistent. Either we should stop trading or we should stop condemning." Yet [as also noted above] we have continued to do both. Take even that brief flurry of activity which, in late 1977, found the Trudeau government apparently distancing itself, without much fanfare, from direct state involvement in our economic linkages with South Africa; careful investigation (notably by Wayne Cheveldeyoff in a series of articles in Toronto's *Globe and Mail*) of the loopholes in such an initiative soon revealed it to be only a slightly more elaborate form of rhetorical posturing. Despite the rhetoric "business as usual" with white minority rule remains the basic themes of Canadian policy.

This bottom line, then, is familiar, if depressing, stuff. Significantly, however, the more overt focus of the "debate" over Southern African issues tends to lie elsewhere. For example, the Confederation of Church and Business People—a virulently right-wing group of prominent Canadian business types which in recent years has been actively bankrolling a pro-South African backlash against church activism on southern African issue—tends to downplay direct defense of business's role. No doubt aware of the difficulty of presenting any very convincing rationale on behalf of their involvement, such critics most often attempt simply to place anti-apartheid activists on the defensive! Their ploy: an attack on the latter's support (for example, through the Committee to Combat Racism of the World Council of Churches) for the liberation movement of southern Africa—the "Soviet-backed," "terrorist bogey-men of right-wing propaganda. We have seen this with reference to Zimbabwe and Namibia, for example: Morton Shulman's unscrupulous red-baiting in the *Toronto Sun* of OXFAM-Canada for its assistance to SWAPO in the latter territory is a particularly notorious further example. But as the struggle for South Africa escalates, as the ANC and popular movement more generally, become more and more active inside that country, we can expect more of the same there too.

Such right-wing ideologues are wise to take this tack, for it strikes at the Achilles' heel of anti-apartheid work: the difficulty many Canadians have in accepting the inevitability of revolutionary change in southern Africa and in accepting, as well, the legitimacy of those violent means that are necessary—as a counter to the systematic violence of white minority rule—in order to bring about such change. Part of the problem is sheer misinformation, a product of the paper curtain through which Canadians can perceive only in blurred outline what is happening in Africa. One does not have to be very long in South Africa to realize what a small and selective percentage of the story we are getting. Yet, equally important I'm convinced, is a set of mythologies or prejudices ingrained in our culture that cushion the biased press coverage, and make it not only believable but even palatable.

Most obvious is our ubiquitous anti-communism. In part this is an understandable response to the Soviet Union's deformation of the socialist impulse. But in equal measure it is an illusory global preoccupation—and as such promoted quite self-consciously by, among others, the white minority regimes themselves—that makes it impossible for us to evaluate African liberation movements, and their radical demands, on their own merits. Because, almost inevitably, these movements begin to have revolutionary prescriptions for their societies that move beyond the mere substitution of black faces in power for white and because, of necessity, they receive most of their arms from the Eastern bloc (from where else could they hope to get them?), it becomes all too easy to portray them as being "Soviet puppets," or, at best (in the ubiquitous newspaper tag-line), "Soviet-backed." Take the second point first. One thing that my own acquaintance with personnel from these movements, dating back to the early sixties, has impressed upon me is that they have not fought so hard or so long in order to hand their independence over to someone else. Only our own residual paternalism could enable us to interpret the arms link so readily as being one of subordination.

Or take the revolutionary demands themselves: majority rule and, beyond that, redistribution of the land, worker control, some form of socialism. An emanation from the Kremlin? Scarcely, for because the oppressive structures in South Africa are so deeply embedded, so the surgery must be radical. Still, we have an almost overwhelming difficulty in taking these realities seriously. Once again I think it is our own culture that stands in the way. Our own stunted sense of the possibilities for meaningful social change, our own cynicism about the political realm, our own incapacity to imagine any heroic collective purpose for ourselves, indeed our own apparent fear of any such purpose, all these barriers intervene. I have felt these barriers most profoundly recently in the contrast between, on the one hand, the bland outpourings of this year's Canadian election campaign (and public indifference toward it) and, on the other, the palpable sense of a people in motion, consciously making their own history, that I experienced last year in post-liberation Mozambique. Yet it was also apparent to me that militants in South Africa are now bidding to make their own history in a similar way. Is this, possibly, one root of that boredom with things South African noted above? Since, as Canadians, we cannot take seriously the prospect of any profound change in our own lives, we are incapable of grasping that aspiration for such a change can be the dramatic, yet everyday, reality of others.

Moreover, it seems clear that, as regards southern Africa, such incomprehension is underwritten by a low-key yet pervasive ethos of racism in Canada. Put quite bluntly, we have even more difficulty in taking black aspirations for freedom and social change seriously than we do any roughly comparable aspirations on the part of whites. For one thing, we tend to lump all Africa together in a hopeless, uninspiring ball; the horrifying depredations of an Idi Amin in Uganda are then seen as somehow casting doubt upon the legitimacy of demands made by black Africans several thousand miles away. (Of course, this trope marks a favourite public-relations gambit of the white-minority regimes themselves, another that we seem prepared to accept quite readily.) Just imagine the scoffing if one were to argue that the activities of the Greek colonels shed some negative light on the prospects for democracy in, say, France, or that Germany's Nazism has proven that Scandinavians (or even Germans for that matter) aren't quite ready for self-government!

The important point to note here is that it is this racist filter, probably more than other factor, that enables us to accept so uncritically the picture of those engaged in revolutionary activity in southern Africa as being mere "terrorists."[66] Few of us are pacifists, and indeed when European liberation movements like the Dutch and French undergrounds in the 1940s, fought against fascism (Germany and its local collaborators) Canadians not only applauded but also sent troops to help. Yet the enemy in South

Africa is clearly the same: it is no accident that John Vorster was interned in South Africa during the Second World War as a pro-Nazi sympathizer. Surely there are many more Canadians than have thus far made themselves heard who can have a colour-blind response to the genuine historical parallel between two such similar struggles for freedom.[67]

But such a response will not come readily. I have mentioned crude and demagogic "anti-communism," our own inchoate sense of self-defeat, and racism as being dimensions of the problem; obviously this is a potent brew, demobilizing in the extreme. Indeed, if my observations are at all accurate, they underscore the deadly seriousness of the task that now confronts those of us—it is, after all, the vast majority of Canadians—who have no real stake, no vested interest, in apartheid. Deadly serious because, if we are ever to take the steps necessary to keep Canada from finding itself on the wrong side of the emerging confrontation in South Africa, our struggle must be waged not only against the established resolve and great weight of our corporate and governmental structures, but also deep within ourselves.

Isandhlwana

In this year, the symbol of Isandhlwana may be of some assistance in any such attempt to rise above our own prejudices and to identify wholeheartedly with those in South Africa who feel they have no choice but to fight for their freedom. For Isandhlwana, on January 22, 1879, was the scene of the greatest military victory of the Zulu nation against the on-rushing Afrikaner and British hordes, there latter bent on seizing the Africans' land and, ultimately, yoking them to the country's white-driven economic machine. Moving with lightening speed from the coast the Zulu impis (armies) then regrouped stealthily and charged what was the main staging-camp of the British army of conquest; after fierce fighting the British force was decimated. Friedrich Engels was one of the few nineteenth century observers who gave this victory the kind of prominence it deserved, noting that the Zulu had done

> what no European army can do. Armed only with lances and spears, without firearms, under a hail of bullets from the breechloaders of the English infantry—acknowledged the best in the world at fighting in close order—they advanced right up the bayonets and more than once threw the line into disorder and even broke them, in spite of the enormous inequality of weapons and in spite of the fact that they have no military service and know nothing of drill.

True, the military might of the imperial centre was ultimately to crush all such warriors, in Natal and elsewhere in southern Africa, who were armed only "with lances and spears." Nonetheless, Africans had shown themselves to be quite capable of taking up successfully the gage of the conquerors and would be prepared to do so again. Small wonder that the ANC has chosen to celebrate this year as the centenary of that historic battle—terming 1979 the Year of the Spear.

To say that my own visit to Isandhlwana was a "highlight of my trip" to South Africa would smack too much of the travel brochure. Yet it is certainly true. Bouncing along the rough road leading to the site, we arrived at the battlefield, deep in the heart of Zululand, as the sun was beginning to set. In the strange, dusty half-light that is the African dusk, the white-pained cairns, erected here and there across the plain and up a stark, gnarled hill to mark the various places where British troopers had fallen, offered a pitiless commentary on the vain-glories of Empire. And the eerie silence, broken only by the distant moan of cattle shuffling home to their kraals, seemed, nonetheless, to echo with the sound of feet as the warriors once again pounded across the plain toward the hill—and toward their oppressors. I was giddy: one felt one could almost reach out and touch the long relentless arc of South African history in such a place.

From the sublime to the grimly ridiculous. Later that night I sat, not many miles away, in the "whites-only" bar in Babanango, a small town located within a strip of rich, river-bottom, whites-only farmland that cuts like a scar across the most fertile part of Zululand. White skin-colour earns an assumption of virtue and solidarity in such a setting so there was no need to strain to overhear locals speaking apprehensively of the rash of sabotage—mostly barn burnings and carried out, no doubt, by their own "kaffirs"—that had recently taken place in the neighbourhood. Hard not to recognize in even these attempts by Africans to fight back the same will that sparked the anger of the Soweto students and the ANC's military actions at Rustenburg, Zeerust and Thabazimbi. Hard not to hear the echo from Isandhlwana, the spirit of resistance to seizure and oppression still alive in the land of apartheid. Can we Canadians not identify with that spirit? Is it so difficult to be thankful for the fact that Africans, as they continue their fight, now "know something of drill" and are armed, economically and militarily, with other more effective weapons than the spear?

CHAPTER THREE

The Long 1980s (to 1994)

The End of the Beginning

The 1980s. To 1994. Yes, take that latter year as marking the end of the 1980s since it was only then that the struggle in which those of us at TCLSAC (and so many more comrades elsewhere) had been involved for decades came to apparent culmination with the victory, in a post-apartheid South Africa, of the ANC, and the ascendance of Nelson Mandela (a man had spent so many years in prison for daring to demand his people's freedom) to the presidency of the new South Africa. Of course, we had already seen elsewhere in the region—in Angola, in Mozambique and in Zimbabwe—just how ambiguous such a victory could prove to be. Here, moreover, was a sobering learning experience that would merely be replayed as we contemplated (see chapters 4 and 5, below) the similarly troubled trajectories of both South Africa and Namibia through the 1990s and into the new century.

But to such considerations we will return. For meanwhile, and throughout "the long 1980s," our work at TCLSAC continued to expand outwards from our original focus on Portugal's African colonies, building on initiatives that we had already begun to take vis-à-vis southern Africa as a whole. We underscored the role of Falconbridge and other companies stealing non-renewable mineral resources from Namibia and emphasized the parallels between the historic role of the Hudson's Bay Company in Canada and its current (illegal) role in Namibia in pursuit, for coats, of the fur of karakul sheep. Indeed, we even managed to arrange for a delegation from Namibia's SWAPO movement to visit Canada's north to exchange views and experiences with representatives of Canada's own native people there.

We also emphasized the outrageous nature of the UK's half-hearted approach to the illegal white Smith regime that had seized power in Rhodesia and Canada's all-too-mild acquiescence in it, using the occasion of their holding a Commonwealth conference held in Ottawa in 1973 to organize, with others, a counter-conference dedicated to the theme: "Zimbabwe: the Missing Delegation." Representatives of both Zimbabwean liberations movements (ZANU and ZAPU) addressed us, as did those from other of the liberation movements and even some from official delegations at the Commonwealth Conference itself, such as John Malecela, the Foreign Minister of Tanzania.

We were to write more skeptically about Zimbabwe's future as the '70s wore on and the country neared victory over the cancerous Smith regime. As noted in the previous chapter, I myself wrote, in 1977, a controversial article supporting the emergent ZIPA movement against the claims of both ZANU and ZAPU in the mid-1970s. And in a second article, written in 1980 at the time of Zimbabwe's independence I gave a tepid welcome, one full of nervous misgivings, to Robert Mugabe and his new ZANU government. Indeed, in light of the future record of that sad government and of Mugabe's emergence as a full-blown despot, I look back, sadly, on the fact that my comments of the time were almost entirely accurate. Meanwhile, however, we as a group became ever more active with respect to South Africa itself.

True, I did continue in my own writing, both scholarly and popular, during the 1980s, to cover a range of sites in southern Africa (notably Mozambique and Rhodesia/Zimbabwe), but my interests were increasingly drawn to "the belly of the beast" itself. Indeed, spurred on by my trip to South Africa—and I could never obtain a legal visa from the apartheid government for a legal return visit (but see below, in this chapter)—I found myself collaborating with Stephen Gelb, a South African student and activist studying in Canada and also working for TCLSAC. Our book, *The Crisis in South Africa*[68] was a particularly gratifying one to have written and, up to the present, I continue to field comments from

South Africans as to how important the book was to them at the time, the volume itself often squirreled away, I was told, well out of sight, under floorboards and the like, since it was banned by the apartheid government during the dark years of struggle against the police state.

But there was also an extension of the work we had begun with our *Words and Deeds* volume as we now continued to research Canada's complicit links with South Africa itself. For there was a myth of Canada that needed to be deconstructed; this was the myth, assiduously cultivated by politicians and pundits alike, that Canada was in fact actually a sensitive, humane and benign "middle power"—in, but in some vague way not of, the imperial camp. Canada as middle power? In TCLSAC, we had no such illusions about Canada, having identified, in *Words and Deeds*, a pattern of "rhetorical commitment to the cause of popular freedom on the one hand and 'business as usual' with the oppressive white minority regimes on the other."

Thus, as we had demonstrated in detail in that book, Canada's support for Portuguese rule took three inter-related forms: economic, military and political.[69] Now, as we reoriented our principle focus of campaigning towards South Africa, I felt moved to reiterate the book's central point: "Note the title of the earlier book: *Words and Deeds*. The phrase captures the essence of Canada's role, an essence that even Prime Minister Trudeau, in one of his rare moments of candour, also underlined several years ago." And here I cited once again Trudeau's curious aphorism regarding Canada's relationship with South Africa: "It's not consistent. Either we should stop trading or we should stop condemning." Yet in practice, "Canada under Pearson's and Trudeau's leadership had continued to do both."

A KEY ISSUE, ONE AMONG SEVERAL APPROPRIATE ONES, quickly became the issue of international bank loans to South Africa, something in which Canadian banks were deeply involved—the response was a focus of campaigns similar to those aimed at the role of Gulf Oil (Canada) in Angola a few years earlier. Annual General Meetings again became a target, as did carefully counterfeited bank slips made out to the South African government that we slipped onto bank customer-service tables all over town. We also sought to write as widely as possible about the issue of these bank loans, seeking to link the struggles in southern Africa as directly to Canadian realities as we could. Indeed, in an article of the time (published in the 1970s, as it happened, but framing work that we were to continue with throughout the 1980s)—"Canadian Bank Loans to South Africa," in the Swedish published volume *Canada, Scandinavia and Southern Africa*[70]—I continued on from the above-mentioned citations of both dos Santos and Trudeau to argue as follows:

THERE ARE A NUMBER OF THEMES that could be pursued here: our long-term record of silent complicity within NATO regarding the military linkages established between western capitalist countries and, not just Portugal, but also South Africa, or our penchant for downgrading the claims of liberation movements to represent the legitimate aspirations of their people and to use the only means, necessarily non-peaceful, for the latter's liberation (our occasional gesture of humanitarian aid introducing only a minor qualification to this pattern). One could also explore the reasons for our having played the role we have: the imperatives of our domestic dependent economy and the instrumentalization of our state to service the activities of multi-nationals working from a Canadian base; the logic of our own indigenous and unrepentantly capitalist system; our political (and entirely uncritical) encapsulation within the "western alliance" under the thumb of the United State (thanks in no small part to the activities of the exemplary Lester Pearson); our cultural imprisonment within the ideological framework of modern liberalism, domestic and global. And so on.

But here our subject is the banks and it is, in fact, the actual substance of our economic stance towards South Africa and not our rhetoric that is the primary issue. For, as Trudeau has himself admitted, it is precisely here that the gap between words and deeds is most evident. Most recently Trudeau's own words have again spoken volumes. Despite his articulation of the usual pieties at last June's Commonwealth conference Trudeau was pressed to go further. The Canadian press then characterized him as "firmly resisting the urgings of black Commonwealth leaders to clamp down on the operations of Canadian companies in southern Africa" and quoted him as saying that "as far as the private sector is concerned we will not interfere in trade nor investment." Geoffrey Stevens of the *Globe and Mail* took him up on one aspect of this question in a refreshing manner:

> Mr. Trudeau is on shakier grounds when it comes of some of Canada's own double standards. Mr. Kaunda has urged the commonwealth to unite to end the "exploitation and plunder of Namibian wealth." At his press conference yesterday, Mr. Trudeau was asked whether he supported that appeal and whether, if he did, the Canadian government would take action against Falconbridge Nickel operations in Namibia (which is illegally controlled by South Africa). The Prime Minister replied that his federal government has caused crown corporations to withdraw from South Africa, but he said no action is contemplated on Falconbridge. "As far as the private sector is concerned, we are not interfering in existing trade and investment." This distinction between publicly owned and privately owned Canadian companies is not likely to impress any African.

Nor should it impress any of the rest of us.

To be sure, the times they are a-changing in Southern Africa. Vis-à-vis Portugal in Africa Canada was prepared to follow, in hand-me-down fashion, the preachments of Kissinger infamous support of the status quo in his notorious National security memorandum #39. But Kissinger's own game plan was soon in flux. Too late in Mozambique, too late in Angola, to guarantee neo-colonial regimes, Kissinger sought to move more quickly in Rhodesia and Namibia to ensure the transition to pliable black governments before the escalation of the struggles there opened up genuine revolutionary possibilities. As he put the point to the Senate Foreign Relations Committee in May 1976, "we have a stake... in not having the whole continent become radical and move in a direction which is incompatible with Western interests. That is the issue." Or as his then side-kick Anthony Crosland emphasized with reference to the Rhodesia-focussed Geneva conference spawned by Kissinger: "If the British government gave up hope, there would be no doubt who would eventually win on the battlefield. But if the issue were settled on the battlefield it would seriously lessen the chance of bringing about a *moderate African regime* in Rhodesia and would open the way for *more radical solutions* and external intervention on the part of others" (emphases added).

Not much has changed with the ascension of Carter to the Presidency. The premises for African action were spelt out clearly by US Ambassador to the UN Andrew Young when he was asked the following question last year: "Some foreign policy observers have said that the United States has two foreign policy options in southern Africa, one being neocolonialism and the other being out-right support of the minority government in South Africa. Could you comment on this idea and what kind of options we have in southern Africa?" His rather startling answer (presented without any apparent irony):

> I don't even see that many. I don't think that the United States has but one option, and that is neocolonialism.

But whatever this formulation might be thought to mean for Rhodesia/ Zimbabwe and Namibia in Young's mind, any such pronouncement is much more complex and difficult to pin down for South Africa. Surely, he seems to be saying, some kind of liberalization is possible there too: South Africa as Selma, Alabama. Unfortunately for Young this is not an historical comparison that stands up very well to scrutiny, yet it is necessary to note it here despite that fact. For it is within the framework of such a shifting American policy that one must locate Canada's initiatives of December last, initiatives that earned Canada's southern African policy a considerable amount of international attention. First and foremost, they stand as a signal that the West is nervous about the direction of development there, and about the escalation of confrontation that is in train. In this respect, Canada is not far off Andrew Young's wavelength. Secondarily, of course, such initiatives are also a signal to any in Black Africa who will listen that Canada remains on the offensive for freedom

On the offensive, perhaps, but once again largely rhetorically. When seriously scrutinized the policies announced in December reveal themselves to be far more symbol than substance. Thus the work of the now re-called Trade Commissioners in facilitating Canada-South Africa economic links will merely be carried on by locally hired personnel, while the withdrawal of Export Development Corporation facilities affected only one long dormant account and not the more crucial government to business account. No word yet on the trade preferences that bring South African sugar to Canada on a protected basis, no word on the tax-relief afforded Falconbridge on its illegal Namibia operations. There is every indication that Industry, Trade and Commerce will continue to facilitate trade tours of businessmen to South Africa and the like, even if we can expect rather fewer of the fulsome articles that have been periodically published in Commerce Canada extolling the virtues of the South African investment climate. No indication, certainly, of any positive action to stem Canadian corporate activity in South Africa, no indication of any concern as to the propriety of Canadian banks loans to the South African government. As Trudeau indicated in London, the private sector remains sacrosanct. Moreover, as External Affairs Department spokesmen have made perfectly clear (e.g., Mr. Harry Carter speaking recently in Toronto) this kind of token gesture is all that can be expected by way of government action for the foreseeable future.

What, then, of the links of Canada's private sector to the south African economy, links about which the Canadian government waxes so indifferent and claims such impotence. Though any number of corporations might be focused upon, the above-mentioned involvement of Canadian banks in direct loans to the South African government is a particularly apt target for a number of reasons.

The large bank loans—now running to a total of 2-3 billion dollars—made available to South Africa by various consortia in recent years have been of great significance in strengthening the latter's economy (and the entire repressive apparatus that it underwrites) at a very crucial time. Certainly it would be difficult to overestimate the importance of the extensive credit made available by the international financial community in the "dark days" after Sharpeville. If the economy (and the state) is in somewhat parallel straits at the present time—in fact, if anything, the "crisis" is probably more structural now than in the early 60s and therefore more serious—then success in forestalling the activities of the banks involved on these loans must represent an especially weighty blow against apartheid. All the more so when one considers that such loans are directed to such important ends as meeting shortfalls on balance of payments and financing the state's Iron and Steel Corporation—of obvious significance to South Africa's armaments industry—and the Electricity Supply Commission—overseer of South Africa's growing nuclear capacity, among other things.

The negative implications of such loans for the bulk of the population in South Africa is unequivocal. Though there are strong and, I think, even overwhelming arguments against any form of western economic involvement in Africa—after all, we have Vorster's assurance that "each trade agreement, each back loan, each new investment is another brick in the wall of our continued existence"—the direct transfer of monies to strengthen the oppressive South African state yields even fewer ambiguities than all other economic links. As the Canadian Task Force on the Churches and Corporate Responsibility has put the point: "To say that some South African Government departments or agencies can operate to the benefit of black South Africans is to fly in the face of history. Apartheid is the official policy of the South African government and of all its departments and agencies."

The banks are particularly central institutions in our own domestic economy, of course. Indeed, if there is an indigenous core to our capitalist class the work of Naylor, Clement and others would suggest that it lies in the financial sector. Thus in pinpointing the role of the banks and in combatting them, Canadians who seek to aid in the liberation of southern Africa may well find themselves contributing to their own liberation.

For the banks, while powerful, are also vulnerable. Unlike corporations such as Falconbridge that have little reason to solicit public support, Canadian banks are very much concerned with matters of "corporate image" and with institutional advertising. Like Gulf Oil Canada Ltd., a target of support groups several years ago because of its Angola entanglements, the banks may feel the cool wind of protest more quickly than some other corporations. Certainly the experience in Holland, where two of the largest Dutch banks agreed to suspend all loans to South Africa after an intense protest campaign there, suggests the potential for the success of popular resistance to such activity does exist.

There are already many groups and individuals across Canada who are active in the bank campaign and there is promise that even more popular energies—directed against the banks and against the government—can be released by such a campaign. Here we run ahead of our story, but it is a significant point to which we will return.

To undertake the kind of detailed analysis of the current vulnerability of the South African economy necessary to fully situate the importance of foreign loans would require a paper in itself. Suffice to note here that a fundamental factor is deep contradictions that run right through the heart of the South African economy. Though profits are premised on cheap labour, the very cheapness of the labour and the attendant structure of maldistribution domestically makes for a market constraint; moreover, adventures abroad, like that in Angola, and the breakdown of détente have made the expansion of markets into Black Africa a slower process than had been hoped by South African leaders. Yet, simultaneously, so sophisticated has South African secondary industrialization become that the import bill for machinery and advanced technology has steadily increased.

To these factors must be added the unsettling fluctuations of the gold price, plus the due bills for those vast infrastructural projects that the South African government undertook at a time when that price was at its zenith. In addition, the inflow of capital on private account, while by no means stopped, is a more uncertain element in the wake of Soweto. And then there is the vast and tremendously expensive expansion of the military machine. As the *Christian Science Monitor* observed of one of the most recent loans by an international consortium: it comes "... at a time when South Africa is suffering from a decline in its financial fortunes ... Racial unrest has created uncertainty about South Africa's future stability and has contributed to a slowdown in foreign investment."

What are the facts of Canadian bank involvement in the vast network of international banking consortia that were established in the 1970s to channel money to South Africa? Evidence of both the loans themselves and of the role of Canadian banks first surfaced when documents (the so-called "Frankfurt documents") were first leaked (in 1973) from within the U.S.-based multinational firm, the European-American Banking Corporation. The materials revealed, in the words of a brief from the Corporate Information Center in the United States, that "a group of forty banks from the United States, Europe and Canada have been jointly involved in direct loans totaling over $210 million to the South African government and its agencies since late 1970." Three of Canada's five major chartered banks—the Canadian Imperial Bank of Commerce, the Toronto-Dominion Bank, and the Bank of Montreal—were found to be involved, in at least one case (a loan to ISCOR) putting up over 50% of the amount involved between them. (A fourth Canadian bank—the Royal Bank of Canada—was found to be implicated in later loans.)

This much we know as hard fact—but this was still early days in the loans to South Africa game. The volume of money involved has increased enormously and so, one must assume, has the stake of Canadian banks. Not that it is easy to find out the further facts of the matter. The four banks have been most cagey indeed about making information available, pleading "client confidentiality" and "established business practices" when fending off inquiries from church delegations and other interested parties. Some information does filter through. When, in March 1976, a consortium loan to ESCOM was announced by Citibank officials the latter mentioned Canadian bank involvement. And South African sources tied Canadian banks into other 1976 loans of up to $338 million, with possible additional involvements in a major balance of payments loan that same year. Yet only the Bank of Montreal has been (even minimally) candid, answering a 1977 Annual General Meeting question about transfers with the comment: "Yes, we still have outstanding loans with that client."

Others have been more evasive in their responses to the probings by the Task Force on the Churches and Corporate Responsibility (see that group's excellent pamphlet *Banking on Apartheid* from which the following quotes are drawn):

> Toronto Dominion Bank: "The Bank's policy has remained the same... the limited request of the churches not to grant bank loans to the South African government is an oversimplification of the issue...there would not be much business in South Africa in that case."[!]
>
> Canadian Imperial Bank of Commerce: "We examine all applications, and from time to time we make loans but we will not disclose them."
>
> Royal Bank: "We are convinced our fundamental policy is sound, ethical and responsible, and it has not changed since last year...We anticipate and accept responsibility for the direct and indirect economic and social consequences of our economic decisions."

Certainly none will deny the significance of such loans. And all will go to elaborate lengths to defend these "hypothetical" loans as liberalizing or non-political or as carefully chosen to be only of benefit to all the people of South Africa!

The case against the banks is clear, then, although inevitably neither they nor the Canadian government are prepared to take that case very seriously. Fortunately, however, the matter does not end there. Other Canadians are not so sanguine about this issue and are much more responsive to the virtually unanimous call to end such loans (and other western economic involvements) by all South Africans who have sought seriously the overthrow of the apartheid system there—liberation movements like the African National Congress (ANC), political organizations like the South African Student Organization (SASO) and the Black People's Convention (BPC) and liberal critics that have been active in recent years like the Christian Institute of South Africa. And there is also a constituency in Canada who will rally against Canada's destructive links to South Africa, and against the Canadian government if need be, one that found expression in the Black Paper of 1971 and in the People's Forum on Southern Africa held at the time of the Ottawa Commonwealth Conference of 1973. Such a constituency is now beginning to find renewed expression in the campaign against the bank loans.

The initial impetus for this campaign came from the churches. Fortified by the undertakings of American and European churches on the issue and building on the exemplary research work of Renate Pratt and others, the aforementioned Task Force on the Churches and

Corporate Responsibility—an ecumenical body including representatives from the Anglican, Catholic, Lutheran, Presbyterian and United Churches—launched its effort several years ago, working to educate and rally its own constituency while also carrying on a dialogue, through private meetings and interventions at AGMs, with bank officials. Their premise: "Bank loans to the government of South Africa and its subsidiary agencies are a vote in cash for apartheid." This theme has been picked up by activists in other spheres, for example at several universities, notably at the University of Toronto; moreover, the Ontario Federation of Students, representing 140,000 college and university students, has condemned the banks' policies and has removed its funds from the banks concerned. Other provincial student federations are following suit, as is the National Union of Students, the organization that represents all post-secondary students in Canada.

Non-governmental organizations throughout Canada, such as OXFAM and CUSO, are demanding that Canadian banks cease their loans and are conducting campaigns to focus public pressure, while a number of support groups are beginning to launch direct action campaigns around the issue—keying to demonstrations and the like around such dates as March 21 (Sharpeville) and June 16 (Soweto). Some twenty support group from across the country held a meeting, jointly sponsored by CUSO and TCLSAC, in December 1977, to co-ordinate their activities and to plan future strategies. And there are growing indications that trade unions will also be more aggressively involved in such a campaign, building on the precedent of the speech by Joe Morris (president of the Canadian Labour Congress) to the United Nations' Special Committee on Apartheid when he affirmed that "... if we condemn apartheid, we must also condemn those investing in it: those directly or indirectly helping to maintain this rabid system."

Obviously these actions are not at the core of our governmental life, nor are those who press them forward likely soon to become part of a movement that can realistically hope to seriously challenge the parameters of imperial dictate, capitalist rationality and bourgeois dominance that shape, in the last analysis, our South African policy. But it would be a mistake to ignore them altogether. Indeed, it would be unfortunate if our overall concern with "policy options" were to direct itself only to the possible actions of governments. Unfortunate not only because, with reference to Canada, this is a particularly grey and unpromising area, but also because concerned elements of the citizenry have "policy options" beyond what our state is constrained to do. By resisting the government and the corporations, such elements can certainly give resonance to the actions of the peoples of southern Africa who are fighting for their freedom—a sense of solidarity that is important to the latter as Frelimo's aforementioned invitation to TCLPAC/TCLSAC, rather than the Canadian government, to attend and to celebrate its independence in 1975 gave eloquent testimony.

Furthermore, by keeping alive the question of southern Africa, by exposing government duplicity and corporate opportunism, by forcing as many dealings as possible into the light of day, these concerned actors, if unlikely to fulfill their fondest hopes, can at least make a contribution to restraining the powerful from doing the worst they might otherwise do. They can also contribute, through such actions, to the enlightenment of more and more of their fellow citizens regarding the realities of the southern African situation. This is of considerable importance, especially when one realizes that, whatever the short term accomplishments of such activists, they must probably think of themselves primarily as preparing for the (inevitable) day when the South African situation escalates even further. Then it will probably be necessary to resist particularly strenuously the logic of a Canadian political economy that would otherwise draw Canada ever further onto the wrong side of that struggle. It seems to me important that all concerned Canadians must take seriously their own individual responsibilities—their own "policy options"—in light of such a possible scenario.

BUT THOUGH WE AT TCLSAC were increasingly working on South Africa, a country still under the bondage of apartheid, our group never lost interest in Mozambique. Indeed, together with my family, I was to spend the year, 1980-81, teaching in Maputo in the Frelimo Party School and at the Universidade de Eduardo Mondlane, in the Faculty of Marxism-Leninism ("Try putting that on your CV," I joked to friends on my return to Toronto). It was an instructive experience, one I wrote of in the introductory chapters of a book of essays (*A Difficult Road: The Transition to Socialism in Mozambique*) that I edited, essays written by various expatriate comrades who were also working in Mozambique and in diverse sectors.[71] As for my own "sector," it was "ideological work." Particularly evident, as I had feared in advance of going to teach there, was "the disturbing gap between the 'practical Marxism' that I had seen to characterize Frelimo's own developing ideology and the more theoretically elaborated [sic] framework taken over (somewhat uncritically) from Eastern European textbooks and teachers [some now to be my own colleagues] in the post-independence years." The uneasiness of this mix was soon clear to me from the pedagogical programmes themselves, from their formidable degree of abstraction, and from the mechanical and lifeless (in fact, undialectical) manner in which they sought to explain social interconnections.

My job, however, was to help develop syllabi and teaching programmes and materials that would help overcome such problems, problems grasped clearly by Frelimo leaders who publicly bemoaned a "revolutionary verbalism" and abstract formulas that did not "clarify ... the situation which presently exists in our country." I sought to lecture in the spirit of such leaders and against any such revolutionary verbalism; I also had the opportunity, while in Maputo, to capture something of what I felt this might mean in a book, written in Portuguese with the help of two Mozambican colleagues and friends, Jose Paulo Borges Coelho and Zegui Negrao, and published at the University: *O Marxismo-Leninismo no Contexto Moçambicano*. Of course, I'm not certain just what ground we managed to win for the consolidation of progressive revolutionary theory and a more serviceable Marxism in Mozambique through such efforts. In any case, the tide of progressive possibility had begun to run against the left nationally, regionally and globally. For the country itself was soon under an ever more intensified siege by RENAMO's domestic, though Rhodesian-spawned and South African-backed, counter-revolutionaries, by apartheid South Africa's even wider regional offensive and by Reagan's United States, the latter now intent on the "roll-back" of revolutionary states around the world.

A sobering experience, then, but sobering on other fronts as well. I have lost a number of friends to the "thirty years war for southern African liberation" over the course of it and I've written about the subject elsewhere, most overtly in my appreciation of Eduardo Mondlane, Frelimo's first president, on the occasion of the thirtieth anniversary of his assassination by the Portuguese state, an event that had originally taken place in the 1960s while I was living in Dar, the site of the murder. And also in my memorial to Samora Machel, successor to Mondlane as Frelimo president and first president of an independent Mozambique, killed, in all probability, through the manipulation of radar signals by the South African state, in an air-crash while returning from Zambia (along with, among several others, one of his trusted advisors and my very good friend, Aquino da Bragança). The piece recalling Eduardo is included in the following chapter while the second has been republished as an appendix to my recent volume, *Empire and Decolonization*, (to which I refer the interested reader).

The death of a friend also haunted my Maputo stay, one that occurred during the very last days of my period working there: the assassination of the exemplary South African exile Ruth First, by now a colleague of mine at Mozambique's university. On this occasion there could be little doubt—and subsequent events would prove it definitively—that this was a killing organized, quite ruthlessly, by the South African state (the very apartheid state that would soon have a hand in the death of Machel). Thus, years later and in the wake of the liberation of South Africa, that country's "Truth and Liberation Commission" opened the books on First's assassination, a process that soon found Craig Williamson, a master agent of the apartheid police, "confessing" to having organized the bomb that took Ruth's life. This was something he brazenly testified, in the presence of two of Ruth's daughters, that he had done in line with his "official duties." As a result, for better or worse, he was subject to amnesty with respect to this action! (A chilling account of an earlier, less formal meeting with Williamson is to be found in a book by Gillian Slovo, one of Ruth's daughters, and entitled *Every Secret Thing* [London: Little-Brown, 1997].) Moreover, in another atrocity in Maputo—not unlike that which befell Ruth—a second friend of mine, also South African exile, Albie Sachs, lost his arm in a South Africa-spawned car-bomb rigged to kill him outside his block of flats. I reflected on Ruth's death in the piece written close to the time for *This Magazine* (17, 5, December, 1983), originally entitled "Laying Ghosts to Rest: Ruth First and South Africa's War":

THE REALITY OF SIEGE WAS THE MOST STRIKING THING about Mozambique when I visited there earlier this year for the Fourth Congress of the Front for the Liberation of Mozambique (Frelimo). If anything the sense of siege had intensified since a year earlier when I lived and worked there. Mozambique is a major target of South Africa's aggressive war of destabilization against its black-majority neighbours. The means? Direct intervention, but also extensive support for the self-styled Movement of National Resistance, a band of local renegades (complemented by ex-Portuguese policemen mercenaries and South African "advisors"); its tactics are intimidation of the rural population and destruction of vital socioeconomic infrastructure.

I had returned to Mozambique for Frelimo's Fourth Congress and the party did not allow such grim realities to undermine its activities. There was a high level of discussion and very frank self-criticism by party members both at top leadership level and from the grassroots [see below]. There was a promise of fresh and innovative economic and political strategies designed to overcome weaknesses evident in recent years. As in Nicaragua, however, war clouds threatened to obscure that promise. It was useful to be reminded first hand of that fact. Note, here, however, that my return to Mozambique also had a further personal meaning for me since it meant laying to rest a private ghost as well—albeit one closely linked to the fact of South Africa's war.

Ruth First

For on August 17, 1982, on the very eve of my departure from Maputo after the year of working there referred to above, my friend and colleague Ruth First was assassinated by a letter bomb received in her office, merely moments before she was to have hosted a farewell reception to mark my departure from the country that weekend after a period working there. A few months later, back in Canada, I received an invitation from the organizers of the American African Studies' Association to present a eulogy to Ruth at the association's annual meeting. A difficult task but an appropriate occasion. The setting: Washington's Capitol Hilton Hotel, just down the road from Reagan's White House and in a vast ballroom which only minutes before had seen Chester Crocker, the administration's senior Africa-hand, flabbily rationalizing the United States' kid-gloves treatment of apartheid South Africa to another panel session of the same ASA meeting. Now I had the rostrum to say something of the other side of that struggle. And Oliver Tambo, president of the African National Congress, the pre-eminent force for positive change in that country, would follow me, to speak briefly of Ruth First, but then, eloquently, of the present state of his movement's struggle against white-minority rule and racial capitalism. Let me repeat here what I said then:

"I applaud, as we all do, the initiative taken by this conference's organizers in arranging a memorial meeting to honour Ruth First and I thank them for the invitation to speak here. I feel deeply honoured as well, conscious of the fact that there are many others in this room whose lives were deeply touched by Ruth and who might equally well be speaking from this platform. I only hope that my few words can capture some small part of what Ruth First meant to so many of us.

"Fortunately we are honoured in also having with us here one of Ruth's closest friends and comrades, Oliver Tambo, president of the African National Congress of South Africa, one who is perhaps better qualified than anyone to speak of her service to the South African revolution, for which service, in the end, the South African government took her life. His very presence reminds us of Ruth First's role in the front ranks of that revolutionary struggle since the 1940s: as an editor (with such important publications, ultimately banned, as *The Guardian* and *Fighting Talk*), a writer, a political organizer, a mobilizer of the freedom struggle both within and without South Africa. As I'm certain that Comrade Tambo will have something more to say on this score, I can proceed to remind you of a second important dimension of her work.

"Again, however, it scarcely seems necessary to remind an audience of students of Africa of her intellectual contribution not only to the Southern African revolution but also to raising the intellectual and moral level of our own discourse. Consider, among many other writings, her early exposé of South Africa's role in Namibia (*South-West Africa*, 1963), her harrowing personal account of her own period of solitary confinement in a South African jail (*117 Days*, 1965), her revelations, with her co-authors, as to *The South African Connection* (1972) with western capitalism, her landmark study of militarism in independent Africa (*The Barrel of a Gun*, 1970), her recent blending of socialist and feminist perspectives in the biography of Olive Schreiner which she co-authored (*Olive Schreiner*, 1980).

"There is a third aspect of her career, its most recent phase, which may bear special emphasis, however; it is, in any case, the one that I can speak about most confidently at first hand. I refer to her role at the University of Eduardo Mondlane in Mozambique where, friends for some years previously, we became colleagues. Indeed, in the end, I was two minutes late for a farewell party which she had arranged in my honour, and in those two minutes, in her office in the Centre of African Studies, she died, opening a parcel-bomb, at South Africa's hand.

"I would therefore like to underscore the importance of Ruth's Maputo years, and their broader significance. For in the past half-decade or so her involvement in the struggle to construct socialism in Mozambique paralleled and equaled her involvement in the continuing struggle for South African freedom—though, of course, she would have made no such distinction between the two struggles.

"In this regard it bears emphasizing that Ruth First was a brilliant social scientist—albeit a revolutionary social scientist (and again she would have made no real distinction between the two, between her roles as revolutionary and as social scientist). For, as a social scientist, she knew that there was no substitute for clear thinking and hard work—for a genuine science. She knew that solidly grounded revolutionary endeavour required and demanded no less.

"There can be no doubt that the Centre of African Studies at the University of Eduardo Mondlane exemplified, in a powerful way, this kind of commitment. Indeed it was and is an institution whose vital contribution—in terms of research and teaching linked to the construction of Mozambican socialism—represented to a considerable degree a victory for her strength of will, a victory for her intellectual drive and force in her role as research director. Moreover, the UNESCO Conference on Problems and Priorities in Social Science Training in Southern Africa which she had organized in the week before she died was specifically dedicated to a discussion of the advancement of a revolutionary social science throughout the Southern Africa region; in fact, its occurrence may have been one of the things that made her, at the specific moment at which she died, so tempting a target for the South Africans.

"For I think it is important to realize that this attack on Ruth's person was not just an attack upon herself, or even upon the African National Congress—though it was, of course, both of these things. It was also an attack upon Mozambique, an attack upon the Centre of African Studies and against the scientific work which it exemplified, an attack upon the ability of Mozambique successfully to build socialism. It was yet another aspect of South Africa's brutal war of destabilization in the region. When we hear the bland protestations which we heard last night and again this morning from State Department representatives regarding

U.S. commitment to non-violence in Southern Africa, we should think of Ruth First and remind ourselves that the ideology of "constructive engagement" and the reality of financial support (like the recent IMF loan) emanating from the U.S. are merely fuelling the military machine which killed her.

"May I be permitted to conclude on a more personal note. I doubt that there is anyone who knew Ruth First well who didn't have difficult moments with her. She was tough, demanding, even occasionally domineering. She was forged in a hard school, a revolutionary socialist and a woman fighting consistently and unflaggingly against racism, chauvinism and capitalist exploitation in the teeth of one of the most brutal regimes the world has ever seen and, fortunately for us all, she was ready to fight back for what she believed in.

"Besides, even when one looked back at moments of inter-personal tension one had had with her it was also with the realization that such tensions were not arbitrary ones, that almost invariably something important, intellectually and politically, was at stake. The seriousness of her engagement, the intensity of her concern, could never be doubted. Nor, if you were struggling to be as serious yourself, could such moments cast any doubt upon her personal concern, her compassion, her continuing solidarity in the next round of whatever struggle, public or personal, was in train.

"Now almost two months have passed since that August day in Maputo and, strangely, I still hear, from time to time, her voice echoing quite clearly and tangibly in my ears, snatches of earlier conversations and the like. I know this reflects the strength and continuing impact of her vibrant and powerful personality.

"Perhaps others here will have experienced this as well and, of course, for each of us who hears it this will be a private voice. Yet, knowing Ruth, we need not doubt that it is also a political voice, a voice exhorting all of us, here and elsewhere, as "Africanists," as scientists, as activists, to continue the struggle for which she gave her life."

Laying to rest that ghost on my recent visit to Mozambique was, in fact, a prosaic enough moment. I had to leave Maputo only days after the assassination and before the funeral. Now I was walking down the hall to Ruth's office where I sat so often in the past but had last seen only from the road as a gaping hole in the outer wall of the building. Not surprisingly, I found it humming with activity, serving at the office of the centre's secretariat. How to avoid cliché: life goes on, the struggle continues. I thought of the three people whom I had known well in both political and personal contexts who had fallen to the assassin: Ruth; Eduardo Mondlane, Frelimo's first president (killed in 1969 in Dar es Salaam where I was living at the time by a book bomb sent by the Portuguese); Walter Rodney the Guyanese historian and activist who had been my next-door neighbour for many years in Tanzania (*This Magazine*, Vol. 14 No. 5). Was I, was the movement, "stronger at the broken places" in the wake of such horrors? Probably not. But, of course, there is no real alternative but to act as if we are, to get on with it. We owe such comrades at least that much.

Home Thoughts

Perhaps a Canadian footnote to Ruth First's death is worth mentioning. The evening after the assassination, still in the shock, tired from a previous night spent assisting the police investigation, I was summoned by a neighbour to the telephone. My mother, perhaps, having heard the news? Instead it was the CBC's "As It Happens." Not certain how much I had myself under control but reluctant to miss an opportunity to speak to Canadians on Ruth's behalf, I agreed to be interviewed.

Charlotte Gobeil on the line seemed to accept my initial premise that it was, undoubtedly, South Africa, who was responsible for the act. Then the kicker. Weren't she and her husband (Joe Slovo, a prominent ANC activist) throwing bombs at the South Africans? Wasn't this just a case of tit for tat, a case, Gobeil implied, of First getting back a little bit of her own medicine? A wave of nausea swept over me. I had forgotten what a sea of bullshit one often had to wade through in the Canadian media in order to make a meaningful point. Too often an interview on an issue of substance means fending off the interviewer long enough to establish a few essential alternative premises on the basis of which, before the interview is over, one might hope to make a meaningful point or two. A year in southern Africa—never having to argue, for example, the obvious premise that apartheid, like Nazism before it, must be overthrown—had dulled my sparring skills.

Leave aside the fact that Ruth First had nothing whatsoever to do with the military side of ANC activity. Leave aside, too, the fact that the ANC, as it has improved its military capacity in recent years, has focused on military targets and has not indulged in the kind of terrorist activity directed at individuals that the South African government has unleashed in the region in recent years. No, the most depressing aspect in all this was the kind of moral blindness that could equate the violent defence of South Africa's racist and exploitative status quo by the apartheid state with the efforts of the oppressed to overthrow that oppressive system. Perhaps the ignoring of South Africa's war by our media has a silver lining! When our media does focus on such matters its racist and reactionary preoccupations often make its "contribution" to enlightenment worse than no news at all.

And then, back in Canada from the recent Frelimo Congress (see below), I hear "As It Happens" strike again. The ANC has, dramatically, exploded a bomb at the Pretoria headquarters of the South African Air Force, and South Africa "retaliates" with an air raid into Mozambique which kills a number of Mozambican civilians. Bill Cameron has Pik Botha, the South African foreign minister, on the line. Botha presents the raid as being of exemplary value, seeking to teach the Mozambicans to keep a tighter rein on the ANC.

Cameron passively allows Botha his platform. Nothing is said of the fact that the ANC has no military bases in Mozambique and self-evidently does not wait upon Mozambique for its marching orders. In any case, Cameron might have added, the main springboard for ANC action is its own political network inside South Africa: it is the repressive nature of South Africa's domestic situation which dictates the terms of black people's revolutionary response there. Indeed, building on his false premises, Botha is even allowed the opportunity to twit Mozambique for violating the "civilized norms" of cross-border relations between states! Of course at this point our man Cameron springs in with a reference to Ruth First's assassination and South Africa's relationship of puppet-master to the MNR inside Mozambique, doesn't he? Not a chance.

To be fair, some of the coverage by the Canadian media of these recent events was a little better than this (though even at its best tending to be maddeningly "even-handed"). Better, however, than the response, reported from Canadian government officials who continued to mumble, even at this late date, about the virtues of "non-violence" as if there were some practical content to such a pious stance. Unfortunately for such ostriches, there is no avoiding the fact that in Southern Africa it is now, more clearly than ever, a question of which side you are on.

A newspaper report this week finds Alan Boesak, a South African "Coloured" theologian, putting the essential point quite clearly—in a speech to the World Council of Churches meeting in Vancouver. "The churches always had theories of just war. They always believed that a moment would arise when oppressed people reach a point where they have no alternative...These churches should not turn pacifist when it's black people who find themselves in that situation...These churches are being dishonest and hypocritical. When oppressed people pick up weapons, churches must choose for the oppressed people." And not just churches.

But, as noted, I was also in Mozambique in 1985, at Frelimo's invitation, to celebrate the tenth anniversary of the country's independence. I wrote of this in *Southern Africa Report* (1, #1 and 1, #2) and began my account by evoking the original independence celebration in 1975 (recounted in chapter 2, above) and also linking it to an even earlier trip I had made to the liberated areas in 1962 (the account of which is also to be found in chapter 2). In Tete in 1962 I had "experienced the heady sense of a people taking control of its own destiny, a people making its own history." In 1975, I had had "that same sense, in trumps." Now, in 1985, I felt forced to ask myself: could ten years really have passed since that first independence day? In some ways it seemed like only yesterday. Yet in other ways it had been a long ten years:

Certainly Mozambican leaders I talked to in 1975 had had no illusions about the difficulties that lay ahead, the challenges which they anticipated would far outstrip anything they had confronted during the armed struggle. They had seized the country from the most backward of all colonialisms; moreover, they could see signs that even that legacy of extreme underdevelopment was to be further exacerbated by the panicky and vindictive flight of the Portuguese, those who had so exclusively harboured to themselves the few skills and resources which colonial society had to offer to the post-colonial development effort. Such leaders knew, too, that the regional environment in which they must seek to advance their revolutionary project would be a hostile one, with the white-minority regimes of both Rhodesia and South Africa posing long-term threats.

These facts did penetrate the euphoria of the first days in 1975—although then, in truth, only tangentially. We were too busy celebrating. Besides, it was tempting to think that everything was possible after so famous a victory. From the vantage-point of 1985, however, it is evident that such hard facts have become less notional, more real, with each passing year. The cruelty of the political and economic vise in which Mozambique now finds itself means that there is far less room for euphoria this independence day.

I have kept in close touch with the Mozambique revolution during the ten years since that first, glorious celebration, visiting on numerous occasions (including, once again as an invited guest, at the time of the Fourth Congress) and even working there, teaching at the Frelimo Party School in 1981-82. I have had a privileged opportunity to witness at close hand both the accomplishments and the failures, the strengths and the weaknesses, of the first decade of independence. It is on the basis of this experience that I can also affirm—a point made in the lead article of another recent issue of *Southern Africa Report*—the crucial importance, the devastating impact, of the war of destabilization which continues to be waged against Mozambique and the absolute primacy that this factor should have in our minds as we mark the tenth anniversary.

Nonetheless, recent visits had dramatized for me the extreme difficulties of the present moment in Mozambique. As noted, the war continues, the list of Mozambique's external enemies is a daunting one, the economy refuses any very spectacular upturn. At the same time, I did see positive signs. Particularly in the centre of the country, where the war has been waged the longest, Frelimo has begun to succeed in its attempt to find a more effective military strategy. The key lies in finding a contemporary equivalent of that rooting of the war effort in the exertions of the local populations themselves that were so important to Frelimo's success in the days of armed struggle against the Portuguese.

Thus, in the central provinces, the grouping of such populations in defensible villages and their organization into effective militias seems to be advancing. Even more innovative has been the development of military units intermediate between local militias and the army per se, units made up of local people but given a higher degree of military training than mere militia members; returned to their localities where they will have a particularly clear familial and economic stake in the war effort, these citizen soldiers continue to operate under army discipline, available for offensive action against the armed bandits. Important steps, needless to say, despite the hard reality that every kind of military effort continues to be constrained by the severe economic limits within which the Frelimo government is operating.

There was also a sophistication in the analyses made by Mozambican political leaders regarding their attempts to manoeuvre for breathing-space on the international plane which might surprise many of the country's left critics. Certainly the leaders I talked with (including President Machel) presented a pretty full catalogue of the probable forces ranged against them, while also weighing quite coolly the odds for and against their complicated strategy, mentioned in our lead article, of trying to play off neo-colonizers against militarists in the imperial camp. Frank, too, was the appraisal of the limited number of cards Mozambique has to play in this game, and of the possible risks to long-term socialist goals of tactical concessions made to neo-colonialism. As one Minister and friend put the point to me, there does exist the danger of Frelimo waking up one day and discovering that *"nos nao somos nos"* (we are no longer ourselves)!

Sobriety, too, characterized the economic calculations of many of the country's economic planners, calculations now made within the framework of a new overall policy guideline, that of the *Economia da Guerra* (War Economy). Of course, this guideline is very far removed, because of the imperatives of war, from the high hopes for a renovated economic strategy that marked Frelimo's Fourth Congress in 1983. Moreover, on this front too, the apparent imperatives of pragmatism and survival economics seem sometimes to threaten a blurring of the socialist vision. Nonetheless, the current crisis has also served to bring Mozambican planning ever more firmly down to earth, to a confrontation with the real possibilities of production at the district and provincial levels under the very hard conditions, economic and logistical, which exist. While obviously focussed upon the immediate demands of underwriting the war effort economically, such a trend may also have the long term effect of helping to make planning for economic development a far less abstract and far more effective exercise in Mozambique than it has sometimes been in the past.

These things having been said, you will find no easy optimism here. Merely a sense that it is impossible to "factor out" from the analysis of the present conjuncture a consideration of the historical process which has produced FRELIMO and grounded the movement in a popular revolution. The leadership cadre who launched that revolutionary process is still in place, frayed at the edges certainly, older (although, one suspects, wiser), girded [or so it seemed] for one further attempt to recast the foundations of its revolution. And the link—replete with tensions and contradictions but forged in struggle—which has joined Frelimo to the popular classes in Mozambique also remains in place, stretched, perhaps, to the breaking point but in place.

Such assertions are not premissed on mere faith; it is the analysis of the long arc of Mozambican development that underpins them. Nor can there be any question of underestimating the odds against the successful attainment of Frelimo's goals. Nonetheless, in Mozambique—the phrase has worn thin through repetition, but is still true—a luta continua, the struggle continues.

And there was, of course, the celebration of the tenth anniversary itself. It was, indeed, a "boa festa."

Thus, on the evening of the 24th, an impressive gala, staged by Mozambique's national dance troupe. In the morning hours of the 25th itself President Samora Machel is joined by five other African presidents (from Tanzania, Zambia, Cape Verde, Angola and Botswana) and one Prime Minister (Robert Mugabe of Zimbabwe) who are guests for the celebrations in laying wreaths at the Heroes' Monument in Maputo. Then a mammoth, impressively organized, march past of thousands of Mozambicans, from schools, from youth and women's organizations, from various workplaces. That afternoon, a reception at the Polana Hotel, the President speaking briefly, members of the Politburo leading the dancing as a giant birthday cake is cut and distributed. Later in the week: the premiere of Mozambique's first feature-length film, *The Time of the Leopards*, a film which evokes the days of armed struggle against the Portuguese, and another premiere, the production of a play by the noted Angolan writer, Pepetela, by the country's leading theatre group.

Yet, inevitably, there is also a more sombre counterpoint to the week's events. It serves to remind us, even in the full flush of celebration, of just how harsh are the realities of the current moment in Mozambique. Thus independence day in Manhiga district, less than seventy kilometres from the capital, finds the "armed bandits" of the MNR—South Africa's principal contribution to Mozambique's first ten years of independence—attacking a bus and clubbing 27 people to death. A few days later, in much the same locale, a convoy is hit, five busses come under heavy fire, thirty-nine killed, over one hundred wounded. More prosaically, though no less importantly: even as we eat our fill at the Polana we know that, given the depths of the country's economic crisis, few others in Maputo will have enough to eat this week. Beyond survival—although under the circumstances in which Mozambique finds itself this latter is no small accomplishment—there seemed little enough, in all conscience, to celebrate. A decade which had begun with so much hope had become, by its end, a long and very difficult one.

> Did you see it?
> It passed
> near enough
> to touch
> a whisper of the future.
> Red sky in the morning,
> oppressor's warning.
> A dream,
> so beautiful.
> You know it when you touch it
> here and there
> in the cracks of a society
> scorched by the past,
> charred in the present
> by a thousand pyromaniacs.
> Is it gone
> with the sun?
> No, but it's a cold night
> and we must build a fire of our own:
> to drive away the wild animals,
> to warm the people.

In fact the efforts, evoked in my poem "To build a fire of our own," to reignite the Mozambican revolution do continue; such efforts are being mounted by Frelimo on both the international and the domestic fronts. As I noted above, Frelimo leaders see the domestic front as being primary to seeking to regroup economically, politically and militarily. And with some signs of the beginnings of success [albeit, as time would reveal, not quite enough success]. Thus the most recent reports from Mozambique (September) bring news of a particularly dramatic victory in the field, the smashing, with help from Zimbabwean forces, of the substantial central base of the MNR, known as "Casa Banana," in the Gorongosa Mountains of Sofala Province.

But the diplomatic initiatives are also continuing in an attempt, by that route too, to lift some of the weight of South African aggression from Mozambique's shoulders. Our *Southern Africa Report* (SAR) spoke of Frelimo's efforts to exploit a possible division "both in South Africa and in the international capitalist world... between one group of policy-makers who think they can now ensnare a severely weakened

Frelimo in the toils of neocolonialism and another group who prefer to pursue the overthrow of the present government by force." If able to use judicious concession to strengthen the case of the former group, Mozambique might perhaps hope to survive in order to continue the fight for its progressive development strategy—albeit on a terrain only slightly more promising than that of imperialist aggression: that of neocolonial penetration.

Dramatic evidence of the existence of just such a split in the imperial camp surfaced soon after my previous SAR article appeared. Thus, even as right-wing Senator Jesse Helms worked in the Senate to severely qualify proposed American aid to "Marxist" Mozambique, no less a figure than Melvin Laird, a former U.S. Secretary of Defense, penned an op-ed piece in the *Washington Post* (June 17, 1985) calling for a much more active American "opening to Mozambique", a "balanced relationship that includes diplomatic contacts, private investment, trade, economic and humanitarian assistance and a modest military training and assistance program". As Laird elaborated the point:

> I recognize there are those who argue that the United States should have nothing to do with a self-styled Marxist state. I disagree. The only way we can advance U.S. strategic goals in the Third World is if we compete in relevant ways—on the ground, through our programs, our presence, our diplomacy. The United States should be ready to respond constructively to openings that advance our interests whenever they occur.

Just where the Reagan administration actually stands with respect to this policy divide over imperial strategy towards Mozambique is less clear. But when President Machel met with Ronald Reagan in Washington in late September it was the delicate game of attempting to tilt the American government in the direction of Laird's "liberal-imperialist" option that he came to play. He did bring with him strong additional evidence (some of it captured at Casa Banana) of South Africa's continuing complicity with the MNR—despite the signing of the Nkomati Accord in March 1984, and Mozambique's subsequent compliance with the Accord's main terms. (Indeed such evidence soon forced South African Foreign Minister Pik Botha to admit publicly that his government had built an air-strip for the MNR and had made supply drops from planes and had taken MNR officials in and out of Mozambique by submarine, though Botha termed these merely "technical violations of the Accord"!) But just what kind of response Machel could expect to have from the U.S. government—which many suspect, in any case, of having its own links with the MNR—is just one of the many questions left unanswered as Mozambique's second independence decade begins.

FROM THE VERY EARLIEST DAYS OF TCLPAC/TCLSAC we had made every effort to link our activities vis-à-vis southern Africa with on-going struggles elsewhere, notably in Latin America where we had a natural affinity with the preoccupations and undertakings not only of militants in Latin America itself (and the many in exile in Toronto) but also with Canadian activists, notably in the Latin American Working Group (LAWG). Such links were manifested in a number of dramatic evenings of our "Cinema of Solidarity" film series, for example, but were also to carry me, as "revolutionary traveller," to meetings in Cuba and in Nicaragua (then under the leadership of the Sandinistas). I described one such visit under the title "Under Fire II" in both *This Magazine* (December, 1984) and *Monthly Review* (March, 1985).

DÉJÀ VU. NICARAGUA HAD TOO MUCH THE FEEL FOR ME of Mozambique two or three years ago, on the way to the Nkomati Accord with South Africa: an inspiring struggle, a humane and vital revolution, being slowly bled to death. A Jesuit priest, now working in Nicaragua's agrarian reform sector but also active in Chile before the coup, put the point to me with scalding simplicity. "In Chile," he said, "the Americans made a mistake. They cut off the revolution too abruptly. They killed the revolution but, as we can see from recent developments there, they didn't kill the dream. In Nicaragua they're trying to kill the dream."

Of course, the possibilities of Reagan attempting a quick kill remains. Nicaraguans are bracing themselves for a possible invasion, as well they should. But in the meantime the American-backed Contras are not merely, perhaps not even primarily, a military threat per se—though people are dying. They're also part and parcel of the overall strategy of slow strangulation—attacking economic targets and disrupting normal economic life on the one hand, draining off scarce Sandinista resources (internal funds, foreign exchange, personnel) into the defense effort on the other. Such wrecking complements an all too familiar gamut of international economic pressures which have been brought into play as well: leaning on debts, boycotting exports and the like. It's hard to know who wrote the textbook on this kind of economic warfare, South Africa, or the United States; it does at least seem certain they have compared notes. (Ironically, just as this article was going to press, one such "text-book" did surface, a ninety-page manual in Spanish entitled "Psychological Operation in Guerrilla War"; apparently prepared by the CIA for its Nicaraguan henchmen, it urges, among other horrors, the [provoking of] riots or shootings, which lead to the killing of one or more persons who will be seen as "martyrs" and the hiring of professional criminals "to carry out specific selective jobs," including the "neutralization" of Nicaraguan judges and the like. Reporting this, even a *Globe and Mail* editorial writer [October 18] felt moved to note that we should not "dismiss [Sandanista] concerns as imaginary!" To put it mildly.) And the result in Nicaragua does begin to approximate that achieved by the South Africans in Mozambique, even if the process has not yet gone nearly so far: an economy in tatters, with lack of foreign exchange a severe constraint, a goods shortage, rising prices.

Needless to say, these developments hit the proverbial "man (and woman) in the street" pretty hard. Such economic difficulties were the first thing many people wanted to talk about as I walked about Managua. Even when they could see the American-cum contra role in all of this, some people grumbled—not going over to the other side, it seemed, but a little less wholeheartedly enthusiastic about the revolution than before. Some of the blame for economic crisis must stick to socialism, so the Americans apparently calculate. Who'll dare to raise their heads for another fifty years after we get through, who'll dare to dream: this too seems part of the calculation. When I gave a public talk in Managua about South Africa's war of aggression in Mozambique, Nicaraguans shook their heads; the parallels jumped off the page. I was sobered by one related fact: how little information flows from North to South, how much communication, even between two outposts of revolution, is filtered through the metropole. Small wonder that the full scope of South Africa's war was so little known in Nicaragua. After all, how many North Americans knew there was a vicious war—with a sharp economic edge—going on in Mozambique until, out of the blue, earlier this year, there was a peace treaty!

We know rather more about Central America, but not enough. Or, more likely, we don't care enough. I'm struck by the brutalization of debate about international affairs that has occurred in North America, a downward spiral from the high-water mark of moral discourse about such matters that characterized the immediate post-Vietnam period. Clearly, the various precedents of "gloves-off" imperial assertion—Israel in the Middle East, South Africa in its own region, the U.K. in the Malvinas, the U.S. in Grenada and now in Central America—have taken their toll. Small wonder that the Los Angeles Games were so chillingly reminiscent of their 1936 Munich counterpart. And so obviously so. As one *Toronto Star* sports writer, not generally renowned for his deep political thinking, wondered aloud in his last column from L.A.: where is all the xenophobia going to be directed next?

Nicaragua is a prime candidate, of course, especially if the bleeding goes too slowly (and if some of Nicaragua's allies continue to stand sufficiently firm). For when all is said and done, one came away from Nicaragua with the distinct impression that it would not go under quickly, despite the odds. There are too many good people, Nicaraguans and others (not least among the latter a very strong band of Canadians), doing good things there—in health, in education, in agricultural development, in so many other sectors. But it's tough, make no mistake about that.

A Workshop

I was in Nicaragua for a reason. The Ministry of Agrarian Reform, in conjunction with the Jesuit-sponsored *Instituto de Investigaciones Economicas y Sociales*, had invited fifteen or twenty of us from various parts of the world to Managua for a workshop on "Problems of the Transition to Socialism in Small Peripheral Economies." For six days, from morn to midnight, we debated the issues with our Nicaraguan counterparts. All the "big questions" were raised, though two in particular kept swimming to the surface. One of these might be labelled, if I may be forgiven an academicism, the "economics of socialism under siege." How to keep alive the long-term goal of a socialist restructuring of the economy while reeling under the blows of ruthless economic aggression? How to advance the interests of the desperately poor of the society, the workers and the peasants, while making sufficient short-term concessions to entrepreneurial elements and to keep at least some of them on-side politically and certain important sectors of the economy functioning?

Hard work, not merely for intellectuals cogitating such matters but, more importantly, for the practitioners of the transition. The hard work showed on the face of Jaime Wheelock, one of the nine commandants who lead the Nicaraguan revolution, when he came to talk with us at one of our evening sessions. The Minister of Agrarian Reform, he was now spending most of his time back in military harness, organizing the defence against the Contras in the Sixth Region. His face was grey with exhaustion, tired not merely from a few nights without sleep, but much more deeply, his face mirroring those of old friends among the Mozambican leadership when I've seen them in recent years as they lived the South African siege. It's a bad time, a Friday evening after a hard week's work, and Wheelock is in an almost elegiac mood. Perhaps he's guying us, the intellectual observers of the passing scene, just a little bit when he says, "Transition to socialism? There's no transition to socialism here. We're surviving, that's all. We're living from Friday to Friday!" But there's realism in what he says too, a chilling realism.

No one stays downbeat for long in Nicaragua, though. There's too much to do. Even in our workshop. Perhaps it was fortunate that our second major preoccupation offered more positive inspiration; let's call it the question of the "democratization of every nook and cranny of the transformed society." Historically, the practice has been much less inspiring as, all too often, socialist aspirations have collapsed in upon themselves, offering up a drab, authoritarian denouement to the high hopes with which the process began. There are reasons for this, not the least the kind of siege by the capitalist world that we've been talking about, a constant factor which has stalked all socialist experiments, putting them on the defensive and narrowing their possibilities. But such an explanation doesn't make the reality any more comforting.

Perhaps the most exciting thing about the Nicaraguans is just how alert they themselves are to this problem. Not that in the struggle to democratize the revolution there is anything that Ambassador Jeanne Kirkpatrick could be expected to comprehend. It may even be that the current electoral exercise is as much a tactical concession to firm up an international constituency as it is anything else. But speaking to our workshop the Sandinista Front's electoral organizers described how the election had taken on a very positive resonance for them. They had had to revitalize their grassroots organization quite dramatically to reach out to the people, for example. They also found themselves having to answer very tough questions from the opposition—and from the people generally; from such a process, the Front could only be expected to learn and to grow.

Pluralism is a risky business under fire, of course. Much of the opposition is pretty unscrupulous, not least the National Democratic Coordinator (CDN) of Arturo Cruz; with its own links to the Contras, this group's escalating and largely arbitrary demands for more electoral space are both patently provocative and of self-evidently "made-in-Washington" provenance. And *La Prensa*, the opposition newspaper, is busily churning out a demagogic line of uniformly destructive criticism every day; indeed it seems to have nominated itself (or been nominated?) for the same kind of role played by *The Gleaner* in Manley's Jamaica and by *El Mercurio* in pre-coup Chile. Under such circumstances it is difficult for revolutionaries not to think back, precisely, to the Chilean precedent and to act to preempt the dangers involved. Yet *La Prensa* grinds on. The Independent Liberal Party, which is participating in the election, criticizes openly from the right. From another point of the spectrum (one hesitates to identify it as being to the left of the Front!) two different Communist parties and a Maoist one also level attacks. (This latter was, for me, a particularly genial aspect of pluralism in Nicaragua: the shrill certainties of such protagonists packaged up in their little groupuscules, rather than infecting the more open, and much more revolutionary, character of the Sandinista Front itself.)

Even more important, perhaps, was the glimpse I had of democratic life inside the Front. As I talked over lunch with one union leader, for example, it became apparent that there was no mere "transmission belt" from the political leadership to his rank and file. He took the national imperatives—the imperatives of economic planning, defense, unity—which the Front represented seriously, but he took the needs and demands of the agricultural workers whom he represented equally seriously. He seemed well aware that the transition to socialism is poised on a knife edge, the demands of leadership (the need to give direction, thrust, strength to the revolution) in permanent tension with the need for mass action and for popular control (to breathe life into the revolution, to keep the leadership honest). Nor is this a tension, a contradiction, that can be resolved once and for all. It comes with the territory, it is the politics of the transition to socialism. My luncheon partner was living this "contradiction" as creatively as could be imagined.

Our workshop took the theme of socialism and democracy seriously too, as seriously as our Nicaraguan hosts clearly intended us to do. Much was said of real interest, not glib, not judgmental, merely serious. I sensed that in this we were taking much of our inspiration from what was happening around us: the feeling of open creativity, despite the fact of being "under fire," was palpable in Nicaragua. I was to have my sense of this reinforced in the days after the workshop when I visited, among other locales, the Sandinistas' cadre training school on the outskirts of

Managua. I'd taught in the Frelimo party school in Mozambique, so I was particularly eager to see what was happening here. And there were illuminating similarities.

Like Frelimo, the Sandinistas are trying to give their cadres a theoretical grounding in the Marxist tradition as a necessary undergirding for their practice. As in the Mozambican case, the most readily available version of that tradition comes from Eastern Europe, yet, in this form, many of the strengths of the tradition lie twisted out of recognizable shape. Mozambicans have been aware of this and, as I know from first-hand experience, have struggled to find their own voice on the terrain of Marxism. I was delighted to meet Nicaraguans engaged in the same task, understaffed for this purpose as in so many other sectors, but striving to innovate. In this regard, I liked the quote I found prominently displayed on the wall of their school, a quote from the Nicaraguan writer and activist, Ricardo Morales Aviles, after whom the school had been named: "We have to study our history and our present reality as Marxists; we have to study Marxism as Nicaraguans!" I liked that quote. Siege aside, I liked what I saw in Nicaragua.

The Real Irresponsibility

Back in Canada I listen to Bruce Cockburn's album, *Stealing Fire*. On it there are three magnificent songs inspired by his own visit to Central America last year. Their essence: "in the flash of this moment/you're the best of what we are/ don't let them stop you now/Nicaragua." Not surprisingly, I find the songs more moving than ever in the wake of my visit. And I think back to when the album first came out, recalling a minor matter of the time, stuck in my brain ever since but with new resonance now. It concerned one of those songs, one entitled "If I had a rocket launcher." The lyrics invoke, poetically and powerfully, some of the horrors of Central America's suffering under the U.S. heel, such as a helicopter raid on a refugee village. The punch line: "If I had a rocket launcher...some sonofabitch would die!"

I thought it a powerful song when I first heard it, all the more so coming from Cockburn. He has always been a fantastic guitarist, a fine and sensitive musician. And as a lyricist he's manifested, from the outset, an interesting political sensibility. Still he drifted out of the orbit of my interest when, a few years ago, his Christian preoccupations became a bit too heavy duty for my taste, taking on something of a "born-again" cast (albeit without the oft-attendant right-wing political overtones). For me he got a little mushy, all "god" and "peace" and "sensitivity."

A matter of taste, self-evidently. But this background did make Cockburn's gut response to American aggression in Central America all the more powerful—for its not being entirely predictable. I'd say, too, that his response is the appropriate one; if you care about human decency in Central America, "fight back" is the only answer. Yet it's difficult for Canadians to wriggle their way far enough past the American smokescreen, largely duplicated in our own media, to see the truth of the situation, difficult for us to shake off the coils of our comfort long enough to see that some people have no choice but to fight for what they believe in. Here we return to that "minor matter" mentioned above. Because the kicker to this story is not so much Cockburn's song as a review of the album written by Liam Lacey in *The Globe and Mail* those several months ago. He labelled the "rocket launcher" song "vile and irresponsible," thereby offering, within the modest confines of the record review, a brief and sobering glimpse of what massive incomprehension Central Americans are up against in North America. You shoulda been there, Liam. Right on, Bruce. Stay angry.

DURING THE 1980S WE CONTINUED TO CAMPAIGN ACTIVELY in Toronto around Southern African issues, around, for example (as flagged above), the issue of bank loans to the apartheid regime in South Africa and the involvement of certain Canadian banks in consortia dedicated to that practice. We also maintained active contact with the liberation movements in southern Africa, of course, and were increasingly appalled at the smug, sanctimonious and dismissive attitude of the Canadian government towards their claims and the actions they felt compelled to take in order to achieve their freedom. ANC President Oliver Tambo's visit to Canada, described below, underscores our government's willful blindness on this issue, recounted in an article for *Southern Africa Report* (October, 1987) entitled, advisedly, "Tambo, not Rambo: The ANC's President in Toronto."

ON SATURDAY, AUGUST 29, a few hours before he addressed a public rally in front of the Ontario Parliament Buildings in Toronto, Oliver Tambo met at Anglican Church House with a group of anti-apartheid activists, drawn from church, labour, NGO and support group circles. There was time for a full and frank discussion of a wide range of issues of mutual concern. The chief purpose of the present article is to share the substance of that session with readers who were not in attendance. But first, a few words about context.

Earlier in August Canada's Secretary of State for External Affairs, Joe Clark, visited southern Africa. He made clear his commitment to the "Front-line States" in their defense against South African aggression, even passing on an invitation to non-member Mozambique to participate as an observer at October's Commonwealth Conference in Vancouver. He professed himself once again to be no friend of apartheid and appeared to be greeted very coldly indeed by his South African opposite number, Foreign Minister Pik Botha. Clark received a much warmer reception in Lusaka when he met with representatives of the African National Congress. Perhaps it was there, too, that he finally pinned down the date of ANC President Oliver Tambo's long-awaited visit to Canada at the Canadian government's invitation. In any case, it was only two weeks later that Tambo arrived in Canada.

Tambo was well received by the anti-apartheid / non-governmental organization network in Canada. Indeed the warmth of his reception at a well-attended informal get-together at Toronto lawyer Charles Roach's house on the Wednesday evening of his arrival in Canada would be difficult to describe. And such warmth was duplicated at other "unofficial" sessions in Ottawa and at the above-mentioned public rally, hastily organized but remarkably effective nonetheless. Much less warm was his reception by his official hosts, the Canadian government. Thus Joe Clark, in his comments on the visit, managed to convey the impression to the media that he was at least as concerned about the ANC's resort to violence and its links to "Communism" as he was about the horrors of apartheid.[72] Moreover, it appears that, in private, Brian Mulroney's approach was not very much more enlightened.

Tambo meets Mulroney

When he spoke to us that Saturday morning, the day after his meeting with Mulroney and Clark, Tambo, seasoned diplomat that he is, chose his words carefully. The ANC, he stressed, had welcomed Canada's recent support for a sanctions programme against South Africa and had been impressed, in particular, with Mulroney's persistent pressing of the issue at the seven nations Economic Summit earlier this year. He hoped now to encourage the Canadian government to play an even more active role in pushing for "comprehensive sanctions" at such forthcoming meetings as those of the "Francophonie" and the Commonwealth. It would be unfortunate if the intransigence of the British and the Americans on this question (including their persistent vetoes of U.N.-sponsored mandatory sanctions proposals) were to discourage Canada from following through on this question. The example of the Nordic countries in acting "comprehensively" despite U.N. vetoes might prove helpful to Canadians, he suggested.

Yet Tambo was exposed to an even more deep-seated limitation in Canada's position. For the Canadian government, he suggested, apparently views sanctions as designed to preempt altogether the need for popular-cum-armed struggle in South Africa—a view very different from that of the ANC which, more realistically, sees sanctions as "complementary" to that necessary struggle. In this latter view, the role of sanctions is to weaken the side of the oppression and thus, in the long run, to undermine the apartheid state's ability to resist indefinitely. Tambo had hoped that Canadians saw themselves to be supporting, by means of sanctions, a just and legitimate struggle for freedom that takes many forms, including the resort to the use of force of arms. Now he learned at first hand from Mulroney that the ANC's "violence" was a major problem for him!

Tambo was not altogether successful in hiding a note of annoyance here, especially as he recounted the moment when Mulroney confronted him with the South African government's advertisement from that day's *Globe and Mail*, one which demagogically misrepresented the ANC's armed struggle as mere "terrorism." "With all due respect", Tambo said, "I do not think the Canadians should look to what the South African government is saying about the ANC to determine its own strategy." The majority of the people in the world, he pointed out, don't care what the South African government says and refuse to evaluate the ANC by shifting their gaze from the central reality of apartheid's unyielding violence—which is, after all, the reality which the ANC must confront in choosing its own tactics. "Are there no justified acts of violence in the world?" he asked. Could this be merely a pretext for some watering down of support for sanctions?

To be sure, the Prime Minister presented the matter to Tambo partly in terms of tactical considerations of his own. Mulroney claimed that he could not really hope to persuade Thatcher to move on the sanctions question as long as the ANC engaged in violence. Tambo did not need to point out to us that this was to misrepresent the nature and depth of Thatcher's hostility to sanctions or indeed any other form of significant action against apartheid. Instead Tambo, politely but ironically, permitted himself only the comment that he had never heard that argument before. As for Mulroney and Clark's own punctilious distaste for revolutionary violence in South Africa, it was left for others in the room to point out how unlikely it was that these two were merely uninformed about the extent of the apartheid regime's intransigence or naive about the kinds of real pressures which would be necessary to shake the regime. Tambo himself refrained from pressing the point.

Tambo also saw the long arm of Pretoria's propaganda machine in the kind of fixation with the question of "Communism" which he had experienced on this visit. Certainly he was prepared to make no apologies for the presence of Communists in the ranks of the ANC. He noted that "we are all fighting the same enemy" while also pointing out, correctly, that there is "not a tittle of evidence" for the bizarre charge that the ANC is controlled by Moscow and/or "the Communists." The West fought side by side with Stalin against Hitler, but we who are fighting another Hitler in our own country are asked to drive the Communists out. Why, he asked, is that? Why is Pretoria being tacitly defended by this kind of argument? Is it because it is a white regime, we wonder? And is this kind of red-baiting also being slotted in as one more pretext to pull away from a firm commitment to sanctions? Such were the questions that Tambo left us with.

The strength of the resistance

Of course, there was much more to the ANC President's presentation than a series of bemused reflections on the preoccupations of the Canadian government, useful though these reflections were to the assembled Canadians who must deal with that government on a day-today basis. Actually, the central and primary thrust of Tambo's talk was to underscore, in rich detail, the continuing strength of the resistance in South Africa—in spite of the brutal repression that the apartheid regime has brought to bear under its several States of Emergency. Although government censorship chokes off a clear image of the activities of the forces of resistance the truth is, Tambo affirmed, that "the more the repression grows, the more determined we are."

He reminded us of the advances made despite the States of Emergency. Thus the greatest trade union movement in the history of South Africa (COSATU) was born during the emergency and one of its affiliates (the National Union of Mineworkers) has just engaged in the greatest strike in South African history. The impressive organization of youth, SAYCO, was launched this year in the very teeth of the Emergency as will be a new federation of women. And the United Democratic Front refuses to be driven from the field despite every effort by the government to destroy it. At the same time, the armed wing of the struggle has also advanced, there having been more armed actions in the past seven months than during any comparable period. Not that such armed action includes the practice of "necklacing," much as the South African government and some sections of the media might like to imply otherwise. "No member of MK (*Umkhonto we Sizwe*, the ANC's armed wing) has ever necklaced anybody," Tambo said. "We have an army of trained cadres whose orders are to attack military and the police and to avoid attacking civilians."

In short, Tambo affirmed that the political and armed struggles are two sides of the same coin, premised on the understanding that "apartheid must be abolished." Here was, in effect, Tambo's reply to Mulroney and Clark: a point must be reached "where apartheid is so costly that its defenders back off." How is this to be achieved? "We have proven that the key lies in struggle." True, the state has acted viciously in retaliation, attempting to destroy the ANC inside and outside South Africa by means of assassinations, armed raids, kidnappings and the like. And they have had to modify their domestic policies, avoiding new installments of apartheid on occasion while introducing some modifications. Hence, the dropping of certain of the pass laws (albeit many important aspects of them have been introduced in new form). But, said Tambo, "the government had already experienced great difficulty in enforcing these laws against the people's will." Besides, the demand of the people is not merely for the modification of this or that repugnant law. "The demand of the people is for power."

President Tambo had less to say about the nature of post-apartheid South Africa, although he did respond at some length to questions about the future of democracy and socialism there. Consistent with the ANC's oft-stated position he affirmed that "there will be political parties of all shades of opinion" and the people will decide democratically what their futures hold. As regards economic matters, Tambo's answers may have been a little too conciliatory (even if calculatedly so) for some in the room. Thus, he argued that meetings with South African business people, among others, have produced a satisfactory level of agreement regarding the ANC's position that "the economy must serve the people," that it be "strong" but also that "the wealth be distributed equitably."

He drew attention to the nationalization planks of the Freedom Charter, while also noting that there is no strict blueprint as to how rapidly any such programmes would be pursued or how comprehensively. As for the statement by Galvin Relly that the South African economy is so structured that it would be destroyed by nationalizations, Tambo underscored the extent to which the apartheid state itself already holds a very substantial stake in the economy. The ANC's goal is a "mixed economy," said Tambo, reiterating that businessmen, black and white, are relatively comfortable with the ANC. There was, in short, virtually no reference to the possibility that some kind of on-going post-apartheid class struggle might be necessary in order to guarantee an "equitable" future—although the importance of the strike activities of the mineworkers, underway at the moment of his talk, was singled out for special emphasis.

Obviously, there were a number of open questions being flagged here regarding South Africa's long-term socioeconomic future, questions that will, no doubt, continue to be wrestled with both within and without the ANC. And, in any case, there is still the apartheid system to be overthrown before such questions can be placed absolutely squarely on the agenda. Yet with respect to this stage of the struggle, it came as no surprise to those gathered at Anglican Church House to find Oliver Tambo still rock solid in the front line—bringing to Canadians a clear message of militancy. It seems certain that all of us there in the room felt moved by his eloquence and his example to rededicate ourselves to taking his message ever more effectively to other Canadians, including to those political leaders who refused to listen carefully and sympathetically, on this occasion, to the message from Tambo's own lips.

THROUGH THE 1980S, I CONTINUED, WITH TCLSAC, my anti-apartheid activities on a range of fronts, seeking to contest Canadian policy, both governmental and corporate. I had written other related work, especially on the situation in South Africa, as well.[73] And I continued to follow the ebb and flow of Canadian policy closely too, aware that this had become an increasingly revealing index of just what the balance of forces within South Africa was beginning to look like. Thus I wrote in the August-September, 1988, issue of *This Magazine* of "The Mysteries of the Dark Cabinet," and asking the question: "What is behind the Mulroney government's surprising stand on South Africa."

ALTHOUGH WE DON'T HEAR SO MUCH ABOUT IT NOWADAYS, there have been moments in the past few years when Canada appeared to be in the forefront of the struggle for a democratic South Africa. And the issue seemed much higher on the Conservative political agenda than it had ever been situated under the Liberals.

Intimates would argue that Mulroney had been moved by a gut-level distaste for racism, especially of the heavily institutionalized apartheid variety. But Commonwealth politics also helped persuade Mulroney to take the high road on South Africa. After all, his first dance steps on the international stage were taken at the 1985 Commonwealth heads-of-state meetings in Nassau where the South African issue was a prominent concern. Mulroney had been lobbied in advance by African leaders. He was impressed by Bishop Tutu when Tutu visited Canada in late 1984; the visit of Tanzanian president, Julius Nyerere, just before the Nassau meetings also had a strong impact. And wasn't the Commonwealth one of the arenas in which Pierre Elliot Trudeau had so often shone. Here was a chance to upstage the old show-man himself.

The Nassau conference, which appointed a "group of eminent persons" to investigate the situation in South Africa, also hinted at a stronger Canadian line on sanctions in South Africa. Then, at the U.N., the die of a progressive Canadian anti-apartheid policy seemed to be cast. If there is no fundamental change in South Africa, Mulroney declared in his October 1985 address, "we are prepared to invoke total sanctions against that country and its repressive regime... If there is no progress in the dismantling of apartheid, our relations with South Africa may have to be severed absolutely!" African delegates crowded around after this speech to shake the prime minister's hand.

Note the timing of all this, however. The urgency now attached to the South African question was not something whistled up by Mulroney and others from a standing start. It was imposed on the international community by the actions of South Africans themselves!

The resurrection of resistance in South Africa from the ashes of the sixties has been dramatic. It surfaced first in the working class actions of the early seventies in Durban and then in the assertions of the students in Soweto in 1976. The media image of this emerging democratic movement—even when presented sympathetically—tended to be the rock-throwing crowd. But underneath was a different, far more promising, reality—a massive surge of creative political activity. From the late seventies onwards, a dense and formidable network of organizations was created: trade unions, student and parent organizations, women's groups, community-based "civic associations," national-level umbrella bodies like the United Democratic Front and a revitalized African National Congress (ANC) underground. This infrastructure of resistance and a growing sense of popular self-confidence could not be easily crushed and, indeed, came to underpin the massive nation-wide insurrection that began in the Transvaal in September 1984.

Debate wracked South African ruling circles about how best to deal with this insurrection. Eventually the state opted for intensified repression rather than meaningful change as the primary means for coping with democratic demands. But in liberal circles, not least amongst certain enlightened businesspeople, the option of substantive reform as a means of preempting revolution was being explored. In the words of Anglo-American executive Zac de Beer: "We all understand how years of apartheid have caused many black to reject the economic as well as political system...We dare not allow the baby of free enterprise to be thrown out with the bathwater of apartheid." Re-enter, at this point, the Eminent Person's group (EPG), which reported back to the Commonwealth in mid-1986.

Predictably, the South African government had thumbed its nose at the EPG. Not so predictably the group—co-chaired by Malcolm Fraser, the deeply conservative former Australian Prime Minister—wrote an eloquent and tough-minded report calling for an extension of sanctions against South Africa to force it to its senses before the confrontation there escalated out of control. The EPG feared more violence and bloodshed, but Fraser, in particular, sounded much the same note as Zac de Beer. In Fraser's words, in an escalating conflict "moderation would be swept aside...The government that emerged from all of this would be extremely radical, probably Marxist, and would nationalize all western business interests."

It seems clear that Mulroney responded with great interest to this reading of the South African situation. To the goal of ingratiating himself with the Black Commonwealth was now added the role of spearheading the forces of enlightened capitalism. Mulroney sought (unsuccessfully) to convince Margaret Thatcher of the wisdom of the position at the August 1986 Commonwealth mini-summit convened to follow up on the EPG report. He had hoped that Thatcher would link the U.K. to the new Commonwealth-sponsored package of sanctions which was now forthcoming. And he was to press the same kind of case at the Venice

G-7 meeting of the major industrialized countries in 1987, although again to little avail.

Such negative results were not altogether surprising. Certainly Thatcher and Reagan are both racist in ways that Mulroney is not and, for that reason alone, were less likely to be "enlightened" in their capitalist-inspired planning vis-à-vis South Africa. Moreover, Britain and the U.S. each has a much larger stake in South Africa than does Canada. Of course, this might merely have made them even more keen to act preemptively to safeguard capital's long-term future there. But, in fact, both thought the risks of revolution were not yet acute enough to warrant the short-term economic costs of a tough sanctions policy. Meanwhile, Mulroney's government was left to make its own actions conform with its rhetoric and its apparent reading of the South African situation.

And, from 1985 on, some significant steps were taken. Carleton University's Linda Freeman, a leading commentator on Canada's southern African policies, noted in the October 1986 issue of *Southern African Report* that "while the sanctions adopted so far are not comprehensive and they are not mandatory, they exist and they represent progress." She mentions the banning of imports of South African steel, iron, coal, uranium and agricultural products, the stopping of government purchases of South African products and of government contracts with South-African owned firms and the abrogation of the Canada-South Africa double taxation agreement. But, as the government's enthusiasm for sanctions waned, Freeman could point out (in the December issue of the *Report*) that "the sanctions which have been adopted constitute the easy first step of sanctions and it is telling that the government has suggested that there is very little left to do." In fact, according to Freeman's figures, we have banned only one-quarter of our total trade with South Africa.

Still, sanctions had at least been placed more firmly on the Canadian agenda than at any previous point. Far more indicative of Tory policies has been the government's difficulties in taking any other step vis-à-vis South Africa, in particular the step of more actively and directly supporting the popular struggle itself. Indeed, sanctions have been presented, almost exclusively, as being some kind of "peaceful alternative" in South Africa.

The facts, unfortunately, are otherwise. As Chief Albert Luthuli, Nobel Peace Prize winner and one-time ANC president said many years ago, effective sanctions can be expected merely to "shorten the day of bloodshed," to so weaken the apartheid state as to make it possible for those battling for democracy to advance more quickly, less painfully. This plus the fact that sanctions only become a really pressing issue in western countries when the popular movement in South Africa is on the offensive. There is, in short, no substitute in South Africa for popular struggle.

Even Joe Clark came close to acknowledging this point. As he said to an anti-apartheid conference in Montreal in February 1987, "Certainly it seems to us that a policy based solely on sanctions would not mount the pressure we need. For one thing, we see little likelihood of the governments of major economies applying sanctions on the scale that would be required to force Pretoria to change. That result may come in time, and certainly Canada will use our influence to build the weight of sanctions, but it is not realistic to expect an impenetrable wall to be set up suddenly, or even quickly."

Yet what could be expected, alternatively, to "mount the pressure we need"? No real answer has been forthcoming from either Clark or Mulroney. Certainly one will wait in vain for any indication from Clark that the answer might be "popular struggle." Witness Clark's response to the *Toronto Star*'s Carol Goar in September 1987 when asked why South Africa had become such a prominent international issue: "Then, about three years ago, there was what Clark called 'a spontaneous focusing of world opinion' on the apartheid issue. 'I don't know why it happened,' he said. 'It's partly the media. A lot of people became aware of a greater urgency to change, maybe even the greater possibility of change in southern Africa'." Spontaneous focusing, indeed. Clark was speaking virtually three years to the day from the outbreak of the Transvaal uprising that first signalled the massive and sustained upsurge of the South African people, an upsurge that, ineluctably, drew the attention of the world!

How much easier, from such an uninformed starting-point, to then blame the victim in South Africa for the apartheid government's intransigence. Here's Clark again, writing in the *Star* at about the same time as his own recent trip to South Africa: "In my conversations with both the ANC and (South African) foreign minister Pik Botha, I raised again the "Possible Negotiating Concept" developed by the Commonwealth group last year. That concept foundered on the question of violence, especially the South African government's insistence that the black opposition renounce violence as a prelude to talks. It is clear this remains a stumbling block." Talks? A South African government ready for talks, at this stage, about a genuine democratization of South Africa?

It would be difficult to imagine a more misleading—be it willful or half-witted—formulation as to the source of the problem in South Africa than this.

Prime Minister Mulroney had appeared capable, at least momentarily, of getting closer to the heart of the matter on his own trip to South Africa earlier in 1987. There, in an affable interchange with the presidents of the Commonwealth front-line states (Zimbabwe's Robert Mugabe, Zambia's Kenneth Kaunda and Botswana's Quett Masire), Mulroney pointed the finger of blame firmly at Pretoria, admitting that "the absence of progress in dialogue...confirms me in my sad conclusion...that the way of dialogue is not making progress but is regressing." More importantly, he professed to "understand" why, under the circumstances, black African leaders should feel the use of violence to be necessary to overthrow the racist South African government, even if, he said, he could not "condone" it. Not that the broad range of tactics pursued by the democratic movements in South Africa can be reduced to armed action. But the growth of the ANC's capacity to neutralize state terrorism by force of arms will continue to be important. Mulroney's tentative steps towards viewing things from the vantage-point of the oppressed did seem to be a step in the right direction, a step toward a more sympathetic understanding of the imperatives of real struggle in South Africa.

Unfortunately, this was not, in the end, to be the direction in which the tide of official opinion was running in Ottawa. Clark's own signals have been mixed but he did manage to convey to the Montreal meeting in February and to the media on his return from Africa in August, 1987, that his worries about the ANC's resort to violence and its links to "Communism" rivaled his concern about the horrors of apartheid. Even more depressing evidence of this trend was forthcoming when ANC President Oliver Tambo came to Canada that same August, in the run-up to the Vancouver Commonwealth Conference, at the Canadian government's own invitation. Who could have predicted the churlish reception he would receive, red-baited and scolded by both Mulroney and Clark for his commitment to violence as one necessary tactic to be used in South Africa.

I then included in the original article a further synopsis of the Tambo meeting with Mulroney and Clark in Ottawa and of Tambo's account of it the next day to Toronto-based anti-apartheid movement activists that I attended (as recounted in the text that immediately precedes the present one in this chapter), concluding with the various questions that Tambo then raised with us with regard both to the nature of his reception and to Canadian policy more generally. I continued the present article as follows:

Unfortunately, [the questions Tambo thus raised] were not to be laid to rest in subsequent months. True, Mulroney and company did sustain a high level of anti-apartheid rhetoric though the Vancouver Commonwealth summit in October—ensuring that black Commonwealth anger at that meeting would be directed exclusively against the rigidly inflexible Thatcher. But since then the South African issue has been increasingly downgraded and the promised further initiatives in implementing sanctions has remained in abeyance. Indeed, as Linda Freeman argued, Canada's sanctions have still not cut all that deep; we continue to export sulphur there, among other things, and still allow Canadian subsidiaries and consulting firms to operate in South Africa.

Moreover, to take merely one example cited by Freeman, the 1986 purchase by Wardair of three airbuses from South African Airways "was about equivalent to the revenue lost in South Africa from Canadian import sanctions." Small wonder she can conclude that "Canada's choice of sanctions has been anything but comprehensive and its ability and willingness to monitor compliance with existing sanctions highly suspect." But then this is also the opinion of Glenn Babb, South Africa's notorious ex-ambassador to Canada, who could crow on his return to South Africa in early 1987 that the threat of Canadian sanctions had "receded" markedly.

Even the further intensification of South Africa's brutal emergency which saw the banning of eighteen key above ground democratic organizations in South Africa in February of this year (1988) prompted little response. True, both Mulroney and Clark professed to find Pretoria's new actions reprehensible; Clark was even moved to suggest some revision of his comfortable rejection of any violent action by those South Africans opposed to apartheid. "They [the bannings] leave little else," he said. But with the situation so clearly deteriorating further in South Africa, one could be forgiven for dusting off Mulroney's 1985 United Nations speech and asking what has happened to its brave promises. Why not, at the very least, further sanctions? Why no response to opposition demands to downgrade, if not sever, Canada's diplomatic links with South Africa? Why, most recently, and only one short year after the Venice G-7 meeting, virtually no mention by Mulroney of the South African issue at his own carefully crafted Toronto summit? Why was

Mulroney's brief term as ringmaster of an enlightened capitalist strategy toward South Africa apparently coming to an end.

One could offer a variety of explanations. Had Venice taught the Prime Minister not to get too far out in front of his capitalist allies, particularly the U.S.? Wasn't the Vancouver Commonwealth meeting now over, any potential embarrassment on Canadian soil forestalled? What of pressures from the right wing of the Tory party, from which grouping so many MPs and others have travelled to the land of apartheid, most often at South African government expense, to "see for themselves"? What of the drag of External Affairs, where old-guard senior bureaucrats appear to be critical of Mulroney's "adventurism" on the South African issue, and of his "unfriendly" stance toward the British? What of Joe Clark, prepared himself it would seem, to peddle the more cautious External line? And hasn't Mulroney enough other things on his plate, what with free trade, Meech Lake and domestic scandal to occupy him elsewhere?

All true enough. But there is something else too. The moment in South Africa that evoked Mulroney's enthusiasm for quarter-backing a liberal-capitalist response to apartheid's crisis is gone [albeit temporarily as events would prove], gone with the Emergency inflicted nation-wide in South Africa since 1986, the emergency with its media controls and its brutal attempt to suppress outright the democratic opposition. South Africa has made certain that the television images that so fuelled western popular indignation are no longer available. So it is true, at least for the moment, that there is less to see. The sophisticated development of the apartheid state's National Security Management System, its sweeping programme of arrest, detention without trial, torture and assassination, its use of ruthless vigilantes (like those orchestrated by Chief Gatsha Buthelezi) from among the black population against the democratic movement has seen to that.

There has been, in short, a set-back in South Africa, even if, fortunately, this is not the 1960s when an earlier emergency did crush, for a decade, a (much weaker) movement for emancipation. The present-day movement has a stronger organizational base and is psychologically and organizationally better fortified. Of course, it must now find much more effective means to ground itself at the base, must arm itself better, co-ordinate itself better. There seems little doubt that it will eventually do so. Moreover, the economic crisis that underpins the political crisis of the apartheid system cannot be resolved by mere repression alone. What goes around will eventually come around.

Nonetheless, it must be admitted that Pretoria has gained time for itself by means of the emergency, with even the most liberal of business-people now passively falling in behind the government as repression is seen to "work" and as the threat of revolution recedes. The same is true, it would seem, of that other summer-time soldier for change in South Africa, Brian Mulroney. Canada has given some direct help at the margins of the movement in South Africa (for detainee family support inside the country, for instance, and even, via CIDA, for some Canadian NGO-sponsored programs linked to the ANC). We have also upgraded our assistance to the "front-line states," themselves under aggressive siege by South Africa.

Yet it is also clear that the more intractable the situation becomes in South Africa and the more crucial to the cause of transformation becomes the struggle being mounted by the popular movement, the more difficult it is to avoid the overt taking of sides. Some western countries—the Scandinavian counties in particular—have moved a considerable distance toward choosing, assertively, the side of the popular movement, while educating their own electorate of the necessity to do so. However, this is an example our own government is reluctant to follow. The Canadian anti-apartheid movement must continue to insist that it do so, even if recent experience suggests that, ultimately, it is only the revitalization of the movement in South Africa itself that can force a Tory government here to reengage seriously with the apartheid question.

As we know, this lull in the pace of change did not last long. The movement in South Africa did regroup and revitalize itself. Equally important, reformist elements in the business community actually stayed on course, seeking to carry not only "enlightened" elements with the National Party establishment but also important players within the ANC itself with them in the direction of significant political changes—albeit profoundly reformist ones that would serve to safe-guard the continuing, if modified and dramatically deracialized, hegemony of capitalism. True, Canada had been temporarily derailed, its enthusiasm (both verbal and, to some degree, substantive) for sanctions in good part dribbling away, as Freeman has clearly documented (she speaks of some achievements but also of a record of "weaknesses, compromises and ambiguities") in her magisterial *The Ambiguous Champion: Canada and South Africa in the Trudeau and Mulroney Years* (Toronto: University of Toronto

Press, 1997). As a result, our role as any kind of real player in the on-rushing project of false decolonization (false liberation, one would be tempted to say, were not the overthrow of rawly racist rule not so significant in and of itself) was thus blurred. On the other hand, we did hang onto these sanctions we had managed to put into place (until 1993) rather longer that many other countries. Moreover, official Canada, both governmental and corporate, was soon happy enough to become an eager participant in the process of recolonizing South Africa for global capital that would, unfortunately, accompany that country's release from racist overrule.

NONETHELESS, THE STRUGGLE INSIDE THE COUNTRY was still raging throughout this period and, indeed, as the 1980s wore on, I began to sense that I really had to see apartheid in its latter-day manifestations for myself. I therefore decided in 1988 to do so. The following account of that trip, entitled "Without Proper Papers: Inside South Africa," was published in 1989, once again in both *This Magazine* and *Monthly Review*.

I HAD NOT BEEN TO SOUTH AFRICA FOR ALMOST A DECADE, unable to obtain a visa from the apartheid government. In July of last year I decided I should go anyway. It wasn't the first time I've crossed a frontier without proper papers. But in 1972 when I visited the liberated areas of Mozambique during the war against the Portuguese, I was accompanied by a column of Frelimo guerrillas. This time I was on my own.

There were a few moments of tension—decades of reading thrillers should have left me better prepared—yet the details of entry and exit don't really matter. Pretty small potatoes, in any case, compared to the dangers South African activists must confront daily as they seek new ways to beat back the brutal repression of South Africa's current officially declared "Emergency." More important was the opportunity to witness at close hand the impact of that repression, to explore the changing social context that situates it, to get some hint of how the broad movement for a democratic South Africa is attempting to regroup on difficult terrain. After all, not even the Canadian Broadcasting Corporation or the *Globe and Mail* are presently allowed into South Africa, having been specific targets of a more generalized news shutdown that has helped Pretoria take apartheid out of the headlines in recent months. In this context a certain measure of risk seemed a small price to pay for the sharp impressions to be gleaned from a month inside South Africa.

A decade since my last visit. Almost a decade, too, since I wrote of that earlier trip in the pages of *This Magazine* ("In the Belly of the Beast," November/December, 1979). Unfortunately much of what I wrote then might merely be repeated here. "Things in South Africa," I then affirmed, "are as bad as all that. And far from improving they're getting worse... In the townships the scope of arbitrary administrative power over the lives of urban Africans can be seen to grow broader every day, while the government is quite explicit about the fact that any apparent reforms are an alternative to, not a step towards, majority rule." Equally true in 1988. My last visit occurred in the wake of the dramatic Soweto uprising of 1976. The intervening decade has seen a continuing escalation of resistance, finding a new high-water mark in the near-insurrection of 1984–85, an upsurge far more dramatic than the Soweto events. But again, my observation in that earlier article regarding Soweto has present-day resonance: "such protest ultimately did lack the focus and the clout to really endanger the state in a fundamental way."

Indeed, it was hard to escape the sense, during this visit, that the past few years have witnessed a setback in South Africa. The nationwide emergency regulations imposed since 1986 have introduced a level of repression and state terror even more severe than that which followed in the immediate aftermath of the Soweto events. So severe, in fact, that their impact invites comparisons with a previous period of emergency, that of the early 1960s, when, in the wake of the Sharpeville massacre, the state was able to smash the democratic movement, physically and psychologically, for a decade. As a result, the movement for genuine change in South Africa has been forced to retreat some considerable distance from the euphoric mood of the mid-1980s, when people even talked about the likely nature of a post-apartheid South Africa.

Yet if the democratic movement is bloodied, it is also unbowed. In 1978, I could affirm that "post-Soweto South Africa is not post-Sharpeville South Africa," and the escalating political activity of subsequent years bore out my assessment. In 1988, as I moved around South Africa—to Johannesburg, to Durban, to Cape Town and to a number of places in between— and as I talked with a wide range of South African trade union and community activists, I found today's South Africa to be even less a "post-Sharpeville South Africa." Whatever the recent setbacks, the events of the past ten years have had the overall effect of strengthening the movement, psychologically and organizationally, for the long haul—an important point, which I'll come back to.

First impressions? In downtown Johannesburg, I did see more blacks—in some restaurants and theaters and on the streets at all hours—than I had ten years ago. Blacks are settling in the urban areas at a pace that the government's ongoing "removal" policies can never hope to arrest. One geographer told me that Durban is now the fastest growing city in the world, and it was not hard to believe him after a day spent touring the sprawling shantytowns of that city. And so-called "grey areas" of mixed-residence have sprung up in Jo'burg, for example, in defiance of the notorious Group Areas Act (though the government now threatens to act more sharply to contain such trends).

Yet the pervasive racism of the society remains very close to the surface, visible in even the most trivial of contexts. An article in Johannesburg's leading newspaper on the "world's fastest sprinter"—a local policeman not named Ben Johnson or Carl Lewis—requires a second reading before one realizes that it is talking about the world's fastest white sprinter. A golden-haired girl smiling out from another front-page article is described as being "all dolled up for the matric dance—a big event in every girl's life"!

Unfortunately other aspects of the "commonsense" of South Africa's untransformed racist system are less laughable, much more grim. I had many intense and thoughtful discussions with activist friends about how to reorganize the democratic movement in the black townships. So often, however, we had to bring ourselves up short, to remind ourselves of just how many of those who might be expected to implement such tactics in this or that township have been killed, arrested, or driven very deep underground in the past several years. I knew the litany from abroad, of course: the mass detentions and torture, often of the very young, the Goniwe killing in Cradock, the assassination of Victoria Mxenge, the Mayekiso trial, and the harassment of the Sharpeville Six. But those I talked with had similar stories to tell and often quite personal burdens to bear. After all, the active pursuit of full color-blind democratic rights is still among the most serious of crimes in South Africa, and it is precisely this "crime" that the emergency regulations, with their more full-blown militarization of South African society, have been designed to curb.

Significantly, the state's tactics extend beyond militarization and police violence to the setting of elements of the black community against each other—and, with some success, to destabilizing neighboring states such as Mozambique and Angola. In Durban and Cape Town, I observed at close hand the real nature of the "black on black violence" that fuels Pretoria's propaganda machine. Invariably, it is a matter of the state making common cause with privileged black strata in the repression of the democratic movement: I heard the grim tales of active police connivance with the "warlords" of Cape Town slum boss Johnson Ngxobongwana in the smashing of the Old Crossroads squatter settlement several years ago, for example, and of their tacit alliance with the brutal Chief Buthelezi and his Inkatha movement as the latter has taken the offensive in recent months in Pietermaritzburg. Of course, one did not need to go to South Africa to know that Buthelezi is not the leader of some uniform entity of "six million Zulu" as *ABC Nightline* host Ted Koppel and Toronto's *Globe and Mail* often seek to present him; no more should his murderous tactics in defense of his own turf have earned him the label of moderate with which such sources also tend to grace him. Nonetheless, it was chilling to hear from Zulu trade union and United Democratic Front (UDF) activists that they would just as soon fall into the clutches of the South African police as those of Buthelezi and his henchmen.

There are also political divisions that cut across the racial divide on the white side of the political equation, although it is not entirely clear how significant they may prove to be. While I was there, the six-year prison sentence given to a young draftee named David Bruce for refusing to undertake his military service became big news with substantial impact. Bypassing any religious or pacifist arguments in his own defense, Bruce stated quite simply that he would do nothing to defend apartheid. Within days, another 143 draft-eligible youths from across the country had associated themselves with Bruce's stance. Indeed, the growing support for the End Conscription Campaign (ECC) moved the military, momentarily, to discuss with it some form of compromise through an expanded definition of acceptable alternative service. Typically, however, compromise was not to be the state's preferred option. Only days after my return to Canada, I learned that the ECC had been banned.

Yet whatever optimism such a division within the white community might nurture seems far outweighed by the spectacle of government and business closing ranks. In the mid-1980s, confronted by a rising popular movement, some businesspeople did become more reform-minded, counselling some significant deracialization in order to preempt the possibility of the resistance movement becoming ever more revolutionary and—horror of horrors—socialist. Now, as I breakfasted with one young, activist Afrikaner business reformer, I found him expressing deep frustration at how quickly his colleagues had fallen in behind the state's repressive strategy once that strategy had been seen to "work," at least in the short run, in forestalling resistance.

He also confirmed my sense that it is not so much the pull of political parties to the right—the very visible Conservative Party (CP), the neo-fascist Afrikaner Weerstand Beweging (AWB)—that constrains the National Party's reformist inclinations. Rather, the root of the problem is that party's own intransigent stand against any real and substantive transformation—read "democratization" of the South African situation. To be sure, driving around South Africa I could see quite clearly the social roots of an ultra-Right, see them in the relative poverty of marginal white working-class neighborhoods in a city like Johannesburg or in the dusty towns of the platteland, a long way from the affluence of such leafy suburbs as Houghton and Sandton. Here were whites who had nothing but privileged pigmentation going for them in their attempt to safeguard their socioeconomic positions against the advance of the black population across the color bar; they view each and every whiff of change with deep suspicion. Yet my business acquaintance was prepared to lump the CP and the AWB with the National Party (and indeed with many white liberal groupings to the left of the Nats) as all being parties of mere reform! "Reform," in his lexicon, as distinct from "transform," signifies marginal adjustments in the status quo designed to make the essentials of that status quo easier to defend. The result: too few of even his own business colleagues are prepared to embrace the strategy—potentially opportune if admittedly risky—of democratizing South Africa's capitalist system.

There is a good deal of bluff to the apartheid government's intransigence, of course. Its hard line is not quite as successful as it likes to pretend. Repression cannot will away resistance from below. Nor can it solve deep-seated economic problems. It was common knowledge inside South Africa while I was there that underlying the government's recently more flexible approach towards the situation in Angola and Namibia was the hard reality of military setback in Angola and an inability to meet the escalating costs of such a wasting war. There is also evidence of vulnerability in the paranoia in ruling circles regarding sanctions. Indeed, anyone who still doubts the potential impact of anti-apartheid action from abroad should read the South African press for a couple of weeks and note the near panic that any sign of serious sanctions arouses.

Just before I left Canada, for example, a small group of us at York University had questioned South African participation in the international tennis tournament soon to be held on the campus. Within days—thanks to hard work by anti-apartheid activists and the fact that the Commonwealth foreign ministers were about to meet in Toronto—the Canadian government had been forced to exclude the South Africans. A significant victory certainly, but it seemed equally significant to find news of this victory blazoned across the front pages of South African newspapers during the course of my visit there. Even more frenzied was the response in the white establishment press and in political circles to U.S. presidential candidate Mike Dukakis' strongly stated commitment to the cause of sanctions. In fact, sitting in South Africa, one might have been forgiven for thinking sanctions to be the only issue in the U.S. campaign.

Yet bluffs, like repression itself, can work, buy time, reassure potential sources of support. Western governments and business interests have little enough genuine enthusiasm for sanctions in any case. If South Africa can be made to seem less urgently in need of some preemptive compromise with revolutionary energies even that minimal degree of commitment may begin to wane. There are signs, for example, that the international banks, deeply concerned, not so long ago, about South Africa's "stability," are beginning to creep back, bringing the financial succor the apartheid state craves. The international anti-apartheid network must do what it can to resist any such trend. Yet it is the perceived strength of the democratic movement inside South Africa itself that will do most to dissuade such international economic actors from reengaging. What then, in the South Africa caught in perpetual emergency, are that movement's prospects?

I spoke with trade union officials, from national office holders and local organizers to shop stewards gathered for a meeting in a modest West Rand office; with UDF spokespersons, some of them staying just one jump ahead of the law; with students linked to the broad ranks of township youth; with activists, black and white, in a range of support and advice organizations; with academics, the best of them trying to make their expertise relevant to the revitalization of the popular movement. All admitted that their spirits have wavered under the relentless onslaught of the apartheid state. At the same time, virtually everyone I met refused to concede that the state had won anything more than a round in the struggle. The continued existence of this mood of intense commitment to struggle, a sentiment reiterated over and over again in my presence, was the most dramatic news I have to report from a month on the road.

There is, of course, the vibrant memory of the drama that occurred not so many months ago and of the powerful political energies unleashed in that "insurrectionary moment." There is a conviction, too, that such energy is still at large in South Africa, a conviction grounded not in mere hope but in tangible realities. The country remains pockmarked by ongoing rent and school boycotts, for example. But particularly salient and still a topic of urgent conversation during my visit was the successful "stay-away" of June of this year. In defiance of the Emergency and of the February bannings of most above-ground democratic political organizations, the three-day stay-away saw as many as 2.5 to 3 million people off work at its peak. The flag of resistance had been shown, visibly reinvigorating people's spirits. But the achievement, jointly engineered by the trade unions and the popular political structures, had also visibly shocked the powers that be, forcing both government and business to reconsider, at least momentarily, some of the more draconian aspects of their newly proposed labor legislation.

To be sure, a few people I talked with seemed to think that raw energy might still prove to be sufficient, that it was merely a matter of time before another spark would once again ignite the South African powder keg, this time exploding the whole sordid system. Certainly, the government is aware of the dangers of such sparks, fearful, for example, of the moment when Nelson Mandela might "die on them" in prison. (It is, of course, equally fearful of the possible implications of setting him free and hence remains frozen in indecision). More often, however, I discovered a mood of self-criticism to be at large within the movement, a feeling that last time the headlong escalation of the insurrection both underestimated the state's strength and too quickly outstripped the ability to give spreading resistance clear focus and maximum effect. Not that this fact had been entirely overlooked at the time; the months before the emergency had seen a growing awareness of the need to consolidate a stronger organizational base (street committees and people's courts, for example) in the townships. But the emergency has reinforced the point, even if, unfortunately, that very emergency means there is now much less room than previously for moving openly to consolidate such structures.

As a result, the question of how to strengthen the resistance movement was much on the minds of those with whom I spoke. Trade unions have a certain advantage in these terms, which is one reason why they have emerged as ever more politically central in the current phase (if also as increasingly important targets of state repression). They have the immediate need to mobilize and focus their members' energies for day-to-day struggles with capital over wages and working conditions. Yet in doing so they also create an organizational beachhead for more sweeping and potentially revolutionary confrontations with the state in future moments of crisis. Given the overall repressive atmosphere, township political organizations are more hard pressed to find equivalent modes of effective short-term action, ones that permit interim victories and build confidence among the people of their potential for wresting even more sweeping forms of democratic empowerment from the powers that be.

It was for this reason, apparently, that some UDF activists even briefly floated, for discussion, the idea of participating in local blacks-only elections and thereby seizing hold of state-structured township councils as one possible way of giving fresh focus to popular resistance to the state. Ultimately the idea was rejected, since the councils are, in fact, so tightly controlled by the apartheid administrative apparatus that they grant the democratic forces little real space for maneuver. In fact, only the most obvious of collaborators concluded otherwise, while Bishop Tutu and others, at some risk to themselves, called for a renewed boycott of such structures in the October elections. For its part, the state used its emergency powers (and considerable manipulation of the electoral procedures) to neutralize the boycott and to attempt—with no great success, as things turned out—to manufacture the appearance of support for those few blacks prepared to help it make its system work. Continuing boycott of the councils makes sense, I think, but some further discussion of the merits of the boycott made sense too. In any case, this was merely one example among the many I found of the readiness of South African democrats to scrutinize past practice in their effort to devise new and more relevant tactics.

There seemed, in fact, to be even greater tolerance within the resistance movement, more possibilities of comparing notes and learning from shared experience. Even if most (though not all) democratic activists accept the centrality to the movement of the UDF, with its close ties to the Freedom Charter tradition and the African National Congress

(ANC), there are those who have found that organization to be sometimes rather overbearing in its political approach. Interventions by Charterist spokespersons in the 1987 annual meeting of the country's leading trade union, COSATU, were criticized along those lines, for example. Yet last year's meeting in May provided a much more open forum for differences of opinion on key questions than had been the case only a year previously. And the meeting also pointed the way forward to a COSATU-sponsored September conference of a broad spectrum of unions and political organizations that would carry the discussion of relevant strategies and tactics further.

A broad spectrum? There are, of course, continuing divisions and differences of opinion even among those who seek to change South Africa. However much the country's evolution has been frozen by racism, it has become a complex and highly differentiated society. Union representatives spoke with me not only of class divisions within the black population, between workers and the small but growing middle class, but also of potential tensions and differentiation of interest between organized workers (with the relative privilege that the mere possession of a job affords them) and the vast army of the unemployed. There are also differences of emphasis between those with nationalist and those with socialist preoccupations (what does "transformation" really mean), between those with an exclusivist "black consciousness" agenda and those with a multi-racial one, between those who stress, under present conditions, the priority of underground activity and those who still find major scope for above-ground initiatives. But within the cacophony it was the resilience, the sober second thoughts, the openness to questioning, that most caught my ear and exemplified the promise of the present moment.

Unfortunately, come September, the COSATU-sponsored "all-in" conference was banned amid yet another round of detentions and restrictions against anti-apartheid activists and senior trade union officials. How difficult it is, under such circumstances, to find the necessary space to question and regroup. How difficult, too, to speak of wholly peaceful solutions instead of "armed struggle" against so malign and unyielding a state. Indeed, few I talked with seemed to doubt that armed struggle is one essential ingredient of the confrontation with apartheid, or that it is the ANC who will mobilize it. But practical questions remain, a point driven home to me by one particularly discomfiting coincidence: as I sat eating my lunch in a fast-food restaurant in one suburb of Johannesburg, a bomb went off, killing and maiming several people, in a similar establishment in another suburb of Johannesburg not many kilometers away. Interviews with certain ANC personnel cited in South African papers at the time raised the specter of anti-civilian terrorism emerging as a new tactic to "bring the war home" to the white population (although black civilians have also been the victims of the few instances of this kind of action). But who were the perpetrators of such incidents? And what impact do they have on the consciousness of both the black and white populations? These questions attracted intense debate; I was to obtain some answers on my way back to Canada.

Safely out of South Africa, I headed to Zambia to speak with external representatives of one of the key actors back inside, the African National Congress. For the ANC's part, armed action, while felt to be no more than complementary to broader kinds of political work, is nonetheless considered essential both to neutralizing the state's repressive apparatus and to heightening the saliency of resistance both at home and abroad. But "hard targets," not mere random terrorism designed to match the apartheid regime's own terror tactics, remain front and centre. True, they admitted, ANC military cadres had been frustrated at the movement's failure to deliver a knockout blow militarily during the insurrection, and there is sharp debate about how best to make the apartheid state pay for its brutal actions. Moreover, some "soft target" incidents— when not the work of right-wing provocateurs—may well represent mistakes made by guerrillas on the ground. And government intransigence may yet lead to an even more anarchic pattern of violence in South Africa. Still, the ANC seems fully committed to avoiding this kind of denouement, with the differences of emphasis among ANC activists that I was able to detect being less about the tactics of retaliatory violence than about other crucial questions.[74]

Not surprisingly, these latter paralleled debates that I had found to be taking place inside the country. What priority is to be assigned to internal mobilization for struggle on the one hand as against the mobilization of external pressure on the other? Should we place more emphasis, in the short run, on the laying down of a much firmer organizational base or on reaccelerating the pace of insurrectionary confrontation? Should we be searching, first and foremost, for allies across a broad spectrum of classes or placing more militant working-class demands at the centre of our concerns? Obviously, none of these are really either/or questions (although choices of emphasis on these matters do make a difference), and the policy debate that swirled around them within the ANC seemed to be unfolding in a reflective manner appropriate to the difficulties of the moment. Too bad, I thought (and not for the first time), that the South African government seeks only to sow chaos in defense of its blighted system rather than allow the creative capacities so evident in the ranks of the democratic movement full play in the building of a new South Africa. Perhaps this will be the ultimate indictment by historians of that government and its allies: the creative energies diverted, the years wasted, the blood spilt, because of its arrogant delaying of the "inevitable." Still, for the moment and in the period of struggle necessary to create the very possibility of a post-apartheid reconstruction, how important it is that there remains enough talent on the side of liberation to promise a continuing renewal of that struggle.

The downside of my trip? A decade ago I had written of my earlier visit that "after studying South Africa off and on for twenty years I saw little that I didn't expect to see. Yet how much more real—and how chilling." Chilling indeed. As I learned in southern Africa in the summer of 1988, Pretoria's intransigence means that the "inevitable" democratic transformation of South Africa will take rather longer than had been hoped and the costs of transformation will be even greater than I had feared. Chilling, but also inspiring. For there was an "up side," one which bore out my initial hunch that a few risks were worth running in order to touch, once again and at first hand, the "long, relentless arc of South African history." I had stolen a month from Pretoria and I had passed close enough to the cutting edge of revolution in that country—the people, the organizations, and the powerful yet indefinable ambience of resistance—to have sufficient reason to accentuate the positive. I had come away with the knowledge that, whatever the odds, the struggle to realize "transformation" is in good hands. And that these South African "hands"—the people, the organizations, the very spirit of revolution itself—deserve our support.

MEANWHILE THE END-GAME OF THE STRUGGLE seemed set to roll on into the early 1990s—and not only in South Africa itself but also within anti-apartheid circles in Canada and elsewhere. After all, the anti-apartheid movement had always been an uneasy but, nonetheless, entirely workable alliance between those who conceived the struggle in southern Africa as being primarily, even fairly exclusively, against the institutionalized racism that characterized the regimes there, and those who, like many of us in TCLSAC, saw the enemy as being, as much or more, the capitalist system, both local and worldwide, that interacted with racial oligarchy to advance its profits. Now as some new kind of South Africa seemed increasingly inevitable the Canadian government itself became more "reform-minded." This was part of a global turn that also witnessed an increasing awareness on the part of Margaret Thatcher of the long-term danger posed to capitalism's stake in the country from the continued radicalization of the anti-apartheid struggle that delay in meeting minimal demands for racial justice might bring.

As we now know, throughout the 1980s similar calculations were increasingly moving both South African capitalists and "responsible" politicians there—and even, as subsequent events would demonstrate, the ANC itself—toward the kind of compromise that would produce an extremely modest outcome to the liberation struggle in that country: the end of overt and institutionalized racist rule on the one–hand, but business as usual on the other. The real losers: the impoverished mass of black South Africans. A particular shock for us, though, was how quickly the anti-apartheid movement itself now melted away, disinclined to contemplate a "next liberation struggle" that might carry the fight beyond apartheid and on to challenging the inequities of capitalism, worldwide and local, itself. A dramatic sign of this in Canada was the "'Taking Strides' Consultative Conference" held in Ottawa in May, 1990, one that I attended and wrote about in *Southern Africa Report* (v. 6, #1, July, 1990), under the title "The I Love Lucy Show" (after Luci Edwards, whose role in the Conference will be quite evident in the text itself which follows—though her name should be spelled "Luci," not "Lucy" [my mistake, though it made for a good title!]).

CANADIAN ANTI-APARTHEID ACTIVISTS who gathered in Ottawa in May for their third national conference were hoping for great things—new ideas, new approaches, perhaps the formation of a national network. Only some of that emerged. And along with their disappointment, participants took home with them a feeling that the movement, created and nourished by grassroots activists since the late 60s, was in serious danger of being domesticated.

The title chosen for the Ottawa meeting sought to capture the moment: "Taking Strides—Towards a Non-racial Democratic South Africa" and stated the "main objective" to be "to come up with concrete means of intensifying support for the democratization of South Africa through improved support for the African National Congress and intensified application of Canadian sanctions against South Africa." Or, in the words of one of the other directive documents of the conference, the Forum's goal was "to bring together anti-apartheid activists from across the country to develop strategies to (a) strengthen support for sustained/increased sanctions and (b) to strengthen support for the ANC and democratic forces inside South Africa."

There were some good reasons to think the results of the Forum were positive. We seem to be closer to the establishment of a national anti-apartheid network. The meeting also re-affirmed our insistence that the Canadian government act ever more firmly against the South African government—and for the ANC.

Conference directives ignored

Yet this was not the whole story. Both the "successes" of the conference have a negative side. Some directives established by the conference for setting up the national network have already been ignored. And however firmly the conference participants may feel about the role of the Canadian government, External Affairs was clearly there to talk, not to listen.

Organizing for the meeting was done by the NGO-dominated Inter-Agency Working Group on Southern Africa (IAWGSA), established as a committee of the Canadian Council for International Cooperation (CCIC) and representing some twenty NGOs. It worked through a steering committee that also drew in several additional members—one each from the anti-apartheid networks in B.C., the West and the Atlantic region and a representative from the African National Congress. This committee in turn set an agenda, commissioned a series of background papers and invited the 100-plus participants, who included representatives from member organizations of IAWGSA, anti-apartheid coalitions and groups from across Canada, the ANC and SACTU and other South Africans. And finally, the committee identified a number of "resource persons" and "facilitators" for the working groups into which the Forum was to break from time to time.

Even in the run-up to the Conference, there were signs of behind-the-scenes manoeuvrings by NGO delegates on the Steering Committee that suggested an attempt to narrow and control the Forum's agenda.

The whole idea of having "resource people" was put in doubt by several on the steering committee, at the eleventh hour of preparation for the Forum. They apparently feared that designated resource people like Ottawa's Linda Freeman, Calgary's Don Ray and myself would be a bit too outspokenly critical of Canadian government policy. Although the Steering Committee entertained the idea of cancelling participation by the resource people, they rejected that in favour of warning us against "dominating" discussions.

These manoeuvrings were not readily visible to conference delegates, but in the very first plenary there were visible signals that all was not well. Two delegates from South Africa spoke—Paulus Mashatile of the United Democratic Front and Nomvula Mokonyane of the Federation of Transvaal Women. (The third scheduled South African, Moses Mayekiso of COSATU and the Alexandra Civic Organization was unavoidably delayed and spoke the next morning). But no spokesperson from the Canadian anti-apartheid movement was invited as the third speaker. The only other speaker chosen by the Steering Committee was Lucy Edwards, head of the "Southern African Task Force" of the Ministry of External Affairs. Edwards didn't say much that hadn't been heard before. She presented Canadian sanctions in the most positive light, ignoring statistics that show trade with South Africa continues to increase. She milked the government role in establishing the Mandela Fund for all it was worth and suggested that there was money for "non-political" ANC activities.

No anti-apartheid voice

Many delegates were aghast that no one of comparable stature from the anti-apartheid movement was given a position on the platform to challenge Edwards' remarks—and the Canadian government. Certainly, Linda Freeman (who annually chronicles the shortcomings of Canadian government policy in SAR) would have been an obvious candidate for this task. Suzanne Dansereau of CIDMAA and Dennis Lewycky in Ottawa had also written an informative background paper on the subject for the conference.

This background paper, and others prepared and paid for by the Forum, were included in delegate kits, but were never referred to throughout the course of the conference. Some critical questions for the speakers did come from the floor and Peter Mahlangu, the ANC's representative in Canada who was also at the dais, took the opportunity to query some of Edwards' more outrageous statements as to the exemplary nature of Canada's sanctions performance.

The Canadian government's record is not the worst in the world. Clark has resisted the temptation to abandon the idea of sanctions until there are much stronger signs of what he terms "irreversible change." But there are also severe limits to how far Canada is prepared to go and there is a Canadian government agenda that seeks to limit change in South Africa as much as it seeks to facilitate it. The Forum would have been an excellent opportunity for activists from across Canada to reach a common and critical understanding of official Canada's policies. It was an opportunity lost.

"Mistakes were made"

In response to strong criticism from the next day's working groups of the decision to give Lucy Edwards a platform, the Conference's steering committee admitted a "mistake" had been made. But the evidence suggests it was more than a mistake. Key members of that committee—Ted Scott, former Anglican Church Primate and government-appointee to 1985's Commonwealth Eminent Persons' Group, and Ann Mitchell, executive director of the Ottawa-based International Defense and Aid Fund of South Africa (IDAFSA)—were frank in private conversation about their feeling that a "conciliatory" approach to the Canadian government is in order, rather than what they feel is the old-fashioned "confrontational" approach.

These differences are not new. Ted Scott, despite his long and honourable history of anti-apartheid work, has always been seen by church militants as something of a mixed blessing. His commitment to the southern African cause has helped legitimate anti-apartheid work, in the eyes of government and parishioners. But it is testimony to his "acceptability" with government that he now holds a number of key positions in the proliferating NGOs. He is considered the de facto church representative to External Affairs, he is on the board of the South African Education Trust Fund, president of the IDAFSA and, since earlier this year, chair of IAWGSA. But he has remained conservative in his political outlook and something of a "loose cannon" in his political style. Are the benefits he brings to the movement (not least the credibility he lends it) outweighed by his role in helping, however unconsciously, to domesticate it?

Something of the ambiguous feelings the movement has towards Scott's role surfaced in the Forum when Lucy Edwards herself announced that Scott would be briefing Joe Clark on the Monday following the Forum on the results of its deliberations. Most delegates seemed to feel Scott's willy-nilly appointment as sole conference spokesperson to the federal government was not quite adequate as a way of representing the views of the assembled anti-apartheid movement.

Different strategies needed

There is room for different strategies by different anti-apartheid groups in dealing with the Canadian government. It's too simple to see Ann Mitchell's preference for taming the anti-apartheid movement as springing directly from the fact that IDAFSA is the beneficiary of Canadian government funding. But most of us are experienced enough as activists to know that receiving government money plays a role in the decisions you make about your work. It was hard for SAR workers who were present at the Forum to escape the feeling that some of the machinations there exemplified the dangers identified in an earlier *SAR* article ("Buying Silence?," February, 1990).

In any case, the real loss to the conference was the fact that virtually none of these issues were debated by delegates to the Forum. Of course, part of this may also have been due to the Forum's structure. In the laudable pursuit of a genuine democratization of the proceedings, emphasis fell upon the six to eight workshop sessions for doing the bulk of the Forum's work. In many of these, questions about the underlying premises of our activities did surface. But the energy generated in the groups rarely found its way back to the brief plenary sessions interspersed throughout the two full days of the Forum.

However, by the end of the conference some momentum had been recouped from the first day. The basic mood of the delegates, particularly from the broad anti-apartheid network and from Canada's regions, was much more sceptical of the Canadian government's southern Africa record and consequently more confrontational than some of the Steering Committee may have wished. In its final communique, the Conference did "call on the Canadian government to adopt a clearer and bolder approach in support of democracy in South Africa," including "maintaining and extending the economic sanctions against South Africa; downgrading diplomatic relations with official South Africa; and upgrading relations with the ANC and the anti-apartheid movement in South Africa."

ANC agenda

The ANC had its own agenda at the Forum, some signs of which also surfaced during the period of run-up to the Ottawa meeting. The ANC representative on the conference steering committee queried the propriety of a paper prepared by SAR at the request of the conference coordinator.

The problem? The paper raised the question of socialism in South Africa too overtly and was too critical in its examination of the various forces working for and against the long-term socioeconomic transformation of the South Africa that is now in the making.

What seemed even more crucial to ANC preoccupations was its concern to further institutionalize its centrality—perhaps even to guarantee for itself exclusive standing—at the core of the Canadian anti-apartheid movement. There's no argument against the proposition that the ANC is the key political actor for democratic change in South Africa at present, and so deserves the full support of all Canadians and of the Canadian government. But there are other questions to be raised about South Africa by anti-apartheid activists. One of the most important is what degree of exclusivity of support for the ANC is advisable. The descriptive phrases in the two guidelines for the conference quoted earlier speak, in one case, of "support for the ANC," in the other of "support for the ANC and democratic forces inside South Africa." The conference seemed to oscillate back and forth between these two positions. The tension between the two formulae was one that remained implicit in much that occurred during the conference, but was one more point that was never really talked through. In consequence, the potential implication of such issues for the terms of our support work was largely lost.

Building a "civil society"

The case for "pluralistic support" is not an easy point to make in a context like the Ottawa Forum. Both the ANC delegation and some Canadian participants in the Forum tended to regard any qualification of support for the ANC as hostility. Yet those who raised the question were not agents of forces like the Pan-Africanist Congress or Inkatha. They saw themselves close in spirit to the position of Moses Mayekiso, the COSATU representative who spoke Saturday morning and confirmed that this issue is up for debate within South Africa itself.

Without querying the crucial importance of the ANC, Mayekiso made the strongest of cases for the existence in South Africa of autonomous trade unions and civic associations. These organizations, he argued, deserve the direct support of Canadians both in their capacity as prominent voices for democratic change in its own right and as a force for keeping the long-term necessity for socioeconomic transformation on the agenda of even a formally democratized South Africa.

Other prominent ANC members have voiced similar points of view. Joe Slovo, a member of the ANC negotiating team meeting with De Klerk, has written of his concern that in the failed "socialisms" of Eastern Europe a key weakness was that "the trade union movement became an adjunct of the state and party" and that women's and youth organizations "instead of being guided by the aspirations and interests of their constituencies ... were turned into support bases for the ongoing dictates of the state and party apparatus" with entirely negative results. "Old-style commandism and sectarianism" must give way to "effective autonomy" and "political pluralism," says Slovo.

The same position can be found in statements by ANC National Executive member Aziz Pahad, who recently said that the ANC must become a broad front in order to wrest political rights from the De Klerk government: "A front cannot just be a get-together of all tendencies where there are no ideological battles taking place. The very nature of a front is that you fight for positions." In short, in addition to support for the ANC, support for the building of a strong and diverse "civil society" (in Mayekiso's phrase) must be seen as an essential part of an effort to create effective political and socioeconomic democracy in South Africa—whatever political party may be in power.

ANC role in national network

The majority of delegates to the Forum did not see the importance of such questions—although a related matter did surface more heatedly. It was the question of how the ongoing relationship between the ANC and the new national anti-apartheid network-in-the-making is to be institutionalized. The ANC saw itself as becoming not just an integral member of that network but also a member of any national coordinating committee that is now to be established.

Only in the Ontario regional caucus was this premise seriously questioned. Some Ontario delegates felt the idea of the ANC becoming an actual member of a Canadian organization, let alone a member of its coordinating committee, to be both unprecedented in support-work experience and to be questionable practice in political terms. One delegate wondered what might happen in a situation where either the ANC disagreed with the anti-apartheid network or the anti-apartheid network disagreed with the ANC. The ANC is being forced to develop very complex relationships with the Canadian government. It's not too difficult to imagine a situation in which the ANC, for perfectly good diplomatic reasons, found it advisable to take a softer public line towards the Canadian government than the Canadian anti-apartheid movement was prepared to do. Wouldn't an arms-length relationship be more advisable all round? was the argument. In the end, in the Ontario caucus, the principle of ANC inclusion as a member of the national coordinating committee carried the day by straw vote.

In the final plenary, the majority for ANC inclusion was overwhelming, most delegates feeling comfortable with a definition, in practice, of anti-apartheid activists as a virtual support network for the ANC. Peter Mahlangu declined the voting rights on the coordinating committee that some delegates now urged upon him, arguing that, in any case, with the ANC on the committee, and the practice of consensus decision-making, such rights would be superfluous. Yet almost immediately thereafter Mahlangu was on his feet again, querying the use in the final communique of the phrase "it is important to support the democratic anti-apartheid organizations" (used once, in a text with numerous other direct references to the ANC) as insufficiently specific with regard to the primacy of the ANC.

The strong support by conference delegates for ANC centrality tended to overshadow an uneasiness on the part of others, including those from some of the larger constituencies within the network (the churches, for example, and TCLSAC), with the ANC-Canada's propensity [similar to that of its parent organization vis-à-vis South Africa itself!] to seek to control outcomes. These constituencies have formed their own direct links with South African counterparts in ways that manifest some of the best support work by Canadians.[75] This work is increasing in importance because of the growing number of western interests—including the Canadian government—looking for "reasonable" voices they can support. The anti-apartheid movement must intensify its own work, making sure that the voices and needs of women, workers, youths and others who demand real transformation don't get muffled.

Nelson Mandela Fund

All members of the network will support the ANC pretty unreservedly and, if the network can put new resources at the ANC's disposal, that will be a laudable outcome. There is already in existence the Nelson Mandela Fund, a non-governmental initiative to collect untied funds in Canada to be put at the disposal of the ANC. This was originally suggested by Joe Clark as an alternative to direct governmental support for the ANC's political struggle. It may also have been his attempt to simultaneously distance the Canadian government from overt political support for the ANC, while scoring points with the movement for taking its cause seriously. It is therefore something of a two-edged sword for those who seek to expose the contradictory nature of Tory foreign and domestic policies.

Beyond the Mandela Fund there is also the question of possible direct Canadian governmental assistance to the ANC. Lucy Edwards fudged this issue at the Forum, ignoring the government's bleak record on this front over the years. But she did suggest the door is now wide open for the Canadian government to back the movement's "non-political" activities. And finally, what about the ANC's "Relocation Fund"? It was designed by the ANC as a global initiative to help facilitate the return to South Africa of thousands of exiles and refugees and identified in the Forum's final communique as a priority item. Shouldn't the Canadian government be expected to contribute to that Fund—and shouldn't it be pressured to do so?

There is, in short, plenty of work awaiting the new network. How soon will that network become a concrete reality? That brings us to the last disturbing aspect of the conference.

The "how" of the new network

The need to propose some mechanism for following through on Forum decisions should have been foreseen by organizers. Apparently it wasn't. In the final plenary, after regional groups had discussed and presented what they felt the national network was to look like, delegates had to decide who would organize the Forum's recommendations, including the new network. Some delegates wanted a brand new interim executive, with strong representation from grassroots forces, to avoid the Ottawa-centric nature of so much of the Forum activity. A stalemate was developing.

But many participants were within minutes of departing for the airport. The pressure to find a solution very quickly was strong. One delegate suggested it be left in the hands of the conference Steering Committee. Even without any discussion, the unpopularity of that suggestion was obvious. A change was made—leave it to the expanded committee (comprised of the Steering Committee plus about eight more people who had acted as "facilitators" at the forum and who did represent a rather wider regional and sectoral spread than the Steering Committee alone). Many objected to giving the conference organizers such a pivotal role in setting up the national network. But there was a vote, and the Conference Committee became the proposed network's Interim Committee by a narrow margin. Ironically, when this Interim Committee met immediately after the final plenary session, a resolution, put forward by a member of the original Steering Committee, proposed that the work be left solely to that Committee. Objections were made, but they were overruled. And so the very group that had brought us the "I Love Lucy Show," and that has the most to lose in a high-profile, vocal, critical anti-apartheid network, is at the helm, its most important task the drawing up of a model for a national anti-apartheid network.

If the Consultative Forum did anything, it exposed the complexity of issues around anti-apartheid work in Canada. Many of those issues have not been fully explored by activists. In the months to follow many anti-apartheid groups will meet as regions, to carry forward their own work. Eventually they will be called on to examine—and accept or reject—the structure that the network's Interim Committee will propose. That means that this important issue—what we want the network to do and how we want to do it—will be back on our plates within the next few months. It will need all our attention, plus close consultation between regions, to make sure that it truly reflects the wishes of all true activists.

DESPITE OUR CONFUSIONS IN CANADA, the transition in South Africa itself of course moved forward, if somewhat rockily. Now, however, the actual substance of that transition (democracy? capitalism? socialism?) became a subject of much heated debate—both within South Africa and without. The idea of bringing various trade unionists from both Canada and South Africa to discuss such important questions seemed a good one[76] and fortunately we were able to get funding for such a workshop from a broad range of Canadian trade unions, from the IDRC, and from various units at my own university, York. [77] I summarized this unusual and extremely instructive event in *Southern Africa Report* (9, 1, July, 1993) under the title "'Workers of the World,' Debate: A South Africa/Canada Workshop" and it could be of interest to some present readers.

There was one dimension of it that was of a particular interest anecdotally—but, we can now see, of rather broader resonance. For while we were not, at TCLSAC, fully informed of the negotiations that the ANC was carrying on with capital itself and the dramatic compromises being made by the movement—even as it engaged, on another front, in its end-game negotiations with the racist apartheid state—there was some evidence of an increasingly rightward tilt on the part of the ANC even at the York workshop itself. Particularly striking, in this respect, was the demeanour of the representative the ANC chose to send to Toronto in response to our invitation. He was a person (Tito Mboweni) who was to go on to become a very major player in the economic team—and soon to be both the Minister of Labour in the ANC government and then the Governor of the crucial South African Reserve Bank—assigned to oversee the economy.

Yet, interestingly, from the beginning of his visit to Canada he was sharply critical of me and my fellow organizers regarding the quality of the hospitality he was receiving. The university residence accommodation in which we lodged him and his colleagues (including a number of the Canadian delegates) contrasted sharply with the penthouse treatment he had received the only other time he had visited Toronto, on which occasion he had been hosted by Toronto lawyer and corporate fixer, "Fast Eddie" Goodman. Last time, too, he had had business-class air service all the way and he insisted upon our upgrading his ticket to that level again!

The most telling incident of all came, however, in one of the sessions of the Workshop itself. Here the possibilities of forging a progressive and a socialist economic future for South Africa were being debated. Our ANC friend's contribution was, as it turned out, to be an extended joke about FRELIMO in Mozambique, obviously chosen to provide a cautionary tale as to the possible futures open to South Africa. Mboweni entered into an elaborate yarn which found a Mozambican fisherman catching a big fish and then, on his walk back home, discovering that there was, at the bare-shelved shops, no oil and no wood available for the cooking, no matches to light any fire in the first place, and no rice to be purchased to accompany the meal. Discouraged, the fisherman returns to the sea and throws the fish back in. Then, as the fish swims away, he makes one final leap to the surface, raises a fin militantly and shouts: "Viva FRELIMO."

A mildly funny joke, perhaps, if you bracketed off the context of the workshop we were engaged in. In the event, a kind of embarrassed silence followed. But the real answer came over dinner that night. I said mildly that I wondered at the appropriateness of such a joke presented in such an unvarnished manner in the context of the serious discussion we were having. Our ANC guest was in the process of laughing off my perhaps rather po-faced comment when another South African union representative, a black comrade from Cape Town, said "You know, Tito, when you made that comment and I thought of all the sacrifices Mozambicans had made for our liberation, I felt sick at my stomach." Conversation ground to a halt. It could come as no shock, then, to soon read (as cited earlier) in Hein Marais' carefully crafted book of a few years later that "by 1994... the left had lost the macroeconomic battle"!

MEANWHILE, "THE LONG 1980S" DRAGGED ON—despite the fact of the unbanning of the ANC and of Nelson Mandela's release in 1990 from prison—through the tense violence-scarred period of negotiations and constitution-making in South Africa (up to the nation-wide elections of 1994). Personally, though, I did find that I could now return to South Africa—this time armed with a visa. And for me it was a wonderful moment, and not only in terms of the new possibilities that seemed to be opening up in South Africa. It also formed a perfect pendant to a violent decade that had opened for me with the assassination of Ruth First (as seen at the outset of this chapter). For the event in question, what drew me to South Africa specifically at this time was, in fact, a "Ruth First Memorial Colloquium," one to feature a stellar lineup of Ruth's friends and comrades in attendance and now to be held on the terrain of a new South Africa-in-the-making! I wrote both about the event and the larger picture of South Africa that the trip enabled me to piece together in an article entitled "Mass Action: South Africa's Second Referendum" for *Southern Africa Report* (8, 2, November 1992). I reminded my readers (as I have recorded earlier in this chapter) that ten years before—August 17, 1982—I had been there when Ruth "was struck down by the South African government, victim of a parcel bomb delivered to her office at the Centre of African Studies in Maputo, Mozambique" I then noted that "since her death an annual Ruth

First Memorial Lecture has been given in Maputo but this year, on the tenth anniversary of her death, it seemed appropriate to bring the event home." I then continued:

ACCORDINGLY, A "RUTH FIRST MEMORIAL COLLOQUIUM" was planned, to be held at the University of the Western Cape in Cape Town, and intended to explore the theme "The Possibilities of Radical Transformation in Southern Africa: Theory and Policy." I was honoured to have been invited to attend and address the colloquium workshop—and I was even able, at last, to obtain a visa and thus take part in the events!

The two days of workshops were enormously interesting; I'll say something more about them below. Nonetheless, the centre-piece was the public event set for the 17th itself (the first evening of the colloquium), a mass rally at UWC where some 4000 people gathered to hear Nelson Mandela honour Ruth, an old friend and colleague. Others were there as well—Oliver Tambo, Govan Mbeki, Pallo Jordan, Graça Machel from Mozambique, Nadine Gordimer, Ruth's husband Joe Slovo and two of her daughters (including Shawn, who authored the screenplay of A World Apart, the film about Ruth First's early years in South Africa)—and several spoke. But it was Mandela himself who spoke most eloquently about Ruth First's life in the democratic movement—and who also linked her death most dramatically to the present moment. His theme: the continuing role of the South African state in meting out, either directly or by proxy, the cruellest forms of repression, including death, to those who challenge it.

The energy in the hall was astonishing, an earnest of just how eagerly black South Africans seek to embrace their freedom. But Mandela's message was also sobering, a grim reminder of how difficult the transition to a new and democratic South Africa has become. Indeed, a parallel tension—between the energy available for change and the repression that continues to thwart such change—framed my trip itself. I arrived in South Africa in the immediate aftermath of the dramatic week of mass action (early August) and left just days before the cruel events at Bisho in the Ciskei (early September), the callous shooting of ANC demonstrators by that Bantustan's military junta. The drive for democracy, the opposition to it by those in positions of power: it was difficult to escape the conclusion that, under present circumstances, any such transition threatens to remain firmly stalemated. And in a festering condition of stalemate, things don't just stand still. They can deteriorate.

De Klerk: architect of stalemate

What needs underscoring here is that the principle architect of the current stalemate has been President F. W. de Klerk himself. De Klerk quite simply does not want to see any meaningful institutionalization of democratic structures—with the significant empowerment of blacks that would inevitably accompany it—in South Africa. This is the one thing most South Africans I talked to were agreed upon. Contrary to the misleading expectations raised by much western press coverage, de Klerk used the breathing space his referendum victory earned him within the white polity merely to stall, in CODESA and elsewhere, on majority demands. This, and the ongoing pattern of state-sponsored terrorism (e.g., Boipatong), were what had brought negotiations to a shuddering halt by the middle of the year.

Such stalling need come as no surprise, of course. After all, one of the National Party's principle slogans during the referendum campaign was "If you're afraid of majority rule, vote yes." Yet some foreign observers have been tempted to see de Klerk's emphasis on "white vetoes" and extreme decentralization of power as reflecting a judicious, even laudable, effort to curb the excesses of simple majoritarianism (editorials in Toronto's *Globe and Mail*—of December 21, 1991, and March 19, 1992—have been previously identified by SAR as prime examples of this tendency). South Africans know better. They realize that the ANC is itself open to discussion of various kinds of reasonable constitutional compromise—although not of the sort that would simply cripple the ability of any post-apartheid government to redress apartheid's grim socioeconomic legacy. And they sense, equally clearly, that de Klerk's principle interest is not in "good government" but, even at this late date, in white government.

This is the context in which other recent developments must be understood. Yet how difficult it seems to be for overseas journalists to concede the obvious. Take the recent article by the usually far more reliable *Globe and Mail* foreign affairs analyst Linda Hossie on the implications of the Bisho massacre, an article which greeted me almost immediately upon my return to Toronto from South Africa ("Tied together in a tug of war," *Globe and Mail*, September 14). By her account, the ANC had created, more or less out of whole cloth, the drive towards "mass action" that so panicked the Ciskei leadership. How easy to forget that it was the mass actions of the 1970s and 1980s that themselves pitch-forked the ANC back into prominence and helped free Mandela.

In fact, by June, the situation had become one in which the ANC had to run in order to keep pace with its followers! For the fact is that, two and a half years after Mandela's release, people in the Ciskei homeland still suffer under a cruel military dictatorship, one sustained, quite visibly, by the Pretoria regime and without a shred of legitimacy of its own. Indeed, virtually all the black South Africans I spoke with during my recent trip felt themselves to be further away from a democratic resolution of their situation than they were in February 1990. Why is it so difficult for outsiders to take this fact seriously, they asked me. Is it because we are black?

The logic of mass action

Small wonder that direct action to accelerate the process of change broke out on so many fronts in South Africa in recent months: the Ciskei demonstration was merely one example of a general escalation of confrontational politics on the part of the ANC and its allies (notably the trade union movement). This found its fullest expression to date not in the Ciskei but in August's successful week of nation-wide mass action, highlighted by a two-day general strike that saw as many as four million workers stay at home. The press in Canada did not greet this event with anything like the fanfare that accompanied de Klerk's referendum triumph some months earlier. Yet I found South Africans themselves quick to suggest that the results of this "second referendum" were, in many ways, more significant than de Klerk's own victory. It underscored the fact that the vast majority of blacks in South Africa are, quite simply, staunch in their democratic demands—and that the ANC stands as the chief political vehicle of such demands.

Ms. Hossie, in the article referred to above, will have none of this. Instead, she chooses to see the ANC as "working against itself, with two strategies in collision—one favouring mass action and another attempting to maintain negotiations." And she imagines hardliners and moderates within the movement to be deeply split over this issue. Yet the ANC leaders (of very diverse ideological stripe) I spoke with felt the two strategies to be fundamentally complementary, arguing convincingly that mass action was the only card they had left to play in order to pressure de Klerk to move forward. International sanctions have, regrettably, all but withered away, while the ANC has, unilaterally, demobilized any capacity it may once have had to wage effective guerrilla struggle. What other way has there been to focus the white government's attention on the demands of the vast majority of the South African population? The ANC's critics, including Ms. Hossie, have no answer to this question.

True, there are some differences of opinion within the democratic movement as to just what mix of "mass action" and "negotiations" might prove to be most effective. Some leaders probably are tempted by the allure of "elite-pacting"—a "done-deal" behind closed doors—as the principal way forward in South Africa and may be inclined to see mass action as a secondary tactic, a kind of "tap" to be turned on and off if, as and when occasion dictates. At the other extreme, a certain romanticism has sometimes marked the approach of those who are much more firmly committed to the centrality of the mass action approach. Thus, despite the fresh revelations every day of the cruellest kind of state-sanctioned repression in South Africa I still heard a great deal of talk amongst activists about the possible relevance of the "Leipzig way" for South Africa. After all, mass action in pursuit of democratic demands worked in Eastern Europe, didn't it? Why not in South Africa?[78]

But, clearly, conditions are not the same. For the most part, when push came to shove in Eastern Europe the erstwhile communist regimes had neither the will nor the capacity to slash back against broad, democratically inspired coalitions. The ANC finds in de Klerk, his security establishment and its vicious allies—including homeland heavies like Gatsha Buthelezi and the Ciskei's Oupa Gqozo—much more ruthless and intransigent defenders of the status quo. Note, then, that de Klerk's intransigence is a roadblock that confronts all those who make up the democratic movement and one that continues to bind them together. To magnify what are really quite modest tactical differences into major contradictions within that movement (as Hossie does) is, once again, to lose sight of where the main responsibility for lack of democratic progress in South Africa lies.

Negotiations: the real issues

Clarity on this issue became all the more important as, in early October, de Klerk and Mandela began to grope their way back toward negotiations. For those committed to a democratic future in South Africa it would be nice to think that de Klerk has been chastened by mass action and the results of the "second referendum" and that he will return to the table ready to accept more of "the inevitable" than has been the case heretofore. Understandably, it is only on the assumption that he has that the ANC might itself be once again ready to participate—and not primarily, as Ms. Hossie and other media pundits would have it, because it has been "shocked [by the Ciskeian events] ... into recognizing that they must start talking again"! Talking about what? To encourage readers to imagine some kind of retreat from the threshold of reasonable and meaningful democratic demands on the part of the ANC would be seriously to mislead them.

Fortunately, there are also others, notably in some corners of the business community (both within South Africa and abroad), who have also begun to recognize that de Klerk's constitutional sleights-of-hand, so unacceptable to the majority, merely produce political gridlock. Such gridlock, in turn, spells chaos and from conditions of chaos few can expect to profit. Some of these players realize that only by having a relatively strong ANC preside over the present transition can any new dispensation be legitimated in the eyes of most black South Africans. Moreover, they are increasingly confident that the economic clout of capital and the discipline of the global market-place can be expected to cow the ANC into adopting moderate socioeconomic policies, whatever the nature of the new constitution.

Of course, they may be unduly confident in this regard. As I found during my trip, there remain many—both within the ANC and within the powerful labour movement—who are sceptical as to whether solutions that are primarily market-led can produce either growth or equity under present South African conditions. Certainly, this was the thrust of much of the discussion at the Ruth First colloquium itself in which the gathering of activists and academics both from South Africa and abroad sought to give renewed content to socialist aspirations in a new South Africa—sought, in short, to speak to South Africa's future problems in a voice that Ruth First herself ("committed revolutionary, journalist and academic") would have recognized.

Debating transformation

My own contribution to the colloquium was an attempt to make sense of actual socioeconomic struggles now being engaged in South Africa as representing a promising project of "structural reform." I noted the extent to which those engaged in such struggles both sought, self-consciously, to keep alive a sense of long-term transformation even when engaged in relatively modest reforms and also saw a contribution to the cumulative empowerment of the popular classes as a necessary ingredient of any reform worth the effort. Along some such lines, I argued, South African radicals are developing a practice that could avoid "the twin dangers of, one the one hand, a romantic (and ultimately all-too-rhetorical) ultra-revolutionary approach and, on the other, collapse into a mild reformism that will do little to alter the balance of inherited class power and conservative/ technocratic decision-making." And I was gratified to find that my own emphases found resonance in the presentations of others who also discerned the seeds of a practice of "radical" or "revolutionary reform" emerging in present day South Africa.

It was apparent that the pull on the ANC leadership towards "moderation" in a post-apartheid South Africa is strong. This led several of the most vocal participants in the colloquium (both veteran revolutionary and long-time ANC critic Neville Alexander and left-leaning ANC economic advisor Lawrence Harris) to disparage the likelihood that the ANC will ever push its egalitarian demands beyond the purely political realm and seek in any very dramatic way to democratize the economy along socialist lines.[79] Perhaps so! Nonetheless, it was interesting to hear the debate about the transformation of South Africa joined at such a high level as was the case at the Ruth First colloquium.

Moreover, one sensed that differences—both within the popular movement and between that movement and the representatives of other interests in society—over just such crucial socioeconomic issues are likely to define much of the content of the democratic politics of a new South Africa. But what "new South Africa"? It was difficult, this summer, for me to escape the sense that South Africans are still an uncomfortably long way from entering the post-apartheid moment. Perhaps "liberal centre" and "radical left" do increasingly agree that only a firmly democratic political system can promise the stable context for the debate and struggle that the country's future requires—an important advance, if true. But how unfortunate—and how fraught with danger—that F. W. de Klerk still refuses to embrace any such understanding.

As it happened, the various machinations of De Klerk and his cronies proved, in terms of constitution-making, to be of little obvious and immediate avail. Soon there was to be an election, and the ANC and Mandela would advance ineluctably into office. A famous victory indeed, although just how qualified it would prove to be was not yet entirely apparent. Only the evidence of the post-apartheid period would force some of us to write a great deal more about that, as the next two chapters will suggest.

---

1. In this chapter as in all subsequent chapters the various texts of the time that are included here as "freeze-frames" (see introduction) appear in sans serif; those sections in printed serif text are freshly written for these volumes. Similarly, all those footnotes printed in sans serif text in this footnote section,

as keyed to this and all following chapters, are reproduced as they appeared in the original publication of the texts incorporated in the various chapters; those in serif text are new to this volume.

2. The two passages cited here are from my essay "Julius Nyerere's Socialism: Learning from Tanzania" in *The Next Liberation Struggle: Capitalism, Socialism and Democracy in Southern Africa* (Toronto, New York, London and Durban: Between-the-Lines, Monthly Review Press, Merlin Press, and University of KwaZulu-Natal Press, 2005).
3. Some readers may find the overall argument that backs such assertions worth investigating both in the recent essay just mentioned (ch. 7 in *The Next Liberation Struggle*, ibid.) as well as in a myriad of my writings on Tanzania closer to the time (not least my extended essay "Tanzania: African Socialism in One-Country," that is chapter 6 in Giovanni Arrighi and John S. Saul, *Essays on the Political Economy of Africa* (New York: Monthly Review Press, 1972).
4. This paper, entitled "An Approach to the University College Problems" (n.d.) and labelled "Confidential," is in my possession.
5. See "Conference on the Role of the University College, Dar es Salaam, in a Socialist Tanzania: Proposals for Discussion Submitted by a Group of Staff," March 9, 1967 (in the author's possession).
6. As cited in footnote 4, above.
7. As cited in footnote 5, above.
8. "High-Level Manpower for Socialism," being chapter 6 in Idrian Resnick (ed.), *Revolution by Education*, (Arusha: Longman of Tanzania, 1968).
9. The reference here is to the quote from George Sorel that served as an epigraph to my original article in the Resnick volume cited above: "Every time I have approached a question I have found that my inquiries ended by giving rise to new problems, and the further I pushed my investigations the more disquieting these new problems became. But philosophy is perhaps after all only the recognition of the abysses which lie on each side of the footpath that the vulgar follow with the serenity of somnambulists."
10. On this later Atkinson College/York University experience and its link to my intellectual formation in East Africa, see my chapter, "Thanks for the Memory," in Brenda Spotton Visano and Kristen Taylor (eds.), *Room to Grow: Celebrating Atkinson's Living Legacy* (Toronto: York University, 2009).
11. See the two volume collection *Socialism in Tanzania* (Nairobi: East African Publishing House, 1972 and 1973, volumes that I jointly edited with Lionel Cliffe), and the several other volumes in which I also played some editorial role: *Towards Socialist Planning: Tanzania Studies #1* (Dar es Salaam: Tanzania Publishing House, 1972); *Socialism and Participation: Tanzania's 1970 National Elections* (Dar es Salaam: Tanzania Publishing House, 1974); and *Rural Cooperation in Tanzania* (Dar es Salaam: Tanzania Publishing House, 1975)
12. Arrighi and Saul, *op. cit.*
13. As noted in the text, this shortened version of our argument appeared under the title "Socialism and Economic Development in Tropical Africa" in *Monthly Review* (May, 1969). As then described by the editors of *Monthly Review* "this is a condensation of a much longer article with the same title that appeared in the *Journal of Modern African Studies*, VI, 2 (1968)," which appeared also, in the same

extended form, as chapter 1 in Arrighi and Saul, *op. cit*; for a closely linked text, see also, in the latter volume, chapter 2, "Nationalism and Revolution in Sub-Saharan Africa."

14. On this general subject see also G. Arrighi, "International Corporations, Labor Aristocracies, and Economic Development in Tropical Africa," in Arrighi and Saul, op. cit.
15. Cf. Ignacy Sachs, "On Growth Potential, Proportional Growth, and Perverse Growth" in *Czechoslovak Economic Papers* (Prague), VII, 1966.
16. Cf. Peter Worsley, *The Third World*, London, 1964, ch. 4. For a detailed critique of "populism," see John S. Saul, "On African Populism," in Arrighi and Saul, *op. cit.*
17. Roger Murray, "Militarism in Africa," *New Left Review*, 38 (1966).
18. See Samir Amin, *Trois experiences africaines de developpement* (Paris, 1965).
19. Bob Fitch and Mary Oppenheimer, *Ghana: End of an Illusion* (New York: Monthly Review Press, 1966).
20. See Roger Murray, "Militarism in Africa," *ibid.*
21. This article is also reprinted, together with much other material of interest by a wide range of authors (including Shivji's own original text) in Lionel Cliffe and John S. Saul (eds.), *Socialism in Tanzania*: Vol. 1, *Politics*, and Vol. 2, *Policies* (Nairobi: East African Publishing House, 1972 and 1973).
22. Shivji's piece was originally published in *Maji Maji*, #1 (January, 1971), pp. 9-15, being itself an extended and revised version of a review article that originally appeared in *The Standard* (Dar es Salaam), October 23, 1970. It was soon republished, together with the debate to which I have alluded and which it soon spawned, both as a book, *The Silent Class Struggle* (Dar es Salaam: Tanzanian Publishing House, 1973) and as an extended concluding section in Cliffe and Saul (eds.), *op. cit.* Shivji's manner of conceptualizing the Tanzanian problematic seems to have been characteristic of the work of the Cheche socialists: see also Karim Hirji whose related article a related article, "Salient Implications of the Silent Class Struggle" (Cheche, #3 [October, 1970]), suggests, controversially, that "the neo-colonial bureaucracy is in fact seen to have a social base in the international bourgeoisie whose interests it objectively serves." A wide variety of alternative formulations emerged from a stimulating exchange of articles and letters concerning the nature of Tanzanian politics in general and of TANU in particular in *The Nationalist* (Dar es Salaam) in October-November, 1970.
23. We very soon saw, for example, that when a real rural force of this nature began to emerge from below in the form of the Ruvuma Development Association the President was merely content to support the party's initiative to smash it, thereby flashing a clear and dispiriting signal as the scope and depth of both democratic and socialist commitment in the long term. In addition, the subsequent crushing of workers' attempts to realize effective participation and real power from below at the Mount Carmel Rubber Factory and elsewhere soon put paid to that hope as well. See, on the fate of the ujamaa programme, Leander Schneider's powerful 2003 doctoral dissertation for Columbia University: "Developmentalism and its failings: why rural development went wrong in 1960s and 1970s Tanzania," a dissertation with regard to which I was pleased to serve as External Examiner.
24. The two brief passages regarding Akivaga and Temu are to be found in "Julius Nyerere's Socialism," *op. cit.*, pp. 149-50 and 156.

25. This longer extract is also drawn from *ibid,* pp. 156-7.
26. Frantz Fanon was a particular inspiration. During my years in Dar I had drawn a great deal on the ideas of the great doctor and writer from Martinique, an extraordinary person and extremely prescient thinker closely linked with the Algerian revolution in the 1950s and with other fronts of struggle on the continent. His writings—particularly the brilliant third chapter, "The Pitfalls of National Consciousness" in his irreplaceable *Wretched of the Earth* (I still have my now frayed, first paper-back edition [1967], Penguin on my desk as I write this, more than forty years later)—helped to anchor and frame my lectures and writings during my Tanzanian years, and beyond. In fact, I even tried to codify the main insights I had found in his works in a brief paper, distributed to my students, that I entitled "A Paradigm for Fanonist Analysis." Now, search as I might, I can find no copy of that paper in my records or I would have been tempted to include it here!
27. This, and the second quotation below from Phil Ehrensaft, are drawn from his "Semi-Industrial Capitalism in the Third World: Implications for Social Research in Africa," a cyclostyled copy of was included in a course kit distributed in the East African Society and Environment Course, University of Dar es Salaam, 1971-2 (I cannot now retrace its original publication details).
28. For my much later elaboration of a closely related approach, one undertaken with Colin Leys, see our "Sub-Saharan Africa in Global Capitalism"," now chapter one to *The Next Liberation Struggle* (*op. cit.*), as well as our entry on "Dependency" in D. A. Clark (ed.), *The Elgar Companion to Development Studies* (Cheltenham and Northampton: Edward Elgar Publishing, 2006).
29. This quote, read in the course of presenting this lecture, is from Okot p'Bitek, "Indigenous Ills," in *Transition* (Kampala), 7, 1 (August-September, 1967).
30. From Okot p'Bitek, *Song of Lowino* (Nairobi: East African Publishing House, 1966)), ch. 11 ("The Buffalos of Poverty Knock the People Down"), p. 195.
31. From Amilcar Cabral, "Brief Analysis of the Social Structure of Guinea," in his *Revolution in Guinea: An African People's Struggle* (London: Stage 1, 1969); see, in this same volume, the essay entitled "The Weapon of Theory," also written by Cabral, whose work overall is amongst the most impressive of any African revolutionary intellectual in the past century; tragically he was assassinated in Conakry by the Portuguese colonial power who worked with internal dissidents of his own party on so doing in January 20, 1973.
32. Note that I have, throughout the book, for convenience sake, primarily presented the movement under the name "Frelimo," although prior to Mozambique's independence its name as a liberation movement was rendered as FRELIMO—an acronym for the Frente da Libertaçao de Moçambique/Front for the Liberation of Mozambique. Only after independence, when the movement became a political party, was it actually named and identified as, simply, Frelimo. One other lexigraphical practice employed in the book as a whole bears mentioning. The term "southern Africa" is often variably rendered as "Southern Africa;" since the former usage seems, arguably, more grammatically correct, I have attempted to consistently so spell it, changing my own previous usage in texts where necessary.

33. I had, of course, already written of Frelimo and its struggle in my essays "FRELIMO and the Mozambique Revolution," which is ch. 8 in Arrighi and Saul, *Essays on the Political Economy of Africa* (New York, Monthly Review Press, 1973).

34. I went to Tete with three comrades from the Committee for Freedom in Mozambique, Angola, and Guinea (CFMAG) of the UK. FRELIMO had been fighting fiercely to claim the area we visited less than two years previously, a fact which made the level of social and political infrastructure we found there all the more impressive. By the time of our arrival, the Portuguese could penetrate the area only rarely, and then only by jet plane and helicopter, in order to destroy crops or to make short-lived raids.

35. For Mabote, "a soldier who has not been mobilized politically is like a dismantled weapon." Or, as one soldier (who had once served as a draftee in the Portuguese army before deserting) put it when contrasting his work there with his FRELIMO activities: "Then I was able to see only straight in front, but not to the sides."

36. For a more analytical approach to the dialectic established between peasant and cadre in building a base for revolution in Mozambique, see my "African Peasantries and Revolutionary Change" in *Review of African Political Economy*, I, 1 (August 1974), especially Section IV.

37. *Ibid.*, where the question of the collectivist components of peasant-based revolution in Africa is another of the themes discussed.

38. In particular, it is being codified in the speeches of Samora Machel, as evidenced in Barry Munslow (ed.), *Samora Machel, An African Revolutionary: Selected Speeches and Writings* (London: Zed Books, 1985).

39. I am currently preparing a fuller and more analytical account of such efforts by ourselves in TCLSAC, and others in Canada and elsewhere, for Arbeiter Ring that will be entitled *Anti-Apartheid and Liberation Support: Southern Africa, Canada and the World.*

40. TCLSAC, *Words and Deeds: Canada, Portugal and Africa* (Toronto: TCLSAC, 1976).

41. See, for example, J. Bowyer Bell's book with this title, *The Myth of the Guerilla* (New York: Knopf, 1971), and subtitled "Revolutionary Theory and Malpractice"; Bell's volume contains a particularly ugly and misleading chapter on southern Africa.

42. As follows: "Mitchell Sharp, when Secretary of State for External Affairs in Canada, was fond of preaching the virtues of patience to Africans suffering under white-minority domination in Southern Africa. Canada does not believe in violence; Peaceful solutions are preferable—and, of course, possible. This was sheer demagogy, willfully ignoring both the violence inherent in the very practice of colonial oppression by the Portuguese and the fact that wars of national liberation in Angola, Mozambique and Guinea-Bissau were already more than ten years old (now only to be won or lost, not denied!) Sharp's position merely represented an attempt to undermine the credibility of the liberation movements at the U.N. and elsewhere, and to deny to the African population the sole method left to them by intransigent whites to advance their cause."

43. There remained, as I also noted, one piece of unfinished business, the fate of the islands of Cape Verde, considered by the PAIGC as part of one country in the making. The PAIGC did ultimately aucceed in making this claim good, in fact, albeit only temporarily as the future was not to be kind to a united Guinea and Cape Verde, nor indeed to either of its individual components. I also commented in the original article on the fact that Cape Verde was at the

moment seized of a severe crisis (a manifestation of the Sahel's more general famine) that Portugal had previously merely ignored and with regard to which the PAIGC was then seeking assistance.

44. John S. Saul, "Transforming the Struggle in Zimbabwe" (1977), now chapter 5 of Saul, *The State and Revolution in Eastern Africa* (New York and London: Monthly Review Press, 1979).
45. John S. Saul, "Zimbabwe: The Next Round" (1980), now chapter 4 of Saul, *Socialist ideology and the Struggle for Southern Africa* (Trenton, N.J.: Africa World Press, 1990).
46. John S. Saul and Richard Saunders, "Mugabe, Gramsci and Zimbabwe at Twenty-Five" (2005), now chapter 6 in Saul, *The Next Liberation Struggle* (Toronto, New York, London and Durban: Between-the-Lines, Monthly Review Press, Merlin Press, and University of KwaZulu-Natal Press, 2005).
47. See Roger Murray's article, "South Africa Grabs Opportunity to Bash SWAPO," *African Development*, January 1976.
48. The speech was reprinted in its entirety in *The Review of African Political Economy*, 4 (1975).
49. John Saxby's own illuminating account of the Mozambican celebrations from which this quote was taken was circulated in mimeographed form by TCLSAC at the time.
50. For an account of the revolutionary process that has given rise to such a movement in Mozambique see my two previous articles in *Monthly Review* (March 1973 and September 1974).
51. The Cabora Bassa arrangement seems to represent as well a gesture of solidarity towards the new Portuguese government that would be placed in a difficult financial position by outright nationalization. Instead, the Portuguese will continue to control the dam, retiring their debts by selling power to South Africa, and passing the dam to Mozambique at term—by which time it is intended that Mozambicans will themselves be ready to use the power domestically.
52. One additional, rather chilling, feature of our trip to Zambezia was a visit to the Frelimo office in Quelimane, formerly the PIDE (the secret police) headquarters. It had been called the "house of death" in colonial times—i.e., only a few months previously—and we saw some of the torture apparatus and propaganda material found in the building. Its choice as an office by Frelimo was as much symbolic as practical of course; the occupation was a tangible exemplification, for local people, of the reality of liberation. For us, it served as a reminder that, for all our preoccupation with Frelimo's future plans, we should not underestimate the importance of what has already been accomplished.
53. My chance to talk with the rector, Fernando Ganhao, was brief. The university, having been shut down for a month for the purpose, well over half the faculty, students and staff, the Rector included, were leaving the next day to join workers' brigades in the country-side.
54. A current issue of *The Guardian* (New York, October 15, 1975) also quotes Chissano: "In a recent visit to the United Nations to address the General Assembly, Mozambique Foreign Minister [later President], Joaquim Chissano, was introduced to Henry Kissinger...'I hear you people in Mozambique are revolutionaries,' Kissinger greeted Chissano, pumping his hand. 'Yes we are,' Chissano quietly replied. 'And we mean it.'" [Time would dictate a very different, indeed quite non-revolutionary, fate for both Mozambique and Chissano, however.]

55. In a related manner, "non-official" delegations from the United States were welcomed in lieu of an invitation to the American government.

56. Losing to the Zimbabwean liberation forces on the ground inside Rhodesia/Zimbabwe, Smith and the army have adopted the classic tactic of desperation (a la Vietnam): attempting to pulverize the "base areas"—the latter being very broadly defined, of course. There is probably a motif of vengeance against Mozambique that is at play as well, and that helps broaden the havoc created. Many of those pulling the trigger for Rhodesia are ex-Portuguese and police personnel from pre-independence Mozambique, as well as right-wing detritus from elsewhere, with their own scores to settle. In addition, some of the Rhodesian terror seems directed at frightening off *cooperantes*—expatriates on contract—who are currently helping Mozambique in its reconstruction efforts.

57. No less interesting was another argument heard from planners for an emphasis on industrialization: it will develop the working class, and this can only prove a "political stronghold " of the revolution. But such an emphasis is not surprising in light of the active role that workers are being encouraged to take in the actual running of the industries themselves.

58. Only a detailed recounting of such interviews would be sufficient to really make the point, but, once again, the comparison with Tanzania was instructive for me. One saw an encouragement in Mozambique of precisely the kind of militancy that tended to be feared rather than supported in Tanzania. As another interesting point of contrast, it is worth noting that the expressed intention that the party headquarters in Mozambique be further strengthened with a fresh complement of technically-trained cadres—"red" but quite adequately "expert." Not for Marcellino dos Santos (Minister of the Plan *and* Secretary for Party Economic Policy) the half-baked "realism" which has elsewhere suggested that, in light of overall human-power constraints, this would be an unnecessary duplication of functions. For, as he affirmed to me, it is only by enlarging its capacities that the party can really hope to make specific its goals and continue to bring them to bear on the day-to-day policy-making of the bureaucracy.

59. Significantly, some of the fresh drive to rethink agricultural policies came from within the Ministry of Agriculture itself, from younger agriculturalists working in the regions and closer to the peasants.

60. This is the terrain whose complexity was particularly evident for me at the University of Eduardo Mondlane where a variety of brands of Marxism are on display, some of them much, much more promising than others. But the struggle—a necessary part of the broader struggle against any trend toward bureaucratization of the revolutionary impulse—was beginning to unfold in other sectors as well.

61. As Charles Stimac, of Canadians Concerned about South Africa and one of the organizers of the demonstration, was quoted in the *Globe* article as saying, the protesters wanted the game stopped because the game itself was "against the international boycott of South African participation in sport": the match was, he continued, a "backdoor technique" of the South African government to gain approval for its sports teams, with the hope of eventually being able to participate in international sports again. "When a team from South Africa arrives in Canada this close to the Olympics [Stimac] said, 'that's planned as hell' and is a 'conspiracy against Canada and against the Olympics.'"

62. The picture itself, for those interested, now accompanies a more recent article of mine entitled "Liberation Support and Anti-Apartheid Work as Seeds of

Global Consciousness: The Birth of Solidarity with Southern African Struggles," in Karen Dubinsky, et. al., *New World Coming: The Sixties and the Shaping of Global Conciousness* (Toronto: Between the Lines, 2009) at p. 137.

63. England's Lord Goodman succinctly summarized this aspect of the South African reality when he noted: "It is the only society of which I have knowledge where no private virtue, no public worth, no intellectual or physical gifts can redeem you throughout your life from the inferiority brought about by an accident of birth."

64. In an important recent book, John Kane-Berman, assistant editor of South Africa's prestigious *Financial Mail* concludes that "there can be little doubt... resettlement and the Bantustan policy are leading South Africa to a tragedy greater than any that apartheid has yet inflicted upon the country" (*Soweto: Black Revolt, White Reaction*, p. 252).

65. Andrew Young has stated quite explicitly that his proposed alternative to white minority rule in southern Africa is, in his term, "neo-colonialism," political power for black moderates with "business as usual" in the economic sphere. Yet one senses that western policy-makers must lie awake nights trying to imagine a "reform" scenario for South Africa—in order to take the steam out of the kettle—equivalent to their proposals for streamlining transition in Zimbabwe and Namibia. And even there western attempts to absorb the liberation movements and preempt their radicalization has not been markedly successful [sic]. How much more difficult, given the even more deep-seated intransigence of whites and the even more pressing necessity of root-and-branch socioeconomic revolution, is this in South Africa!

66. No doubt the racism implicit in this formulation has also helped reinforce the glib application to southern Africa of anti-communist globalism: Can Africans, something whispers from behind the arras of our prejudice, really be capable of making their own history—or is not some other sinister force involved?

67. In a recent article on Harvard University's debate over the issue of divestment vis-à-vis South Africa, Anthony Lewis of *The New York Times* suggested another related parallel: "...generalities (about over-involvement of the university in causes) cannot apply in the extreme situation when not to act is to be guilty of complicity in evil. It was not morally possible to ignore the character of Hitler's Germany in 1939. And if there were a country today that made its Jewish citizens live in ghettoes, forbade them to vote and made Jewish men and women live apart from their wives and families, American universities and other institutions would not want to be associated with it. The especial, the extreme, character of South Africa is that imposes such disabilities on black people."

68. *The Crisis in South Africa* (and, in a second edition, under the same title but with additional materials) published by both Monthly Review Press and Heinemann [New York and London: 1981 and 1986]).

69 "Economically our bodies corporate and governmental partook readily, and greedily, of the spoils available from the superexploitation which Portuguese hegemony guaranteed in its African holdings. In doing so, we chose to ignore that such economic activity also helped bankroll an otherwise shaky Portuguese economy in its feckless military endeavours. Militarily, though uncritical acceptance of the NATO connection which married the arsenal of the West to Portuguese colonial purposes, Canada made itself, willy-nilly, a partner of the Portuguese. Perhaps most galling of all, on the diplomatic front our spokespersons also served the cause of Portuguese oppression and Western imperialism well by undermining, systematically, the claims of the liberation

movements—and of the African people—to their rightful primacy in arbitrating the fate of their own countries... In short, Canada's official record with respect to Portugal's African colonies was a bleak one indeed" (*TCLSAC, Words and Deeds: Canada, Portugal and Africa* [Toronto: TCLSAC, 1976], pp. 6-7). The four substantive chapters of this volume are also well worth reading by those interested in exploring in detail the obscenities of Canada's foreign policy of the time. They are: Chapter 1, "Business as Usual: Canadian Economic support for Portugal in Africa (1960-1973); Chapter 2, "Larceny by Proxy: Gulf Oil (Canada) Ltd. and Angola"; Chapter 3: "Canada and NATO's African Wars"; and Chapter 4, "Liberals and Liberation."

70. D. Anglin, T. Shaw, and C. Widstrand [eds.], *Canada, Scandinavia and Southern Africa* (Uppsala: Nordiskafrikainstitutet, 1978.)

71. See John S. Saul (ed.), *A Difficult Road: The Transition to Socialism in Mozambique* (New York: Monthly Review Press, 1985); in addition to introductory materials and a conclusion by the present author, it contains six case studies of different aspects of Mozambique's socioeconomic situation by various authors, two of whom—Judith Marshall and Barry Pinsky—were also TCLSAC members working in Mozambique.

72. The inability or unwillingness of the Canadian government to grasp the central point of this paragraph—the fact that popular struggle is the most crucial element in the anti-apartheid arsenal—was no more graphically witnessed than in Joe Clark's recent interview on Southern Africa policy with Carol Goar of the *Toronto Star* (September 15, 1987). Goar finds that the external affairs minister "cannot explain South Africa's extraordinary prominence on the world's stage... About three years ago, there was what Clark calls 'a spontaneous focussing of world opinion on the apartheid issue. I don't know why it happened. It's partly the media."' No mention of the fact that exactly three years ago the Vaal uprising triggered off the most massive upsurge of popular resistance in South African history, one that has sustained itself for three years!

73. There was, for example, my aforementioned book with Gelb, *The Crisis in South Africa*, for 1982 publication. I had also seen through the press a second edition for which I now wrote a new and updated introduction and concluding chapter in 1986, and had written a number of additional essays on that country in the *New Left Review*, the *Socialist Register*, and elsewhere.

74. Little did I know—and, not surprisingly, I was not told in Zambia at the time—that both Mandela inside SA and the ANC leadership outside were not only deeply engaged in discussions about a possible settlement with both South African businessmen and with the Nationalist Party government but even nearing a settlement—albeit one that would still not come easily even after Mandela's release from prison and the ANC's own return from exile and one that would involve compromise on both sides. In fact, as we shall discuss in the following two chapters, such compromises would even involve, some have said, a very real "sell-out" on the part of the ANC as regards the kinds of structural socioeconomic changes many thought necessary to realize the genuine liberation of the mass of South Africans from the grimly hierarchical realities of both racial and class oppression as carried over from the apartheid days.

75. The propriety of doing this was a long-standing issue of debate within the anti-apartheid movement; for example—and much to the annoyance of many Canadian anti-apartheid activists—the ANC's attitude towards the latter

activists' support of important trade unions that were militantly active on the ground in South Africa but not linked to the by now largely defunct ANC-affiliate, SACTU, was, for extended periods, quite hostile. "Direct links stink" was the ANC's grossly misleading formulation as regards this matter.

76. The spirit with which we approached this workshop was well summarized the CAW's Sam Gindin (who also attended the workshop), as quoted at length in the immediately prior issue of *SAR* (May, 1993) in the interview-article "Mutually Searching: Trade Union Strategies, South Africa and Canada."
77. There was funding from a broad range of Canadian sources, including a number of trade unions. A number of the South African delegates also participated in a successful TCLSAC-sponsored public meeting on "Economic Strategies for a New South Africa" and at several panels, on related themes, of the Canadian Association of African Studies which happened to be meeting in Toronto at that time.
78. A presentation at the Ruth First Memorial Colloquium by ANC/SACP activist Jeremy Cronin entitled, precisely, "The Boat, the Tap and the Leipzig Way: A Critique of Some Strategic Assumptions in our Ranks" was particularly illuminating regarding the debate within the democratic movement over such tactical questions.
79. See the useful account of the colloquium proceedings by journalist Gaye Davis in *The Weekly Mail*, August 21-27, 1992, entitled "Can socialism survive the new SA?"

Part Two
The Struggle Continues

PREFACE

Half Empty or Half Full?

I spent the 1990s still deeply involved in southern African concerns, helping edit our *Southern Africa Report* magazine and writing and speaking extensively, both in *SAR* and in other venues. Moreover, at the century's turn, I still found myself as engaged as ever, even though *SAR* was to come to the end of its run in 2000 after fifteen years of solid reportage and commentary. Still engaged: this was true concretely, in my practice (as the first-hand reports from South Africa that conclude chapter 4 and begin the following chapter will indicate), but also in terms of my ongoing efforts to make for myself some broader sense of the changing realities through which I was living. It is true, for example, that by 2000 it had become apparent that I had, in effect, hitched my wagon to a somewhat fading star; the hopes, dreams and analyses that led many of us to see in the struggles for liberation in southern Africa a promise of genuine liberation and development for the populations of the countries in the region that had felt forced to fight, courageously and dramatically, for their freedom, were now visibly waning. For it was depressingly clear that the "false decolonization" Fanon had seen as the fate of many of the newly independent former colonies of his time was merely being repeated in southern Africa.

I wrote of this sadly (chapter 4) with regard to Mozambique, a country that had focused my emotional energies for so long. And, as also noted, I engaged, with my friend Colin Leys, in a searching investigation of developments, both historical and more contemporaneous, in Namibia. I also kept a watching brief on Zimbabwe as the egregious Robert Mugabe and his cronies led that country ever closer to chaos and self-destruction. But it was to South Africa that my attention was increasingly drawn as Mandela (for all the courage he had previously exemplified), Mbeki and others gracelessly squandered any opening to a much brighter future for most South Africans that their own efforts and those of their compatriots had opened up by 1994.

I wrestled with such developments during the 1990s and, by the first decade of the century, I found that there were two responses I could make. One was to tell it like it is, as I did in a talk, first presented in South Africa itself (and later published), "The Strange Death of Liberated Southern Africa."[1] In that text, I sought to divine just what combination of cruel inheritance, overweening global capitalist power, and opportunism/lack of will on the part of southern Africa's new rulers had produced the region's grim outcome. For, despite the positive good of freedom from white political overrule, this outcome (a form of recolonization under the domination of western capitalism) had come to scar the futures of the bulk of the southern African population. Two of my previously published pieces in particular[2] defined my own response to this bleak outlook and, as noted, I will further allude to them in chapter 5 (below).

A second response was to seek out the resistances to this outcome that were forming on the ground, and this inquiry led me to entitle another recent book of mine *The Next Liberation Struggle*. Moreover, this book was merely a first attempt to assess the history that I had myself been privileged (if tormented) to live through. Soon I had signed a number of book contracts to seek, beyond the present volume, to analyze this past and discuss some of its present implications—fully aware that this was likely to prove difficult, deeply contradictory, and eminently challenging terrain.

Thus, on the one hand, I have no difficulty in hailing victory. I remember clearly my own introduction to southern Africa, many years ago, not long after I arrived in Tanzania in fact. I was in Mbeya, in southwest Tanzania, pursuing my research of agriculture marketing cooperatives in that country, and planned to continue such investigations in the Tanzanian districts of Sumbawanga,

Mpanda and Kigoma on the shores of Lake Tanganyika, further to the north and west. There was a problem, however. Tanzania's own road from Mbeya to Msuya has long since been rendered impassable by rains and general wear and tear; to continue my journey I would have to go via Zambia, cutting across that country's northeast corner and, then reentering Tanzania, take the coastal road to reach Sumbawanga.

There were fears that the various towns along Lake Tanganyika in Tanzania might be short of petrol, so, having taken on board several large jerry-cans of the precious stuff, I set out. Reaching the Zambian town of Abercorn, a good sized settlement of perhaps ten thousand or so inhabitants, around lunchtime, I soon spotted a hotel that I made for directly. Bear in mind that Zambia had been until very recently a kind of second tier white-settler colony (being, for a period, an unwilling prisoner of the white inhabitants' plot to secure their own privileged future in the region and the country, the Central African Federation). Zambia had managed to win its independence in spite of this, but many of the cultural attributes of the white south still haunted the place—and not least at the Abercorn hotel. The hotel's dining room was crowded (with whites!) as I entered and the headwaiter asked if I would mind sharing a table with another patron. Of course not. So I was shown to a seat opposite a well turned out Englishman, just finishing up his contract with the civil service he said, complete with long socks, bony knees, shorts and a crisp white shirt: a complete colonial officer kit, don't you know. He seemed decent enough and by way of launching a friendly foray of small talk I asked him, innocently enough, how many people lived in Abercorn. "Oh, a couple of hundred," he said. "There used to be five or six hundred but a lot of them have left." Only whites were to be thought of as "people, apparently," even here well north of the Zambezi—north of Mozambique and Angola, of Zimbabwe, Namibia and South Africa, north of all these fronts of struggle still to come—I reflected to myself in astonishment. Welcome to the continent's "White South," I thought.

But how to honour the story of genuine liberation that such an anecdote evokes, while telling the simultaneous story of the very much less than full freedom that, in any meaningful sense, is the lot of most residents of liberated southern Africa? How to tell that second story too, without losing sight of the first? This is, quite simply, the biggest problem for any participant-observer of the southern African liberation struggle: has the cup of liberation been half-empty or half-full? How can one adopt a vantage point, true to the undoubted victories of the past,that also enables one to evaluate, honestly and critically, a less than happy present?

For the liberation support movement that has shaped my life in Canada had also merely faded away—with "victory" (see chapter 6). It is, of course, difficult not to continue to adopt a negative approach to Canada's ongoing history: to our role in western capital's continuing subordination of southern Africa, for example. And we could also query our current war in, say, Afghanistan, adventures that find our leaders smug, self-righteous, and every bit as bilious as were, with their own smug certainties, the Trudeaus and the Sharpes evoked in chapter 2 (above). Not that some Canadians are not resisting this kind of worldview and its consequences. But not enough of us. And, certainly, not (yet) effectively enough.

CHAPTER FOUR

The 1990s

Southern Africa, Free at Last?

Let us, here, begin the 1990s in 1994. For the moment of South Africa's first "liberated" election was one that many of us, not least the vast mass of South Africans, had struggled for and looked forward to for many years. I was extremely moved to be in South Africa for the election and to write, as I did for the piece that I include here, about this dramatic moment, in *Southern Africa Report* (9, 5/10, 1, July, 1994). Given the continuing challenges that faced South Africa my article was entitled, appropriately enough, "Now for the Hard Part."

"NOW FOR THE HARD PART." So, in more or less the same words and within a half an hour of each other, Pallo Jordan and Joe Slovo greeted me at the Carlton Centre on the day the ANC readied itself to declare victory in the recent elections and become South Africa's new government. True enough, perhaps. Yet few would begrudge the ANC the euphoria, gleeful and unbounded, that gripped the hotel's ballroom later that evening in the wake of Nelson Mandela's historic pronouncement. Certainly, in a lifetime of accompanying the ups and downs of African politics, I had never experienced anything quite like it: a gigantic surge of energy that I knew, from television monitors banked in the corners of the room, was spreading to the streets outside the hotel, and beyond—to the crowded black township of Alexandra, for example, and to the more distant rural areas of the Northwestern Transvaal, places where I had accompanied the voting only a few days before. We danced and laughed, all of us, embraced, and danced again.

My memory drifted back thirty years, to the ANC's dusty offices in Dar es Salaam, Tanzania, where I had first met, as exiles from their own country, many of the people now dancing in the Carlton ballroom. I knew something of the long, uneven, but ultimately heroic journey that had finally brought them here to Johannesburg and to the brink of power. But I had also been privileged to witness at close hand, as a Canadian "electoral observer," the equally dramatic events of the preceding week: the ultimate assertion of their claim to freedom by so many of South Africa's black people as, in their vast numbers, they stood, in endless queues, patiently and with great dignity, to cast their ballots.

I participated in this great moment as a member of one of several delegations organized by Canadian non-governmental organizations (in my case, by the Toronto-based Rooftops Canada) to "observe," officially, the mounting of the elections. We were sanctioned—like many other such groups (ranging from United Nations and Commonwealth missions to innumerable "NGOs" from around the world)—by the Independent Electoral Commission to accompany the voting and the counting and to help ascertain whether the whole process was "free and fair." Our five-person team thus found itself with privileged access to the event, frequenting numerous polling stations throughout the three days of the election, while also monitoring queues and, finally, some of the long, drawn-out drama of the final tabulation.

"Free and fair" enough

It would be easy to highlight the numerous foul-ups in the proceedings—although one wonders how even our own finely honed electoral apparatus would have coped with a sudden expansion of the Canadian voting population by the five or six times South African officials had to cope with! The imagination with which so many, recently mobilized to the electoral team from all walks of life, coped with the logistical difficulties involved in mounting such an exercise was impressive.

So, too, was the forbearance of virtually all parties involved in the elections, something that made it possible to interpret rules with the degree of measured flexibility that seemed so appropriate. It was this, in turn, that helped translate a sense of the importance of the occasion into a growing acceptance that the process was, certainly, free and fair enough. Sprawling, loose-limbed, often chaotic, the drama of the event as a "liberation election" stood out above all else. A personal case in point: on one occasion we fulfilled one of our duties by monitoring, behind the screen, a presiding officer as she asked a certain aged and illiterate voter where he wanted his "x" to be placed. I expect that as long as I live my ears will harbour the echo of his fervent, almost whispered, response: "Mandela."

There were lingering anomalies, even dangers, in some of the results, of course. For example, it was difficult to feel entirely sanguine about the electoral outcome in the Western Cape, where apartheid's long-term success in setting Coloureds against Africans was stoked, successfully, by a National Party campaign that bordered on mere racism (see David McDonald's account of the Western Cape election elsewhere in this issue). And, in Natal, even the probability that a dramatic measure of voting fraud had been perpetrated by the Inkatha Freedom Party could not blunt the fact that the often brutal IFP had considerable support there.

The ANC has decided—at least for the moment—not to press its case on the fraud issue and to accept the Natal electoral outcome, warts and all. Will this ensure the continuing commitment of Chief Buthelezi and his IFP colleagues to now press their various claims willingly through the channels provided by South 'Africa's fledgling democratic institutions? And will the many ANC-aligned Zulu who have been victims of the IFP's cruel tactics in the past feel confident to commit their own futures to that possibility? In Natal, perhaps, the future is anything but bright, but time alone will tell.

The hard part

Moreover, beyond these unknowns there hovers an even more fundamental question: what could those vast numbers in their patient queues actually hope for, in terms of changes in the often grim reality of their own daily lives, from the "liberation election" that their long walk to the polls had so dramatically become? South Africa remains, election or no, amongst the most unequal societies in the world, vast wealth juxtaposed to abject poverty and with such inequalities still largely inscribed along racial lines. What can the ANC government be expected to do about the extremely undemocratic nature of the socioeconomic structure it must now, as policy-maker, confront?

Of course, of all the parties to the election only the ANC had run on anything like a coherent policy programme, one embodied in its "Reconstruction and Development Programme." Here, in fact, is a programme at whose core lies acknowledgement that the black population's legitimate expectations are not to be merely dismissed as "unrealistic," that its democratic voice must continue to be heard, and that its "basic needs" must be met. Small wonder that one of the most energizing of moments on Victory Eve was when Mandela departed from his written text to underscore vigorously the ANC's once and future commitment to this very RDP.

The RDP is less clear as to the means of doing all that it promises, of course. Will the ANC, bound by prior agreement to a "government of national unity" with its former opponents and confronted with a bureaucratic apparatus until recently entirely unsympathetic to its aims, find room for imaginative manoeuvre on such fronts? And what of the forbidding global context in which it finds itself? Must the ANC merely accept the dictate of market outcomes, worldwide and local, as the bottom line of its development aspirations?

Or can it, as many of its supporters within the trade union movement and within the other popularly-based institutions of "civil society" insisted when we spoke together, use the state to at least steer the business community in directions deemed necessary to realize more humane results? Unfortunately, the answers to such questions are not altogether promising ones—as I argue in a second article in these pages, one prepared for the *Work in Progress* symposium which has now become part of this issue of SAR (see below). Here, of course, the chief emphasis can safely be on celebrating, without apology, the dramatic moment of political democratization that we have just witnessed in South Africa. Still, we should also pause to remind ourselves that the economics of South African liberation remains to be defined in most of its essentials. The western solidarity network, now being rebuilt on the foundations of the old anti-apartheid movement, must find increasingly imaginative ways to link itself to South Africans' struggles to forge such a definition.

MOREOVER, I FOUND SPECIAL SIGNIFICANCE in the fact that the account would appear in a special issue of *SAR* that we were honoured to publish jointly with the final issue of *Work in Progress*, a crucial South African magazine from the days of anti-apartheid struggle. I myself had every issue of the magazine back to its beginnings in the 1970s, having received its first numbers from Gerry Maré and Glenn Moss, its first editors, when we met for coffee in Johannesburg more than twenty-five years before during my visit to South Africa recounted in chapter 2. I was particularly pleased (though saddened) to be asked to contribute to its very last number (co-published, as mentioned, with *Southern Africa Report* as

SAR/WIP, volume 9, #4/vol. 10, #1, July 1994). Already by 1994, however, writing of the transition in South Africa was becoming a sobering undertaking and a far cry from the hopes for a post-apartheid future that Glenn, Gerry and I had shared in 1978.

This was true even of the ANC's original socioeconomic strategy document "The Reconstruction and Development Programme" (subtitled "A Policy Framework, African National Congress") that housed such significant ambiguities that I felt forced, once asked, to comment upon them. My piece was entitled, under the title I shared with Bill Freund, "The RDP: Two Reviews," with my Part II being: "Half Empty." Yet how much more dispiriting would things become when the RDP itself was jettisoned only a couple of years later in favour of the ANC's euphemistically titled "Growth, Employment and Reconstruction" document, one that was far more subservient to market-premised neo-liberal and western dictate. The ANC's retreat from meaningful "liberation" for the vast mass of South Africans was one that had led Hein Marais, in commenting on the deals being struck between capital and the ANC in the late 1980s (i.e., even before the "fall" of apartheid), to argue that "by 1994 ... the left had already lost the macroeconomic battle."[3] Here, as I argued the "half empty" side of the debate, my commentary was further captioned by the editors: "There are a lot of good things about the RDP—its heritage of consultation, its intention to uplift, its vow to empower South Africans. If only, warns John S. Saul, the 'plan's central assumptions were a bit less rickety...'" I then proceeded as follows:

IT'S EASY TO BE LABELLED AN "ULTRA-LEFTIST" in South Africa these days. Increasingly, all you have to do is mention the "S" word—socialism—and you're quickly laughed off the stage, in official circles, as an "unrealistic," hopelessly old-fashioned dreamer. Capitalism is, quite literally, the way of the world and with a little finesse and good management all South Africans can share its fruits.

In fact, this seems to have become the conventional wisdom. And rare indeed is the leader in "the new South Africa" (past statements to the contrary notwithstanding) who will publicly demur from that premise. Is this also the anchoring premise of the ANC's Reconstruction and Development Programme (RDP)?

It's certainly one very plausible reading of the document, especially if we take what it doesn't say as seriously as what it does say. For, in the end, the RDP's picture of the South African development effort is relatively contradiction-free; everyone, capitalist and shanty town dweller alike, has more or less the same interests and can be served by more or less the same policies!

I don't want to give the wrong impression. Up to a point, the RDP must be deemed a "good thing." It's a considerable achievement for those who nurtured it from its origins as an "accord" designed to safeguard union priorities within the ANC alliance all the way to its current status: as a broadly progressive programme defined, in so many ways, from below, yet also embraced forcefully by Nelson Mandela and the rest of the ANC leadership.

Substantively, too, the RDP's strengths are real. Its dramatic first section locks into place a clear statement about the centrality of meeting "basic needs," a goal that becomes the chief performance standard against which the success of the new SA can be measured; and all sectors, including the business community, can be held accountable to it.

That's a powerful platform from which to challenge any tendency to accept the slide into a Brazilian-style "fifty-percent solution" (or worse) as being "good enough" for SA. Strong, too, is the later section which pivots the transformation of SA on democratic empowerment.

The latter emphasis also squares well with one of Nelson Mandela's more intriguing recent remarks, when he advised workers at last year's COSATU annual congress to be "vigilant." "How many times," he asked, "has a labour movement supported a liberation movement, only to find itself betrayed on the day of liberation? There are many examples of this in Africa. If the ANC does not deliver the goods you must do to it what you did to the apartheid regime." Empowerment, then ... and yet the question remains: empowerment for what? And—dare one also ask?—over and against whom?

We come, by this route, to the RDP's central section on the economy. Here, it's true, we find some formulations upon which a fairly radical approach to economic reconstruction might be built. "The fundamental principles of our economic policy are democracy, participation and development," the section begins.

"We are convinced," it continues, "that neither a commandist central planning system nor an unfettered free market system can provide adequate solutions to the problems confronting us. Reconstruction and development will be achieved through the leading role of the state, a thriving private sector, and active involvement by all sectors of civil society which in combination will lead to sustainable growth."

Less clear, however, is how readily the authors of the RDP expect the production decisions of "the private sector" to yield a product mix that will actually service the basic needs of the vast mass of South Africans. And, if this does not happen spontaneously—if socially defined and politically driven demand must substitute in significant measure for market-driven imperatives in shaping SA's production structure—what kind of limitations may have to be imposed on the free writ of capital? Unfortunately, such questions are finessed, rather than met head-on, by the RDP.

For the real question is: What if capitalism doesn't really work? I don't mean merely that it might not "work" in moral terms—although it is striking how quickly any qualms have vanished about centering a new SA on what we used, quaintly, to call "exploitation." (Leave that aside. After all, President Mandela has rushed to declare, in his first post-election interview [with the *Sunday Times* editor Ken Owen], the irrelevance of any Marxist frame of reference: "In our economic policies... there is not a single reference to things like nationalization, and this is not accidental. There is not a single slogan that will connect us with any Marxist ideology"!)

What if, quite simply, acceptance of some relatively unalloyed capitalist option won't work even in the limited sense of providing sustainable solutions to SA's economic problems? Unfortunately, there are strong indications that this might well be the case. (Compare, for example, the difficulties elsewhere in Africa and in Latin America of producing either equity or growth by capitalist means.) Indeed, exposing the country to the competitive imperatives of the global marketplace—as the IMF and the foreign investors in whom Mandela and others seem to put such stock might counsel—could prove disastrous.[4]

Of course, it might be considered adequate to answer simply that "socialism" won't work either. There is, after all, the chill formulation of the Polish-American social theorist Adam Przeworski regarding the alternatives that present themselves to countries like SA in today's global context: "Capitalism is irrational; socialism is unfeasible; in the real world people starve—the conclusions we have reached are not encouraging."

Perhaps the more responsible ANC leaders feel that under such circumstances there is no alternative to an accommodation with capitalism. Let's just accept, they seem to be saying, Przeworski's premise that we're damned if we do and damned if we don't. And—socialism being "unfeasible," after all—let's opt for trying to put a more positive, progressive, humane spin on capitalism in SA (however difficult this may have been to achieve elsewhere).

True, there are skeptics who argue that this kind of accommodation with capital has a lot to do with the realities of class formation in contemporary SA. What we're witnessing, they say, is the logical end-product of the "elite-pacting" model of political change which has formed the basis of SA's transition to democracy: the co-optation (the salaries, the houses, the power!) of a significant portion of the ANC leadership into a comfortably middle-class way of viewing the world..."realistically."

Assume for the moment that this view is too cynical. Assume that the ANC leadership's extremely pragmatic approach towards capital marks a carefully considered response to SA's vulnerable economic situation: to the prospect, among other things, that capital, if pushed too hard, will simply take flight. Yet, even then, might we not expect them—and the authors of the RDP itself—to do more to inform their followers that capitalism is indeed irrational (however difficult the realization of "socialism" may be)?

It's true, of course, that some sections of the popular movement seem more enthusiastic and/or resigned than others to the prospect of a capitalist route forward. The Cosatu-linked Industrial Strategy Project, for instance, seems to have made the presumed imperatives of "global competitiveness" and an open, export-oriented economy more of a guiding premise than the Macro-Economic Research Group (MERG) report. The latter at least harks back to the notion of "redistribution through growth" and provides grounds for some more active disciplining of capital by the state. And the RDP itself? The reader may feel that it reflects, first and foremost, a rather uneasy and unresolved blend of both of these two emphases.

Not that one need advocate some kind of ultra-left adventurism as the necessary antidote to the vaguely reformist neo-liberalism that seems to tempt many within the ANC. Elsewhere (in my *Recolonization and Resistance: Southern Africa in the 1990s*[5]) I've argued that the notion of "structural reform"—a circumspect but nonetheless revolutionary project of closing in on the prerogatives of capital and gradually shifting the balance of power over the production process towards the popular classes—epitomizes what some of the best South African progressives still believe is possible.

Take, for instance, the recent statements by important South African socialists like Enoch Godongwana and Pallo Jordan in a debate on "social democracy or democratic socialism" in the *South African Labour Bulletin* (November-December, 1993). Thus, Godongwana acknowledges that "if we want a socialist alternative in the absence of an insurrection, that poses a challenge for us," then goes on to suggest that "we argue a socialist alternative, but within the constraints of saying that we cannot simply storm and seize power tomorrow." Therefore, he says, "we should be creative—how do we make sure that, in the process of struggling for socialism, we assert ourselves as a class with the objective of having a class rule...We must begin, while we assert a leading role in various areas of society, *to build certain alternatives within the capitalist framework that will tend to undermine the capitalist logic*"(emphasis added). Consider, too, Jordan's similar interest in a kind of strategy "which doesn't necessarily imply grabbing hold of the state or nationalization of the commanding heights of the economy, but in a sense establishing a number of strategic bridgeheads which enable you to empower the working class and the oppressed, and from these bridgeheads you begin then to subordinate the capitalist classes to the interests of society in general."[6]

Of course, as it stands, much of this kind of presentation remains at the level of the metaphor. Spelling out what it would have to look like in practice requires real imagination, with respect both to the mechanisms of state action (the use of tariffs, taxes, procurement policies, and the like) and to any action that might spring from civil society (via collective bargaining structures, for example, or through the full range of existing socioeconomic forums).

Nonetheless, the language one uses to frame the challenge confronting South Africans does make a difference. Perhaps, up to a point, capital can be encouraged to service socially defined priorities by invoking a sense of shared national purpose. It would also be unwise to refuse to use profit-defined "incentives," where possible, to achieve the same end. But the fact remains: neither of these mechanisms is likely to be entirely adequate as a substitute for bringing real, countervailing social power—the power of mobilized popular classes—to bear.

It is true that, in this respect, the very vagueness of the RDP's handling of the "production question" may actually have its virtues. There is certainly space within the document for a "Left-rendering" of the project it begins to sketch, one that would emphasize the needs for "democratic pressure" to impose an "economics of basic needs" on capital. But this also means that the document is less what it is than what it might become—if and when the Left regroups sufficiently in SA to keep socialist preoccupations on the agenda.

Of course we must avoid restricting considerations of policy and empowerment to questions of "production." And perhaps my own formulations do run the risk of being cast too exclusively in "leftist"/"workerist" terms. Beyond the silences on how best to deal with capital, there's a lot in the RDP for "progressive forces"—women, environmentalists, land reformers, urban, education and health activists—to chew on as they plot empowering initiatives in their respective spheres. Both within and beyond the ANC, the rebuilding of a movement to press for on-going and deep-cutting transformation must occur across a very broad front of issues and initiatives.

Still, I can't help thinking that the question of how best to deal with the "production problem" remains crucial to determining whether the notion of a full-blown and genuine transformation of the bad old SA is to become truly hegemonic. For if the ANC can't find a way to spring the economy forward (something that even the halfway uncritical acceptance of neo-liberalism and globalist economics simply cannot promise), advance on other fronts will be severely compromised. Could the outcome be an ANC government that is forced to use more and more authoritarian methods to control a populace whose quite legitimate expectations are not met by some variant of business-as-usual? In an untransformed SA, could the playing down of class struggle merely mean that ever-rising levels of criminality and of ethnic, regional and racially driven conflict become the essential stuff of society and politics?

I wonder, then, whether the main problem with the RDP isn't the fact that it avoids clearly identifying class contradictions and evades even the most subdued evocation of the need for class struggle. Instead it inserts the notion of a relatively unproblematic national purpose as the core of the reconstruction and development effort. In doing so, the RDP—despite its undoubted strengths—may merely make it that much more difficult for the ANC's own mass constituency to develop the kind of self-consciousness necessary to ensure its full and most meaningful liberation.

WORSE WAS YET TO COME, HOWEVER. The RDP was only a brief waystation on the headlong South African lurch towards the infamously neo-liberal GEAR strategy document (mentioned above) and an embracing of the full package of market-centred economic premises for an only minimally altered economy. Nelson Mandela was clearly in over his head when it came to the economic front, radical enough sounding on the very first day of his emergence from prison in Cape Town but soon prepared to reverse ground by about 180 degrees. And Thabo Mbeki, his successor, was even worse: "Just call me a Thatcherite," he is quoted (as noted above) as having gleefully pronounced shortly after liberation.

Of course, South Africa's ever-rightward trajectory was of a piece with the rollback of all of those socialist hopes that had seemed once to fire liberation movements across the region. That this was so was not particularly surprising in Angola, Zimbabwe and Namibia: there the movements' left credentials had, even in the phase of the liberation struggle itself, seemed rather suspect. But in Mozambique, where so much more had seemed possible, the reversal of direction really stung. I had been forced to confront this reality at first hand when I went back there to witness, as an international observer on the Oxfam-Canada electoral mission, its so-called "peace election" in 1994. This was an impression I was able further to confirm when I returned to celebrate the twentieth anniversary of Mozambican independence the following year (see below). The election itself I wrote of in *Southern Africa Report* (10, 2, December, 1994) under the title "Mozambique: The 'Peace Election.'"

SIX MONTHS AGO I WAS AN OFFICIAL OBSERVER at the South African election and I reported on that experience in a previous issue of *Southern Africa Report* ("Now for the hard part", *SAR*, July, 1994). In October I returned to southern Africa to witness the mounting of a second election, this time in Mozambique. But the tone of things, on this second occasion, was very different from the first.

In April, the overriding mood of most South Africans had been one of euphoria. Theirs was, after all, a "liberation election," one in which a very large majority of South Africans felt themselves to be voting, quite literally, for their freedom. Unfortunately, Mozambique offered a far more sombre context for exercise of the franchise. Indeed, large numbers of Mozambicans encountered by our Canadian observer teams (CIDA-funded and drawn from such NGOs as OXFAM-Canada and Cooperation Canada-Mozambique) seemed to be voting, first and foremost, for the very idea of voting itself. Their apparent hope: that the election would prove to be an arena within which political differences might, at last, be resolved peacefully, and the violence that has scarred their lives for so long, might end.

For Mozambique is a society now almost completely shattered by a sustained and merciless war, a reality evident to us as we travelled throughout Maputo Province in the days before the election: to Magude, to Matatuine, to Moamba. These districts are pockmarked with landmines, burned-out buildings and the visible flux of displaced people trying to find their way home.

This war was initiated, when it first began more than a decade and a half ago, as part of apartheid South Africa's defensive strategy of actively destabilizing its neighbours. South Africa's target was the government of Frelimo (the Front for the Liberation of Mozambique), the liberation movement that had defeated the Portuguese colonial power in the mid-1970s and established Mozambique's first independence government. And its chief instrument of destabilization was RENAMO (the Resistencia Nacional de Moçambique). Now, as one further step in a difficult peace process, Frelimo and RENAMO were to face each other as electoral, rather than military, combatants.

It was not just Mozambicans who sought peace by this means, of course. The international community has been a central player in the process, with the United Nations itself investing some $95 million in seeing the elections through. And it was also prepared to hand over large sums to RENAMO: to ease its transition from guerrilla organization to political party, it was said, though some skeptics saw it to be a fairly straightforward bid to buy off the movement's leadership in order to ensure some form of stability for the country!

Noteworthy, under such circumstances, was the consensus of virtually all foreign observers (including our Canadian delegation) that the election had been run by Mozambicans with great care and scruple. This, in spite of the enormous logistical difficulties spawned by Mozambique's extreme degree of underdevelopment (and even some difficulties experienced by Frelimo activists in penetrating RENAMO-dominated areas in order to campaign). And when, right in the middle of the three-day voting period, RENAMO's presidential candidate Afonso Dhlakama momentarily dropped out of the race protesting fraud, RENAMO's own senior representatives on the National Electoral Commission confirmed publicly the fairness of the elections. With any luck, it will prove more difficult for RENAMO arbitrarily to disown the electoral process than was the case in Angola where Unita, a movement of roughly similar provenance, arbitrarily rejected a result deemed "free and fair" by international observers and resumed its war against the MPLA government.

Of course, RENAMO also has done surprisingly well in the election. But the fact remains that Frelimo has won, Alberto Joaquim Chissano scoring firmly over Dhlakama in the presidential balloting and the party itself scraping a rather narrower majority in the National Assembly. In consequence, much is now said to ride on Chissano's willingness to incorporate the defeated RENAMO leaders into a coalition government (a deal which might also include governorships for RENAMO people in the five provinces, where their party has carried the national vote).

Equally important are RENAMO's own intentions. Will some of its people choose to stand, once again, and fight? It can be said that Mozambique, in this respect, is no Angola. Many of Renamo's traditional backers—South Africa and Malawi—have changed inalterably, for example. And both the government's forces and those of RENAMO have been considerably depleted, vast numbers of soldiers on both sides bought off by UN demobilization allowances and a visible measure of war weariness. Yet arms caches remain and some soldiers are in readiness—even if there is nothing that approximates to the level of war preparedness that Unita's Jonas Savimbi retained while waiting out the Angolan balloting. At the very least, some have argued, RENAMO is readying itself for a period of "armed negotiations" in which it flashes the card of militarism in order to strike a better deal for itself with the Frelimo government.

What about a coalition government, then? In fact, agreement on a "government of national unity" (on the South African model) was what senior United Nations personnel and western diplomats had been pushing Chissano to embrace in the run-up to the election itself. If anything, and despite Chissano's refusal to concede any such deal prior to the voting, the pressure will have increased in the wake of the results.

There is an irony here, of course. Those who once, for some good reasons, rejected the claims that one-party states can contain the stresses and strains inherent in underdeveloped societies, now seem willing to argue the virtues of "one-government states" for very similar reasons. One might question how quickly one can learn lessons regarding the legitimacy of responsible opposition and the values of a democratic culture under such dispensations.

But perhaps the possible prospect of achieving peace by such a route should take priority. And, in any case, such a resolution may not be as difficult to achieve in the Mozambican case as might at first appear. After all, Mozambique is by now a very different society from what it was when South African destabilization began at the end of the 1970s. As one South African journalist commented of the election, it seemed to be marked by a kind of "moral amnesia." Frelimo's own high purposes at independence seem but a distant memory and RENAMO's history as first Rhodesia's and then South Africa's brutal cat's paw have also been obscured by time.

In addition, Frelimo had been, in part, responsible for making itself vulnerable to attack by RENAMO and by that movement's South African sponsors. Too undemocratic, too insensitive to peasant needs and desires, too indifferent regarding diverse regional and other sectoral demands: so Frelimo's critics have charged. Then, as the war ground on, the government's morale snapped. Mounting corruption and the increasingly arbitrary use of power by both military and civilian authorities threatened to drag Frelimo's project down to RENAMO's own level. As RENAMO itself turned to more conventional politics some of the distance separating the two began to disappear.

True, there is evidence that, in Nampula say, or Tete, some may actually have voted for RENAMO because they feared a return to war if it lost (a vote for "*sobrevivencia*" [survival] rather than "*preferencia*"). And indeed, certain of Dhlakama's statements did warn of this possibility. But there is little doubt that, particularly in the centre of the country, one found a strong anti-government vote. It led at least one observer to wonder aloud to me what might have happened had "a respectable third force got itself together and done some work to present itself as the peace party!"

But this did not happen. Instead, the levelling-down process between the two leading parties was further reinforced by a second factor. The scope for national decision-making is, at least for the moment, defined particularly narrowly in a recolonized country like Mozambique. Economic decision-making rests largely in the hands of the World Bank and the IMF, various aid agencies and a particularly aggressive band of pirate multinationals, and the state itself has been eviscerated. The result: in substantive policy terms, too, there was little enough to divide the two parties.

A coalition government—and some kind of peace—may be in the offing, then. But what else can one say, more broadly, about the kind of politics this situation has begun to produce in Mozambique? How important is the fact that the recent multi-party election in Mozambique has failed to provide Mozambicans with the opportunity to debate their long-term future in any meaningful way? Thus, Frelimo, once the proponent of a clear socialist development alternative, ran a campaign centred on "show-miçios" (a play on the Portuguese word "comiçio"), rallies where show business trappings, the trivialization of issues and the glorification of the candidate took precedence over real substance.

For its part, RENAMO tended to fall back on the rather calculated manipulation of various regional, ethnic, religious and (advanced in the name of "tradition") gender-oppressive particularisms and animosities in building its own electoral base. On one occasion, for example, Dhlakama threatened to "drive the Shangaans [the ethnic majority in southern Mozambique] back to Zululand," setting, in this and other ways, a number of dangerous precedents regarding the texture of future political debate in Mozambique.

Small wonder, under such circumstances, that many voters did indeed find themselves voting as much for peace as for party. Mozambicans deserve peace, of course—and they also deserve much more democracy than they have experienced either under colonialism or in the more recent past. Yet not all forms of democracy are equally empowering of people, and the importation into Mozambique of the electoral model we observed—one too much like our own?—probably had as many costs as benefits in this respect.

True, if this particular stab at democracy does indeed reconcile enemies and produce peace, it will have served a worthwhile purpose. But it was difficult to escape the feeling, in Mozambique last month, that something more is needed. One may hope that the Frelimo government, realizing it has not been overwhelmingly endorsed at the polls by any means, will feel constrained to clean up its act. As it happens, on the occasion of one of his press conferences, Chissano did acknowledge that he would eventually have to move against the rising tide of corruption within the state apparatus. But this was very far from being a major campaign theme. Moreover, the prospect of an influx of RENAMO-sponsored politicians and bureaucrats into a new coalition government hardly strengthens the promise that such a revitalization of the state will occur.

Still, as noted, some kind of lowest common denominator government of national unity may be just enough to satisfy the ubiquitous "western ambassadors" who now loom so large on the Maputo political scene. These are, in any case, no friends of a strong state in Mozambique. But representatives of the Canadian NGOs who were observing the Mozambican election had another reaction, one that found its way into their various reports on the election process.

For they were forcefully reminded, by the visible limitations of political parties and electoral machinations, of an alternative source of possible renewal for Mozambique, one close to the surface of their own experience in that country. In recent years, such organizations (OXFAM-Canada, COCAMO) have been linking up with Mozambicans who are attempting—through the construction of green-zone cooperatives, women's organizations, trade unions and the like—to strengthen their ability to build and control, from the ground up, their own lives. If these latter can succeed in this undertaking, the necessary underpinnings for pressing even more powerful democratic demands upon governments, parties and the electoral process itself will be that much more firmly in place.

In this regard I was myself reminded, while observing the elections, of a conversation I had had a few months earlier with Graça Machel, former minister of education in the Mozambican government and widow of Samora Machel who, as Frelimo leader, had been the country's first president. Saying that she would not herself be standing for the Assembly this time round, she told me that she would, however, be voting for Frelimo. I was taken aback. This was an answer to a question it would not have dawned on me to ask.

Yes, she went on, Frelimo still represents more of a national project—Frelimo's most crucial historical accomplishment, in her view—than any other alternative currently on offer. But in terms of deepening democracy and ensuring the eventual revival of other, more progressive strands of Frelimo's original undertakings for the country, she saw the chief hope to lie in the strengthening, in her phrase, of "the institutions of civil society." And this is the sphere towards which, for the foreseeable future, she intends to direct her own considerable energies.

AS SUGGESTED ABOVE, I was able to reconfirm my sober impressions from a year earlier when I returned to Mozambique as an invited guest to help mark Mozambique's independence anniversary. I wrote of my impressions in a *SAR* article (11, 2, January, 1996) that I entitled, with heavy heart, "Twenty Years After: Recolonization in Mozambique."

JUNE 25, 1995, MARKED THE TWENTIETH ANNIVERSARY of Mozambican independence, the original moment, in 1975, having been the occasion for a joyous celebration that I was privileged to attend. To return to Mozambique this June—and to view the country in the light of the high hopes and expectations which so many of us held for the revolutionary process that Frelimo (the liberation movement in Mozambique) had set in train during its armed struggle against the Portuguese—was an extremely sobering experience, however. Certainly, quite visibly, the anniversary was not one that anybody felt very much like celebrating

This is not surprising. At the moment, by the World Bank's reckoning, Mozambique is the poorest country in the world with a gross domestic product per capita of approximately $60 in 1990. It is also one of the most dependent on foreign assistance, which accounts for two-thirds of its measured GDP. Indeed, aid receipts per capita amounted to approximately $60 in 1990, almost double the figure for sub-Saharan Africa.[7] So Mozambique presents an extreme case, one where, among other things, the state has virtually been destroyed. Currently, it is true, the country is inching its way back towards some kind of political stability, one that, for the moment at least and for the first time in many years, provides the rudiments of peace for Mozambicans. But it is not providing much else for the vast majority of them.

What happened?

Explaining this denouement has become a controversial undertaking. Recently, reviewing some of my own work, Bill Freund has suggested that those of us close to the Frelimo project in the early years lost our "critical edge" in celebrating the movement's "socialist" efforts, and he argues, instead, that "the jury is still out on the structure and character of Frelimo." I don't know: perhaps you really did have to be there! I know of few who were who didn't think that indeed, something "truly stirring" was happening. But such first-hand witness seems to count for little in the current sceptical climate.

Still, I think I'll stick with the opinion of Jorge Rebelo, one of the early Frelimo leaders. A close friend of two former Frelimo Presidents, Eduardo Mondlane and Samora Machel, Rebelo is one Mozambican leader who has managed to retain much of his own personal integrity in the current general climate of *sauve qui peut*. He expressed his thoughts on this twentieth anniversary in an interview that appeared in the Maputo daily *Noticias*:

> We all agreed that we were going to gain independence, but this was not the ultimate object; that was in fact the creation of a progressive society that would bring an end to misery in our country. This was not merely a slogan. It was inside of us. It is for this reason that some of us remain very demoralized with the situation that has brought us to the point where we are today. On the one side however, we think that perhaps it wasn't possible to have done things very differently. But we can't help but be shocked by the distance between that which was our objective and what is the reality today.

Rebelo went on to talk about how sad it was that young people in Mozambique are at the moment lost, without much sense of a future for their society. In response to a final question suggesting that "20 years after independence, and thirty years after joining Frelimo this isn't the country which you dreamed of," Rebelo replied: "Clearly it's not."

Rebelo also recalled leaving a meeting at the Ponta Vermelha Palace just after independence and having President Machel say: "Now we have the power and we can finish with misery in Mozambique in two years." Someone said, "No, two years is too short a time." And Machel replied, "Okay, three years then." "We have to say now," Rebelo continued, "that this was a bit of voluntarism (voluntarismo) on our part. We were imagining things that in reality were not possible. But that's what we wanted to do."

Of course, Rebelo is signalling both the leadership's sincerity of intention and the fact that profound errors of judgment and mistakes in policy were made—springing, not least, from this kind of "voluntarism" and leading Frelimo to try to do too much, too fast. There was also an arrogance of purpose that encouraged the Frelimo leadership to do things much less democratically than they might, and should, have done... as well as a vision of socialism far too exclusively cast in an eastern European mode. But, as we also know, there was the desperately difficult situation left by the Portuguese and, above all, there was South African destabilization: willfully attempting not only to assert control over Frelimo's actions, but even to break the back of Mozambican society.

Still, whatever balance sheet one strikes on this history, the fact remains that it has left a Mozambique dependent in its poverty on the behest of the World Bank, the IMF and the external aid community. And it leaves a leadership which has certainly lost touch with the aspirations of ordinary people. As Graça Machel, the widow of Samora Machel and an important political actor in Mozambique in her own right as a minister in the first Frelimo government and now active in the NGO sector, put it forcefully to me during my recent stay there: "Workers and peasants don't count for anything in this country anymore."

True, in the 1980s, the Mozambican leadership tried to find ways of dealing with the external financial institutions in such a way as to protect achievements in social spheres like education and health, while keeping some kind of state involvement in the direction of the economy. Thus the country's first economic recovery program sought to finesse the World Bank and others into allowing space within which to give a more humane face to the compulsory restructuring that was going on.

Recolonization

This didn't last long, however—and soon privatization had become the alpha and omega of policy. The state is being forced back in every sphere, while many of those who staff the state are looking for their own ways into the private sector: the Minister of Finance announces the privatization of the two main state-controlled banks; the cotton industry is turned over to large cotton concessionary enterprises, driven by firms like Lonrho, who have established private fiefdoms along the lines of the prazos that existed in the nineteenth century; forests are stripped; and land is being granted, in the name of increased productivity, to South African farmers who are fleeing the advent of black power in their own country.

Much recent writing on Mozambique—as, for example, Joseph Hanlon's eloquent *Who Calls The Shots?* or David Plank's important article, cited above—focuses on the extent to which policy is being dictated from outside. Moreover, Plank introduces the concept of "recolonization" quite self-consciously into the discussion as something more than a mere metaphor, suggesting on the basis of his findings in Mozambique, that there and elsewhere "the most likely successor to post-colonial sovereignty will be neo-colonial vassalage, in which Western powers assume direct and open-ended control over the administration, security and economic policies of 'deteriorated' states under the banner of the U.N. and various donors."[8]

He also compares this kind of "recolonization" suggestively with the earlier form of colonialism that Frelimo had first rebelled against; it seems worth quoting him at length on this subject for SAR readers.

> Although the abject status of several African states is being characterized as a new form of colonialism, there are three fundamental differences between Mozambique's past and present situation.
>
> First the relationship that is now emerging between the country and its donors is less overtly intrusive than direct administration by a colonial

> power, but its effects are more pervasive. The bonds of debt and dependence that tie Mozambique to its donors were entered into voluntarily by a nominally sovereign state and may in principle be repudiated at any time. The policy changes prescribed by the principal donors aimed to accelerate the integration of Mozambique into the global market and to transform the domestic economy to this end. Beyond this, however, the West's policy prescriptions implied dramatic social and political consequences, including the exacerbation of social inequalities, the aggrandizement of local and expatriate elites and the subversion of prevailing political arrangements. Attempts by the World Bank and other agencies to remake the Mozambican state in their own image, accompanied by their insistence on the reduction and redirection of public expenditure suggest the extent of changes that are in prospect.
>
> Second, the relationship now being constructed between Mozambique and its donors is potentially far more durable than traditional colonialism. The country's subordinate status is currently rooted not in discredited ideologies of racial superiority, imperial destiny or Christian mission, but in the precepts of modern economic orthodoxy. Dominion is exercised not by the agents of a colonial power, but by the technically sophisticated and politically disinterested economists of the IMF, the World Bank and of bilateral aid agencies, whose prescriptions are determined not by parochial national interests but by economic analysis. Resisting the power of the major donors is consequently difficult, because Mozambique's subordination is portrayed as a natural consequence of global economic trends rather than an imposition by a specific colonial power.
>
> Finally, the new relationship has no place for the reciprocal obligations that in principle characterize colonialism ... The absence of formal political ties between Mozambique and its donors leave the Government powerless to refuse the policy prescriptions of the principal aid agencies, because the flow of funds must be maintained at virtually any cost ... The donors enjoy considerably more autonomy than they would if bound by the statutory obligations to traditional colonialism, while Mozambique is in some respects more dependent on them than it was on Portugal before 1975.

While this is an accurate picture of what has happened to Mozambique—inside from the outside, as it were—there are also Mozambicans who are buying into this process to their own advantage. Still, they are not all that many, given the overall state of the economy, and the advanced condition of collapse of most state-centred social provisioning. Take the health and education systems, for example—once the pride of the early post- independence years. Both systems are being privatized precipitously, where they are not just rotting away, and, self-evidently, this is happening at the expense of the interests of the poorest of the poor.

It is also difficult to be entirely sanguine about the rush to embrace "traditional authority" as one of the bases for local politics. True, Frelimo did often overlook, in a high-handed manner, the claims to some kind of integrity of existing rural social and political structures. Let's remember, though, the flip-side, that this was done, at least in part, in the interests of certain kinds of social change—including, amongst other things, the transformation of gender relations—that will now be much more difficult to realize if "tradition" is to become too central a touchstone of policy. And there is also a whole range of regional, ethnic and other identities that Frelimo also tended to override rather high-handedly, as threats to what it felt to be a necessary sense of national purpose. Perhaps, in so dealing with these identities, Frelimo actually heightened the possibility that they would eventually become politicized in divisive ways. But the fact remains that there are equally important, present-day reasons why such identities now threaten to surge forward uncontrollably into the political realm.

Globalization and "democracy"

The souring of "identity politics" can be one of the most critical symptoms of the economic and social stagnation generated by the negative impact of "globalization." Societies rot out from underneath when political options that evoke the existence of some shared sense of societal purpose are not available. It is then that people are tempted to fall back on the lowest common denominators of sociopolitical identity to give resonance to their lives. It is in such a world, in fact, that the Rwandas and Yugoslavias can become the face of many countries' future (see, on this subject, Bernard Barber's recent volume, *Jihad vs. McWorld*).

Yet what sense of collective purpose can arise in a Mozambique where, as one member of parliament described the situation, "the biggest moment of Mozambican politics this year was when the government went to Paris to meet with the donors. That was where parliament really was held in Mozambique this year, the donor meeting in Paris." As another MP explained, unlike other countries and parliaments, "we accept that our budget is really set by donors at the annual Paris conference. We accept that our priority is to develop a donor-acceptable budget." The claim he then advanced for elected politicians was correspondingly modest: "But the assembly must be part of that process, that is what democracy means in Mozambique."

That, and an electoral process which did at least as much to disempower Mozambicans as it did the reverse[9]: what can be the substance of a "democratic" debate in which the crucial policy options are delivered on a plate from Paris to all parties! Not that we need then trivialize the importance of the breathing space that peace and a certain kind of democratization have brought to Mozambique. The virtues of peace are self-evident. And there are also benefits to be found in consolidating even the most formal of democratic structures: as one erstwhile senior Frelimo politician—himself an architect of some of the most undemocratic features of Frelimo's strategy—admitted to me self-critically, if there had existed the present kind of democratic structures in the old days (including the far greater freedom of the press that now exists) obvious abuses of authority like the disastrous "Operation Production" of 1983 would not have been possible. Moreover, as Ken Wilson argued firmly in the most recent issue of *SAR* (November, 1995), the room for manoeuvre for local communities, for trade unions, for women's organizations, that is provided within a more open political system has permitted some revival of positive energies at the base of the system as well—even if the precise extent and impact of the revival he identifies remain to be seen.

For the moment, however, it is a less edifying kind of politics that often prevails, notably the grinding on of the bleak polarization between Frelimo and RENAMO, with hints of renewed violence always in the air. But there are also tensions, apparently, within Frelimo itself—focusing principally, it is suggested, on the struggle between one faction, centred around President Chissano and his cabinet, and another, centred around Frelimo leaders in the legislative assembly. It is acknowledged that such intra-Frelimo factionalism is probably linked, in part, to a jockeying for position over who shall be Frelimo presidential candidate "next time." At the same time, there are those who argue that more substantive strategic issues are also, increasingly, at stake.

For this parliamentary faction has also been seen as beginning, in however rudimentary a fashion, to exemplify the ambitions of a "national bourgeoisie," one that might defend, against the presumed imperatives of globalization, the claims of a national [read: "national bourgeois"] interest. Indeed, the advocacy of this kind of economic nationalism can easily pass for progressive politics in Mozambican intellectual circles these days, the alternative language of socialism having been so profoundly discredited. I was struck, for example, by the vigour with which the well-known Mozambican journalist Carlos Cardoso argued the case, at the time of my visit, on behalf of domestic cashew processors defending their interests against the World Bank's preferred strategy of opening up the trade in unprocessed cashews directly to India—even though this latter strategy would actually assure the peasant producers of higher prices.

Interestingly, one Canadian diplomat with whom I talked found danger precisely where Cardoso found hope: he feared that "the nationalists" might actually use parliament to disrupt the plans of a newly ascendant cadre of efficient, technocratically inclined Ministers within the Cabinet, a cadre on whom he (and, he suggested, other Western interests) have pinned their hopes. Not that he was terribly worried about such nationalists, it must be admitted. In the end, most observers agree that the promise/danger of some putative national bourgeoisie quarterbacking the emergence of a more independent and economically buoyant Mozambique under present circumstances is not a strong one—not least because those who might be thought of as possible candidates for such a role tend to behave more like pirates and/or racial demagogues than like potential captains of industry.

No, on the whole, Westerners in Maputo seem to feel pretty confident of the intellectual hegemony they have established over (and the community of interests they have established with) the present Frelimo leaders, only wishing, perhaps, that more of them were a bit more competent... and some of them a bit less corrupt. Such Westerners seem to have little doubt of the leadership's general acceptance of the wisdom of World Bank/IMF nostrums. And they have particular enthusiasm for the close and comfortable links of the most competent (and least corrupt) of this leadership group to their counterparts in the international financial institutions (some of whom, it bears noting, are themselves Mozambicans, often of formerly left-wing provenance, who are now comfortably ensconced in the IFIs!). There is only one real problem, of course: as suggested earlier, there is little sign that the "market utopianism" of such Frelimo cadres—however ascendant—can and will produce positive economic outcomes for the country.

A celebration?

Twenty years after? This year, in Maputo, there seemed little enough ground for optimism, or, as suggested earlier, for celebration. Not that many in Mozambique would wish the country back to the period of authoritarian rule—however much some of that authoritarian structure may have been crafted, by Frelimo, in "a good cause." Yet there was a sad irony in the observation of a Mozambican friend, a journalist and a firm supporter of freedom, not least of the press, in his country. Certainly, he wished for no return to the bad old days of government dictation of the "party line" to his newspaper. Yet, he confessed, he couldn't escape the feeling that the workers and peasants in Mozambique had actually had more power under the "old" Frelimo regime. Then, he said, the leadership took their interests seriously, their voices actually were heard more clearly than they are now, under liberal democracy: in the present system their votes are merely canvassed in a competitive manner that has little to do with advancing their life chances or helping them to clarify their socioeconomic options.

In short, both periods—that of old "Frelimo state" and that of the new—have their downside. One could conclude, nonetheless, with the observation that what has been lost, most visibly, from the early period of post-independence Mozambican history, is something terribly important. It is, precisely, a strong sense of public purpose, one premised on the envisaging of society-wide transformations that might actually change the lives of the vast majority of Mozambicans in positive ways.

Are such Mozambicans, like so many others around the world, now merely locked into the apparent iron logic of present-day capitalist-driven globalization—with their leaders also left, as they claim, with no choice but to follow that logic? This is, of course, the apparent "commonsense" of the matter evoked so negatively by Colin Leys (as cited in the editorial that frames the present issue of SAR). It is also the ethos that can move a theorist like Adam Przeworski to observe grimly, of the current epoch, that "capitalism is irrational, socialism is unfeasible, in the real world, people starve—the conclusions we have reached are not encouraging." Faced with this "logic," can we ever hope, anywhere, to move beyond merely muttering an uneasy variant on an old slogan, "Dare to struggle, dare to whine"?

It is, of course, difficult to imagine that so bleak a prospect as Mozambique currently offers up can last forever—though it is equally difficult to see any ready way forward, either nationally or globally. (The picture at the national level is discouraging enough, as the situation so visible on the ground in Mozambique attests, but add to that the fact that, as Perry Anderson argues, "the case against capitalism is strongest on the very plane where the reach of socialism is weakest—at the level of the world system as a whole"!) Perhaps the most that can be said is that the bleak realities we have identified will not disappear of their own accord. In fact, the one thing that was absolutely clear to the visitor to Mozambique in 1995 was that it will now be necessary for Mozambicans to revive, slowly but surely, the kind of positive energies and sense of mission—resisting (re)colonization, (re)imagining the future, (re)asserting the claims of the social—that brought them independence twenty years ago. But that is true not merely for Mozambique.

I HAD BEEN TOO CLOSE TO THE STRUGGLE for freedom in Mozambique not to continue to be haunted by the complexities of its later trajectory but also, as stated in the previous chapter when discussing the loss of Ruth First, by the loss of other friends, both from within the Mozambican revolutionary camp: Eduardo Mondlane, Frelimo's first president, assassinated by the Portuguese in Dar es Salaam in 1968 and Samora Machel, independent Mozambique's first president, killed in a plane crash apparently engineered by South Africa's apartheid state. I was to reflect many years later upon the meaning of Mondlane's life and death—and of the ongoing travails of a post-independence Mozambique. I had been invited to speak at a workshop held to honour his memory at his own alma mater, one very far from his native Mozambique: Oberlin College in Ohio. I entitled my talk on that occasion, as I did its later publication in the *Review of African Political Economy*, "Eduardo Mondlane and the rise and fall of Mozambican socialism," from which I extract some paragraphs here.[10]

HOWEVER TEMPTING AN EXERCISE it may be when contemplating the abrupt removal from the historical process of so exemplary and important a person as Eduardo Mondlane, speculation as to "what might have been" had he lived is likely to be an exercise of only limited value. In the present case, this is true even for the analysis of the pre-independence period in which Mondlane both made his political contribution and also died. The tensions within Frelimo had been temporarily papered over at the 1968 Congress, but they were far from being resolved, indeed they may even have helped produce Mondlane's assassination. Had he lived, would be have been able to finesse the Kavandames and the

Simangos more deftly and resolve more amicably the key strategic questions that were dividing the movement? And, if this were not possible (I rather doubt it was), would he at least have been able to orchestrate the rising ascendancy of those directly linked to the military wing of the movement (and to the dynamics of popularly rooted guerrilla struggle) in a positive manner on at least two fronts: to have allowed the military struggle to advance successfully (as it did) while also to have helped preempt the dangers of hierarchy and authoritarianism that the necessary militarization of the Mozambican struggle seems, in retrospect, to have carried with it?

But if these are impossibly speculative concerns how much more so are questions about "what might have been" had Mondlane lived to usher Mozambique into independence? True, this latter question has not failed to be asked, and it has not been debated merely as a matter of academic speculation either: it has actually been, from time to time, the stuff of post-independence political propaganda and electoral sloganeering, RENAMO itself having attempted from time to time to claim for itself and away from Frelimo the mantle of Mondlane: that is, the mantle of Eduardo Mondlane the good Mozambican nationalist, the nationalist who would not have been as "Communist" as Samora Machel and his most immediate political entourage (most of whose members had been Mondlane's own most immediate colleagues and proteges, it should be noted) had proven to be.

We have, of course, the countervailing evidence of one of Mondlane's last political statements, preserved on tape by Aquino da Bragança from which tape I myself transcribed it and subsequently translated it into English:

> I am now convinced that Frelimo has a clearer political line than ever before... the common basis that we had when we formed Frelimo was hatred of colonialism and the belief in the necessity to destroy the colonial structure and to establish a new social structure. But what type of social structure, what type of organization we would have, no one knew. No, some did know, some did have ideas, but they had rather theoretical notions that were themselves transformed in the struggle.
>
> Now, however, there is a qualitative transformation in thinking that has emerged during the past six years which permits me to conclude that at present Frelimo is much more socialist, revolutionary and progressive than ever and that the line, the tendency, is now more arid more in the direction of socialism of the Marxist-Leninist variety. Why? Because the conditions of life in Mozambique. The type of enemy which we have,

> does not give us any other alternative. I do think, without compromising Frelimo which still has not made an official announcement declaring itself Marxist-Leninist, I can say that Frelimo is inclining itself more and more in this direction because the conditions in which we struggle and work demand it.[11]
>
> Moreover, as Mondlane argued in the same interview, it would be "impossible to create a capitalist Mozambique" because "it would be ridiculous to struggle for the people to struggle to destroy the economic structure of the enemy and then reconstitute it in such a way as to serve the enemy." And he also stressed the importance of "learning from the concrete experience, including the errors, of the socialist countries which since 1917 have worked and lived the socialist experience."

In my introduction to a new edition of Mondlane's book *The Struggle for Mozambique*, published in the early 1980s,[12] I noted that I had taken such statements to reflect accurately the most positive strand of ideological development within Frelimo during the period of armed struggle, the strand that became dominant in the struggle for control of the movement after Mondlane's own death. I also cited (as I have done above) Jorge Rebelo's recent celebration of the key premises he felt lay behind Frelimo's actions of the time. And I myself concluded that "just what Mondlane thought to be conveyed by the term "Marxism-Leninism," what he felt, more specifically, to have been the key "errors" of the "socialist countries," and (had he lived) in just what ways his own continued reflection on such matters might have played concretely into Frelimo's post-liberation practice are things we can never know." But could we not suggest that such a process of reflection—as undertaken by him and by others in the movement and that he encouraged—could well have prompted judicious action that might have spared Frelimo some of the policy errors it undoubtedly did commit in its pursuit of a socialist future for Mozambique (errors I then itemized in the paragraphs that followed in my memorial presentation).

Yet I did not really take my task to be an evaluation (something I had done elsewhere in any case) of the neo-liberal turn by Mozambique that has been attendant upon the peacemaking process in that country—a turn that continues to define current policies there. Rejecting Chester Crocker's smug assertion that the

Frelimo leadership had merely abandoned its "Afro-Marxist fantasies" (as distinct from being beaten into submission) I expressed my continued agreement with David Plank, as quoted earlier in this chapter,[13] when he asserted that Mozambique had most recently experienced a particularly dramatic form of "recolonization" (his word) that was potentially even more pervasive and difficult to shake off than was the Portuguese version of colonialism. As I then continued:

Can we at least ask how Eduardo Mondlane might have fared in these heavy seas of "destabilization" and "rollback" and "recolonization"? As stated earlier there are diminishing returns to efforts to speculate about such a question. Still, one must suspect that he would have been pushing, for reasons already discussed, to find room for manoeuvre—within the global economy, within the region, and within the damaged economy and society left behind by the Portuguese in Mozambique itself—to advance more rather than less progressive, even socialist, policies to meet the needs of ordinary Mozambicans. In short, no more recent image of Mondlane as "neo-liberal" *avant la lettre*—whether that image be wielded by spokespersons for RENAMO or, as is quite conceivable nowadays, by spokespersons for the new Frelimo—can really stand up to close scrutiny.

This may be of some significance. As we know, it would be naive at this late date to argue that the era of the old "Frelimo state" and its "left developmental dictatorship"—with deeply compromised economic, social and political policies—did not have its grievous flaws.[14] Nonetheless, reflecting on the first thirty-plus years of Mozambican independence—years marked most recently by destabilization, by internal war and by "peacemaking"[15]—one could still conclude with the observation that what has been lost, most visibly, from the liberation struggle itself but also from the earliest period of post-independence Mozambican history is something terribly important. It is, precisely, the loss of too much of the sense of social and public purpose that once prevailed, a purpose premised on the envisaging of society-wide transformations that could actually change the lives of the vast majority of Mozambicans in positive ways. That such commitment to the collective weal has been lost will bring no tears to the eyes of a Chester Crocker, perhaps. But the fact remains that its loss has been the price both of the kind of war inflicted on Mozambique and of the kind of peace achieved there. If development in any meaningful sense is ever to occur in their country Mozambicans will eventually have to rediscover just such a sense of purpose, I think. And in doing so they will have to rediscover, among other things, something of the socialist legacy of Eduardo Mondlane.

But what about another question of contemporary resonance, what about the question: "Mondlane the democrat"? No less speculative than the question: "Mondlane: socialist or neo-liberal?," this question does nonetheless provoke thoughts about post-independence Mozambique, not least in its socialist phase, that carry us onto especially interesting analytical terrain. For in retrospect it might be argued that, insofar as Mozambique's future lay in Frelimo's own hands at the moment of independence, the most fundamental flaw in its project, even more fundamental than its weakness in the sphere of economic policy-making, was precisely its weakness in the sphere of democratic theory and practice.

Not that Frelimo ignored this issue altogether. Indeed, the Frelimo leadership revelled in the fact that a great deal of its military success came from listening to and working with the people on the ground as the movement advanced its armed struggle. Moreover, one of its most dramatic policy initiatives in the very first days of its holding power was the attempt to deepen the populace's own sense of fundamental empowerment through the establishment of the *"grupos dinamizadores"* in urban neighbourhoods, rural villages and in workplaces. But the messiness of such democratic processes-in-the-making did not greatly appeal to those used to the military orderliness of Nachingwea camp. It proved all too easy for Frelimo leaders, in their arrogance of power (albeit often, at least in the early days, with the very best of intentions and with full commitment to the popular cause) to convince themselves that they knew best, and absolutely, what was required. Moreover, this was an organizational trajectory that the adoption of official "Marxism-Leninism" with its stern Stalinist rationale for vanguardism and its firm sense of historical certainty could only reinforce.

For the fact remains that opposition was often merely crushed and that mass organizations (the women's organization and the trade unions and the like) ostensibly created as mechanisms of popular empowerment all too quickly became more like transmission belts for delivery of the party line. Critical debate that should have been the lifeblood of a revolutionary process all but dried up in a stale and predictable media. "Tradition" (seen to have its negative side in spheres like gender relations and exaggerated deference to old-style authority), religious conservatism, and ethnic and regional sensitivities became, as examples of "obscurantismo," only so many negative constraints to be overridden from on high, rather than being viewed as the deep-seated social realities they were, to be worked upon politically, balancing leadership against mass initiatives, in much more nuanced and open-ended ways. At its most grotesque this tendency was revealed in the "solution" to problems of urban overcrowding that became *"Operaçao Produçao."* Here was a prime example of the kind of transformative tactics that, in their negative impact, would ultimately provide hostages to RENAMO and also help to rot out much of the high moral purpose that had originally inspired Frelimo.

This is not to be wise after the event. Writing in the early 1980s in an introduction to the new edition of Mondlane's book, *The Struggle for Mozambique*, mentioned earlier, I had already evoked such thoughts, seeing them as being as relevant to contemplating the then still (somewhat) open future of Mozambican socialism as they may now be to writing that socialist experiment's epitaph. I noted a number of "danger signs" that threatened the vigour of the emancipatory process that Frelimo professed to value, including considerable "inertia in facilitating mass action and self-organization by the workers and peasants"; "the over valuing of top-down interventions and administrative solutions"; and "the adoption of an 'official Marxism' whose 'sterile definitions' could serve "to deaden Marx's emancipatory message." Such tendencies seemed to me to cut against the profoundly democratic thrust both of Mondlane's book and of his political proclivities more generally. As I then wrote in concluding my introduction, Mondlane's own socialist, even "Marxist-Leninist" premises (as expressed to Bragança in the interview cited above), remain "framed by his book, by its insistence that Frelimo's political project cannot exist outside of or above the Mozambican people itself" and that "as long as the sensibility that informs Mondlane's book remains at the centre of Frelimo's practice, there is a strong likelihood that the country's goals will be achieved"![16]

Once again, we cannot say for a certainty what would have become of Mondlane's own highly developed democratic sensibility under the pressures that sprang from the kinds of regional conflagration, institutional disorder and economic difficulty that his successors had to face, not to mention from the temptations of power that ensnared so many of his African counterparts (to go no further afield). What we can say is that his immediate successors, the Frelimo leadership, did not manifest nearly enough of this democratic sensibility in their socialist years (or more recently, for that matter), as a number of the old militants from that period have confessed quite ruefully to me in recent interviews. To be sure, it is difficult to isolate out this one factor, the failure of democratic sensibility, from all the other relevant variables. Nonetheless, the costs of its absence were probably quite high.

Of course, even if this point is granted, it does not follow that the formal democratic institutions now in place are any more empowering for ordinary Mozambicans than were the political structures established by socialist Frelimo. (Here, in making my argument, I draw upon an essay included immediately above, and directly, as it happens, from a passage to be found on p. 272). I allow the same formulation to stand here both to retain the flow of the present text and also to reinforce what is, I feel, a most relevant point. For I continued to find "a sad irony in the observation of a Mozambican friend, a journalist and a firm supporter of freedom," yet someone who couldn't "escape the feeling that the workers and peasants had actually had more power under the 'old' Frelimo regime than they had now." Then, he said, the leadership took their interests more seriously (even if they never found ways to institutionalize a genuinely "popular democracy" in any very effective way), and their voices were actually heard more clearly than they are now, under liberal democracy.

Thus, perhaps, the witches' brew that the potent combination of formally liberal-democratic institutions and socioeconomic recolonization can produce, a proof that even if the existence of multi-party elections is one necessary condition for democratizing a country it is very far from being a sufficient one. Harken then to contemporary efforts to rebuild the Mozambican polity from the ground up, to help empower civil society, not least those of its members who are among the poorest of the poor, to make the kinds of demands on the Mozambican state that may ultimately force it to recover something of its founders' social vision, the vision of, among others, Eduardo Mondlane, as I have argued here. It is no accident that two widows of two former presidents of Frelimo, martyrs both, have been amongst those who have been engaged in such work from time to time. I speak, of course, of Graca Machel and Janet Mondlane. In this work, and in the work of others in Mozambique who have become similarly engaged, can we doubt that we hear echoes of the voice, the democratic voice, of Eduardo Mondlane?

I WOULD CONTINUE TO WRITE about the tangled circumstances in a more contemporary southern Africa, republishing, for example, my eulogy to a second fallen comrade and close friend who was also, evidence would suggest, assassinated (in this case by the then guardians of the apartheid state): Samora Machel, liberated Mozambique's first president.[17] But in republishing it (eventually as an appendix to my book *Empire and Decolonization*) I had the opportunity to reflect ruefully—in an afterword later appended to the original eulogy—on the fate of a by then very firmly recolonized Mozambique.[18] I was also invited, throughout the 1990s, to speak on a number of occasions about post-apartheid South Africa's celebrated Truth and Reconciliation Commission—a dramatic undertaking about which, however, it was difficult not to have mixed feelings. In support of such a critical position I was able to quote a number of other sharp observers who agreed with my misgivings; thus I concluded one such presentation, at York University, as follows:

> **THE TRC [I ARGUED] IS FAR MORE A SYMPTOM** than a cause of the much broader and deeper limitations of the transition process in South Africa. For what the TRC does help to hide from sight is not merely the guilt of virtually all whites (and some others in all racial categories) as regards their connivance, both active and tacit, in the apartheid system, but, more specifically, the institutional interests of class oppression that benefited, behind the scenes as it were, from the grim workings of the apartheid security state—a not unimportant point given that many of the instruments of such class oppression are still very much in place. Moreover, such a skeptical reading not only of the TRC but also of the transition itself in South Africa, informs a number of pertinent writings on contemporary South Africa which also suggest that the TRC's primary focus on case-by-case exposure of abuses of power by malignant state officials has served to blur any adequate focus on the far more powerful class, racial and other interests that had underwritten the unjust structures of the apartheid era.

Thus, Mahmood Mamdani, while noting the fact that only relatively perfunctory hearings occurred on the role of such institutional actors as the judiciary, the media and the business community under apartheid, suggests that the central preoccupation of the TRC with the perpetrators of violence themselves, helped mask the broader sociological distinction between the beneficiaries of apartheid and its victims. "In its eagerness to reinforce the new order...the TRC created a diminished truth that, in effect, wrote the majority of apartheid's victims out of its version of history" and thus "failed to open a social debate on possible futures for a post-apartheid South Africa."

Moreover, as Colin Bundy has asked in a similar vein: "Does the TRC's highlighting of individual memories actually facilitate social amnesia? Do we run the risk of defining a praiseworthy new order as one in which police may no longer enjoy impunity to torture opponents but failing to specify that ordinary citizens should not be poor and illiterate and powerless against being pushed around by state officials and employers?" And isn't this, therefore a brand of "'truth and reconciliation' [that is] not merely the product of a compromise but historically compromised," one likely to produce a "form of nation-building...that can only yield a lopsided structure—two nations disguised as one, a hybrid social formation consisting of increasingly deracialized insiders and persistently black outsiders?"

In a similar vein, Stephen Robins is concerned that if, as he suspects, the TRC had helped permit "the systematic socioeconomic legacies of apartheid to recede from public discourse" this has had "important implications in terms of contemporary public debate on social tranformation and economic policy": for whatever the range of truths that were revealed by the TRC process "we may be forced to admit that these are not necessarily the sorts of truths that are most useful to setting the present generation of impoverished South Africans free."

Fortunately, I was soon in South Africa again myself. In 1999 I was an observer of the second national election in post-apartheid South Africa—the first post-Mandela election. This time Thabo Mbeki was to be the president if, as it was fully expected to do (and did), the ANC won. I had asked myself, in evaluating the RDP earlier in the decade (above), whether the cup of liberation in South Africa was to be most appropriately considered on the ANC's watch to be half empty or half full. Now, as the ANC, with its re-election, confirmed itself in power I did so again. But the fact was that I had begun to suspect strongly that the former descriptor—half empty—was by far the more appropriate one and this fast crystallizing premise would inform my writing during the coming decade. Now, on the brink of the millennium, in 1999, I wrote briefly on the election in *SAR* (14, 4, August, 1999): "'Normalization'? The South African Election."

The concept of "normalization" has been much used in conventional circles to describe the consolidation of liberal-democratic practice that seems to be taking place in South Africa. But what does this so-called "normalization" entail precisely? In fact, with regard to any such conceptualization, evaluating the recent election is no easy matter. Do those who use this concept wish to suggest that the political cup in South Africa is half empty? or is it deemed to be half full [to evoke a metaphor employed earlier in this volume]? Both interpretations have some plausibility.

Of course, as an election observer at both the 1994 and the 1999 elections, I did not expect the 1999 version to have quite the same human drama as was on display in 1994. 1994 was, after all, the occasion of the Freedom election, its essence unrepeatable in quite such historically charged terms. The 1994 election was much more decorous: well attended, peaceful, largely respectful among the parties contesting the outcome. This kind of "normalization" must have seemed no bad thing to South Africans who have witnessed so much politically charged carnage in recent decades.

True, some have seen a threat in the fact that what electoral politics has consolidated in South Africa is a one-party dominant tilt, a dominance that is cast, moreover, in primarily racial terms—with the ANC overwhelmingly the party of South African "Africans" (except in Kwa-Zulu/Natal where, however, an accommodation between the ANC and the Inkatha Freedom Party seems to be holding) and the Democratic Party, the relatively small opposition, having purchased its success in large part by playing the racial (white, and to some extent, in the Cape, "Coloured") card.

Yet far more worrisome, I think, is another kind of dominance: the one-ideology dominant tilt of the elections that have just transpired and the fact that the ANC's hegemony has been won in the name of a neo-liberal economic strategy—one, it should be noted, that no other party of significant following (least of all the DP) sought to contest during the election—that has little promise of transforming the lives of the vast majority of ordinary South Africans.

Perhaps it was not, strictly speaking, the voters' intention to so sanction neo-liberalism. But one ANC politician did put the point quite clearly on television as the results poured in: "Our platform was GEAR," he said. Or, as another argued in the heat of the campaign: "Fiscal and monetary constraint and liberalized trade and capital movements...that aim at the structural repositioning of S.A.'s economy in response to globalization, whatever their long-term benefits, have severe short-term costs for the constituencies of voters who are among the chief supports of the governing party. The ANC has, however, indicated, that it will persist on its chosen path. As one British banker put the point, in the wake of the election, to the *Washington Post*: "[New S.A. President] Mbeki holds things close to the chest and makes decisions in a secretive way. However, he is not a populist and has been a 'Thatcherite' in his fiscal ideas. His experience in exile introduced him to the financial world—he is unlikely to abandon these close ties to business developed in the years abroad."

In his excellent recent book, *Fault Lines: Journeys into the New South Africa* (Berkeley and Los Angeles: University of California Press, 1999), David Goodman finds one of his informants, a brash emergent African entrepreneur named Tumi Modise, stating quite frankly and unequivocally: "Race is not the issue anymore. It's class." Yet while this seems to be, to a signal degree, objectively true of the new South Africa, it is still far from being subjectively so. In this election, both the "commonsense" of neo-liberalism (normalization indeed!) and—probably even more importantly—the continuing resonance of African nationalism (and of the ANC's past political achievements) helped to obscure that fact. Surely the development policy debate must eventually occur in South Africa in much more sophisticated and contested terms than the ANC's policy programme, and its electoral hegemony, encouraged this time round.

Such, at least, is the "half empty" reading of the import of these elections, seen, from this optic, as having served to damp down the measure of class consciousness and class conflict that is so necessary to the vast majority of South Africans' eventually securing their futures. Note, however, the one saving grace of the election considered in this way. For while it is true that the ANC tacitly played the neo-liberal card and continued to court the international marketplace for all it was worth, it did run (as Pottie suggests), in the most public terms it offered, on the platform of "delivery"—a theme that also formed the core of newly minted president Thabo Mbeki's inauguration speech. Should its chosen strategy fail to deliver on the promises thus made to its popular constituency, the debate in future elections might well prove to be cast in terms of a much wider range of strategic alternatives.

I ALSO WAS PREPARED, as the new millennium dawned, to return to South Africa—to the University of the Witwatersrand ("Wits") in Johannesburg—to work for a term or two. In this way I hoped to see, even closer to hand and at greater length, just what was happening. Of course, I had already undertaken several study visits to South Africa since 1994 and also kept in close touch with developments there as I continued to serve with the editorial committee of *Southern African Report* throughout the 1990s. When I now went to Wits, however, it proved to be a particularly eye-opening experience, one that further alerted me to the fact that developments in South Africa under the stewardship of global capitalism and of the ANC, were even less positive than I had dared to acknowledge from afar. It was on this basis that I felt emboldened to pen, while there, a series of sharply critical writings on developments in South Africa crafted for the Johannesburg-based newspaper, *The Mail and Guardian*. The first of these was published in the *M&G*, June 23 to 29, 2000) and entitled "The ANC's tragic leap to the right." In fact, these reflections served to round off the 1990s for me even as they opened a door to the sobering reflections that the new millennium was to force upon me.

AFTER A TERM TEACHING SOCIOLOGY at the University of the Witwatersrand in Johannesburg, my strongest impression of the new South Africa was just how easy, in many circles, it has become to be considered an "ultra-leftist."

Should I have expected more? My own contacts with the South African struggle go back a long way, to the mid-sixties when I taught in Dar es Salaam and had my first direct links with the region's liberation movements, including the ANC. And I was still at it thirty-five years later as part of the editorial team for the Toronto-based publication *Southern*

Africa Report, the main activity now pursued by our Toronto Committee for the Liberation of Southern Africa (TCLSAC) that we founded in 1972. Many's the damp basement or draughty church hall where I heard ANC representatives, including the country's current president (Thabo Mbeki), speak in "the old days."

Anybody at all close to the movement for liberation over all those years knew that there were tensions within it as to what might happen after the overthrow of apartheid: the theories of "colonialism of a special type" and "the two-stage revolution" seemed to signal as much. Moreover, as noted earlier, Mbeki himself had written forcefully (as early as 1984, in the *Canadian Journal of African Studies* no less) that "the ANC is not a socialist party. It has never pretended to be one, it has never said it was, and it is not trying to be. It will not become one by decree for the purpose of pleasing its 'left' critics."

True, as Mbeki then continued, the ANC represented the "notion of both an all-class front and the determined mobilization of the black proletariat and peasantry,"—with this working class to be viewed as "a conscious vanguard class, capable of advancing its own democratic interests." But for supporters such apparently contradictory formulations posed questions. Were we merely dealing with "petit-bourgeois nationalism" of the kind Frantz Fanon had seen as being so prone to facilitating a "false decolonization" elsewhere in Africa? Or was this a movement that promised a far more transformative politics? In fact, even those who were somewhat more skeptical about the revolutionary vocation of the ANC leadership per se thought (along the lines of the second of Mbeki's formulation just quoted) that enough energy had begun to be released from below in South Africa (not least from a burgeoning trade union movement) that radical, even socialist, outcomes were quite likely. Time (and struggle!) alone would tell.

But perhaps time has already told its tale—at least for the moment. Hence my own conclusion in striking an interim overall balance sheet on the "South African revolution": A tragedy is being enacted in South Africa, as much a metaphor for our times as Rwanda and Yugoslavia, and, even if not so immediately searing of the spirit, it is perhaps a more revealing one. For in the teeth of high expectations arising from the successful struggle against a malignant apartheid state, a very large percentage of the population—amongst them many of the most desperately poor in the world—are being sacrificed on the altar of the neo-liberal logic of global capitalism. There is absolutely no reason to assume that the vast majority of people in South Africa will find their lives improved by the policies that are being adopted in their name by the present ANC government. Indeed, something quite the reverse is the far more likely outcome.

Capitalism is irrational?

But what am I really bemoaning in this passage? Is it the fact that the world has changed, that capitalism is everywhere hegemonic, and that socialism, as a world historical alternative, has been more or less obliterated, that explains this outcome? Are we merely forced back, in such a context, to the grim epigram [quoted earlier in this chapter] of the Polish-American theorist, Adam Przeworski: "Capitalism is irrational; socialism is unfeasible; in the real world people starve—the conclusions we have reached are not encouraging."

Capitalism is irrational? How else to explain a situation in South Africa (but it is also true on a global scale) where the vast majority of people are desperate in their poverty for a wide range of the simplest goods and services on the one hand and a very large percentage of people (most often the same people) are equally desperate for jobs on the other. Why can't these two central pieces to the South African puzzle simply be put together, you ask? Why must they be joined so indirectly and inefficiently through the circuits of global capital and the process of generating surplus value (profits) for the few with the power to dictate terms and guarantee their own massive cut of the action?

No one needs to be reminded of these facts perhaps, not in a world where (according to one set of UN figures) the share of the world's income of the richest twenty percent of the world's population has risen to a staggering eighty-five percent while the share of the poorest twenty percent has declined to 1.4 percent. But of course in South Africa itself the already vast gap between rich and poor has also continued, by most accounts, to widen since 1994. True, a few more blacks have joined the whites at the top of the table. But is there really so very much consolation to be found in that?

No question, whatever Trevor Manuel and the business press may say, such outcomes are—there is no other word for it—irrational. And yes, in the "real world" of South Africa people do starve. This is not a surprising outcome. Not so long ago, Colin Leys and I produced a survey of the capitalist prospect in Africa in which we concluded that the result for Africa is "relegation to the margins of the global economy, with no visible prospect for continental development along capitalist lines...Africa's development and the dynamics of global capitalism are no longer convergent, if they ever were." The point stands, I think.

What of South Africa itself in this respect? In his own analysis of Africa the highly regarded sociologist Manuel Castells (a recent visitor to South Africa) sees somewhat more room for South African manoeuvre within global capitalism than is the case elsewhere on the continent. He argues this because of the country's size and relatively sophisticated economic structure compared with other African countries. And yet even Castells must conclude his analysis of South Africa by evoking the possibility of South Africa falling, like "its ravaged neighbours," into "the abyss of social exclusion." As he writes, "the real problem for South Africa is how to avoid being pushed aside itself by the harsh competition in the new global economy once its economy is open." Since it is unlikely to do so, this is, I fear, Castells' most convincing formulation.

But wait: are these merely examples of the dreaded "Afro-pessimism" that we have all been hearing so much about? I don't think so, although that charge has certainly been levelled at me during my stay in South Africa when I have made such a point. No, I'd say the real "afro-pessimists" are those who state that Africa (including South Africa) has little choice but to tag along behind a global capitalism that actually offers very little by way of development prospects for the continent.

Leaps of faith

Africans—South Africans not least—can do better than that. Current Wits Vice-Chancellor Colin Bundy acknowledged some years ago that to continue to hold out the prospect of a socialist transformation in South Africa may seem to require something of a "leap of faith." But, he continued forcefully, "to imagine that a milder mannered capitalist order can secure a decent future for the majority of South Africans—or that deracializing bourgeois rule will meet the aspirations of exploited and oppressed people—or that South Africa can somehow be absolved of its economic history and enter a future like that of Sweden or Taiwan: now that really requires a leap of faith." Surely, in short, there are stronger grounds upon which to build an "Afro-optimism" than through such a feckless flight to the right.

What about socialism, then? In principle it makes a lot more sense, surely: "From each according to their means, to each according to their needs." But "unfeasible"? I'm not so sure. After all, not so very long ago there were alternatives to neo-liberalism proposed in South Africa, and not merely in Nelson Mandela's celebrated call for nationalizations (which he very soon retracted in the name of accelerated "privatization," as we know) on the very day of his release from prison in 1990.

Recall, for example, "growth through redistribution," a modestly radical proposal once used in ANC circles to suggest a possible first step towards challenging capital and prioritizing the needs of the vast mass of the population within the productive process. As now governor of the Reserve Bank, Tito Moboweni, then phrased it, "The ANC believes that a strategy of 'growth through redistribution' will be the appropriate new path for the South African economy... In our growth path, accumulation depends on the prior redistribution of resources. Major changes will have to take place in existing power relations as a necessary condition for this new growth path."

Or take the 1994 argument of Nelson Mandela (it seems a long time ago now): "We are convinced that left to their own devices the South African business community will not rise to the challenges facing us...While the democratic state will remain and develop the market, we envisage occasions when it will be necessary for it to intervene where growth and development require such intervention." I agree with Mandela here, although I would take the point much further. For unless centres of democratic power can begin to wrest exclusive control over decisions about production out of the hands of capital and begin increasingly to discipline the latter to a larger social purpose than mere profit-making there is not much hope of progress.

And yet, how different from this are the public debates of the moment. Isn't it now: ask not what capital can do for you, but what you can do for capital? All foreign investment and "trickle down effects," stock markets and lotteries. And, of course, "black empowerment"—with this often cast (as the President put it in a recent speech to a meeting of black managers) in terms of a need to "strive to create and strengthen a black capitalist class," a "black bourgeoisie." In fact, Mbeki continued, since "ours is a capitalist society," the "objective of the deracialization of the ownership of productive property" is key to "the struggle against racism in our country."

There's one problem, however, in Mbeki's mind:

> Because we come from the black oppressed, many of us feel embarrassed to state this goal as nakedly as we should. Indeed, our lives are not made easier by those who, seeking to deny [sic] that poverty and wealth in our country continue to carry their racial hues, argue that wealth and income disparities among the black people themselves are as wide as the disparities between black and white. Simply put, the argument is that the rich

> are rich whether they are black of white. The poor are poor whether they are black or white.

All of which, Mbeki continued, "frightens and embarrasses those who are black and might be part of the new rich." Get it? The new black capitalist class are victims—of class analysis.

Of course, I'm not suggesting for a moment that structures of racial inequality aren't an ongoing problem in South Africa. But can the issue of class formation and its long-term social and political implications really be finessed away so easily in the new South Africa? Like them or not, the statistics suggest otherwise: as it happens, "the rich are rich whether they are black or white." In short, one fears that Mbeki's celebrated "African Renaissance" comes to be primarily about the "embourgeoisement" of the favoured few. If so, it could turn out to be a very tawdry thing indeed.

True, a report in a recent issue of the *Mail and Guardian* suggests that some within the ANC (but what about Mbeki himself?) wish to draw away from that position ("ANC backtracks on black bourgeoisie," *M&G*, June 2, 2000). Nonetheless, the current presidential fashion of posing South Africa's challenge in terms of the problem of "poverty" is not much more promising a formulation. Paradoxically, the language of poverty alleviation is not an uncomfortable one for those at the top, looking down, to employ. For who can deny the existence of poverty in South Africa and who isn't charitably against it? But what if the problem were named differently: as the deepening polarization of social classes across the colour line, and as a pattern reinforced by the very logic of a capitalist development strategy? Quite another matter, obviously.

A revolutionary alternative?

Don't get me wrong. I haven't a blueprint for the revolutionary alternative. That can only be worked out, centimetre by centimetre, by South Africans themselves, as engaged in concrete struggles for change. What I can tell, however, is when a blue-print isn't working—and that's the case with present-day South Africa's neo-Thatcherite turn ("Just call me a Thatcherite," as we have seen Mbeki famously to have said at the launching of GEAR).

Nor am I merely arguing this from afar. My hunch is that, through our shared vulnerability, people all over the world are linked in their struggle against global capitalism in a way that we haven't quite seen before (viz., "the spirit of Seattle"). The fact is that global capitalism has, in the name of market realism, and the presumed imperatives of capital, forced on every country one version or another of a costly "race to the bottom." Thus, my own country, Canada, is currently having its vaunted welfare system picked clean, a "death of society by a thousand cuts," as Colin Leys has described the Canadian case.

But then nobody ever thought we had a chance for revolution in Canada: too rich, too comfortably close to the centre of global empire, too smug. Here in South Africa, as even Thabo Mbeki once envisaged it, the chance for something new and more promising has seemed greater. In this regard, some will perhaps find it difficult not to be sympathetic to the current leaders of the ANC, given the global pressures they are under. Nonetheless, it's equally difficult to escape the feeling—historians will decide—that in some important way these leaders have merely blown it.

Please understand. I've no illusions as to the importance of my own personal intervention here. The current leaders of South Africa don't have any reason to care what wizened old veterans of the anti-apartheid struggle think about the course that the liberation struggle has taken. After all, their primary points of reference, as the President's recent grand intercontinental tour clearly indicated, are now the Clintons, the Blairs and the Schroeders, the doyens of the International Financial Institutions, the WTO and the global business community. In such a context, the anti-apartheid movement, with its hopes of ongoing progressive transformation in post-apartheid South Africa, is definitely yesterday's news.

Nevertheless, some of us can't help thinking that history isn't over, that the second stage of South Africa's vaunted "two-stage revolution" may yet be at hand. Indeed, I seem to detect in many spheres—including within the ANC itself—signs that the left is beginning to reclaim space and to regain its self-confidence. Is it too "Afro-optimistic" to think, for example, that the several million workers who stayed away from work in protest on May 10 represent as much a wave of the future as they do a voice of conscience from the past? And what of the growing number of younger South Africans (like some of the students I have met while teaching at Wits) who are heartily sick of crime and unemployment, of social degradation and inequality, of retrenchments, marketization and the smug embrace of neo-liberalism? Might they not increasingly become tomorrow's news? I certainly hope so.

CHAPTER 5

The 2000s

Once More into the Breach

While I was in Johannesburg, at the dawn of the new millennium, I chose to present a second think piece, under the title "Towards a (small "a") alliance" to a workshop of academics and activists I helped organize at Wits just before my departure from the university and from the country. This workshop drew together various Jo'burg-based activists and a group of Wits' teachers to discuss the current state of the struggle in South Africa. I was also to write, upon my return to Canada and along the same lines, the balancesheet on the new South Africa I felt I could now more confidently strike on the basis of first-hand experience.

Thus my "Cry for the Beloved Country," published in the *Monthly Review*, became of some salience in the discussion of South Africa's post-apartheid trajectory, earning a range of responses (many of them quite hostile, of which several are discussed, alongside the inclusion of my original article, in my *Africa: The Next Liberation Struggle*). Nonetheless, I received many much more positive responses, including a particularly thoughtful and revealing one from Rusty Bernstein (a storied veteran campaigner of the ANC and the SACP) that was subsequently to be published in a leading South African journal, *Transformation* #64 (Durban, 2007). Let me begin here, however, with a second paper I also wrote (like the piece with which I concluded the previous chapter) at the time of my 2000 period of work in Johannesburg. For the two pieces together helped open the door to the challenging work of review and reflection that would lie ahead of me in the new century.

TEACHING FOR A TERM IN SOUTH AFRICA, I attended many political meetings—at the Workers' Library in Johannesburg and at other venues. Most heat was generated when the question of the Alliance [which housed the ANC, the SACP and the Congress of South African Trade Unions/COSATU] with a capital "A" was discussed. Those who spoke debated the merits of the ANC and of the wisdom of COSATU continuing to work through its tripartite relationship with the ANC and the SACP. Unfortunately, all too often the arguments for and against various strategic choices around these issues tended to be presented in very abstract terms, more often than not as long, boring and predictable recitations of platforms and positions from micro-parties ranging from centre left to far left.

Significantly, much the more interesting discussions (more light than heat!) occurred when the issue was a concrete one (a particular example of retrenchments, for example, or a reflection, say, on the impact developments in Zimbabwe were having on the land-hungry in South Africa). Comrades with heavy party political axes to grind tended to be silent or not to attend at all on such occasions and a more reflective and circumspect mood prevailed amongst those, often middle-level, cadres from within the unions and other such organizations, who did speak up.

Not that their inputs were any less serious than those of their more ideologically driven comrades. Quite the contrary. I even began to think that there might be a lesson here: perhaps the moment hadn't yet arrived for resolving the very largest of political questions in South Africa, perhaps something else needed doing first.

A range of resistances

What I thought I saw in such meetings, but also heard in conversations with numerous activists from many sectors during my stay, was that a range of resistances to orthodoxy, specifically neo-liberal orthodoxy, and to the bureaucratization of the erstwhile mass democratic movement, was beginning to spring up across the country. Such resistances were often modest, even sometimes rather isolated, and certainly not finding very effective voice through the party and governmental structures ostensibly available to them. But they are no less real for all that. And potentially, they help constitute a base for a new popular movement for progressive change in South Africa.

One should not, of course, romanticize the possibilities of reconstructing such a base. The popular forces are currently at a low ebb, as an important article by Shamim Meer[19] has recently reminded us: "A striking feature of the post-election period has been the demobilization of civil society. As the anti-apartheid struggle has waned, the organizations that sustained it have lost ground and influence in public life. Trade unions, civic associations, youth and women's organizations—in which the struggle was grounded—are all weaker." How much is rebuilding an effective popular movement therefore a matter of starting all over again, from scratch?

Not quite. Meer goes on to make the obvious point: "The poverty and inequality associated with apartheid— and which fuelled the struggle—remain." And to affirm, as she does, that awareness of this situation is also real enough. As Beyers Naude put the point several years ago, "While GEAR is a 'party political issue,' when it affects the poor the church has no option but to intervene." Or, as another church leader added, "The church should go back to the trenches, because it seems that is the language the government understands." This kind of sensibility continues to percolate through church circles, providing much of the clout for the growing strength of a local Jubilee 2000 campaign that focuses on the question of apartheid debt, and complementing other exemplary initiatives like the Campaign Against Neoliberalism in South Africa (CANSA).

And what of the townships? While it is true that the South African National Civics Organization (SANCO) is amongst those organizations hit hardest by post-apartheid institutional decay, circles of township militants, focused on issues of schools, health facilities and services, remain. New voices are beginning to be heard that ask tough questions and could give renewed life to broader urban-based initiatives. In addition, some fledgling reactivation of grassroots women's organizations—significantly demobilized both by too sanguine assumptions about the extent of the victory achieved by feminism and by the movement of many militants into the state—has also begun to occur.

Peasant-linked NGOs like the influential National Land Committee and the rural Development Services Network have pushed land and water issues, helped generate a "rural people's charter" and now taken fresh energy from recent land-related developments in neighbouring Zimbabwe. Moreover, these latter two organizations are among those feeding into the umbrella body, the South African Non-Governmental Organizations Coalition (SANGOCO), that has undertaken a number of signal initiatives, including, in the past few years, a revealing set of nation-wide public "Poverty Hearings" and floating the idea of an "Economics

Commission" of its own in order to help design a new framework for economic and social policies.

The trade unions

And then there are the trade unions, still very much at the centre of the revival of left politics in South Africa, however harshly they have been buffeted by the impact of neo-liberal economics (overall job losses, privatization, retrenchments) and by the insults directed at them all too frequently by the ANC top brass. However compromised some may feel the COSATU leadership to be, the organization is still able to pull out the numbers, as it did in May when upwards of four million workers stayed home and many hundreds of thousands demonstrated in the major cities. And it can still produce ringing and defiant pronouncements like that by COSATU general secretary Zwelinzima Vavi promising further mass action if government and business "fail to respond positively to COSATU's demands to stem job losses, stop privatization and for the state to play a direct role in correcting marked imbalances." As Vavi asks, "The economy is not working for us. GEAR is not working. How can we support this?"

But where is COSATU most likely to find allies in seeking to push such issues more forcefully? Perhaps not readily—and certainly not exclusively—within the (capital "A") Alliance. Indeed, it seems that the most pressing question facing COSATU right now may be how to find more effective ways of reaching downward and outwards to those actors in other sectors of society who also feel the pinch of neo-liberalism. And, in attempting to do so, wouldn't it be a smart move to dust off the language, so potent in the 1980s, of "progressive/working-class civil society" and to think in terms of rebuilding more systematically from below a movement of mass-based popular resistance to the strategic direction that post-apartheid South Africa has taken?

Looking for signs that the further forging of this kind of (small "a") alliance might actually be occurring I took heart from a news item in the business press (in the *Financial Mail*, May 19, 2000, to be exact) that I read towards the end of my stay in South Africa. The article focused on the fact that "organizations aligned to the ANC-led Alliance have regrouped into a formidable lobby which, judging by their frustration with government policy, could develop into SA's real political opposition."

This initiative was taken, it was said, to underscore the fact that "the real opposition in SA is not to be found in parliament, but in extra-parliamentary politics—as was the case before the ANC's unbanning in

1990." COSATU, Jubilee 2000 and SANGOCO are among those identified as key actors in this initiative, with the spirit behind it captured in the words of SANGOCO executive director, Albie Dithlake, a key figure in the group: "The debate on economic and social policy needs to be broadened. We need a reconfiguration of the nature of politics in SA. A realignment of politics will allow space for fresh input into the economic debate."

A "structured movement" of the left?

What this can mean in practice remains to be seen. But I found in it startling echoes of debates that are also taking place back in my own country, Canada, regarding the possible rebuilding from the ground up of a movement for progressive social change. Indeed, writings by Sam Gindin, Canada's pre-eminent trade union intellectual, offered a language that helped me make sense of my South African experience once I returned home. Gindin recommends for Canada the building of what he calls a "structured movement"—"something transitional that is more than a coalition and less than a party," as he puts it. Hadn't I just been witnessing in South Africa promising signs of just this kind of structured movement-in-the-making?

Interestingly, Gindin argues that the much debated "party question" (the NDP? a new party of the left?) be postponed for, say, five or six years in Canada, while the left movement/alliance—without abandoning its immediate concerns regarding self-defence and more appropriate policies—give priority to the development of its "political capacities." As for these capacities, they are specified by Gindin in terms of growth in "our understanding, our ability to win others over, the creation of new forums and structures for studying, working and fighting together." A movement, rejuvenated along these lines, says Gindin, will find itself laying the groundwork for an "alternative politics"—a politics that differs from the practices of currently established political parties in Canada (but also, might one add, from the present practices of the ANC in South Africa) in terms of "how it organizes, educates and mobilizes; the depth of its challenge to the status quo; the emphasis it puts on developing a counter-culture; its faith in the potential of ordinary people."

In South Africa, too, much more will have to be done to build a critical mass of such bottom-up assertions before the outlines of the organizational structures that might best focus such assertions and carry them forward can be identified. Perhaps a certain agnosticism is in order as to just where a growing (small "a") alliance will eventually find its most effective political expression. Could it be revitalizing, from within, the ANC—a party whose leadership has now taken a socioeconomic path that promises little to the vast mass of South Africans. Could it be, equally dauntingly, through the resuscitation of the SACP, or possibly by means of creating some other new political organization altogether? Again, it seems much too early to say.

Any ideas in the meantime? I know South Africans concerned to rebuild a progressive movement are generating plenty of them. One quite concrete suggestion did surface out of discussions I had with comrades in South Africa, however. I recalled the old Labour Monitoring Group that did so much in the 1980s to publicize trade union assertions not only to the outside world but also to the workers themselves. Wouldn't it be useful, we wondered, to establish some kind of "Mobilization Monitoring Group" whose principal task would be to record carefully the widening range of resistance sector by sector and circulate the record as often and as widely as feasible? Greater knowledge of mutual struggles through some kind of newsletter (as comprehensive as possible in its coverage but low in editorial content and modest in its political claims) could help give further resonance and enhanced confidence to those severally involved in popular activism around the country.

But of course this is merely one very modest proposal amongst many that might contribute to creating an ever more expansive sense of shared resistance on the part of those already engaged in struggle. And such initiatives would be seeking further to nurture the consciousness of a growing movement, further to structure that movement, and further to build towards the kind of "alternative politics" that might hope to regain the progressive momentum that seems, for the moment, to have been sidelined in South Africa. Starting from scratch? Not exactly perhaps, but something very much like it. Still, South Africans have been here before: first apartheid, now neo-liberalism. The struggle continues.

I WAS TO RETURN TO SOUTH AFRICA only two years after my period of teaching there for a counter-conference organized by various popular movements that stood outside the orbit of the ANC and were increasingly suspicious of it. The official event was the World Summit on Social Development, the WSSD, with the counter-conference designed to question the host ANC government's bona fides in this regard. And, in the demonstrations of the time, especially the march described below, I did glimpse a new spirit alight in South Africa and felt sufficiently encouraged to entitle a subsequent short piece on the events with the question: "The ANC's Project 'Exhausted'?" For there was certainly something afoot, even if the task of actually constructing a new and counter-hegemonic opposition movement to the ANC remains, to the present, a daunting one.

IT WAS, ON AUGUST 31 [2002], right in the middle of the dramatic "unofficial" march from Alex (the impoverished former "black township" set away from the heart of Johannesburg) to Sandton (a posh suburb of that same city which now serves as South Africa's business capital and where, indeed, the "official" WSSD conference that we were protesting was being held). I was stopped there for a television interview by the well-known Canadian writer and activist, Naomi Klein. She immediately asked the most probing of questions, one I had myself been puzzling over in the weeks leading up to the event. "As a long-time anti-apartheid activist in Canada," she asked, "are you surprised to find yourself now participating in a march against the ANC?"

I replied that, of course, I had been surprised—shocked, really—when, a week earlier, South African policemen fired into a peaceful candlelight march near the Wits campus to protest the arrest of several local activists. The severe burns suffered by a young Canadian comrade (Karen Cocq) who, marching near me, was hit by a percussion bomb shot directly at her, served as a grim wake-up call as to what the post-apartheid state was now capable of.

But the present march was different, a joyful event full of promise in both its numbers (at least 20,000, said the BBC, and I believe it) and its spirit. Many of us, I answered Klein, had suspected all along that it might prove easier to lay formal apartheid to rest than to tackle the capitalist-induced inequalities that were also part of the old order. But, I continued, it was difficult not to see in the energies of the thousands surging forward on this day precisely the same spirit of resistance to inequality and injustice that those of us in the anti-apartheid movement abroad had been privileged to associate ourselves with in the 1970s and 1980s.

Indeed, as I reflected to myself later, the very fact that such energies had come into focus against the ANC and its neo-liberal policies was actually the key to the promise that the march exemplified.

The verdict

For surely the jury is now in on the ANC leadership's overall project, the twinning of neo-liberal economics with the doubtful corollary that the needs of the masses really will be served by the trickle-down effects of increased capitalist success. Despite the noble efforts of many dedicated people in the middle ranks of state and party, the stark drumbeat of high unemployment and deepening inequality prevails and the much heralded provision of services begins to seem paltry, fragile and, for an ever higher percentage of people, unaffordable and hence unattainable.

Although it is true, for starters, that the global economy provides a harsh and unforgiving environment for African development efforts and this makes it even more difficult to believe that pursuing, on bended NEPAD, the holy grail of foreign investment and G8 largesse is anything more than a chimera. If the ANC can't come up with something better than this—something rather more resistant to the lowest common denominator of market logic than anything the Mbekis, the Manuels and the Erwins seem capable of divining—then how seriously can the erstwhile liberation movement now in power expect to be taken by ordinary South Africans?

Small wonder that groups like the Anti-Privatization Forum, the Soweto Electricity Crisis Committee, the Western Cape Anti-Eviction Campaign, the Concerned Citizens' Forum in Durban, and the Landless People's Movement have stepped forward in the past few years to focus the involvement of people in active resistance to their own government's bankrupt policies. It was their energies that also lent such force to the August 31 march.

In fact, the ANC as presently led and constituted has little to say to such people and such groupings, and it is not clear that the SACP or even the bulk of the trade union leadership, locked into their ("capital A") Alliance, have much to say either. Might one not suspect that the ANC project, the Alliance's project, is—as one South African friend said to me—"exhausted"?

Exhausted?

When I taught in South Africa a couple of years ago, I sensed the beginning of a sea change in South African politics and actually wrote about it in South Africa itself, in the *Mail and Guardian* (see above). True, the process of building an alternative politics was then just beginning, and it was certainly far from clear whether the fresh stirrings of popular discontent already visible would find their most effective expression within or without the ANC and its Alliance.

Leaving that question open, I nonetheless felt that I discerned the makings of a (small "a") alliance capable of drawing the trade unions into common cause with other actors in "civil society" (the churches, SANGOCO, and the like) to bring pressure to bear on the ANC-controlled state (and, beyond that, on capital, worldwide and local) in order to realize more humane and effectively developmental possibilities in South Africa.

Ironically, the groups I had then identified were the very groups that found themselves lured by the ANC into its own abortive "official" march on WSSD (a march correctly described as "a massive flop" by one South African newspaper) instead of linking up with the stirring demonstration of strength mounted, that same day, by the Social Movements' Ndaba. Indeed—since I wrote in 2000 (above)—it is other groups (notably those itemized above) that have stepped forward to give real substance to the radical promise of "working-class civil society." It begins to appear that COSATU and the NGOs will have to run to keep up with their sometime constituency as that constituency now turns left.

"The Tide is Turning"?

Of course, it would be foolish to underestimate the strength of the ANC's own continuing legitimacy, as the party of liberation, in many quarters, and the extent to which it still focuses the positive energies of many who would nonetheless wish it were rather more progressive than it has become. Equally foolish to underestimate how far a "Zanufied" ANC leadership might yet be prepared to go in order to protect its turf.

It would also be naive to overestimate the strength and unity of the new movements, the breadth of their reach, and the current level of their organizational capacity. There is, without doubt, a great deal of work to be done in order to seal the promise of a more progressive and appropriate politics in South Africa.

Perhaps it is too early, then, to say that "the tide is turning" (as one of the leaders of the march from Alex to Sandton enthusiastically shouted out to me along the route). Nonetheless, it is difficult to have been on that march and not sense that it served as a significant sign-post on the road to a post-neo-liberal and post-nationalist politics in South Africa—and as an impressive rallying point for forces that might yet get things back on track in South Africa. That is, in fact, the main message that many of us from abroad would be taking back to our constituencies from our days in Johannesburg and at the WSSD.

I ALSO DID A LOT OF SPEAKING OVER THE YEARS in pursuit of both my academic work and my political work. I won't bore the reader with an endless recitation of such presentations, as I spoke, from time to time and at various points in the evolution of both my own thinking and of the struggle in southern Africa, in most parts of Canada, many in the US and the UK, and elsewhere in Western Europe, too. Still, one somewhat more recent presentation in Canada stands out in my memory, one made at a workshop held by the Canadian Labour Congress (CLC) to explore, as the cover of the slim volume that included my text and that came out of the event announces, "the relationship between the labour movement and parties of the left in Canada and other countries."

I recalled having helped host in Toronto a meeting between South African and Canadian trade unionists about a decade earlier (as mentioned in the previous chapter), during South Africa's tough transition phase that would eventually see the ANC become the country's newly elected government. Now I sat on a panel with Zwelinzima Vavi, the head of South Africa's Congress of South African Trade Unions, the massive union that was in alliance with the ANC that has now been in power for almost a decade. I added the following remarks, pressing points I had lately been making in South Africa itself. They were later published (after some pruning by the original editor, they are here again lightly edited for inclusion in the present volume) in a booklet from the CLC entitled *Labour and Social Democracy: International Perspectives* (edited by Paul Leduc Browne).

HOW DOES LABOUR BEST REPRESENT its members politically? When you look back at the South African case, it becomes apparent—and we have learned this already from Comrade Vavi's presentation—that the way in which COSATU has primarily sought to represent its members politically is through the alliance that it has forged with the ANC (although a broader range of tactics and strategies have also been deployed).

Perhaps Mr. Vavi has been slightly diplomatic in some of the things he has said: his own difficulties in South Africa to some degree belie the picture he is presenting, although he made it very clear that the marriage that has emerged in South Africa between the liberation movement, the ANC, and the trade unions is not an entirely happy one.

As somebody said to me: it's all very well that the marriage should continue and that there is no divorce, but what is to happen if the relationship involved spousal abuse? For, if you want to press the metaphor so far, there are signs that the ANC's drift to the right is not so much a "drift" as a forced march to the right, towards a neo-liberal socioeconomic strategy, one that has involved the clear abuse of its partner, the labour movement.

A look at Africa today—Africa generally, not just South Africa—makes it immediately apparent that Africa has no scope for meaningful development within the frame of the global capitalist system, as it currently exists. Thanks to structural adjustment and diverse kinds of bullying by the World Bank, the IMF and various Western governments, Africa's weak economies are being forced to *compete* on an unequal, non-level playing field, something they quite simply cannot do successfully. They are, in the process, being ripped off by global capitalism.

For it is impossible to avoid the question in Africa as to whether the capitalist strategy of development actually works. One can repeat until the cows come home that the choice between capitalism and socialism is old hat, that it has been displaced by history, and so on and so forth, but, if you are in Africa, you cannot avoid facing that question. My colleague Greg Albo at York University has said that the choice globally—but it is certainly the choice in Africa- may actually be between a utopian capitalism and a realistic socialism!

In short, I would suggest that the need to transform global economic structures and African societies in a leftward direction is paramount. It is not surprising, then, that many Africans are beginning to sense that there is no way forward within the structures of global capitalism that currently exist: the history of Africa has placed it at the receiving end of a system that does not give it much scope for development by merely following standard economic models. In Africa at least, the question of socialism versus capitalism therefore *must be* on the agenda, not to be shuffled aside by simply saying that the Soviet Union did not work—if that was your idea of socialism (not mine!)—or that the Berlin Wall has fallen.

In South Africa, such questions were posed in a particularly dramatic way. True, South Africa has what is without doubt the most developed economy in Africa. But even South Africa's position within the global economy is far from being an unequivocally positive one. Nor can the country's problems be readily cured by merely swallowing the neo-liberal strategic nostrums that are currently being urged upon all governments in Africa. And yet, truth to tell, the ANC leadership has simply chosen a pretty unqualified neo-liberal economic strategy there.

[I then quoted once again from my recent *Monthly Review* article on South Africa on what I called the "sad denouement" of what otherwise looked to have been a successful liberation struggle—and to a range of statistics documenting the fact that "while the economic gaps between black and white has narrowed somewhat in South Africa, the gap between rich and poor is widening. This means that some blacks are moving into the upper circles of wealth, but that most blacks find their incomes falling." And I concluded that "South Africa's is an economy in difficulty, then. And one thing, in particular, is very far from clear: the very idea that neo-liberalism offers a viable way forward with its prescription of opening up the economy even further to privatization of a wide range of public assets and services, and of legislating increased labour flexibility (i.e., further vulnerability to capitalism)."]

Where does COSATU (I then asked) fit into this picture? In fact, its marriage to the ANC is a recent one, COSATU having for many years followed its own independent course. Even when the United Democratic Front, which was much closer to the ANC, emerged in the 1980s, COSATU did not join it. Indeed, it was not until the actual period of transition in the early 1990s that COSATU forged a formal alliance with the ANC. Moreover, to return to our earlier metaphor, the marriage has been stormy. COSATU has provided much of the electoral punch, in terms of both organization and personnel, that has enabled the ANC to win its elections. There is no doubt about that. In addition, as suggested above, COSATU's actions have also led to some modification of what could otherwise have been very stern labour legislation. Yet in terms of economic policy, COSATU has not, by and large, been able to stop the march of the ANC towards a neo-liberal, capital-oriented strategy—even if it has, sometimes, been quite critical of it.

For, as hinted, the GEAR strategy that replaced the RDP as the ANC's main strategy directive is essentially an extraordinarily neo-liberal design for managing the overall economy. [I then reiterated, among other such statements, Mbeki's celebrated "Just call me a Thatcherite" line.] Yet, as Comrade Vavi wrote at the time: "The economy is not working for us. GEAR is not working. How can we support this? This is a jobless bloodbath." These were the words he used. Nonetheless, this is what is happening in South Africa.

In the year 2000, during which I was working in South Africa, four million workers stayed home for a short period to protest the government's policies. The streets of Johannesburg, Durban and Cape Town were jammed with workers demonstrating. And many unions have stood up too: the Metal Workers has even raised questions occasionally as to the possible need for a socialist strategy; the Teachers' Union has been very critical of educational policy in the ANC's South Africa; the organization of the Municipal Workers has been a major force in trying to resist the sweeping privatization that is taking place in South African communities; and so on.

What is their reward for this? They have been chastised at COSATU meetings, and denounced, in very strenuous terms, by Mandela, Mbeki and others, labelled ultra-leftists, wreckers, people who are trying to destroy the economy in the name (at best!) of some abstract socialist cause. These are, in short, indices of what can only be described as, in many ways, an abusive relationship.

It is obviously not for me to say whether the benefits of staying in such a relationship outweigh the costs. Mr. Vavi has already said here that this relationship is not a seamless one, of course, and any careful reading of the situation in South Africa must surely reinforce this view. Moreover, in South Africa this reality has raised the question of whether alternative ways exist for representing union members politically. In this regard, we have heard today about other alliances that COSATU is forging with groups in the broader civil society. This is potentially important for the future of South Africa—but this possible development could also be quite instructive for Canada as well.

When I was working in South Africa, I spoke with many trade-unionists and others about what was happening there. There was, to put it mildly, considerable skepticism about the overall strategy being pursued by the ANC, as well as about the nature of the alliance forged between the latter and the unions. Not that it is entirely easy to walk away from the ANC. Despite its more recent policies, the ANC has earned considerable legitimacy as the major architect of the anti-apartheid struggle and of the change that has taken place in a formerly racist South Africa.

Indeed, its political legitimacy and control make it for the moment hegemonic. It is thus not easily challenged.

Furthermore, although some people do believe it would be better to "walk away" from the ANC and are convinced that there is nothing in its policies for them, others in COSATU (and in other spheres) do not wish to do so. For they believe that it is their ANC too: just because the group presently in power has taken a faulty economic line, it does not follow that others don't feel they have a stake in the ANC too, and that they have a right to expect a different kind of policy from it. They seek ways of bringing pressure to bear upon the ANC. For they do not assume that the ANC will necessarily seek to advance the workers' interests, as Comrade Vavi has made quite clear here today. Increasingly the talk (in certain circles at least) is very much about the need for what I have identified as another kind of alliance, a "small a" alliance that links trade unions with other groups in civil society (women's groups, environmental groups, community action groups and the like) in pursuit of their mutual interests—and in order to ensure the revival of a more meaningfully left politics.

In fact, this is a brand of politics that has become ever more important to the discussions that are currently taking place in South Africa. Indeed, it is beginning to be seen by many that it is not enough to merely "get into power"—although it is nice to do so and probably essential. But there is an equally important question: in gaining power, how can we build up institutions through which to pressure those who come to hold power in our name so as to encourage them to do what we would like to see them do? How do we, in short, establish a movement that focuses popular demand sufficiently strongly and clearly to keep the new leadership under strong pressure from below? For without this it is all too possible that legitimate voices (e.g., those of the workers) get shuffled aside as being those of mere "special interests"—to be trumped by a countervailing rhetorical claim wielded against them, that of a self proclaimed "government of all the people."

It has become clear to many in South Africa that power can be seductive and that it must be unpacked and examined carefully to see how it actually works in practice. Thus, the debate: what kinds of "small 'a'" alliances might be necessary to complement the "big 'A'" Alliance that already exists between COSATU and the ANC? And does this mean bringing worker pressure to bear in, through, and upon the ANC? Or must it eventually lead to the creation of another kind of political formation to the left of the ANC?

These are the kinds of questions that are increasingly being posed for popular forces as they find themselves faced with a government that has moved starkly to the right—in spite of the fact that such "popular forces" have been a major actor in bringing such governments to power. In South Africa this is seen by a growing number as, quite simply, a question that cannot be shirked, any more than can the question as to the kind of economic strategy that might actually work to serve the interest of the vast mass of the population!

As regards this latter question it has begun to be asked increasingly (though many trade unionists have been raising this query all along) as to whether the time has not come to reactivate the language and practice of socialism. How else to deal with a global order that is imposing upon South African policies that are *not* in the interests of people beyond the circles of the elite? Indeed, this seems (as suggested above) simply a matter of juxtaposing the "utopian capitalism" as invoked by the ANC leadership to a "realistic socialism." For a capitalist revolution, bettering the lot of the mass of the population is increasingly seen to be a utopian vision. Not that the realization of socialist development, in the context of a neo-liberal economy and polity, will be easy to achieve. But the costs of not attempting to so are increasingly apparent.

It is, of course, possible to become quite cynical about all this. [Here I again quoted Adam Przeworski's haunting aphorism to the effect that "capitalism is irrational, socialism is unfeasible, in the real world people starve."] For, in Africa, a central reality stands: if you think capitalism will positively transform the continent—as the Canadian government, for example, continues to claim at G8 summits—then you are wrong. As suggested, most of the people I have talked to in COSATU would agree. Precisely what this kind of awareness can mean in practice is, needless to say, a more challenging question. Yet are we forced to take a merely static view: that people are trapped in the "commonsense" of the moment and are incapable of imagining and thinking that new things are possible? Can't we ourselves begin, through political hard work, to help raise the level of popular understanding of, and commitment to, alternatives much more democratic and far more materially and spiritually fulfilling than anything presently existing?

On this front, while I was living and working in South Africa, speaking at great length with various people, I began to introduce Sam Gindin's idea of creating a "structured movement" [as discussed above, in this chapter]—not a party but more than a mere loose alliance. Here was something that might hope to pull together a range of social forces for political purposes, even if it does not, at least for the moment, raise the question of a political party. This has implications here in Canada clearly.[20] But in South Africa, with its recent history of apparently successful popular struggle but also its growing sense of promises and hopes broken and frustrated, this kind of question about the future is even more open. Perhaps it's true that there are not vast numbers of people saying that the Alliance should be smashed and that a new left party must be built. Perhaps there is even more talk about revivifying the ANC from within [as in some of the recent COSATU statements in support of the rise of Joseph Zuma to his possible candidacy for President in 2009]. And perhaps this will work [although Zuma himself appears to be a somewhat doubtful candidate to fill such a radicalizing role].

Nonetheless, as Vavi has pointed out here, there are more people than ever saying that it is indeed time to put real pressure for change upon the ANC. He has also said that trade unions acting alone cannot do it, lest they merely get dismissed as just another special interest group. Instead, some argue, it is necessary to build a movement of unions, of women, of community organizations, of churches and the like, and to begin, together, to become more effective players. True, there is a need for sober realism about all this. But, as we have seen, there is also a great and pressing need in South Africa for the revitalization of left politics that we have been discussing. This is as true in Canada as it is in South Africa, and indeed in most other places in the present-day world.

AS NOTED ABOVE, a period spent teaching in 2000 in South Africa enabled me to write with additional authority about the disturbing trends in that country that I had sensed from afar but could now more confidently document at first hand. I was to write of these, beyond the original pieces I prepared for the *Mail and Guardian*, in a variety of forums over the next few years and, in particular, in the article mentioned at the beginning of this chapter, "Cry for the Beloved Country," and published in *Monthly Review* (52, 8, January, 2001). I have also alluded earlier to the debate that it incited (including Rusty Bernstein's own remarkably supportive letter/commentary), a commentary also notable for Bernstein's own candid testimony as to the sobering anticlimax to ANC victory in South Africa.

But this squared all too neatly with our own experience in TCLSAC of the ANC, and its partner organizations, the South African Communist Party/SACP and the South African Congress of Trade Unions/SACTU) in Canada during the liberation struggle itself. Thus, both the ANC and SACTU (and, notably, for those of us active in anti-apartheid work in Toronto, its energetic SACTU Solidarity Committee in Toronto) were loath to grant the emergent trade unions on the ground in South Africa the kind of credibility and credit we sensed they actually warranted. As we sought to reach out from Canada to such unions we found ourselves haunted by ANC/SACTU incessant reiteration of the theme: "Direct links stink." Unfortunately, in their battle for hearts and minds, SACTU was assisted, paradoxically enough, by the Canadian Labour Congress, itself a haven of right-wing anti-communist sentiment that found itself supporting the right people—the independent trade unions—for the wrong Cold War reasons. And some of the best activists in the union movement, because of their justified suspicions of the CLC, came to support, all too exclusively, SACTU and the SACTU Solidarity Movement rather than the new and vibrant trade unions on the ground!

This was part of a more general problem in fact: an intense suspicion (something viewed with unease by many of us in the anti-apartheid movement in Canada) on the part of the ANC of any energies released from the base in South Africa that were not firmly under the control of its vanguardist organization. As cited above, shortly before his death Rusty Bernstein, the noted ANC/SCAP patriarch, himself offered an extended analysis of "what is going wrong in South Africa, and why," an "understanding" of this being, in his words, "the essential precondition for any rectification, and thus for any return to optimism about South Africa's democratic future." His summary, rooted in more or less the same period as the example I have just given and published in full in *Transformation*, was as follows:

> The drive towards power has corrupted the political equation in various ways. In the late 1980s, when popular resistance revived again inside the country led by the UDF, it led the ANC to see the UDF as an undesirable factor in the struggle for power, and to fatally undermine it as a rival focus for mass mobilization. It has undermined

> the ANC's adherence to the path of mass resistance as a way to liberation, and substituted instead a reliance on manipulation of the levers of administrative power. It has paved the way to a steady decline of a mass-membership ANC as an organizer of the people, and turned it into a career opening to public sector employment and the administrative "gravy train." It has reduced the tripartite ANC-COSATU-CP alliance from the centrifugal centre of national political mobilization to an electoral pact between parties who are constantly constrained to subordinate their constituents' fundamental interests to the overriding purpose of holding on to administrative power. It has impoverished the soil in which ideas leaning towards socialist solutions once flourished and allowed the weed of "free market" ideology to take hold.

This added up to formidable price to be paid by newly "liberated" South Africans, and I will allude to only one other. For imagine the benefits of having instead developed institutions of self-empowerment, beyond the ballot box and the marketplace, that would have helped encourage people to grow a further sense of self-respect and purpose—to develop, in sum, a transformative popular consciousness grounded in a transformative political and economic practice. How much less likely, for example, would have been any withdrawal by ordinary South Africans from the electoral process or their opting for the grim hatreds and morbid identities of mere xenophobia that we have seen in recent years in South Africa? Here, in short, are some of the costs of detaching liberation from the substance of democratic voice, and from the space that could have been opened up if people had been encouraged to find more active and creative participation in the making of their own lives.

As for myself, I was to present a second piece, equally controversial, later in the decade when, in the spring of 2007 I returned to South Africa, my first plane journey since a near-fatal accident several years before. I had recovered sufficiently to be carefully following, by means of published articles, the internet and personal contacts, the grim unfolding of events both in South Africa and in the wider region. During my visit I several times presented—in a talk entitled "The Strange Death of Liberated Southern Africa"—my overall evaluation of recent developments there, including to a gathering of township activists brought together by the Municipal Services Project in Cape Town. (The talk was then published, first in South Africa itself [in *Transformation* #64, as noted] and then in my 2008 collection, *Decolonization and Empire*, where the interested reader can track it down, if so inclined.) Note that I had more or less poached the talk's title from a highly regarded old book by George Dangerfield entitled *The Strange Death of Liberal England*[21]—hoping to give a similarly bleak spin to that catchy title in my own paper. For there was actually a quite substantive resonance to the twin themes. Dangerfield wrote of the period of proto-revolutionary upsurge in Britain on the eve of the First World War—encompassing actions by women, workers, the Irish—and of the role of the Liberal Party, caught up in the maelstrom of the time.

The parallel was by no means entirely apposite, I argued, but one sentence in the book's opening pages did catch my eye. The Liberals, Dangerfield wrote, emerged from the fray "flushed with one of the greatest victories of all time," yet, he added, "from that victory they never recovered." As I then continued: "Something similar could be said of southern Africa more generally: of Frelimo, of the MPLA, of SWAPO, of ZANU and of the ANC. For these movements, although still 'in power,' have now come to preside over the death of the promise that they were once thought to epitomize and their victories, or at least the way they came about, were arguably ones from which they too might never recover—in any meaningful sense. It is with this paradox in mind that I not only have given [I further noted] such a title to the present essay but also the title to one of my recent books—*The Next Liberation Struggle*—a 'next liberation struggle,' for which I live in hope."

Writing this essay provided me with an opportunity to set down some final thoughts on the outcome of the thirty years war for southern African liberation, including countries such as Angola, Zimbabwe and Namibia, sites of that war which have been somewhat less central to my direct research agenda over the years than Mozambique and South Africa. I have, nonetheless, written about these countries and continue to do so,[22] less often about Angola, more often, over a span of some thirty years, on Zimbabwe. Indeed, as noted above, I find what I wrote of

Zimbabwe as early as 1975 and 1980 to be especially haunting and can only regret that my then negative prognostication has proven to be an accurate if, even then, a somewhat understated one.[23]

Perhaps, beyond the cases of South Africa and Mozambique, I have written most intensively on Namibia, including my book, jointly written with Colin Leys and others, *Namibia's Liberation Struggle: The Two-Edged Sword*. The fact is, however, that it was as regards Namibia I was most mistaken in the early years. Indeed, we at TCLSAC were approached on one occasion by a group of Namibians who came to Toronto at one point during their own country's armed struggle as part of a North American information tour. Their mission: to inform us of the authoritarian manner in which SWAPO, the UN-sanctioned liberation movement in Namibia, was harassing and terrorizing dissident voices within SWAPO and the Namibian exile community. We were suspicious of such claims, smelling a South African disinformation ploy, and, in any case, were content to view Namibia, a relatively small country, as more or less a subset of the apartheid South Africa problem, a country that illegally controlled Namibia. It was a tragic error that I came to regret and later attempted to redress in scholarly work with Colin Leys just referred to.[24]

Of course, I also wrote in the essay on the "strange death" of "liberation" elsewhere in the region—in Angola and Mozambique (the latter country's fate having also been much discussed in these pages) and through a probing of the profound anti-climax that an apparently successful end to the anti-apartheid struggle in South Africa has produced. Perhaps I should merely add here that the observations on the ground made during my 2007 visit served merely to reinforce the grim reading of developments in the region that the research for and writing of my original article had forced upon me. Nonetheless, the trip itself—and especially the workshop, in Cape Town, of township activists that had originally extended the invitation for my visit—also confirmed my sense that the struggle for genuine liberation is still alive in South Africa, in spite of the machinations of both global capital and the currently hegemonic ANC elite. Moreover, I was moved, on the evidence from yet another visit there in 2009, to register more recently the same continuing contradictory reality in South

Africa. For assessing on the ground the fallout of the ascendance of Jacob Zuma to the South African presidency in the 2009 election merely reinforced my sense of the limited meaning that liberation has come to have to date in South and southern Africa—a sobering reflection that I had felt forced to also offer when, during this trip, I spoke several times in South Africa.[25]

AND WHAT, TO RETURN TO THAT THEME, of Canada itself, as seen through the lens of a long-time anti-apartheid activist? As it happened, I had been moved to reflect on this question when first asked by my comrades at *SAR*, several years ago, to review the volume *The Ambiguous Champion: Canada and South Africa in the Trudeau and Mulroney Years*, written by a long-time contributor to our own magazine (*SAR*), Linda Freeman. In the review in question, I first considered, via a critique of Freeman, the historical record:[26]

DIPLOMACY IS THE ART OF GOING ABROAD to lie politely for one's country. So the wags would have it. And whatever else one might say about Nelson Mandela's otherwise very moving 1998 visit to Canada there was quite a lot of lying going on. How else to categorize the constant references to Canada's grand and glorious record in the anti-apartheid struggle?

Not that Mandela was the main perpetrator of such fabrications. As often as not he spoke about the record of Canadians in general rather than that of the Canadian government in particular when handing out kudos (although even he trotted out the heroic litany of "Diefenbaker, Trudeau and Mulroney" during his remarkable Skydome appearance and elsewhere). Veterans of the anti-apartheid struggle in this country could take some solace from the possibility that, most often, he was really speaking about us rather than about the Canadian politicians and businessmen with whom he was in fact spending most of his time.

And yet it was just such politicians and businessmen—now basking in the glory of Mandela's presence—who seemed most smugly engaged in facilitating the pretence that Canada had been in Mandela's corner all along. Difficult, it is true, to put on too many airs in the presence of someone who spent twenty-seven years in prison for his belief in racial equality and human dignity and then emerged to embrace his captors in a spirit of reconciliation. Nonetheless, there was a distinct atmosphere of self-congratulation all round about the visit, and, needless to say, not a hint of apology from "official Canada" about the role Canada had actually played in the anti-apartheid struggle.

No apology

Still, apology would have been the most appropriate response. It is the great strength of Linda Freeman's new book, *The Ambiguous Champion: Canada and South Africa in the Trudeau and Mulroney Years*, that it permits of no other conclusion about Canada's record. Moreover, it makes its case with such a wealth of documentation and careful argument that it should stand as the essential touchstone for all future discussion of the topic.

Freeman has come by her expertise honestly. The bibliography reveals that she earned her PhD on the topic of "The Nature of Canadian Interests in Black Southern Africa" as far back as 1978. And readers of SAR will recall her relentless tracking of Canada's southern Africa policy through over a decade of annual surveys in these pages (indeed, her very short list of acknowledgements includes gracious thanks to "the Southern Africa Report collective"). This is a book long in the making, then, but worth the wait since the scholarship it represents is thorough and formidable (the footnotes and bibliography run to 130 pages for example, almost a third the book's length!) and the argument important.

What she does is demonstrate convincingly how compromised Canada's official policy toward white minority rule in southern Africa was over the decades. For example, she usefully debunks the overblown legend of Diefenbaker as scourge of South Africa within the Commonwealth in the early 1960s. And she neatly documents Lester Pearson's role, later in the decade, both in rationalizing for a wider audience Britain's half-hearted response (through the weakest of sanctions packages) to Rhodesia's UDI and in himself resisting any economic measures whatsoever against South Africa.

However, Freeman saves her main fire for Trudeau and Joe Clark. Trudeau remains a great enigma for the progressively minded in Canada, along the lines of: he's so smart, why didn't he do a lot better? In fact, on southern Africa he did worse, as Freeman clearly documents. His was a callous failure of humane principle made all the more galling by his infamous statement of the time that "we should either stop trading or we should stop condemning." But, of course, he continued to do both. A smug prisoner of Canada's presumed capitalist imperatives, Trudeau idly allowed Canada's economic links to apartheid to deepen on his watch and, as Freeman scrupulously documents, permitted the likes of Hedley Bull and his Space Research Institute to bolster South Africa's military arsenal—this despite the UN's mandatory arms embargo of 1977. Nor, as one might anticipate, were things carried out in any more principled a manner during Joe Clark's brief interregnum as Prime Minister.

Theoretical interlude

Of course Canadian anti-apartheid activists, accustomed to Freeman's trenchant articles in the pages of *Southern Africa Report* over the years, will need little persuading as to the merits of her book, in terms both of the comprehensiveness of the data she provides and of the general accuracy of the analysis she presents. No doubt many of you will have already read the book. Rather than gild the lily, then, let me seek instead to engage critically with several of the book's more controversial dimensions—in terms both of its approach and some of its substantive interpretations—that are likely to be of particular interest to those for whom the experience of the anti-apartheid struggle remains an active legacy.

To a considerable degree Freeman allows her careful documentation to drive her argument on these matters. But she is too good a social scientist to pretend that it is really possible for "the facts" merely to speak for themselves. Some theoretical perspective is necessary, even inevitable. Here she chooses, in the first instance, to emphasize the importance to the shaping of Canada's policy by structural determinations, those defined principally by the logic of Canada's capitalist economy and the vested interests, corporate and bureaucratic, linked to that logic. This proves to be a powerful entry point, as a *Globe and Mail* staffer felt forced to acknowledge of her book when first reviewing it last year (Sean Fine, "How Canada failed South Africa," *G&M*, April 11, 1998). Fine concedes Freeman's case that the "politics of balance" (social justice vs. economics) claimed by decision-makers as driving Canada's South African policy was largely "illusory": "The guiding philosophy was that the state should not interfere with the private sector."

Still, Freeman is unwilling to advocate any straightforward brand of economic determinism, emphasizing—as a means both of defending herself against such a charge and of enriching her analysis—the simultaneous importance of certain "autonomous variables." In this regard she makes much of the impact of "discourse," the extent to which the common-sense premises of establishment discussion of South African issues become a factor in their own right in determining outcomes, especially within the foreign-policy-making bureaucracy. And yet what Freeman presents as evidence in this regard is the operation of pretty unmediated capitalist ideology: the reduction of national interests to the unquestioned pursuit of profit.

More convincingly, she notes the impact of the discourse of "non-violence," much trumpeted by "official Canada" to justify its not taking sides more unequivocally—although here too she shows any such preoccupation to have been pretty opportunistically and selectively defined, not least in Cold War terms. Still, if Freeman had pressed her search for intervening variables a little harder she might also have made much more than she does in this book of our pattern of institutionalized racism that made it all too easy for Canadians to deny to Africans the necessary means of their liberation that (for example) we had been more than willing to grant to the maquis of Europe during the Second World War.

Even more important for Freeman as an "autonomous variable," however, is something she calls "politics," this latter said to qualify the impact on policy of established economic interests that seem otherwise to define so much about the supine role of Canada towards apartheid South Africa that she describes. Here the shift in Canadian policy undertaken by Brian Mulroney, the other key player focused on in Freeman's book, becomes a critical test case for her. If structural/economic determination serves to explain so much about most phases of Canadian policy towards South Africa why, Freeman asks, was Mulroney able to go further than any other Prime Minister in acting, rather than merely speaking, tough towards South Africa? For Mulroney did, as Freeman scrupulously documents, carry Canada's sanctions' policy and some related anti-apartheid initiatives to a high-water mark.

The Mulroney moment

The issue may be less complicated than Freeman supposes. One other possible intervening variable (somewhere between economic structure and "politics") she rather surprisingly downplays is class, a factor never systematically embraced in a book that otherwise seeks to stake out radical ground in the study of Canadian foreign policy. And yet what binds businessmen, politicians and higher-level civil servants is the privileged position they share in the upper reaches of the class hierarchy in this society and the (hegemonic) outlook—"discourse"!—they are encouraged to share.

Against this kind of analysis, however, Freeman chooses to frame her radical critique by highlighting what she calls the "structured representation of interests," an approach that risks functioning as a kind of left variant of pluralist theory. Thus, under normal circumstances, some voices—notably those linked to capital—are argued to sound more loudly in the pluralist chorus that drives our politics than others. But when they don't, at least in any very straightforward manner, the reason must be "politics," this term implying, apparently, the impact on policy of a much wider range of political interests. What we were witnessing in the Mulroney case, she argues, is "a response at the political level to the dramatically new conjuncture at home in Canada and abroad in South Africa. In this way, the new policy demonstrated the relative autonomy of the Canadian state from key forces wedded to the policy of the past" (p. 134).

No doubt developments in South Africa itself did change the terrain of decision-making considerably and demanded fresh thinking about appropriate Canadian policies. But how far do the invocation of "the political level" and "relative autonomy" take us in explaining Mulroney's own response? Not far enough, I fear, if Freeman is suggesting that forces from beyond the sphere of ruling class interests had suddenly become central to Canada's policy-making vis-à-vis South Africa. For the fact remains that "key forces" from the past—the hegemonic Canadian capitalist class—dictated outcomes even during this period.

Of course, the terms of such ruling class hegemony cannot be read crudely off the presumption that some entirely straightforward "logic of capital" is at work; class analysis of a far more shrewd and supple kind is required. Political assertions from below do have some impact, for example: but this is primarily because an effectively hegemonic class will be at its most successful when it is able to co-opt and contain such oppositional demands rather than merely seek to repress them. This point is particularly important to our discussion, below, of Freeman's analysis of the Canadian anti-apartheid movement. More central here is the fact that struggles within that hegemonic class (struggles between factions and fractions shaped by differing interests and differing levels of craft and understanding) to define its strategies are often as intense as any struggle between classes. Indeed, in seeking to understand the apparent anomalies of the "Mulroney moment," it is precisely by focusing upon such intra-class struggles that we learn far more than through any insights provided by "radical pluralist theory."

Saving the baby

Thus capital in South Africa itself had long profited from the cheap labour made available by a parallel system of racial oppression. However, what seems evident is that, by the mid-1980s, a profound debate had emerged within the capitalist class, world-wide and local, over how best to deal with the problem that a near-revolutionary South Africa now posed. Cooler heads within that class had begun to have some pretty daring thoughts, in effect echoing the earlier insight of Anglo-American executive Zac de Beer that "we all understand how years of apartheid have caused many blacks to reject the economic as well as the political system ... We dare not allow the baby of free enterprise to be thrown out with the bathwater of apartheid."

Particularly important [as also quoted earlier in this book] in advancing this point of view was Malcolm Fraser, the Conservative former Prime Minister of Australia, who was an extremely vocal member of the Eminent Persons' Group (EPG) assigned by the Commonwealth in the mid-'80s to investigate the South African situation. Echoing the EPG's call for sanctions to force apartheid South Africa to its senses before the confrontation there escalated out of control, Fraser (as cited by Freeman) argued that any such escalation meant "moderation would be swept aside ... The government that emerged from all this would be extremely radical, probably Marxist, and would nationalize all western business interests." As I wrote at the time (in my article "Mysteries of the Dark Cabinet: What is behind the Mulroney government's surprising stand on South Africa?" *This Magazine*, August-September, 1988 [included in chapter 3, above]), "it seems clear that Mulroney responded to this reading of the South African situation. To the goal of ingratiating himself with the black Commonwealth was now added the role of spearheading the forces of enlightened capitalism!" From such a perspective much of the mystery attached to the explanation of Mulroney's anti-apartheid initiative falls away.

To be fair, Freeman does allude to much of this evidence and it is also true that some of the other variables she introduces did have pertinent effects: for example, it probably did make some difference to Mulroney's ability to embrace the side of the intra-capitalist strategic debate he did that he was not a racist like Reagan and Thatcher. Still, Freeman at times seems so intent upon looking elsewhere for additional "political" explanations of Mulroney's choice that she tends to blur the central insight offered by a more firmly grounded class analysis of that choice. Moreover, this latter way of understanding Canadian policy-making is further verified by what happened next: when the South African government seemed to have succeeded at least momentarily in crushing domestic resistance through its Emergencies of the later 1980s its apparent success suggested the possibility of a return to "business as usual" on the old racist terms—and reinforced the less adventurous perspectives both of other capitalist actors in Canada and of other, larger capitalist powers, notably Britain and the United States.

At this point Mulroney's own enthusiasm waned (p. 165), further solidifying a context within which the forces in Canada supportive of a more conventional capitalist approach to South Africa (their lineup usefully itemized by Freeman here) waxed strong once again, and the malignant Clark could emerge as Cabinet point-man for reining in what was now thought to have been too forward a policy. This is not too surprising. After all, even in acknowledging the uniqueness of the Mulroney moment Freeman demonstrates just how short-lived and shallow the high-water mark of Mulroney's anti-apartheid initiative actually was. Now, as that moment faded, she can link her evaluation of Mulroney that much more firmly to her earlier discussion of the likes of Diefenbaker and Trudeau and emphasize the flimsy nature of Mulroney's own claim to the legendary status that has begun to accrue to him on this front (p. 256). And yet, at the same time, it is interesting to note the number of members of the capitalist class who would come to see Mulroney as having been right the first time. Indeed, it was precisely during the late 1980s' period of Mulroney's retreat from his advanced thinking regarding apartheid that certain similarly inclined capitalists in South Africa itself were beginning to press forward successfully the logic of a very similar containment strategy for preempting and taming black aspirations.

THAT SAID, I THEN CONCLUDED MY REVIEW of Freeman's important book with thoughts not merely about the overall pattern of official Canada's stance, past, present and future, towards South Africa, but also about the nature, in retrospect, of the anti-apartheid movement with which we had both been active for so many years. A signal as to the nature of my own future work (now in progress) on the history of liberation support and anti-apartheid work in Canada and elsewhere, such thoughts may nonetheless serve here as a useful, albeit sobering, penultimate conclusion to the first two sections of the present book.

WHAT, WHILE ALL THIS WAS GOING ON, of the Canadian anti-apartheid movement? It bears emphasizing that in her concern to allow "politics" to matter Freeman is led to study carefully the role—one that another writer might have ignored—played by various forces in Canadian society that swam against the current of establishment interest and orthodoxy as regards South Africa. In her book this encourages an important acknowledgement of the often impressive efforts of a wide range of churches, unions, NGOs and liberation support organizations linked to the Canadian anti-apartheid movement, broadly defined. And yet, as hinted earlier, in her search for the "political" explanation for the rise of Mulroney's own anti-apartheid policy—one that, given her approach, must emphasize the broadening and diversifying of the range of relevant political forces in order to explain outcomes—she may give the movement far more credit for producing that enlightened policy than it deserves. Even more clearly, she places far too much blame upon the movement for permitting the subsequent weakening of Mulroney's commitments (she speaks, in this respect, of the negative impact of "the splintering of the movement" in the late 1980s, of the "rut into which [it] seemed to have fallen," and of the extent to which its self-destructive tendencies "removed a key irritant from within civil society" [p. 232]).

For starters, in documenting the range of organizations and individuals involved in anti-apartheid work in Canada Freeman misreads the nature of the movement in important ways. Thus her main point of reference in measuring movement success seems to be the degree of its institutionalization as a national movement. Yet this is not a particularly illuminating angle of vision. True, as she demonstrates, the movement was pulled forward, briefly, towards a more integrated national focus during the heyday of Mulroney's policies. But most anti-apartheid activists had never been naive about what could be accomplished at that level, choosing instead to prioritize efforts in their own diverse constituencies, social and geographical.

After all, the alternative model was the British Anti-Apartheid Movement, its measure of unity facilitated by the compact geography of the UK, but also by a degree of enforced policy conformity (uncritical support of the ANC, for example) that many anti-apartheid activists in Canada would not (quite rightly, in my opinion) countenance. As for the fact that some left-liberal campaigners fell for Clark's venal attempt in the late 1980s to substitute various feel-good gimmicks (his focus on the media question, for example) for any substantial deepening of sanctions, or were coopted by monies momentarily made available by the government for certain kinds of anti-apartheid activities, this was perfectly predictable. Nonetheless, in my experience and in sharp contradiction to the elegiac tone adopted by Freeman about such matters, there was no slackening off of anti-apartheid work in Toronto itself and in many Toronto-based institutions (but this was also true elsewhere in the country) as the 1980s wore on, whatever the decay of the soft unity that had momentarily surfaced nationally amongst very diverse constituencies, regionally, politically and ideologically.

But what about the impact of this movement, however interpreted, on policy? No doubt, in its very diversity, it did make some difference: ironically, Freeman herself—only several pages (p. 248) after her pronouncement of the movement's self-destruction—is to be found hailing the extent to which forces in civil society (churches, unions and the like) stayed the Mulroney government from merely dumping such sanctions as were in place at the point when the negotiations process began in South Africa in 1990! But in the 1980s phase Freeman focuses upon most centrally, the movement's fate was to flow most strongly with the opportunity offered (largely for reasons beyond the movement's own control) by the Mulroney moment and to appear to ebb somewhat when that moment passed. To interpret events otherwise—to "blame the movement" for Mulroney's backsliding, for example—is to miss the main point to be gleaned from an alternative reading of the history of the anti-apartheid movement in Canada.

For the one thing that a structural-cum-class analysis of Canadian policy-making should underscore is just how limited in its impact a reformist approach (including the attempt to reform one particular aspect of Canada's foreign policy) must inevitably be without a far more fundamental transformation of Canadian society and polity. This is the hard lesson that radical anti-apartheid activists kept learning during the years of their activity as they were confronted constantly with the economic-cum-class logic of our country's link to racial capitalism in South Africa. This is not to say that they—we—were wasting our time, nor is it to say that we couldn't have worked both harder and more effectively. It is to suggest, however, that Freeman's pluralistic/"political" qualifications of her main argument risk blurring the very strength of the case (about the overbearing impact on policy of the untransformed socioeconomic structures in this country) she makes most effectively... and usefully.

This as regards the past. What of the present? As I continued:

In the end, interestingly, these latter structures reclaim centrality in her argument about Canadian policy-making. Not the least of the virtues of this important book is Freeman's insistence on carrying her story through, however briefly, to the post-apartheid present—a sign of her welcome insistence throughout on wedding careful scholarship to social and political concern. Moreover, her "Conclusion and Epilogue" demonstrate, once again, the strengths of the structural emphasis within, at its best, her overall argument. For she reveals unerringly the narrow and selfishly market-driven character of Canada's continuing outreach (trade, aid and the rest) to post-apartheid South Africa, making this chapter of far more than historical interest and indeed required reading. Her conclusion is powerful: "In the current conjuncture of neo-liberal fundamentalism, dominant forces in Canada and the West seem even more indifferent to the interests of the vast majority [in South Africa] than they were in the long battle to end apartheid" (p. 304).

Good stuff. Yet even in this last chapter there must be nagging doubts as to the efficacy of the overall framework (marked by its downplaying of class analysis) that Freeman adopts. The South African state under ANC leadership has proven to be a willing recipient of such market-defined, post-apartheid Canadian outreach. Why? Special attention must be paid, in this regard, to the embourgeoisement of a stratum of Africans, within and without the ANC, and the very considerable evidence that this development has contributed mightily to the movement's leadership accepting, in Freeman's words, "policies at odds with the principles of the ANC Freedom Charter" and adopting a brand of "neo-liberal fundamentalism." Was not this precisely the outcome that the deep thinkers within the capitalist class had begun to consider possible in the late 1980s (if not, perhaps, Mulroney himself: whatever the cunning of his broader strategic views, his government crudely downgraded the claims to centrality of the ANC until quite late in the day)? Yet, as Freeman analyzes the ANC (p. 301), first and foremost this "drift to the right in discourse and the approach towards economic policy of senior ministers in the Mandela government, although not entirely uncontested, indicates how narrow the options are"!

This is, at best, only half right. The structural constraints imposed on the ANC by the power of capitalist interests, world-wide and local, are real enough. But the ANC itself has also become part of the problem in many ways, the constraints generated by class formation and class polarization (and by the proto-hegemonic quality of its chosen "discourse") beginning to cut across it just as surely and as sharply as they do across Canadian society and the Canadian political system.

WHAT MORE NEEDS TO BE SAID? And what more, finally, about southern Africa itself? Clearly—a cliché from the past, the old Frelimo slogan "a luta continua," but still apt—the struggle continues, both in southern Africa and in Canada. As for myself, I would continue with some things but not with others. Thus, as I approached my seventieth birthday in 2008 I decided, though already teaching post-retirement, that I would finally yield my place in the spring that year and so, by the date of my birthday, May 4, had indeed returned my final set of papers and submitted my final set of grades. As it happens, I had sought, in my last year or so at York, to shape my courses to mesh more closely than ever with my own research preoccupations and ongoing focus of writing; this was certainly true of my last class. Indeed, the final exam in the course sought to elicit from the students their own thoughts on the very questions that now most preoccupied me. The first question asked: "Who, in your own carefully argued opinion, won the 'Thirty Years War for Southern African Liberation'?" A second queried, in turn: "How likely is it that a 'next liberation struggle' in southern Africa, one waged for a more humane and egalitarian outcome, might soon be launched either across the region or in any of the five countries that we have focused upon in this course? Who (parties? organizations? classes? genders? community actors?) might conceivably be the chief protagonists of any such renewed struggle?"

Now, in deep retirement, I continue to attempt to answer those questions for myself, with various manuscripts (on *South Africa: The Present as History; Southern African Liberation: A History*; and *Anti-Apartheid and Liberation Struggle: Southern Africa, Canada and the World*) already under contract and in progress. Let me merely conclude here with the final paragraphs of my essay "The Strange Death of Liberated Southern Africa," cited above and reprinted elsewhere. For in these paragraphs I offered several hypotheses as to why things had not yet turned out in southern Africa as we had once hoped they would.

[THUS I PRESENTED AS] ONE FINAL POSSIBLE EXPLANATION of the less than revolutionary outcome to liberation struggle in southern Africa: the possibility that the people "at the bottom," although comprising the vast majority of their populations and potentially radically conscious of the unacceptability of their subordination, haven't yet quite figured out how ... to reverse the process of "false decolonization/recolonization" Moreover, indigenous "intellectuals," in the expansive sense of the term employed by Gramsci, haven't yet helped them adequately to do so. To so argue is not to simply to score points against a left that has up to now "failed" but to admit that the challenge that confronts the left is a daunting one. For a reactivated challenge from below would mean, I would suggest, literally "starting from scratch" in order to rebuild new local initiatives, new national movements, new regional/continental undertakings of genuine promise—and also to reinforce global initiatives currently in train. I do think this is happening, I hasten to add, with numerous positive signs, both in South Africa and beyond, of its beginning to do so. But it will continue to be formidably hard work, daunting uphill work. Then again, so was the original liberation struggle itself.

A SOBERING TALE, THEN. As stated earlier: in now attempting, simultaneous with my preparation of the present volume, to write my own history of the thirty-years war for southern African liberation, I move that book towards a final chapter and seek, somewhat forlornly, to shift the title (and rather grey mood) of that chapter from that implied by the title I first gave it, albeit in a rather bleak moment. For in my initial outline the chapter was (as I previously suggested) entitled "who won?."..and I fear that, for me at least, the question stands. We know who lost, of course: the white minorities in positions of formal political power (whether colonially in the Portuguese colonies or quasi-independently in South Africa and perhaps in Zimbabwe). And thank fortune, and hard and brave work, for that.

But who, in contrast, has won? At least for the time being it has been global capitalism, the West and the IFIs (International Financial Institutions), and the local elites, of state and private sector and both white and black. But what about the mass of southern African populations, both urban and rural and largely black? They are not so obviously the winners, I would suggest, and certainly not in any very expansive sense. Indeed, has it not been a kind of defeat for them, too?

True, as we used to say in Mozambique: *a luta continua*. Writing here, we might also say that the struggle continues—continues precisely against the recolonization of southern Africa by the "new empire" that is being driven by global capitalism and its local minions. But does that struggle really continue? Or, put differently, does "a next liberation struggle" look like it is finding any meaningful and promising traction? I have posed these questions elsewhere in terms of agency (just who, in terms of such categories as class, gender and the like, might be realistically expected to act [and how?] to realize progressive purposes and outcomes?), site (where might such prospective bearers of liberatory "agency" be expected to so act: locally, nationally, regionally, globally?) and in terms of what imaginary (for socialism, human rights, democratic voice and/or what else?). There I have sought to frame such questions clearly and sharply and can refer my present readers to that source for further elaboration of these categories and their import.[27] Here I will merely persist in stating that, yes, the struggle does indeed continue. But so, dauntingly, will the challenges to our creativity, our intelligence, and our commitment.

We can perhaps conclude these first two sections of the book with such a call to action, while also reminding ourselves of the sobering comments on the current situation by none other than Archbishop Desmond Tutu, as quoted from a recent *Globe and Mail* article by Stephanie Nolen:

> "One of the most venerated people in South Africa launched a blistering attack on the country's current leaders yesterday, calling them corrupt, arrogant and deeply estranged from the people they govern. Archbishop Desmond Tutu warned that those who rule today could soon lose power, just as the National Party leaders in the apartheid era did, because of the extravagant and vain isolation in which they live. And he said all this with the only two people to rival him in public esteem (Nelson Mandela and Albertina Sisulu) at his side. Archbishop Tutu said that the country's current leaders are 'arrogant, strutting about like a proud peacock seemingly deaf to the cries of those who brought them to power... [They are] like

the Nationalists, thinking that only they possess wisdom or knowledge. At one point the Nationalists, too, seemed immovable and destined to rule forever.'"

Strikingly, such a comment as this by Tutu seems to imply—as does my own writing—that the stage is set for a "next liberation struggle" in southern Africa. Assuming this to be the case, it will continue to be our duty to assist southern Africans as they move to liberate themselves from subservience to the Empire of Capital. And to liberate ourselves from such subservience as well.

---

1. "The Strange Death of Liberated Southern Africa" in *Transformation*, #64, (2007), and, as chapter 5, in Saul, *Decolonization and Empire (op. cit.)*.
2. "Cry for the Beloved Country" in *Monthly Review*, 52 8 (January, 2001), and, as chapter 8, in Saul, *The Next Liberation Struggle* (*op. cit.*); see also "The Strange Death of Liberated Southern Africa" (in Saul, *Decolonization and Empire* (*ibid.*) and as excerpted in chapter 5, below).
3. Hein Marais, *South Africa: Limits to Change* (Cape Town and London: University of Cape Town Press and Zed Books, 1998), p. 156.
4. See, in this regard, Manfred Bienefeld's useful essay, "Structural Adjustment and the Prospects for Democracy in Southern Africa" in David Moore and Gerald Schmitz (eds.) *Crisis and Renewal in Development Discourse* (n.d.).
5. John S. Saul, *Recolonization and Resistance: Southern Africa in the 1990s* (Trenton: Africa World Press, 1993).
6. Note, too, the statement (in the *Financial Times*, February 15, 1994) by Mandela himself, where he says that he does "not believe South African businessmen could be trusted to develop a post-apartheid economy without state intervention": "We are convinced that left to their own devices, the South African business community will not rise to the challenges facing us. While the democratic state will maintain and develop the market, we envisage occasions when it will be necessary for it to intervene where growth and development require such intervention." But this is by no means the invariable tenor of Mandela's comments on the role of the business community, foreign investors or international financial institutions... Nor did the ANC's compromises end there: the studied ambiguities of the RDP as regards the broader choices of the economy's overall direction were soon to be capped by a fresh initiative... and a fresh (if highly misleading) acronym: GEAR (for "Growth, Employment and Redistribution"!), marched the ANC and its policy even further to the right and South African society even further along the path towards a class polarization not merely between black and whites (as had all along been the case, in any event) but amongst the blacks themselves. But I was soon to see this grim spectacle for myself when, in 2000, I travelled to Johannesburg to teach for a period at Wits, the University of Witwatersrand.
7. See David Plank's exemplary article in *The Journal of Modern African Studies* (31, #3 [1993]) entitled "Aid, Debt and the End of Sovereignty: Mozambique and Its Donors."
8. As Plank (*ibid.*) adds, "the interests of many Africans have been served in nation-states ruled by aid-sponsored despots, but there is little reason to suppose that they will

be better served in a world governed by U.N. proconsuls, U.S. marines, and World Bank economists."

9. As I argued in the short article immediately preceding the present one in this chapter, and in chapter 3, "'For fear of being condemned as old fashioned': Liberal Democracy vs. popular democracy in Sub-Saharan Africa" of my *The Next Liberation Struggle* (op. cit.).
10. The full text is available as "Eduardo Mondlane and the rise and fall of Mozambican socialism," in *Review of African Political Economy* and also as an Appendix to my *Decolonization and Empire.*
11. A transcription by the present author of the tape in question.
12. Eduardo Mondlane, *The Struggle for Mozambique* (Harmondsworth, Penguin Books, 1969) and Mondlane, *The Struggle for Mozambique* (London, Zed Press, 1983), the latter being a new edition which includes John S. Saul's, "Forward" and Herbert Shore's important biographical essay "Resistance and Revolution in the Life of Eduardo Mondlane."
13. David Plank, *op. cit.*
14. See, *inter alia*, Saul, "The Frelimo State: From Revolution to Recolonization" in my *Recolonization and Resistance: Southern Africa in the 1990s* (Africa World Press, 1992).
15. See Saul, *The Next Liberation Struggle* (Toronto, New York, London and Durban: Between-the-Lines, Monthly Review Press, Merlin Press and University of Kwazulu/Natal Press, 2005), ch. 4.
16. Saul, in Mondlane (1983), *op. cit.*, p. xx.
17. I originally presented my eulogy to the commemorative service at which many gathered in Trinity/St. Paul's Church in Toronto on Friday, October 24, 1986, to mark Samora Machel's passing. The Tanzanian High Commissioner to Canada, Mr. Ferdinand Ruhinda, was a featured speaker and messages of condolences were presented by a wide range of Toronto-based groups. Samora Machel had touched the lives of many Torontonians, especially those in the Toronto Committee for the Liberation of Southern Africa (TCLSAC), and I was asked to speak on their behalf. The eulogy was published at the time in *Southern Africa Report* (2, 3, December, 1986) and later, with the new appendix mentioned here, in my *Empire and Decolonization* (*op. cit.*). Also killed in the crash was my dear friend Aquino da Bragança to whom I dedicated my 2007 volume of my essays, *Development After Globalization* (*op. cit.*) with the inscription: "For Aquino da Braqança—in death as in life: intellectual stimulus, political touchstone, and friend." And I dedicated my 2006 *Decolonization and Empire* (*op. cit.*) to both Eduardo Mondlane and Samora Machel, with the inscription: "They should have died hereafter."
18. See also chapter 4 ("On War and Peace in Africa: The Mozambican Case") in my *The Next Liberation Struggle* (op. cit.), as well as the various additional articles that I have written on Mozambique since 1986 cited therein (notably "The Frelimo State: From Revolution to Recolonization" in my *Recolonization and Resistance: Southern Africa in the 1990s* [Africa World Press, 1992). See too, inter alia, Alice Dinerman, *Revolution, Counter-Revolution and Revisionism in Postcolonial Africa: The Case of Mozambique, 1975-1994* (London: Routledge, 2006); Bonaventura de Sousa Santos and Teresa Cruz e Silva (eds.), *Moçambique e a Reinvençao da Emancipaçao Social* (Maputo: Centro da Formaçao Juridica e Judiciaria, 2004); and Joao Mosca, *A Experiencia Socialista em Mocambique, 1975-1986* (Lisbon: Instituto Piaget, n.d.). On Machel himself, see Iain Christie, *Machel of Mozambique* (Harare: Zimbabwe Publishing House, 1988) and

Barry Munslow (ed.) *Samora Machel: An African Revolutionary: Selected Speeches and Writings* (London: Zed Press, 1985). On the suspicious circumstances of Samora's death and of the crash which instigated it see "Verdict: Murder by radio," *African Concord,* November 5, 1967, and Christie, *ibid.,* "Introduction," pp. vi-xii

19. Shamim Meer, "The Demobilization of Civil Society: Struggling with New Questions," *Development Update,* 3, 1, 1999).

20. In Canada this might become a question of whether a movement that really began to effectively bring together many Canadians (not least those in trade unions) to demand real change could even be the seed of a new political formation—effective, popular—to the left of the Liberals and New Democratic Party.

21. George Dangerfield, *The Strange Death of Liberal England* (Stanford, CA: Stanford University Press, 1997 [first published 1935]), p. 19.

22. The essay "The Strange Death of Liberated Southern Africa" was first presented at the "Services for All: Theory, Practice, Struggle" conference of the Municipal Services Project in Cape Town, South Africa, March 28, 2007 and, that same week, at a seminar at the University of KwaZulu-Natal, in Durban, South Africa (April 2, 2007); but for a more extended argument see also my book *Southern African Liberation: A History,* forthcoming from the University of Cambridge Press.

23. As cited earlier in this volume, particularly germane here are my "Transforming the Struggle in Zimbabwe" (1977), "Zimbabwe: The Next Round" (1980), and an article I co-authored with Richard Saunders, "Mugabe, Gramsci and Zimbabwe at Twenty-Five" (2005).

24. See Colin Leys and John S. Saul, *Namibia's Liberation Struggle: The Two-Edged Sword* (London: James Currey, 1995), "Liberation without Democracy? The SWAPO Crisis of 1976," *Journal of Southern African Studies* (*JSAS*), 20, 2 (March, 1994) and "Lubango and After: "Forgotten History as Politics in Contemporary Namibia" in *JSAS,* 29, 2 (June, 2003).

25. See my essay, one I presented at the University of Cape Town in 2009 and entitled *"Race, Class, Gender and Voice: Four Terrains of Liberation,"* which is soon to be published.

26. The review originally appeared, in much the same form, under the title "A Class Act: Canada's Anti-apartheid Record" in *SAR,* 14, 2, March, 1999 and then, with minor modification, in 2005 as an appendix to my *The Next Liberation Struggle (op. cit.).* Nonetheless, it bears inclusion here in 2008 as a way of rounding off my thoughts, after more than forty years in the lists of the liberation support and anti-apartheid struggles and of resistance to global capitalist imperialism. However, I have recently reflected further on this record in my public lecture, "Two Fronts of Anti-Apartheid Struggle: South Africa and Canada," presented to a meeting of the South African Association of Canadian Studies in Cape Town, May, 2009; this paper is to be published in revised form in *Transformation* (Durban) in 2010.

27. See "Globalization, Imperialism, Development: False Binaries and Radical Resolutions" in my *Development After Globalization: Theory and Practice for an Embattled South in a New Imperial Age"* (Delhi, London and Durban: The Essays Collective, Zed Press, and University of KwaZulu/Natal, 2006).

Part Three
The Setting and the Self

A) PREFACE

On the Big Picture (the Setting)

I'd already begun to develop the vaguest of heterodox views about Political Science and about the world when I left Toronto, probably thanks principally to my old professor, the eminent Marxist political theorist Brough Macpherson. Indeed, one of my fondest academic memories at U of T was of taking a grad seminar with Brough when we used as a core text a draft copy of his soon-to-be published (and justly celebrated) *The Political Theory of Possessive Individualism*. I remember, a few years later, having coffee with him in New York City and of just how pleased he was that his forthrightly Marxist book, by now just out, had been greeted that week in the *New Yorker* with a praiseful review by none other than Jonathan Miller. But it was Gordon Skilling, to whom I had been a teaching assistant at the U of T, who sent me forward to Princeton with an introduction to Hube Wilson in the Politics Department there, Hube who was to become so influential in my own development. And it was Wilson in turn who provided me with an introduction to Ralph Miliband, another well-known leftist prof and editor of the annual *Socialist Register* (that was eventually to publish so many of my essays over the years), who became a trusted friend and mentor at the London School of Economics when I went off to England.

In short, the grounds for suspicion, both theoretical and practical, of established orthodoxies were sewn. And such suspicion seemed all the more relevant when, after seven years in Tanzania (and the accelerated learning curve I had been on there), I finally did submit a PhD dissertation to my distressingly orthodox committee of professorial examiners at Princeton. For they, quite simply, turned it down. Moreover, their reasons struck me as being particularly scandalous: writing on Tanzania I had failed, I was told, to give proper centrality to the American political science literature on either the one-party state or on modernization theory (these sub-genres both stiff with Cold War complacency, I felt). Besides, my timing was bad. At Princeton, as elsewhere in the US, there was a professoriate (other than Wilson and a few additional noteworthy exceptions) of largely right-liberal persuasion that had come under great fire from students (even those at Princeton!) during the Vietnam War and it was now anxious to reassert its power and the hegemony of its orthodoxy.

But I had been away too long and I felt I had learned too much to jump through such outmoded (as they seemed to me) hoops. As it happens I had finished a thesis set within the frame of left developmental and anti-imperialist theory that I had been evolving with others during my Dar es Salaam years. When I showed the dissertation around to some rather more orthodox senior colleagues in various places other than Princeton, they confirmed it to be more than acceptable. But to transform it to square with the ideological orthodoxies now resurgent at Princeton seemed to mark an impossible retreat for me to make. The result: I never did get my PhD but, with time, managed—as an accompaniment to my southern Africa-related political work—both to get a job at York University's Atkinson College (York's night school for "mature" students which was a hotbed of both interesting mature students and various heterodox academics)[1] and to continue to help further develop, with like-minded colleagues and co-authors around the world, the field of radical development theory.

My more heavily "scientific" books are out there. In them such continuing preoccupations can be further studied if any reader of the present text is interested in so doing. In sum, however, I can say of my own ongoing preoccupations—consistent with my earlier critical perspective on western imperial dominance but a further development of it—has led me to focus increasingly on the emergence of what I have chosen to term an "Empire of Capital," an empire that finds its chief expression in pursuing a continuing subordination of the global South to the imperatives and requirements of "the North" in a manner even less apologetic than at any time since the days of brutal imperial conquest (including, as it did, the slave trade and the like).

I have outlined the dynamics of this new Empire of Capital, the differences between it and the old nationally based imperialisms of the period of classic colonization of the South by the North (the "British Empire," the "French Empire," etc.), and the complexities of its interaction with the simultaneous imperial roles played by present-day national states (US imperialism, for example) in a number of recent books. Here, in this section, I have summarized this argument in a paper especially written for this volume and included in this chapter: "The Empire of Capital, Recolonization and Resistance: Rethinking the Political Economy of Development."

In that essay I also examine the kind of "recolonization" of various Third World countries, especially throughout Africa, that this most recent assertion of capitalism's global power has produced. As I have phrased the point elsewhere, "if the power of the empire of capital was taking on ever more global and imperial dimensions, what could this possibly mean for those at its receiving end, those in a global South who were increasingly unable to defend themselves against the 'free global market' as projected upon them by the US, the IMF, the WTO? What else could it possibly be if not recolonization?" And what of "resistance" from below—the "Next Liberation Struggle," as I have entitled another recent book of my writings on Africa?

In this section (chapter 6), I begin with an assertion of my continuing interest in the broader patterns of imperialism and underdevelopment as evoked in the mid-1990s at a memorial conference held in London in honour of my old teacher and friend Ralph Miliband. I next look, broadly, at the present African conjuncture, incorporating a review-essay on Paul Nugent's recent magisterial book, *Africa Since Independence*. And my final inclusion is a piece mentioned above and written especially for this volume that synthesizes my own broad views on the "development question." Among other things, I there spar (though in comradely fashion) with my old friend and late comrade Giovanni Arrighi whose own position has so widely diverged from my own since we first wrote together (see chapter 1) in the 1960s in Dar es Salaam.[2] But in so doing I present both an overall assessment of the negative character of the current Empire of Capital and of such resistance to it as is emerging as well.

CHAPTER SIX

Global Capitalism, Underdevelopment... and Socialism

a) Recolonization and Resistance: Africa and Beyond

Preoccupied though I was with southern Africa, I tried never to lose track of even "bigger questions," both (i) about matters of approach to the study of global development (and in particular to the fate of "the global South") within the world system, and (ii) about the best manner in which to conceptualize—for both scientific and practical purposes—that system, its outcomes, and the resistances to which it gives rise. This was a part of my teaching vocation, for example, when at Atkinson College I taught for many years our second year introductory course on "Foundations of Social Science," with particular substantive reference to Canadian issues, in the Social Science department. When, as Atkinson waned, I migrated more toward the Political Science department in the Faculty of Arts where I continued to develop broader courses for both graduate and undergraduate students, courses concerned with global development issues that complemented the teaching I was also doing on Africa and, more specifically, southern Africa.

Some of this came into focus when I was honoured in 1995 with an invitation to address a memorial workshop held in remembrance of my old teacher, friend and mentor, Ralph Miliband, who had died the previous year. It was held in London, with his wife Marian and their two sons and other stalwarts, old and young, of the left (Eric Hobsbawm, John Savile, Sheila Rowbotham, Tony Benn, Lynn Segal, Tariq Ali, Leo Panitch, and many more) in attendance. I was asked to give a presentation at the final summary plenary—a presentation designed to place the global South ever more firmly on the intellectual agenda of such an august gathering. In retrospect, I can now see that my presentation also signaled a key stage in the further expansion of my own intellectual itinerary, marking an increased preoccupation with more general reflections on the prospects for development of the global South as set in the context of globalization and of the new "Empire of Capital":

I TAKE IT THAT MY PRESENT TASK on this concluding panel of the workshop is to make certain that we continue to expand our referent to take into account "the rest of the world" beyond Western Europe and North America. I do this a little hesitantly, however. In part this is because of the danger of my appearing to appropriate the voice of those in the global South who are so often at the receiving end of both Western capitalism's worst excesses and the Western Left's most high-handed advice, in part because of the regretted absence of—Ralph's friend, my friend—Joe Slovo from South Africa (himself also recently deceased[3]) who was also to have been on the same final panel and who could have spoken even more authoritatively.

Nonetheless, I have spent my entire adult life—ever since my days here at the London School of Economics when Ralph Miliband was my teacher—engaged in trying to forge intellectual and political links between struggles in what used to be called the "Third World" on the one hand and struggles in the advanced capitalist centres on the other—so I hope that is some kind of qualification. In addition, the fact is that these links are probably more important than ever, in light of the fact that the globalization of capitalism has begun, to some degree, to shift the reality of a geographically defined hierarchy to render us all, wherever we stay, increasingly vulnerable to the depredations of that globalization process.

Like the rest of the speakers today I am also forced to speak in the context of a pervasive new mood on the left and more generally that we need to resist quite self-consciously. In fact—though it may seem a little adventurist to say so—my guiding premise is that the left, in a skeptical age, has to dare to be a bit more old-fashioned than it has recently been inclined to be. In fact, one of Ralph's own great strengths was that he himself dared, in the best sense, to be "old-fashioned": to be old-fashioned, principally, about the centrality of capitalism to the concerns of the left. I think, too, that Ralph's last book, *Socialism for a Sceptical Age*—that has given us the title for this final session of today's Memorial Workshop—is a case in point of this virtuous "old-fashionedness." Let me now attempt to make clearer just what I want to say along these lines.

The general tenor of this new global mood is well known, of course, but I think Colin Leys captured it particularly clearly in a recent article[4] where he uses a most evocative image to make his central point:

> On October 5th, 1994, 25 members of the Church of the Solar Temple killed themselves, or were killed by their leaders, in a house belonging to the Church in Switzerland. The reaction of the media, and of most people, was one of amazement and horror. A community of people had destroyed itself, or has been destroyed by its leaders, in the name of some far-out utopian ideal. We saw it as sick, pathological. If it occurred to anyone that it might be a symbol of what was simultaneously happening to the surrounding, so-called normal, society, I did not see it mentioned. Yet I believe that the self-destruction of the Church of the Solar Temple is a symbol of what is currently happening on the world's stage: that our leaders are directing a process of self-destruction of our societies in the name of a utopia no less irrational than the beliefs of the Church of the Solar Temple, whatever they may have been. This utopia is the idea of a worldwide market in which the people of the world relate to each other directly as individuals, and only as individuals; "globalization" is the process of trying to reach this ideal.
>
> As an idea [Leys continues], this is strictly nonsense. In reality individuals cannot survive on their own; we are social animals, totally dependent for our very psychic stability, let alone the material means of survival, on complex and constant connections with others, i.e., on *society*. The doctrine on which globalization is based, however, is positively opposed to societies. Mrs. Thatcher expressed it accurately, if naively, when she declared that "there is no such thing as 'society,' only individuals and their families." The assumptions on which the [capitalist] globalization process rests, then, are literally absurd. This does not, obviously, mean that the project is unreal. On the contrary, it is well underway.

And he concludes: "Globalization is a policy in the service of an irrational idea, not a realizable world. But in the name of this idea a crucial decision has been made: to accept the freedom of capital to move across national boundaries."

As it happens even the Left seems to have been steamrollered by this mood. There was a time, for example, when, for far too many on the left, too much of what we had to say about capitalism was trite and a little tired—built around the notions of ineluctable contradictions and inevitable collapse, for example—and far too much of what we had to say about socialism was merely triumphalist. Now, ironically, far too much of what we have to say about capitalism is "triumphalist"—even when such sentiments are uttered rather elegiacally—and far too much of what we have to say about socialism is merely trite... and more than a little tired—along the lines, at best, of "it was a good idea, but..."

Here I'm thinking not merely of the residues of Bill Warren's Chicago-style Marxism, a posture that has suggested, especially for the "Third World," that quite a lot of capitalism is pretty good for them out there ("creating a working class," don't you know). Or merely the grim realism of Chicago-based political scientist Adam Przeworski [here I quoted Przeworki again, as I have on several occasions earlier in this book, his chilling formulation being one that I can't quite get out of my head.] For Przeworski, with socialism now being unfeasible, the "irrationalities" of capitalism are about all that we can expect.

I'm also thinking of those elements on the left who are inclined to dabble in the "postmodern"—or, to use the title of an article by Jeffrey Alexander in a recent issue of the *New Left Review*, with the "modern, anti, post and neo." Indeed, it is this article, heralded by *NLR* on its cover under the banner headline "The Reflux of Social Theory" [!] that can provide the one formal citation that I have time to introduce here to capture something of the spirit of the times:

> It is impossible even for already committed intellectuals to ignore the fact that we are witnessing the death of a major alternative not only in social thought but in society itself. In the foreseeable future, it is unlikely that either citizens or elites will try to structure their primary allocative systems in non-market ways.
>
> For their part, social scientists will be far less likely to think of anti-market "socialist societies" as counterfactual alternatives with which to explain their own. They will be less likely to explain economic stratification by implicitly comparing it with an egalitarian distribution produced by publicly rather than privately held property, "a plausible world" that inevitably seems to suggest that economic inequality is produced by the existence of private property itself... Similarly it will become much more difficult to speak about the emptiness of formal democracy, or to explain its limitations by pointing merely to the existence of a dominant economic class, for these explanations, too, require counterfactuals of a traditionally "socialist" kind. In brief, it will be much less easy to explain contemporary social problems by pointing to the capitalist nature of the societies of which they are a part.[5]

Alexander goes on, in the course of his article, to embrace a kind of universalizing modernization theory, one he suggests to be more sophisticated than that provided by Anthony Giddens and other related writers whom he cites—although the subtleties of his distinctions in this regard are a little lost on me. In any case it is the last sentence of the passage I have just quoted that bears most careful scanning here: "In brief, it will be much less easy to explain contemporary social problems by pointing to the capitalist nature of the societies of which they are a part." It is not a sentence that Ralph Miliband would have written—and indeed he did not write anything even remotely like it in his last book. I suggest to you that he was correct not to have done so.

Of course, there are also some very good reasons to be wary of being too "old-fashioned" on the Left. For some of our "old fashions" did leave much to be desired, and neither Ralph nor many other older leftists, myself included, have entirely escaped "blind-spots"—to put it at its most general—on such issues as those of gender, cultural identity, environmental concerns and even the abuse of power/authority *per se*. Nonetheless, it is the depredations of capitalism that continue to have the most powerfully baleful impact on the lives of most residents out there—even if that negative impact is also uneven in its effects, uneven as between classes self-evidently, but also uneven as between women and men, and as between different regions, countries and localities.

Here, as hinted, the recent, apparently diverse, history of "the South" itself does lead to some greater sense of complexity than many of we "Third Worldists" allowed ourselves to acknowledge in the past: we have, on the one hand, the "Asian Tigers," not without their contradictions but surging forward on certain fronts (albeit by using their states as instruments of economic development in an aggressive manner that defies much of the logic of neo-liberalism as forced upon other Third World states by the IMF and the World Bank) and we have, on the other hand, the apparently "hopeless"—I use this words in inverted commas—trajectory of Africa...and of course we have as well the fact of the "third-worldization" of many parts of the so-called capitalist centres.

And yet, as economists like Giovanni Arrighi and Mandfred Bienefeld have shown, the global hierarchy also does retain a geographical siting, still cast largely along lines of "North" and "South" and still bearing the imprint of the West's fortuitous material and military advance out of feudalism and the consequent fact, based on such a chance development, of its global imperial conquest of the rest of the world. Indeed, the world still bears the centre-periphery imprint of that occurrence, and of a high degree of "dependency" as well,[6] even if, as noted earlier, every nation of the world has become ever more vulnerable to the footloose multinationals of the present epoch.

In sum, I would assert that hanging on to a sense of the profoundly capitalist nature of the global "development problem" is perhaps the most urgent challenge we on the Left face, however seriously we also take other concerns. Take a look at the G7 meeting held in Canada just last week. There was no ambiguity amongst the leaders present in Halifax as to the nature of the capitalist spinal column that structures the global system. Nor do the World Bank and the IMF apologize for the fact that they are helping to impose a "master narrative" upon the rest of the world. The IMF, it would seem, hasn't heard about the postmodernists' "death of the author" or "the decentring of discourses." In fact, it has few qualms about thinking of itself as "the author." And certainly it has not heard about the displacement of capitalism to the margins of social causality a la Jeffrey Alexander.

True, the G7 leaders did show themselves in Halifax to be a bit nonplussed regarding how best to bring their own system under control. It is proving very difficult to impose at the global level even the limited measure of order that capital, using Keynesian means, found it possible to impose on otherwise unbridled individual capitalists during capitalism's more successful (and enlightened) moments during this century. This is in part because of the absence of a strong global "state-like entity" through which to organize a more far-sighted bourgeois strategy, in part because of the absence, at the global level, of that popularly based political push from below (and from the Left) that also served to force nationally-based capitalists to introduce certain kinds of defensive reforms in the 1930s. Perhaps this is why the system now proves itself to be, in Przeworski's term (often cited above), as "irrational" as it does at the global level.

Moreover, if it is the case that capitalism can't really work economically for the vast majority of people at the global level, that things don't just stand still socially and politically: they can get worse, as the recent history of Eastern Europe is currently demonstrating to us. Foiled of deliverance along capitalist lines, unconfident (to put it mildly) of the wisdom of attempting to mount any fresh kind of socialist alternative, people fall back on much narrower kinds of identities—those of race, of religion, of nation and of *ethnie*—to give their lives some badly needed compass points and the result can be an even more desperate breakdown of social order than ever. Of course, identity politics is not reducible merely to these its most morbid symptoms. In certain circumstances they can be profoundly ennobling. Nonetheless, "do not paint identity politics red" remains good advice: such politics must be located within a broader project that draws them upwards towards some higher common goal or purpose. And this, I would suggest must be, in some central way, focused upon resistance to capitalism... and therefore, in the end, focused upon the pursuit of socialist goals.

It is for this reason, as well, that we should be skeptical about too readily substituting such concepts as "radical democracy" and the like at the core of our political formulations on the Left. By merely melding what I take to be the central fact of capitalism into a much broader array of contradictions, the notion of "radical democracy" can encourage us to lose sight of that fact, that core reality. That's why I prefer a different line of theoretical advance beyond whatever reductionisms socialist discourse may ever have been guilty of: why I like the sound, for example, of Mary Mellor's notion of a "feminist green socialism" or Leslie Sklair's "democratic feminist socialism." I see no reason, in short, for the socialist Left to make any concessions to the idea that socialist politics must *necessarily* be "essentialist" or "reductionist": socialists are quite capable of learning that democracy is an essential component of socialist advance, that women are oppressed by men in quite specific ways, that racism has its own historicity and dynamic and so on. But let's not forget about capitalism, eh!

But what if socialism is, in Przeworski's familiar formulation, merely "unfeasible"? The answer, and it is Ralph Miliband's answer too, is, quite simply, that we must not accept that premise. The present global system is simply too full of contradictions to last although, as noted, things could get a whole lot worse before—if ever—they start to get better. And while some parts of the world may unravel, we can be certain that even further to the right than the IMF there will be those who seek to capture the language of resistance to globalization for various kinds of fundamentalist purpose, thus adding further fuel to the downward spiral: much speculation in this regard turns around the rise of certain kinds of religious fundamentalism in Third World countries, of course, but note, too, the presidential campaign of Pat Buchanan [and, more recently, the television harangues of the likes of Lou Dobbs] in the United States premised, first and foremost, on the need for American resistance to globalization!

Needless to say, our task on the Left is to seek to channel the response to capitalist contradictions along far more constructive lines—and, as I have said, the sustaining of a socialist comprehension of the workings of the global system can and should be a central aspect of that response.

But what about the sustaining of a socialist politics *per se*? Here a number of questions might be raised, some of which I have rubbed up against in trying to make sense of the compromises that have been forced upon—and, of course, even actively embraced by some members of the organization—the ANC in South Africa. Here especially I wish the late Joe Slovo could be here, as originally planned, to help think this through with us. Nonetheless, as I have written elsewhere,[7] I had divined in South Africa an approach, both to liberation from apartheid and to socialist construction, that sought to avoid the twin perils of an adventurist and unrealistic revolutionism on the one hand and a lapse into mere reformism on the other. Borrowing from the early Gorz and from Kagarlitzky I came to think of this strand of South African thinking as evoking a strategy of "structural reform." Unlike the merely reformist initiatives (of most social democratic parties, for example) this approach involves keeping the goal of long-term transformation of the capitalist system front and centre and it also involves ensuring that each struggle for a particular "reform" is not merely a one-off event but rather one that leaves some residue—organizational, ideological—of permanent popular empowerment in its wake. I sense there is a great deal of room for further imaginative thinking along these lines, both in South Africa (where the post-apartheid denouement has, in fact, been so cruelly disappointing) and further afield.

There is also, as ever, the question of the "agency"[8] that could drive such struggle, a point implicit in much of what has already been said: a class struggle, yes, that's an assertion socialists in a skeptical age must continue to make... even if the range of possible "agents" for progressive change is also capable of being defined more richly than that. I'll return to this point in a moment. Here let me note also that there is an additional question, one posed more pressingly than ever in the current global conjuncture: the question of the appropriate "site" of struggle. For some on the Left, those in Latin America linked to the politics of the "new social movements" for example, or thinkers on Africa like Jean-François Bayart and Jonathan Barker, the most appropriate site of struggle must be the community.[9] But even if this is a useful emphasis up to a point, how quickly the globalizing economy closes in on such communities and shapes—twists, more often than not—their prospects for advance.

Are we forced to think about any relevant new politics primarily at the global level then? Perry Anderson for one suggests as much:

> The case against capitalism is strongest on the very plane where the reach of socialism is weakest—at the level of the world system as a whole... The future belongs to a set of forces that are overtaking the nation-state. So far they have been captured and driven by capital—as, in the past fifty years, internationalism has changed sides. So long as the left fails to win back the initiative here, the current system will be secure.[10]

But does a political project cast at that level merely become wispy and insubstantial in a "real world" that, for many purposes, is still largely structured along national lines? The signs of a rising worldwide movement cast in terms of "anti-capitalist globalization" suggests that a more globally defined struggle might be beginning to take shape, of course. But there are also questions of the nature of politics within regional formations to be considered: what, for example, should a progressive politics at the level of Europe look like if it also takes full account of the situation of those, far more desperate, beyond its borders (or, for that matter, *within* them, as migrant-cum-immigrant labour). And what, finally, of the nation-state itself? Under siege certainly but still often defined by at least enough residual coherence of identity as to make a common language of politics—speaking figuratively but often even literally—possible and even potentially efficacious for progressive purposes (whatever the limitations on national socioeconomic action may be).

In short, there is a whole roster of questions for the Left, and many more questions besides. But may I merely conclude here with one final, mildly heterodox point? I will do so by referring to one of the best books I know about sustaining an "imaginary"—a "counter-factual," in Alexander's term—regarding the prospect of significant structural changes to the global system of capitalism. It is a book that also grounds that "imaginary" in a bracing discussion of concrete, very real, struggles and patterns of resistance. The book, written by Jeremy Brecher and Tim Costello, is entitled *Global Village or Global Pillage: Economic Reconstruction from the Bottom Up* and one striking fact about this book is that it does not even once mention the word "socialism": it's literally not in the index! I don't particularly begrudge the authors this silence, and in any case their book both floats, albeit tacitly, on a Marxist reading of the nature of the global economy and also develops a panoply of euphemisms to argue for something that some of us might rather choose to call socialism.

As it happens, I'm not certain whether the approach adopted by Brecher and Costello is merely a tactical one (for American consumption!) or represents a more principled political stance. Whatever the case in this regard, the voices of Brecher and Costello and of others who seek to challenge local, national and global patterns of class exploitation, of oppressions centred on structures of gender inequality, of differential sexual orientation, and of race, of environmental destruction and the like but who do not choose to think of themselves as socialists must be welcomed. Even as those of us who are socialists insist on the importance of our "old-fashioned" ways there is no good reason for us to revert to the "bad old days" of insisting on the existence of only one true socialism, or, as it is more often put, of only one true Left. Instead, we must build movements—locally, nationally, globally—that are genuinely democratic and as diverse as the Left can be, even as we build towards effective unity of purpose: no easy task but there it is.

What we can insist on—a paradoxical thought for many of us—is that socialist voices actually are also important on the left, even crucially important, we might argue, and that, in the long run, the more socialists the better. In short, the task for socialists is not to attempt to exhaust the meaning of the Left, but, within the Left, to keep alive the idea that there *must* be an alternative to capitalism, and that people's oppression in class terms is still a crucial dimension negatively framing their life chances, especially under the conditions of imperial control, dependency and grinding poverty that infect so much of "the South." This, in turn, demands a massive and ongoing work of education (self-education!) and activism on our part, both within the Left and beyond it. It implies returning to the spirit of Ralph Miliband's final book, returning, in fact, to the spirit of his final paragraphs in the volume:

> For the prospects are not nearly as somber as is often made out. The reason for this lies quite simply in the nature of capitalism and in its failures. Much has been said in these pages in relation to advanced capitalism. But the point applies with even greater force in relation to countries where life tends to be far more nasty, poor, brutish and short. The majority of people in the world live in countries where a wild capitalism prevails, where welfare provision is minimal or non-existent, where drinking water is a luxury denied to masses of people and where sanitary conditions are appalling, where unemployment affects much of the population, where vast numbers of children are put to work at the age of six or seven, where rates of infant mortality are horrendous, where child prostitution is common, and so forth at sickening length.

> At the same time, in the same countries, men in power in the state and in society have it as their main concern to maintain and reinforce a system which gives them and the local bourgeoisie a life of ease and comfort and luxury; and where, [when] they speak of reform, it is always on condition that this should not endanger the prevailing social order. In this they can rely on the support of Western governments and international institutions.
>
> Such a situation [Miliband continues] cannot endure. It simply makes no sense to believe that men and women who know, because of the revolution in communications, that there is a different life to be lived will not in time seek to achieve a different and better life ... the specific demands and the forms of struggle which they will generate will vary greatly from country to country; there is no single "model" of progressive and revolutionary change. But, everywhere, there are common goals and aspirations of the kind that I have sought to describe and define here—for democratic forms where they are denied, and for more democratic forms where they are no more than a screen for oligarchic rule; for the achievement of a social order in which improvements in the condition of the most deprived—often a majority of the population—is the prime concern of governments; for the subordination of the economy to meeting social needs. In all countries, there are people, in numbers large and small, who are moved by the vision of a new social order in which democracy, egalitarianism and cooperation—the essential values of socialism—would be the prevailing principles of social organization. It is in the growth of their numbers and in the success of their struggles that lies the best hope for humankind.[11]

MUCH OF MY RECENT WRITING has borne on broader questions of global development (as encouraged, in particular, by my friend Asad Zaidi of the Three Essays Collective in Delhi who has helped launch both my *Development After Globalization* and *Decolonization and Empire* in the past several years)[12] and on questions of African continental development—even though both my scientific and my political work have most intensively focused on southern Africa (as witness the previous sections of the book). Nonetheless, I welcomed the opportunity provided by an invitation to review (at somewhat greater length than a normal review) for the *Canadian Journal of African Studies* (41, 3, 2008) a book by Paul Nugent on the recent history of the continent as a whole. Here I attempted to set out, one last time, some of my own reflections on a subject that had preoccupied me for more than forty years (recall my piece with Giovanni Arrighi included, above, in chapter 1) and did so under the title "Of Revolutions and Remittances: Paul Nugent's Africa Since Independence."

THIS BOOK, *AFRICA SINCE INDEPENDENCE* (Nugent, 2004),[13] presents a bold and uniquely ambitious recent study of the continent, undertaken at heroic length by Paul Nugent, and discussing it forthrightly here may help reinforce an ongoing debate on how best presently to think about Africa and on how best to act in and upon it. Something of a forgotten continent in both mainstream and left discussion in "the West" since the palmy days of the anti-apartheid movement and the emergence of Nelson Mandela from twenty-seven years in prison to ultimately accede to the presidency in South Africa, there have been, in Africa, only such horrors as those in Rwanda, Zimbabwe and Darfur in addition to the AIDS epidemic to occasionally arouse much Western attention. Indeed, as in 2007, the last major article on Africa to appear even in so important a journal of progressive opinion as the *New Left Review*—to take merely one prominent case in point—was a 2002 article by Giovanni Arrighi, who had once, writing in tandem with the present author [see, *inter alia*, chapter 1 above], argued the necessity of a socialist-premised disengagement from western capitalism as alone promising any meaningful or significant development effort for Africa. In *NLR* he presented himself as being far more resigned.[14]

For Arrighi's view in his 2002 *NLR* article seemed singularly depressed, and depressing. "There may be little that most [African] states can do," he concludes, "to upgrade their economies in the global hierarchy of wealth" (elsewhere in his writing he even argued the existence of a "fixed hierarchy"). He can suggest only that there is, nonetheless, "always something they could do to increase (or decrease) the well-being of the citizenry at any given level of poverty or wealth." Conceding that even in such relatively narrow terms "African ruling groups have probably done far less than was in their power to do," Arrighi nonetheless concludes on what is apparently intended to be an upbeat note: "But it is not clear whether and to what extent they have on the whole been more deficient than the ruling groups of other countries and regions, the United States included. Indeed, if we take into account differentials in wealth and power, it seems likely that they have been comparatively less so" (pp. 35–6). But, even if this were true, it would still stand as pretty modest accomplishment for a destitute continent—and, in any case, Arrighi does not really discuss what strategies pressed by which agents might begin to move "African ruling groups" towards the more benign behaviour he apparently has in mind.

Paul Nugent in his ambitious book under discussion gives us more to chew on of course, a dense and even dizzying exploration (in over some 489 pages plus another 120 pages of notes and bibliography) of a wealth of case studies (there are, after all, more than fifty countries in Africa, of which Nugent excludes from his consideration only those in the "significantly different... North Africa, and some of the islands") that defies easy continent-wide generalization. Defies perhaps, but generalizations there are nonetheless, scattered throughout the book and even more depressing ones than those of Arrighi. As Nugent himself—having, in his words, "dwelt in some detail upon the political upheavals which have afflicted all regions, if not all countries, since the 1980s"—then concludes: "This has not made for edifying reading, but it is important to relate because it marks the final demise of many of the confident assumptions that had been made about African states at independence" [p. 480]. In fact, he also finds precious little to hang any hopes on presently, with the result that his book tails away pretty anticlimactically, with the last paragraph of the entire book dealing with the possible positive contribution of remittances from African emigrants to the metropoles back to their erstwhile native countries. Hence his final sentence (uttered after evoking quite specifically in the preceding sentence "the tremendous resource which the diaspora community represents" in this regard): "If globalization contains many pitfalls, there is also a sense in which it presents abundant opportunities"(p. 489)!

A slim enough reed upon which to premise progress, one might suspect, although perhaps more tangible than the good offices of China that Arrighi sees fit to evoke when faced with the same grim contemporary realities as Nugent—who, incidentally, also gives virtually no credence to, and absolutely no evidence that might support, Arrighi's notion of a possible benign role for Africa's presently incumbent elites! Recall Arrighi's own shift, from his original position in the pages of the "old" NLR in which he first articulated his sophisticated expose of the existent "global hierarchy" and of the West's oligarchic wealth.[15] His conclusion (p. 64) was then equally unequivocal for he continued by arguing that only a process of global socialist emancipation could hope to permit the development game to start over with all players on the kind of equal footing that would permit the otherwise "wretched of the earth" to stand a fair chance; only then, in short, could "a process that has developed to legitimate and enforce world inequalities be turned into a means to the end of promoting greater world equality and solidarity."

Contrast, however, his most recent presentation, now with two co-authors,[16] of much the same argument regarding the existence of such a hierarchy, but with one significant change: this time there is no mention whatsoever of a possible socialist alternative. Instead, the rungs of the global hierarchy are now to be shaken by only one possible force: the emergence of China as a non-white challenger to the west's global economic hegemony—a potential exemplar of "a new model of development that is less wasteful [and, they go on to state, more "just"] than the U.S.-sponsored mass consumption model will be needed in a world of democratic wealth" (p. 27). For it seems that global development is set to become, under China's burgeoning influence, "more equitable, less wasteful, more sustainable," China's rise being seen "as the most hopeful sign that the extreme global inequalities created under European colonial imperialism and consolidation under U.S. hegemony will eventually give way to a more just and equal world."[17] Unfortunately, all the evidence of China's currently aggressive incursions into Africa presents us instead with a clear picture of that country as a self-centred quasi-capitalist interloper, preoccupied virtually exclusively with the extraction of the raw materials it badly needs, even if it means propping up such venal regimes as those in Zimbabwe, Angola, Nigeria and Sudan.[18]

What about Nugent? He does indeed track, in his opening chapters, the situation that Arrighi and I were, with many others, seeking to comprehend in the first decade or so after independence. For his book is nicely paced (if perhaps too dense in its detail for many) to permit the reader to savour, precisely, the range—within the framework of a decolonization process decisively shaped by the inherited economic weakness of Africa's "new nations" vis-à-vis powerful external capitalist centres—of variation on the continent. Thus, after a tour of the decolonization moment in his initial chapters, he highlights, by means of cleverly contrasted case studies drawn from the immediate post-independence years (Tanzania vs. Kenya, Ghana vs. the Ivory Coast, Guinea vs. Senegal), the diverse pulls, in one territory or another, towards either socialism or capitalism. Of course, in both instances the terms must be held firmly within inverted commas. Capitalism, in any sense that might parallel the more successful of the autonomously centered capitalisms existing in the metropoles, was never really permitted or tried. Nor was socialism embarked upon in any very promising sense, being always top-down and autocratic, reflecting both the influence of the Soviet Union and the arrogant predilections of Africa's own leaderships. Small wonder that neither option could be deemed to have been successful.

Note, though, that a more general question seems begged by Nugent here. For one might ask whether either model could ever have been successful given the nature of both the global capitalist economy on the one hand and the nature of the most prominent of the possible "socialist" models (the Soviet one) then most assertively on offer on the other. In any case, the fact remains that both development projects did fail. There was, on the one hand, no obvious base for an entirely successful socialist project—without, that is, the exercise of a much higher degree of ideological and organizational creativity and progressive integrity than was readily forthcoming. But it was also obvious that, under the conditions of continental dependence inherited from a history of colonial subordination, it was equally difficult to envisage in any territory the emergence of some capitalist-oriented class sufficiently vibrant to deal effectively and from a position of relative strength with global capitalism. Yet this was what would have been necessary in order to challenge global capitalism even just enough to bend its parasitic predilections in Africa towards somewhat more capitalistically developmental ends—and to establish a relationship mutually beneficial and responsive to at least some of the needs of Africa's own territories and populations. In short, Africa was vulnerable to the enforced acceptance of global capitalism's worst possible terms. Indeed, so weak was the internal articulation of any class forces likely to be "progressive" (read: developmental) in either socialist or capitalist terms that the continent's unhappy fate, to the present, was sealed: not so much "socialism or capitalism" as "neither socialism nor capitalism," in any meaningfully transformative sense.

Moreover, Nugent also makes it clear—again with numerous apposite case studies—that military rule, a ubiquitous successor in Africa to failed socialist and capitalist civilian regimes, itself offered no alternative for economies warped both by colonialism and immediate post-colonial practices towards continued dependence and underdevelopment. Indeed, social and political decay in most states merely continued apace with virtually no regime surfacing that could really hope to release the creative energies of either the mass of rural and urban dwellers or a viable entrepreneurial class. Instead, as predicted by Fanon,[19] politics came to represent the machinations of elites, building on ethnic, regional and factional foundations and on differential access to means of intimidation. True, Nugent also acknowledges, in an extended chapter on the topic, the promise of liberation struggles (against a much more intransigent form of white and capitalist domination than elsewhere) in southern Africa. The momentary drama of regimes like that in "socialist" Mozambique in the 1970s gave some brief indication of this; thus Norrie Macqueen, writing of both the virtual revolutions that momentarily surfaced from colonial wars against Portugal as well of their ultimate flaring out, has noted:

> Amidst the human and material holocaust suffered by Mozambique and Angola and the violent factionalism of Guiné, the destruction of an idea was completed. The Afro-Marxism of Frelimo, the MPLA and the PAIGC withered and died in the 1980s... but it is one thing for a political idea to have been tested and to fail (and perhaps leave a residue of genuine improvement in its passing); it is quite another for it to disintegrate amidst the externally contrived destruction of people and state. However inapplicable to African realities the schemes of Portugal's guerrilla enemies might eventually prove, they did offer a clear alternative to the cynical manipulation of ethnicity and the neo-colonial complaisance of the kleptocratic elites who increasingly defined African governance in the 1970s and 1980s [and beyond]. Whatever their fate, the projects of the post-independence regimes of lusophone Africa were probably the most principled and decent ever proposed for the continent. They have not been superseded in this regard and seem unlikely to be.[20]

Both MacQueen and Nugent give reasons why the too top-down nature of such an experiment could not, unfortunately, have been expected to withstand the external siege and internal contradiction that befell it. In fact, South Africa seemed to offer more promise within the region and to the continent as a whole, for it was characterized both by an aroused and numerous working-class and by hard-driving urban community assertions that, even more than the leftist rhetoric of the ANC-in-exile, held what seemed to be real possibilities. Yet South Africa, in the extreme neo-liberal denouement of its struggle, became in many ways the most disappointing case of all regional anti-climaxes, albeit a failure that perhaps Nugent deals with a bit too apologetically: the positive "enduring consequences"[328] of liberation struggle, especially in the economic sphere, are less than self-evident in present-day South and southern Africa![21]

What next? Nugent does, in one chapter, take some solace in the "democracy" that began to emerge more prominently in Africa in the 90s. Nonetheless, his scrupulous adherence to the evidence of his own data forces him to give a very skeptical account of the actual empowerment of the people that this entailed. For what we find is a situation marked, at best, by sustained penury but also a ubiquitous politics of intra-elite jockeying for position. Indeed, this has often tended to include the elite's self-interested enflaming of ethnic consciousness (ethnic identity being by no means inevitably fated to become a politically crucial variable, on Nugent's careful account, but ever available to be whistled up, in the absence of more imaginative imagined alternatives, by the political charlatan). And this, with other distempers manipulated to up the stakes of political rivalry, have even led, in many places, to scarring bouts of warlordism and the like. Meanwhile, into the vacuum of purpose and the reality of continental vulnerability that this kind of politics reinforces have rushed the NGOs (and NNGOs). For Nugent is particularly good at revealing the disempowering and too often developmentally quite negative ministrations "on behalf of" the vulnerable inflicted by many such organizations with their ostensibly "well-meaning" agendas. Nugent is also succinctly to-the-point in discussing the harsh reality of AIDS, a curse that racks the continent and to which he gives due salience.

Moreover, there is, buried in the middle of the book, a factor to which he also gives clear and appropriate attention—albeit in the scant twenty pages he devotes to the issue! This, before hurrying on to explore the limits internal to the political process that he is most preoccupied with. For the issue is nothing less than the "recolonization" of the continent (his word, although it has also been used as an appropriate descriptor by others elsewhere) by the forces of global capitalism. Thus "structural adjustment programmes" (SAPs) are presented as being the chief instrument of bringing Africa to heel vis-à-vis a new, more assertive capitalist global hegemony. The results [chapter 8]: the "rolling back" of the state, the "promotion of greater social inequality," the inducing of "the deindustrialization of much of the African continent" and the promoting of remarkably greater "impoverishment" not only in the rural areas but also via "the progressive deterioration in the cities during the 1990s." Indeed, even the so-called "success stories" (Nugent examines especially closely the experiences of both Ghana and Tanzania) "were less than inspirational." Moreover, as a putative response to "Africa's marginalized position in the international division of labour," the neo-liberal "New Partnership for Africa's Development" launched with great ceremony in the new century by African presidents Mbeki, Obassanjo and Wade, is interpreted by Nugent as being merely a route to even greater subordination of the continent [p. 433]. For by now "the freedom of action which seemed to come with independence had narrowed to the point of becoming a virtual fiction" [p. 327].

One would not have been too surprised if this analytical interlude had framed the argument of the whole book. However, even though Nugent does occasionally acknowledge [p. 334] both that the "crisis and disorder" spawned by SAPs and the like may well have been "functional for Africa's political elites"[22] and that external economic interests have also fed comfortably off the chaos, he doesn't sustain the point quite adequately. Perhaps it is that, in the end, recolonization is just too daunting and too ineluctable a reality for Nugent to hold it firmly at the centre of his argument. Thus the final extended chapter deals in typically bracing but humbling detail with Cameroon, Zanzibar, Eritrea and Somalia; Sudan, Angola and Chad; the Great Lakes States and the Congo; Liberia, Sierra Leone, Guinea-Bissau and Cote d'Ivoire. Yet the fact remains that the chapter is primarily preoccupied with finding a political answer to the social fragmentation spawned by "failed" independence ("the path to post-conflict reconciliation and the interplay between conceptions of indigeneity and citizenship," as he puts it in his concluding section [p. 481]). Not, of course, that overcoming social fragmentation is a minor matter in Africa. But can it really be done without simultaneously overcoming the realities of scarcity and redressing the absence of a project of socioeconomic promise to which ordinary people might commit themselves? No more, you might say, than you can forge socioeconomic progress without challenging, at the same time, fragmentation in its own terms.

And you'd be right. Both points are accurate ones. In fact, it is for this very reason that one wishes Nugent had kept both the challenge posed by global economic irrationality and that posed by domestic distemper on the table together right to the end of his book. If you can't really solve one without solving the other then both realities must be confronted more or less simultaneously. Those who would make a difference in Africa must discover how to do both and this is a difficult feat that Nugent doesn't quite manage to illuminate here. Unfortunately in so falling just a little bit short of our expectations the book is symptomatic of a wider issue. For the horizon of imposing meaningful change upon the global workings of capitalism now seems so shrunken—beyond the resistance of equally one-sided and narrow religious fundamentalisms and ethnic-national hysterias—that a vision of any humane secular alternative to the distemper of capitalism seems virtually beyond the contemporary imagination. Even the worldwide resistance to capitalist globalization has become stunted, shocked into torpor by the apparently more immediate reality of the US's imperial adventures in Afghanistan and Iraq. Add, for the Left's consideration, extreme domestic distemper in Africa to the horrors of global economic irrationality and the left's collective mind seems to boggle.

But does history merely stop? Of course one could not have expected Nugent to manufacture out of thin air a principled and popular opposition to such trends where none exists: the goal of his book is, after all, science, not science fiction. Nonetheless his concluding preoccupation with the machinations of political figures, and with the discernible tendency of Africa's power wielders to displace any concern for their continent's marginalized global status and for the fates of their own impoverished populations onto issues of regionalism, religion, ethnicity and the like, is a bit unsettling. For it offers too little real hope for Africans within the difficult situation where they currently find themselves. Fortunately, other writers do find promising stirrings of grassroots resistance on the continent, pointing to the multiple voices from below heard at the recent session of the World Social Forum held in Nairobi (January 18-25, 2007), for example. True, it is probably the case that the centre of global resistance, once briefly seen as, at least in part, residing in the emergent projects of the liberation movements in Southern Africa, has slowly but surely shifted to Latin America: to Venezuela, Ecuador and Bolivia for example. Yet this does not mean that Africans are entirely passive regarding such issues, as writers like Jonathan Barker, Patrick Bond and others have been telling us.[23] One might therefore have hoped that Nugent—without his becoming some bootless Pollyanna of progress and rhetorical revolution—could have examined this dimension in this book, instead of, by the end, becoming so exclusively (and one-sidedly) preoccupied with the subject of order, stability... and remittances.

Still, Nugent does help us to see much of the problem of present-day Africa as being as sobering as it in fact is. There is to be, in his view, no waiting around either for elites who have suddenly become more benign or for China to pull Africa's smouldering irons from the fire. Moreover, the problem Nugent does, in the end, principally pinpoint—that of order and stability—is a real one, even if it is one unlikely to be resolved by a continent as broken and vulnerable as it is by the current workings of capitalist globalization. In short, the world must change... and so must Africa.

Militant Africans know this, of course, although they have not yet found the way to make their own consciousness and the logic of local resistances begin to add up to effectively counter-hegemonic projects. But this is a daunting task for so battered a continent to accomplish. Dare to struggle, dare to whine: sometimes it seems that's all we're left with. But, of course, the slogan actually is: dare to struggle, dare to win. And the best of African activists—like activists elsewhere—are attempting to do just that.

To sum up: in Africa a cruel symbiosis has been established between, on the one hand, a global capitalism (with the World Bank and IMF as its worldwide police force) looking for profitable opportunities (though not often developmental ones in any positively transformative sense) and, on the other, a local political elite, bickering within itself for precedence and privilege while feeding off this global system. Nugent, as we have noted, mentions the one and concludes with the latter, whereas an even more revealing book would have shown the cruel interplay of these two key factors right down to the final paragraph. For the fact remains that the marginalization and catastrophic mal-development of African territories under the aegis of structural adjustment and global capitalist hegemony provide the ideal setting for popular demobilization: away from active engagement in any larger transformative project and towards the predominance of opportunistically induced fracturing of populations by elite manoeuvrings. And these in turn, it must be reiterated, are realities upon which global capitalism can in turn prey.

This grim reality presents a considerable challenge, needless to say, and it is small wonder that so many either retreat or despair in the face of it. Thus, a friend writes of a recent trip that "I feel the scale of resistance or even mere objection to what is being done by neoliberalism and imperialism is pitifully small" ("above all in the North where we are," he adds, although Nugent gives us scant glimpse of any such "objection" as yet being emergent, in any very strong sense, in Africa itself!). I outline three premises of my own work to another friend who has elsewhere criticized me for what he sees to be the unduly "eschatological" tone in my own writing: global capitalism doesn't "work" in Africa, I write; what has been tried in the name of socialism there has also failed; yet Africans, at and from the bottom, can't be written out of history but can and must mount a "next liberation struggle" against their ongoing recolonization. His answer: to agree with both of my first two premises, but to then say of the third: "This is belief and I am not into beliefs anymore."

Yet this latter sentiment is symptomatic, one fears, and not merely at the *New Left Review*. We have suggested above the present limits upon much of the left's imagination and perhaps especially as regards Africa. As we have seen, for Nugent—as for Arrighi—the parameters of any meaningful change in that continent's situation are set so tightly that the prospect of substantive challenge to them is not much worth discussing. Such limits are noted of course, even underscored, but the analysis then merely moves on to more marginal changes—benign elites, helpful remittances—that might, they hope, somewhat affect ordinary people's situations for the better (though not, it seems clear, transform their lives any more radically than that). For theirs is the realism of reformism (I do not, I should underscore, use that term sneeringly), although it is not a "realism" I can either temperamentally "believe" or (more importantly for present purposes) intellectually embrace! Nor is such "realism" really likely to make much positive difference.

b) The New Empire and the Global South

As I reached seventy, I began to realize that I had unfinished business to do in whatever years I had left. And that it was work that might best focus principally on what I knew best: the liberation of southern Africa (and its aftermath), into which region I had traveled, imaginatively, politically and actually, for so many years. I have planned a series of books to that purpose which I hope to complete in whatever years I have left to me.[24] Nonetheless, I was reluctant to abandon the reflections on the broader structures and processes of global, regional and local happenings that so shaped the fate of ordinary people, especially in the global South and that I had recently been thinking about at some length.[25] I therefore sought to draw a set of thoughts together in a summary paper for the inaugural North American conference on "Historical Materialism" in April, 2008, at York University (the conference itself being an outgrowth of an initiative in the UK designed to reassert the continuing validity of a Marxist/progressive slant towards scientific social inquiry). The paper itself was entitled "The Empire of Capital, Recolonization and Resistance: Rethinking the Political Economy of Development in the Global South" and read as follows:

HERE WE WILL LOOK AT THE WAYS in which the present status of the Global South—a term used to refer to those countries beyond the confines of the North Atlantic-centred world of Europe and North America—has come to be considered within the literature on development that has engaged at least some of the attention of global thinkers since the Second World War. The premise is that the real fate of the vast majority of the population in the parts of world denoted by this general category remains harshly bounded by a context of economic backwardness and penury. Indeed, as the countries of the North Atlantic pushed out, from the fifteenth century, on a project of global conquest and colonial domination they constructed a worldwide hierarchy of wealth and entitlement that continues to this day (with Japan and China being virtually the only two countries of "the South" beyond the reach of the most direct kinds of colonization and subordination). Thus, a key premise in this chapter is that the legacy of economies shaped to fit this colonial mould, and the consolidation of the global hierarchy that was attendant upon this unfolding process, remains at the core of the present development problem and of the absence of material advance in the global South.

I. Development?

Not everyone has chosen to see things in this way, of course. Indeed, the predominant mode of "development theory" (and predominant content of the writings of "development theorists") in the decades immediately following the Second World War was decidedly upbeat. Recently decolonized peoples, as well as those in a similar "underdeveloped" situation elsewhere (e.g. in Latin America), could be expected to advance following the pattern already established by the western capitalist economies themselves. This was premised on Keynesian principles which befitted the time, with the state to play a supportive capitalist-oriented role in stimulating both foreign and also local entrepreneurial activity towards the kind of capitalist takeoff that had already occurred in the more (economically) advanced centres. Walt Rostow and similar economists were beacons of this approach but other social scientists slotted in behind this confident vanguard of capitalist-oriented development thinkers, notably the "modernization" school which searched for, and advocated on behalf of, realization of the kind of social, psychological and political prerequisites "necessary" (as western experience had "demonstrated") to now ensure "take-off" in more impoverished parts of the world. Many southern countries adopted this "western" development model, albeit without, on the whole, any great success and indeed the reinforcement of structures of dependent underdevelopment that would come to be labeled "neo-colonial." Indeed, only in parts of Asia where Cold War realities enabled the state to guide the process more authoritatively, even if in a capitalist direction, were there any signs of real economic buoyancy (albeit a great deal of inequality as well).

However, this was a period in which revolutionary challenges to a world dominated by the capitalism that drove the global powers of the North Atlantic were also afoot. This connoted some tendency to halo the attempts by the Soviet Union as having sustained, in the name of "socialism/communism," an even more dramatically state-driven development process of their own, one that was emulated most outspokenly by China, now under the control of its own Communist Party, and by Cuba. Elsewhere, where official Communism per se was viewed more skeptically on the Left and by rising nationalist elites, there was nonetheless a strong tendency to view underdevelopment not as some mere lagging behind of the part of countries outside the global (western and northern) centre but as a situation determined by the very structure of global hierarchy and dependency—one locked into place initially by the colonial subordination of the South (and designed primarily to meet Northern needs for minerals, primary products and profitably one-sided investments).[26] Such a framework for interpretation of a lack of development spawned, in turn, the goal of a possible break with this hierarchy and the prioritizing of autonomous, even socialist, development strategies and the construction of the kind of states thought necessary to carry these forward.

More recent global trends have seen changes however: a sloping away from state-inspired "development" strategies, whether of the capitalist or the socialist varieties. Instead, with the fall of "communism" as at least one possible pole of any contestation over development and the rise of ever rawer and more assertive market-driven economies in the imperial centres the concept of "development" itself has been transformed. It is now less about the possible self-conscious use of political institutions to reshape an economy in order to facilitate either an assertively capitalist or a socialist forward strategy and more about the taking, not least within the global South, of "market signals" from capital, operating, now more than ever, quite freely on a global scale. What has come to be dominant, in short, is what Kozul-Wright and Rayment have come to term "market fundamentalism," arguing that, at great cost to both meaningful economic development and to democratic principles,

> "Stabilize, liberalize and privatize" has, since the debt crisis of the early 1980s, been the mantra chanted at developing countries with quasi-religious conviction by international financial institutions, donor countries and newspaper columnists. Policy debate has increasingly been polarized into the rhetoric of extremes: trade liberalizers versus protectionists, cosmopolitan versus nationalist, the right-thinking versus the wrong-headed, and so on.[27]

A more effective recipe for continuing and growing economic inequality on a worldwide scale would be difficult to imagine.

II. What's the problem?

Here, in fact, lies the very core of the present development problem. And the problem is a real one. As I have noted elsewhere [and, indeed, have also argued, in more detail, in the previous section of this chapter], Arrighi, writing both alone and with others, has made this basic point quite convincingly, speaking of

> a seemingly "iron law" of a global hierarchy of wealth that stays in place no matter what the governments on the lower rungs of the hierarchy do or do not do—regardless, that is, of whether they delink or do not delink from the global circuits of capital, pursue or do not pursue power and status in the interstate system, eliminate or do not eliminate inequalities among their subjects. It seems to me that a necessary step in the direction [of a plausible explanation of this] is to acknowledge that the standards of wealth enjoyed by the West correspond to what Roy Harrod once defined as "oligarchic wealth" in opposition to "democratic wealth."[28]

As we have seen, Arrighi then further developed his argument by suggesting that only a process of global socialist emancipation could hope to permit the development game to start over with all players on the kind of equal footing that would permit the otherwise "wretched of the earth" to stand a fair chance; only then, in short, could "a process that has developed to legitimate and enforce world inequalities be turned into a means to the end of promoting greater world equality and solidarity."

In short, as noted, Arrighi was very much inclined, circa 1990, to see the only answer to the problem of global inequality that he identified so clearly to lie in socialist challenges, both local and global, to the status quo. And yet we have also underscored the startling fact that in a more recent iteration by Arrighi of much the same model of the world he does not mention "socialism" even once as a necessity/possibility, only finding such (minimal) hope of bending the "global hierarchy" in a manner more favourable to the global South to lie (for no very obvious reason, I fear) in the rise of China as a quasi-capitalist competitor to the North Atlantic hegemon.[29] For us, however, the first and consistently reiterated point is the crucial one: there is a hierarchy that privileges the countries and corporations of the global North (and, increasingly, China) through the oligarchic positioning and economic power they command within the global economy. For this outcome is a direct reflex of the latter actors' economic strength, articulated both directly and through a panoply of global institutions (the IMF, the World Bank, and the like) and linked as well to a willingness to use political force, where necessary, to enforce their position.

This seems to me key. Indeed, several years ago Colin Leys and I had (as I quoted at length in several previous passages) underscored Africa's relegation "to the margins of the global economy" to the considerable detriment of its development prospects.[30] In the same context it was also documented that sub-Saharan Africa, with some 650 million people, over ten per cent of the world's population, has just three per cent of its trade and only one per cent of its GDP; and [that] income per head—averaging $460 by the 1990s—has steadily fallen relative to the industrialized world, and is now less than a fiftieth of what it is in the OECD countries. Indeed, by 2003-4 the World Bank could still admit that, despite the much touted (but, in fact, "sputtering") global recovery, the situation is "unlikely to produce growth rates strong enough to cut sharply into unemployment and that, in particular, Africa's extremely slow growth "is far short of the pace necessary to make significant dents in the poverty headcount or to achieve the Millennium Development Goals in health and education."

Moreover, as we continued, we find

- "world demand ... weakening for the export crops that African farmers produce—coffee, cocoa, tea, cotton, sugar, tobacco—and competition from much more productive capitalist agriculture in Asia and Latin America ... intensifying;"
- "industrial country dependence on Africa's minerals and metals is also declining (by about two percent a year)";

- and any "take-off into manufacturing for internal consumption ... blocked by an inability to compete with imports and by tiny domestic markets, [by] collapsing infrastructures, [and by] political risk and poorly trained workforces tending to make manufacturing for export uncompetitive, even at very low wages."

It is small wonder that the Economic Commission for Africa has stated that in most of Africa industrial expansion faces "impossible difficulties." In this context it is virtually impossible to think of the resubordination of Africa to external dictate which has been occurring—one that enforces the adoption of policies conducive to such results and that services almost exclusively the needs of more "advanced" economies for raw materials and minerals—as anything other than a genuine recolonization.

Note however (as I will discuss further below) that I would not wish myself to use this notion of recolonization in some merely incendiary or provocative way but instead as a scientific term of some rigour. To grasp this point it is necessary to ask, first, who is now doing the "colonizing." Here something new is required, a perspective on "Empire" that registers the recent trends of capitalism's activities on a global scale. For the present globalization of capital's writ, although familiar from the long history of western empires, does have something novel about it. It is, quite simply, not as bound to the logic of nationally defined capital and nationally defined social systems as it used to be. Instead it is a capitalist accumulation process, now, more than ever, cast in global terms, with a genuinely transnational capital at its core.

The power of this transnational capital now anchors what is, quite simply, a very real "Empire of Capital," one that seeks to impose its logic on states around the world, especially in the global South. This empire is most directly visible in the actions of transnational capitalists themselves, increasingly bold to prey at will on various vulnerable social formations around the world. Their actions are reinforced, however, by a panoply of global institutions that serve to impose the empire's discipline: the IMF, the World Bank, the WTO. We will have to pay further attention to the governments of advanced capitalist centres in the following paragraph since their actions are not strictly reducible to some entirely obvious logic of capital, but even at their most straightforward they tend to reinforce, through the terms of their aid and debt rescheduling, virtually compulsory subordination of the global South to the "imperatives" of the North's own economic well-being. In addition, locally dominant classes, of both entrepreneurial and state-bureaucratic provenance, come to play an intermediary role on behalf of this new empire. Indeed, what we see operative, at various levels, is what Leslie Sklair has defined, quite simply and accurately, as "the transnational capitalist class"[31]: this class comprises the principle beneficiaries and agents of this new "Empire of Capital."

This is not to say that national bearings of imperialism have been completely superseded by "globalization," even if there is a discernible drift in this direction. For the hierarchy of empire of capital is only in part self-creating and self-sustaining. Self-created and self-sustaining as defined in part by the logic of capitalism, if you like, but also willed and locked into place by the states, the governments in power, of the North and their quasi-international institutions that we have mentioned. For there is an imperialism and it has guns—notably in the hands of the global system's principal agent and beneficiary, the United States. But the actions of those holding the guns cannot be reduced solely to manifestations of the logic of capital per se.

Agents have agendas too, and these are defined at least in part domestically and also on the terrain of the global system of political power and calculation. Differences of opinion about what's important emerge between those with, primarily, economic power (who themselves do not always agree on what is in their own "best interests," either severally or together) and those with primarily political power. Does George Bush speak for capital? If so, what fraction of it? And what else (bizarre religious imaginings for example, or global visions of something he chooses to call "democracy") does he speak for? Certainly the elective affinity between capital and power in the world we are presented with is real enough to justify using the phrase "empire of capital," but there are pertinent contradictions and tensions within the term itself and within the reality it invokes that we must also be aware of.[32] Nonetheless, whatever the precise interactions between the economic and the political imperatives of present-day imperialism, the imposition of the newly defined imperial writ is now, on the whole, merely *dictated to* those social formations at the periphery of the global system.

One final note here. This whole system of "recolonization" by the "Empire of Capital" is far from being without its apologists—and its would-be makers of the prevailing "commonsense," at once "obvious" and ineluctable, of this new Empire. There is, of course, the currently dominant ideological premise that the "free market," self-evidently "rational," can and must be dominant. Thus, despite much earlier predictions of Karl Polanyi and others that such a retreat to the dark ages of primitive capitalism was virtually unimaginable, the "market fundamentalism" of Milton Friedman and his ilk has become the very acme of global "commonsense" in the economic realm. Moreover, the premises of hegemonic neo-liberalism tend to stretch even further than this in the hands of such intellectual evil geniuses of neo-liberalism as Niall Ferguson and Michael Ignatieff.[33] For such spokesmen (Ferguson in this case) of the "Empire of Capital" seem quite content to willfully elide so-called market freedom with political freedom: "There are those who would insist that an empire is by definition incapable of playing such a role; in their eyes, all empires are exploitative in character. Yet there can be—and has been—such a thing as a liberal empire, one that enhances its own security and prosperity precisely by providing the rest of the world with generally beneficial public goods: not only economic freedom, but also the institutions necessary for markets to flourish." And they then press the language of contemporary imperialism quite self-consciously toward a rationale for recolonization:

> I [writes Ferguson] am fundamentally in favor of empire. Indeed, I believe that empire is more necessary in the twenty-first century than ever before. The threats we face are not in themselves new ones. But advances in technology make them more dangerous than ever before...What is required is an agency capable of intervening in the affairs of such states to contain epidemics, depose tyrants, end local wars and eradicate terrorist organizations. This is the self-interested argument for empire. But there is also a complementary altruistic argument. (p. 24)

Here is the good colonialism/recolonization trope at work and the examples of the empire of capital's present arrogance of purpose could easily be multiplied (as I have done elsewhere).[34]

III. Recolonization?

What then, at the receiving end as it were, does "recolonization" look like? There are, for starters, some relevant distinctions to be made. Africa, the continent I know best, does provide, in many respects although by no means uniquely, a kind of worst-case scenario of apparently locked-in penury and, as I have suggested, quite straightforward "recolonization." Recall [from chapter 5] the telling admission by one member of Mozambique's parliament in describing the situation of that country: "The biggest moment of Mozambican politics this year was when the government went to Paris to meet with the donors. That is where our parliament was really held in Mozambique this year, the donor meetings in

Paris." Or, as another MP put it, "We accept that our budget is really set by donors at the annual Paris conference. We accept that our priority is to develop a donor-acceptable budget." Of course, "the assembly must be part of the process, that is what democracy means in Mozambique"![35]

True, Samir Amin, a notable observer of such global realities, has recently made a more general argument, suggesting, in the wake of the demise of the second (communist) world, the wisdom of keeping alive, even under the changing conditions of the present post-Cold War globe, a variant of the First World/Third World trope. True, as he suggests, various global "transformations" have "left us with situations quite different from those that prevailed in 1945." Though a global hierarchy still, all too evidently, exists, the imposition of global competitiveness as the universal condition for all within the global capitalist economy has had differential results, depending on the ability of such countries to become "competitive" (even if within certain severe limits) within such a world system.[36]

In parts of Eastern Europe and in the former Soviet Union, in the countries of East Asia (China, Korea and Taiwan), even, to a degree, in some of the larger countries of Latin America and in India, a degree of "modernization" (although startlingly little domestic equality) has occurred to underpin a measure of "competitiveness" in global terms. This, Amin suggests, is "tomorrow's real periphery." In parts of East Asia, for example, this has tended to occur in countries (South Korea, Hong Kong, Taiwan) which were given, because of Cold War preoccupations, some room for the state to manoeuvre, initially, in order to carve out a certain space for capitalist growth strategies outside the orbit of domineering western capital. Most importantly, in China itself the lingering authoritarianism of a communist past has enabled the state in that vast country to massage into being a capitalism to its own specifications, one that can now "claim to control its relations with the dominant world system" and, one fears, to act imperialistically, in its own sharp pursuit of raw materials, vis-à-vis much of the rest of the global South. Of course, these are societies with gross inequalities, horrific environmental fallout and the like, societies in which a class struggle for human betterment should no doubt be encouraged. But there are worse cases.

These Amin identifies as the locales of a "Fourth World," one even more daunting and depressing in aspect than its "Third World" counterpart. This "world" comprises Africa, but also the Arab-Islamic world, much of Latin America and even such very large Asian countries as Pakistan and Indonesia. For such countries the outlook for their productive insertion into the world system is very bleak indeed. Moreover, it is with reference to such countries that the term "recolonization" applies most aptly, this very term (as noted above) having actually been used quite pointedly of Africa by historian Paul Nugent in his recent magisterial work on the continent's recent history, *Africa Since Independence*.[37] Thus, for Nugent, "structural adjustment programmes" (SAPs) are presented as being the chief instrument of bringing Africa to heel vis-à-vis a new, more assertive capitalist global hegemony.

The results [as itemized in his chapter 8]: the "rolling back" of the state, the "promotion of greater social inequality," the inducing of "the deindustrialization of much of the African continent" and the promoting of remarkably greater "impoverishment" not only in the rural areas but also via "the progressive deterioration in the cities during the 1990s." Indeed, even the so-called "success stories" (Nugent examines especially closely the experiences of both Ghana and Tanzania) "were less than inspirational." Moreover, as a putative response to "Africa's marginalized position in the international division of labour" the neo-liberal "New Partnership for Africa's Development," launched with great ceremony in the new century by African presidents Mbeki, Obassanjo and Wade, is interpreted by Nugent as being merely a route to even greater subordination of the continent. For by now, clearly, "the freedom of action which seemed to come with independence had narrowed" considerably, to say the least.

The context of such recolonization, in Africa and elsewhere, should now be clear. Already, in the heyday of Keynesian/Rostovian developmentalism, it was easy to discern that in most of the world the post Second World War promise had been not just narrowed but lost and that capitalist strength at the centre had continued to trump any real growth and equity on the periphery, in the global South. Now, however, the situation was merely to be exacerbated as the paternalistic thrust of hand-me-down capitalist development was replaced, in the 1980s and 1990s, by a much more hard-boiled version of central capitalist dictate. The state (at the periphery) is dead, long live the market (and, of course, the "free" writ of capital).

In grim reality, of course, the failure of secular visions of progress, either of the right or the left, to make much headway in advancing the lot of the vast mass of the impoverished population of the global South has led to the latter's temptation to fall back on various religious and ethnic markers of their "difference" in order to stake their claims to any meaningful change for the better in their lives. This temptation has in turn been fastened upon and reinforced by opportunist elites of the periphery to press a challenge to "western modernization." Unfortunately, this, in turn, bears little promise for bettering the lot of the poor—even if it has foreshadowed a world, as concretized by the events of 9/11, that is rather less controllable by the imperial centre of the empire of capital than it would like. In contrast, finding a way back to a more promising kind of secular resistance to global capitalism would incorporate, it seems safe to say, a far greater measure of socialist intent. This is a challenge indeed, of course. For this would have to be a socialism of far more democratic provenance than has heretofore characterized, to its cost, challenges to capitalism advanced in the name of such a project. It would also have to announce and practise a programme that brought genuine material betterment to the bulk of the population—this in a world that does not now lend itself easily to realizing such a goal.

Small wonder that Samir Amin, in pointing a way forward, has sought the answer to recolonization and the like in an even more radical decolonization of central capitalist control: in his word, to an actual "delinking" of the economies of the global south from the empire of capital that holds it under its sway.[38] Delinking is, in turn, defined as "the submission of external relations, the opposite of the internal adjustment of the peripheries to the demands of the polarizing worldwide expansion of capital" and it is seen as being "the only realistic alternative [since] reform of the [present] world system is utopian." For "history shows us that it is impossible to 'catch up' within the framework of world capitalism" and that "only a very long transition" beyond the current polarization and beyond presently existing global capitalism will suffice.[39]

But what would it mean to substitute the present political economy of recolonization with an auto-centric socioeconomic alternative that was at once effective, efficient and productive? What would be the programme of a government erected on the premise of a radical delinking from the presently existent and profoundly cancerous global capitalist system? An answer would only begin to be found in a new project of genuine socialist planning—established at a national or regional basis—that sought to smash precisely the crippling (il)logic of such "market limitations" upon development. This, in turn, would suggest the need for a programme that (following the formulations of Clive Thomas) embodied "the progressive convergence of the demand structure of the community and the needs of the population"[40]—this being the very reverse of the market fundamentalist's orthodoxy. One could then ground a "socialism of expanded accumulation"—one that refuses the dilemma that has heretofore faced the many "socialisms" prone to fall into the Stalinist trap of "violently repressing mass consumption" in the name of the supposed requirements of accumulation. For, far from accumulation and mass consumption being warring opposites, the premise would now be that accumulation could be driven forward precisely by finding outlets for production in meeting the growing requirements, the needs, of the mass of the population.

An effective industrialization strategy would thus base its "expanded reproduction" on ever increasing exchanges between city and country, between industry and agriculture, with food and raw materials moving to the cities and with consumer goods and producer goods (with the latter defined to include centrally such modest items as scythes, iron plows, hoes, axes, fertilizers and the like) moving to the countryside. Collective saving geared to investment can then be seen as being drawn essentially, if not exclusively, from an expanding economic pool. Note that such a socialism of expanded reproduction makes the betterment of the people's lot a short-term rather than a long-term project and thus promises a much sounder basis for an effective (rather than merely rhetorical) alliance of workers, peasants and others and for a democratic road to revolutionary socialism.[41]

As Amin (quoted above) has underscored, this is not to make a case for autarchy: judicious and mutually advantageous exchanges with trading partners in the global economy would have their place, earning foreign exchange and trading credits. But the core logic of the specific economy under consideration would be auto-centric. Of course, before this kind of programme of effective delinking could even be tried there would have to exist a radical polity—democratic and revolutionary—not only to sustain such a project once in power but to even launch it in the first instance. But this also poses the question of how exactly such a challenge, one that could ensure the consolidation of movements and regimes prepared to battle against global capitalism, might conceivably be mounted in the world as we presently know it. Needless to say, it would be nice if the powerful imperial centres operated on a logic different from what presently drives them. In fact, this has been the premise of a Trotskyist prioritization of revolution in those centres for decades. But revolution in the First World seems unlikely to happen any time soon. The global South, much the most injured by the present worldwide system, has little option but to act for human betterment now. How to do so? This is a question that is canvassed at much greater length elsewhere, but it is one to which we will begin to sketch some possible answers in the following section.

IV. Resistance?

For where should we look for more promising challenges to the system of recolonization by capital (albeit capital serviced by the singularly unapologetic policeman's role of the western states themselves and their satrapies in the new colonies) that is currently afoot. As stated, I will deal with this important subject only briefly here; nonetheless, several points are worth noting.

First, it would be wise in this respect to take cognizance of the diverse range of circumstances in the global South identified by Amin, above. After all, in those countries that have staked out a measure of competitiveness within the global system and some measure of industrialization, many of the most familiar and promising historical markers of resistance are to be found, not least the growing role of the organized working class as a force of significance. This is less true in other settings, the vast Fourth World of Africa, the Middle East and much of Latin America and Asia, for example, where the resistance to capital will necessarily be somewhat more obliquely defined.

Indeed this is not merely a question of all those peasants out there whose futures are being twisted by the empire of capital. It is also the vast numbers of urban "hangers-on," the unemployed and marginalized—too readily dismissed by Marx and others as mere "lazzeroni" and the like, including many women outside of the "work-force" (albeit alongside an undoubted expanding "feminization of labour")—who not only have an objective interest in revolution, but could, in principle, be linked to it actively, both ideologically and organizationally. Let me cite here Post and Wright who speak eloquently as to the kind of militant quasi-class awareness and potential "class consciousness" on the part of the majority of people of the South that, independently of their role in the "production process" per se, can and must be won. As they argue:

> The working out of capitalism in parts of the periphery prepares not only the minority working class but peasants and other working people, women, youth and minorities for a socialist solution, even though the political manifestation of this may not initially take the form of a socialist movement. In the case of those who are not wage labourers (the classical class associated with that new order) capitalism has still so permeated the social relations which determine their existences, even though it may not have followed the western European pattern of "freeing" their labour power, that to be liberated from it is their only salvation.... The objective need for socialism [by] these elements can be no less than that of the worker

> imprisoned in the factory and disciplined by the whip of unemployment. These prices are paid in even the most "successful" of the underdeveloped countries, [while other countries actually] experience mass destitution. Finding another path has...become a desperate necessity if the alternative of continuing, if not increasing barbarism is to be escaped.[42]

But any stretching of the parameters of a "working class" project will also have to be even more "unorthodox" than that. As I have argued elsewhere,[43] it will need to include a range of diverse identities, and action based upon such identities, that can, with creative work, also be seen—indeed must be seen—as part of a socialist project. Class analysis with a decisive, more inclusive, difference, then: this is capitalism, after all, so working classes matter. But, especially in the global South, capitalism doesn't quite work the way Marx said it should and thought it would. And that reality throws up a mass—though, paradoxically, it is a structured mass, structured by the shared subordination to capital, if only that structure can be rendered more visible to them.

True, resistance to western capitalist hegemony and its recolonization project will not, inevitably, take this left/socialist form. As noted above, given the failure of various secular alternatives (especially postcolonial nationalism but including "socialism"), people who must negotiate their troubled present and future are drawn instead to other possible identifications and projects to validate their own sense of self and their future prospects. There are many such identities potentially available and no shortage of zealots to push them forward. As a result, various fundamentalisms, religious and communal, fill the vacuum that a failed left has permitted to exist.

One of the great challenges facing the left (secular and socialist) will therefore be to help people to understand their social grievances more systematically, and more politically, in anti-capitalist terms. But it will also be to find ways both to acknowledge and to mould grievances and perfectly comprehensible cultural and racial preoccupations that exist at other levels—including, of course, gender-based demands—to complement rather than to displace a class-defined project. This can only be achieved, in short, through imaginative, diligent and non-reductionist political and ideological work. For beyond the obvious dangers of demands cast in merely reductionist terms there is much promise to be found in challenges to western capitalist recolonization that not only assert the continuing imperatives of a global class struggle but that also take firm cognizance of identities rooted in racial, religious and ethno-national belongings.[44]

In sum, there is a need to develop new projects that make sense, in clearly counter-hegemonic terms, with any such new "hegemonies" (ideologies and movements) being necessary to integrate and generalize the many existent and emergent local and sectoral grievances and resistances to a national and regional level. As Leys writes, "I think that many elements of [the requisite] discourse are present in the various discourses of contemporary social movements of all kinds, but constructing them into a unified hegemonic discourse remains largely to be attempted." Similarly, he continues, "any forging of them into hegemonic projects looking for long-term transformation," and into movements capable of imposing themselves upon events and successfully "displacing the power of global mega-corporations and the handful of economic superpowers in the shaping of our world," is bound to be incredibly challenging. Such initiatives are most visible for the moment, perhaps, in Latin America (Venezuela, Ecuador, Bolivia). Nonetheless, it is difficult to accept the fact that the vast majority of the world, now so imprisoned, politically and economically, by the Empire of Capital will not eventually find ever more effective vehicles for expressing their anger and productive energies.[45]

Conclusion

True, it would be easy to be profoundly pessimistic, particularly about the fate of Amin's "Fourth World." The Northern (and Far Eastern!) centres of global capitalism seem increasingly unapologetic about the extent of their power and their selfish willingness to use it largely in their own interests. And the most dramatic response and resistance, for the moment at least, seems to come from al-Qaeda and others of similar fundamentalist persuasion. But these latter can offer no real alternative, at the level of the productive system, to capital-logic. The global South thus seems caught between a rock and a hard place. The need has never been greater for creative left responses to such an apparently bleak situation, one that can both imagine and realize a world of decency, fairness, collective human concern and shared plenty.

SOUNDS TO ME LIKE A CALL, to return to where we began this chapter, for a socialist alternative to the commanding global hegemony of capitalism.

B) PREFACE

On Balance (the Self)

When you take a political stance that finds you constantly beating against the winds of power and of ostensible "common sense" you either find yourself (a) driven mad; (b) prepared merely to throw in the towel (and live happily ever after, at whomsoever's expense it might be); or, instead, (c) holding onto ways to balance your life and your sometimes dispiriting take on the world with an additional range of realities. Myself, I do it, as this section will show, by reading, listening and playing—and by hanging on to friends and family (as my conclusion testifies). I do this not only to retain my *joie de vivre* but also to avoid the dangers attendant upon taking merely a narrowly querulous and censorious stance towards the present state of the world and my life in it. But it's something all of us on the left must wrestle with.

In doing so myself I take comfort from the writing of others of course. To take one example there's Bertholt Brecht's great poem "To Posterity," a kind of personal talisman of mine over many decades. Brecht (in Nazi days and through no choice of his own) was a kind of "revolutionary traveller" himself ("For we went, changing our country more often than our clothes. In the class war, despairing when there was only injustice and no resistance") and a clear-sighted one: "He who laughs has not yet heard the terrible tidings." He was also no romantic and no boaster about either his accomplishments or those of his comrades: "But you, when at last it has come to pass that man can help his fellow man, do not judge us too harshly."[46]

Of similar import was Jan Myrdal whose own memoir, entitled *Confessions of a Disloyal European*, has also been a frequent touchstone of mine (I have included the most relevant extended passage as an appendix in my recent *Empire and Decolonization*). In Afghanistan (some decades ago), Myrdal reveals to an Afghani official at a cocktail party the apparent attempt by a German in the north of that country to recruit Myrdal to assist him in some spying there. As Myrdal then writes, the American who has been drinking beer with them "stared at me. Then he edged away. He looked as if he had seen a snake." Myrdal knew why. "The German trusted me because I was a European. The American felt that I was a traitor to Europe. As for myself, I had passed one of the gates to Asia. My loyalty was no longer an unquestioned loyalty to Europe. And I was quite prepared to let the Afghans take care of [in the words of this Afghan official he spoke to at the party] the German who had been collecting military information in their country."[47]

Colour me, similarly, a "disloyal Canadian," then—if we were to believe for even a moment that the likes of Stephen Harper, or Michael Ignatieff, or Lester B. Pearson, speak authoritatively for who and what we, as Canadians, are. But let me return to Brecht who asks "how can I eat and drink when my food is snatched from the hungry and my glass of water belongs to the thirsty?" Yet, he admits, "I eat and drink." And so do I! And, as this present section demonstrates, I also listen to music, go to plays and operas and movies, and engage (at least until very recently: see below) in vigorous basketball games. And, as my conclusion will demonstrate, I also enjoy the company of family and friends. This despite having heard "the terrible tidings." At what cost, then, has my (relatively) "smooth forehead" ("a smooth forehead betokens a hard heart," writes Brecht) been earned. Perhaps only another, different book—beyond my current capacity to compose—could begin to crack such a riddle. Meanwhile, enjoy this section. If you dare.

CHAPTER SEVEN

Readin', Writin' and Relaxin'

a) On Reading

I've found contentment in writing, even though, given my general predilections, I've had to split much of my writing time between reflections on victory, and on defeat—with perhaps rather more on the latter than the former, I regret to say. Still, my books are my life or at least a goodly part of it. I write, therefore I am.

Well, not quite, as the remainder of this book will attest. For example, I do like to read too, not only professionally but also when relaxing. I guess I always have: my brother tells me I could invariably be found (when I wasn't playing games or out and about, that is) up on the third floor of our house: reading! I can't remember the titles of all those early books very clearly. Certainly I can make no claims to have read Proust in grade school (in fact I'm still working away on him all these years later), or Marx in high school. More likely my fare would be the Hardy Boys or else Gordon Sinclair out on the road, no doubt fictitiously, somewhere. At best, I did read plenty of the Classic Comics versions of *Moby Dick* and other such "formidable" titles, although I do also remember reading an edited version of *War and Peace* and a few like books in high school. However, it was far more likely, at various ages, that I was reading the likes of *Treasure Island* (still a favourite), *Freddy the Pig,* the Horatio Hornblower adventures, and some Sherlock Holmes, and of *Dave Dawson on the China Road* (read if not during the Second World War at least shortly thereafter). And I also fondly remember Canadian titles, mainly provided as they first hit the bookstore shelves by my mother, such as books by Thomas Hambleton (*Forest Ranger; Young Bush Pilot; Abitibi Adventure*) and H. C. Raddall; by John F. Hayes (*Buckskin Colonist* and *Bugle in the Hills*) and Marie McPhedran; by Hubert Evans, (*North to the Unknown*) and Louise Hall Tharp (*Company of Adventurers*); and by C.W. Jefferys whose *The Picture Gallery of Canadian History* appeared in three endlessly fascinating volumes in the 1940s; in fact, I still have copies of each of these diverse relics of vintage Canadiana in my basement!

And I've continued to read fairly widely—I am now able to stock up, when necessary, at my daughter's truly fabulous TYPE bookstore down on Queen Street—with such favourites as *The Charterhouse of Parma, The Magic Mountain, Women in Love, Middlemarch, Nostromo, Man's Fate*, various Thomas Hardy titles, all volumes of Anthony Powell's *Dance to the Music of Time* and virtually everything, too, by Robertson Davies still high on my list. True, such titles comprise a rather arbitrary all-time "hit parade,"—although it is one not entirely randomly selected since all of these titles must stand near the top of any such list of mine. Of somewhat more recent vintage I've enjoyed Richard Ford's Frank Bascombe trilogy and Cormac McCarthy's Border trilogy, as well as diverse books by Michael Ondaatje, M.G. Vassanji, Ian MacEwan and many others (including a valued handful of baseball books: Angell, Boswell and Mark Harris). Still, I'd never try to pass myself off as enough of a heavyweight contender to chance my pen regarding such authors. I leave that kind of thing to my daughter who, alongside her TYPE activities, has a doctorate in English (with a Canadian accent) and is author of a very good book, *Writing the Roaming Subject*, on Canadian writers Ondaatje, Wah, Marlatt and Kiyooka.

Thrillers—even if I've written about them (see below) only intermittently—have been a different kettle of prose for me, a not-so-secret passion, one that helped immeasurably to see me through a recent long recuperation period from an unpleasant accident. Still, I read such books pretty consistently all along, having read, I think, every volume by Ross MacDonald, Dashiell Hammett, Raymond Chandler and Maj Sjowall and Per Wahloo, while wishing that they and others like them were still alive and ready, willing and able to continue to entertain me. But there are lots of present-day writers too that I read, I hope not too indiscriminately, and a number of them I also mention in the present section of this book, a section which actually begins with a venture of my own into a certain kind of meta-fiction, then follows with a pertinent review, and culminates in a essay presenting my thoughts on the difficulties inherent in bringing my twin passions—for revolution and for mystery—together.

Still, even my writing about thrillers has been pretty limited and my passion for them largely pursued as a reader. In fact, the closest I've actually come to writing one myself is the following mock "review" which, in intent, was inspired by my reading of various much more brilliant "literary pieces" (no descriptive noun seems quite adequate to epitomizing them) by Borges, notably his "Pierre Menard, the Author of Don Quixote," a letter-perfect, short exemplar of the form. My own attempt, under the title "A Flag for a Shroud," appeared in *This Magazine*, March, 1978, beginning with the epigraph: "The new crime fiction begins where the masses are, not in their hundreds, but in their hundreds of thousands." I then continued:

THIS EPIGRAPH—SET OPPOSITE THE TITLE PAGE—is a paraphrase of Lenin's celebrated definition of politics, and it greets the startled reader at the beginning of MacKenzie Dawson's new work of detective fiction *A Flag for a Shroud* (MacKenzie Dawson, *A Flag for a Shroud*, Red Maple Publishing, Toronto n.d.). Fortunately it is the only didactic note which the book strikes. Otherwise, on the surface at least, all the familiar trappings of the "private eye" genre are on display for the devotee; brisk and suspenseful plotting, compressed but acute setting of scene, a modicum of violence (and the threat thereof), brittle and witty repartee, vivid characters, each just a little larger than life. And all this set out with a firm and believable sense of our time and our place: imaginary cops-and-robbers in a real bush garden.

Yet the epigraph quoted above is no accident. There is something more to Dawson's book, something that lifts it out of the ordinary run of thrillers and gives it a much broader resonance. For Dawson, in the epigraph, is putting us on notice. He means to take the crisis of his chosen genre seriously. Nor is it accidental that Dawson's "solution" implies the adoption of an overtly political posture. It is not simply that such an approach is, self-evidently, one perfectly suited to Dawson's own personal predilections and commitments. More important, it becomes apparent that politics is, in any case, the sole possible solution to a genre's crisis. The result? With *A Flag for a Shroud* MacKenzie Dawson has produced a private detective novel—right here in Canada!—which now stands as the most advanced outpost on the frontier of what Steven Carter termed to be "experimental mystery fiction."[48]

The Crisis of the Genre

Julian Symons, in his history of the mystery story, *Mortal Consequences*, correctly identifies Dashiell Hammett and Raymond Chandler as the chief creators of the "private eye" thriller. Of the two, it was Chandler who really established the archetype—sustaining Phillip Marlowe's presence over a series of novels and also, in a number of remarkable essays, seeking to theorize the genre he was creating. Like Hammett, he had no illusions about the American milieu of which he wrote. "If being in revolt against a corrupt society constitutes immaturity," he noted sardonically, "then Phillip Marlowe is extremely immature. If seeing dirt where the dirt constitutes an inadequate social adjustment, then Phillip Marlowe has inadequate social adjustment." Where, then, does Marlowe stand? Chandler's evocation of his detective's role as urban knight-errant, as one-man conscience and righter of wrongs, is a familiar one. "Down these mean streets a man must go who is not himself mean, who is neither tarnished nor afraid."

Ironically, Dashiell Hammett—perhaps because his own left-wing political commitments were closer to the surface and more carefully considered—had already foreshadowed in his work the fact that this mythic solution was not viable. His most famous detective-hero, Sam Spade, is no Phillip Marlowe, is not even (in spite of the panache which Humphrey Bogart brought to the role of Spade in *The Maltese Falcon*) a very attractive figure. A corrupt society, unnamed and unassailed, must also corrupt the knight! Of course, despite this knowledge Hammett never let the least hint of a political solution to the social diseases encountered by his detective enter his pages. He merely chose cynicism, rather than naiveté, as the cornerstone of his style. In fact, even Chandler was to echo, privately, a bittersweet version of such cynicism, but, in his case, it became more a kind of despair. Acknowledging to his agent the extent to which his hero belonged to the realm of fantasy, he wrote that he "didn't care whether the mystery was fairly obvious, but... cared about the people, about this strange, corrupt world we live in, and how any man who tried to be honest looks in the end either sentimental or plain foolish."

Still, it was the myth in itself, not the despair, which sprang most forcefully from the pages of Chandler's books. Small wonder that Robert Altman's screen version of one of Chandler's novels (*The Long Goodbye*)—made in the early 70s when American streets had become even meaner than in Chandler's day—could set itself quite self-consciously to explode "Chandler's sentimental foolishness." As Pauline Kael has described the film, "the pulp pretense that Marlowe's chivalrous code was armour has collapsed" and "the one-lone-idealist-in-a-city-crawling-with-rats becomes a schlemiel who thinks he's tough and wise." In Kael's view the Marlowe of the novels "was, in any case, only one step from being a clown, but Chandler pulped his own surrogate and made Marlowe, the Victorian relic, a winner." This is all fair game for Altman, whose "goodbye to the private eye hero is comic and melancholy and full of regrets" but a goodbye nonetheless. Small wonder, she argues, that the film was not a striking popular success: viewers are loathe to "lose... their Bogart icon," they "still want to believe that Galahad is alive and well in Los Angeles."

Of course the genre does live on, despite Altman's assault upon it and despite ever more obvious absurdities of its underlying conceit. Moreover, it would be unduly sombre and humourless to ignore the legitimacy of the escapism that continues to be offered by the most jauntily crafted works in the field. Still, it is the best of these craftsmen who are most unwilling to accept Kael's sweeping generalization that "the detective-novel genre has always verged on self-parody because it gives you nothing under the surface." Dissatisfied with mere flippancy, they have sought to lend their creations at least a modicum of "meaning" and significance.

Thus the most skilled of the heirs of Chandler and Hammett, the Canadian-American crime novelist Ross MacDonald, continues, as he began, to explore the warping effect of money and of "possessive individualism" in capitalist America. Over the years, however, he has chosen to find in Freud rather than in Marx the key to his fictional world. And he has also narrowed his core vision to encompass only a limited range of symbols—centring on time and on family—the endless permutations and combinations of which lend to his later books, for all their virtuosity, a certain claustrophobic similarity. In them we find his detective, Lew Archer, increasingly left on the sidelines, strong to solve the puzzles presented by his cases but powerless to affect the psychic, even cosmic, forces which trap the players in MacDonald's games. As flies to wanton boys are we to the gods...!

The best of recent writers have returned to more broadly social concerns than latter-day Ross MacDonald affords us, though none, prior to MacKenzie Dawson, can be said to have pushed the matter very far. Still, it is refreshing to find in Andrew Bergman's *Hollywood and Levine* a 1940's private eye whose case runs him headlong into young Richard Nixon, the latter just beginning his career as a shady right-wing congressman, but already practicing effectively the kind of slimy politics which were to make him President of the United States.[49] So, too, in Roger Simon's Moses Wine (*The Big Fix* and *Wild Turkey*) we find a hip detective who has lived the consciousness-raising experience of the sixties and whose (partially) liberated mind provides him with some awareness of the broader social forces which structure the seamy world in which he moves. And in Lynn Meyer's *Paperback Thriller* we have in Dr. Sarah Cayse a tough, self-consciously liberated woman psychiatrist who plays a detective-like role with burning urgency.

Best of all we have Robert Parker's Spenser who, in a trio of excellent books (*The Godwulf Manuscript, God Save the Child and Mortal Stakes*), moves believably through the United States of the seventies, his movement marked by such attractive features as his clear eye for those ubiquitous grey areas where government, business and the underworld overlap and his involvement in several refreshingly non-exploitative relationships with women. Indeed the Spenser novels are carried off with such remarkable style that we can almost overlook the fact that Spenser moves alone and, like a latter-day Marlowe, finds the motivation for his actions in a private code of honour. Of course it is not the least attractive of Spenser's qualities that he is himself aware of the fragility of his posture, as his intriguing exchange with his friend Susan Silverman at the conclusion of *Mortal Stakes* makes clear. This is certainly one more reason why Spenser books make such good reading. Nonetheless, such awareness does not quite represent an answer to Pauline Kael's critique.

MacKenzie Dawson's Project

The message is clear. The most attractive of the contemporary private eyes —at large in a post-Vietnam, post-Watergate America—have an even clearer awareness than Marlowe or Spade of the corruption of their society. Yet such increased awareness tends to seal them ever more firmly into the archetypal posture of Chandler's knight. Enter, then, MacKenzie Dawson; it is precisely at this point that the full significance of his approach can be most readily grasped. For Dawson, as suggested at the outset of the article, has seized unerringly upon the full meaning of the private detective's contemporary plight and in consequence has been able to suggest a direction for the genre which gives promise of providing a solution to the crisis. This is not a critical judgment that can be sustained in the abstract, however. In fact, it can be best established by exploring with care Dawson's own novel, *A Flag for a Shroud*. I trust the reader will agree that the importance of the issue at stake excuses the necessity of revealing here more of the book's plot than would normally be considered good form in reviewing a book of this sort. Note too, that such a paraphrase must be done in a painfully schematic manner; I am acutely conscious of the fact that I must do less than full justice to what serious mystery story readers will recognize to be the rich, generic texture of Dawson's novel.

In *A Flag for a Shroud* Nick Shannon, private-eye, is called into what seems, on the surface, to be a routine 'missing daughter' caper, the subject having last been seen in a popular resort area north of Toronto. Shannon quickly senses that there is something too pat about the puzzle. However, his attention is diverted when a series of leaks and happenstances suggest that more interesting events are transpiring at a private lodge far out in the lake. The site is the summer home of Alexander Ralston, Governor of the Bank of Canada. One thing leading to another, Shannon soon finds himself on the island as a surreptitious nocturnal witness to the arrival, by light seaplane, of several senior American officials, including the U.S. ambassador to Canada, for a secret conclave with the Governor!

Shannon, whose own political credentials as a left-nationalist of Marxian persuasion have been deftly, even casually, established in earlier pages, finds such a turn of events much more important than the case which originally placed him on the scene. He is soon back in Toronto, checking with contacts in the nether regions of government and business as to the possible implications of such a meeting. He finds that a rocky and dependent Canadian economy is experiencing a severe balance of payments crisis and the Canadian dollar is showing the strain in the international money market. The Americans, through the International Monetary Fund and other mechanisms, seek the classic solution: a cutback in social services, more emphasis on primary product exports, an even more open door to foreign investment by the multinationals. Yet such action by the government would seem to cut against the grain of current policy: a recent Cabinet shuffle has placed a vaguely nationalist grouping, centred around a kind of latter-day Walter Gordon, in a position of increased prominence. There has even been speculation about such possibilities as nationalization of the energy industry or some real, rather than merely notional, constraints upon American investment.

This lends urgency to Shannon's sense that the American initiative he witnessed is of sinister import, clearly designed to tip such a balance of forces, by whatever means necessary, in a more firmly continentalist direction. Leaking the story to the press, he awaits further developments—which are not long in coming. Elaborate, but not quite convincing denials from the Canadian side, a passable alibi, and much bluster, from the American ambassador, a series of hassles for Shannon from the RCMP and other shadowy agencies (hassles which have a frightening ring of truth to them). Fearing a situation of mere stand-off, Shannon decides to return to the island to look for some further, inalterably incriminating, evidence.

Caught in the act by military police operating as the Governor's private army on the island—they are led by a particularly sadistic officer, one Erik Melnyk, whom Shannon has apparently met before and, will, no doubt, meet again—Shannon is brought into the presence of the Governor himself. The latter is in an expansive mood and, after a stylish verbal skirmish with Shannon on matters of applied political economy, he reveals to Shannon that it has all been a set-up: the missing daughter was merely a come-on and the nocturnal tryst between Canadian and "American" top brass play-acted—right down to the importation of a look-alike for the American ambassador—precisely for Shannon's benefit. It had been anticipated, and desired, that he would then draw the incident into the public eye:

> Don't you see the fix we were in. The P.M. can't be seen to be too deferential to American directives just at the moment. What's more, for its own reasons—something to do with Southern Africa, I believe—the American government is reluctant to rattle its own sabre just now. So we decided to play the American card ourselves.

The Governor is confident that, despite the various denials surrounding the incident, enough of the evidence unearthed by Shannon has struck home to convince the "gnomes" of Wall Street and Zurich of Canada's ultimate responsiveness to America's dictate. The international bankers will feel safe to ignore the government's nationalist rhetoric and, proceeding on the assumption that this country is really playing ball after all, ease off on some of their financial push against Canadian currency.

> Look at the dollar, rallied strongly in the last couple of weeks. We've bought a lot of time thanks to you, Shannon, and we can now set about

> putting our house in acceptable order quietly and without the distraction of too much immediate international pressure. You've bailed us out, my friend.

So confident is the Governor that Shannon is free to go. Who would believe such a tortured yarn? As a result, it's a pretty dejected sleuth who paddles back to the landing. "Game and match to the ruling class?" he wonders aloud. But at the landing an angry crowd has gathered to demand explanations from the Governor. Shannon learns that a similar group is on Parliament Hill, that rallies are to be held in Vancouver, Winnipeg, Toronto and Halifax protesting American intervention, that a network of unions and citizens' organizations is forming around the issue. The Governor and his cronies in power have been playing to one audience: the gnomes of international finance and the multinational corporations. But even Shannon has momentarily forgotten that there is another witness to events, a constituency that the Governor may have underestimated at his peril—the mass of Canadian working people. It is at this point that Dawson brings his tale to an end. Shannon's case is concluded. The political struggle continues.

Private Eye, Public Eye

The significance of such an ending scarcely needs underscoring. As Dawson himself has put the point in a recent television interview, his detective is different because, unlike Chandler's knight, he has, potentially, a constituency for his concern. It is a mass base of increasingly conscious people, understanding the corruption of their society, which can alone give resonance to the detective's otherwise private quest. Only such a constituency can save his attempt "to be honest" from "looking in the end either sentimental or plain foolish." This, then, is the significance of the Lenin-like epigraph, quoted above, with which *A Flag for a Shroud* begins.

Not that Dawson has said the last word on the subject. He is clearly at the beginning, not the end, of his creative project in the fictional world of the private detective. A comparison may be illuminating here. Thus, in a closely related field—the police procedural novel—the Swedish team of Maj Sjowall and Per Wahloo have recently written what one is compelled to recognize as the definitive Marxist classic of the genre, a classic for this and, in all probability, any other season. But *The Terrorists* is the summation of nine earlier volumes in the inspector Martin Beck series (and of a number of prior crime stories written by Wahloo as a single before that).

In contrast, the full ideological and organizational implications of Shannon's detective-cum-political work have scarcely begun to be spelt out. There are clear hints in *Flag* that Shannon's anti-imperialist nationalism will be even more firmly wedded, in subsequent volumes, to socialism and to class struggle than to any mere populism, and there are hints, too, in some of *Flag*'s dialogue, as to Dawson's awareness that mere spontaneity in resisting the dark forces at work within and upon contemporary Canada is no substitute for political organization. And Dawson has himself been quoted as saying that Shannon will soon be called on to probe more systematically the nature of the interface in Canada between the government and the business community. Indeed, in the interview mentioned above, Dawson startled *Canada AM* hostess Helen Hutchinson by observing that in preparation for his next novel he had been scanning, with much interest and edification, the recent weighty and sociological tomes by Wallace Clement and Leo Panitch on the Canadian state and the corporate elite!

Yet whatever may remain to be done, it seems safe to conclude that, with *A Flag for a Shroud,* we possess the vital clue: that at last is a way forward for the private eye. In fact, it is almost embarrassingly obvious, now that Dawson has wielded his literary sword, that only a radical politics can cut the Gordian knot that binds the fictional investigator. But why, it may be finally asked, should it have fallen to a Canadian author to take this crucial step where other skilled practitioners—working mainly, in the case of the private eye novel, in the United States—have failed. It seems certain that the reality of our cultural dependence—so obvious a feature of the Canadian condition—forms part of the explanation. In such a milieu there is every temptation for most artists to adopt uncritically the literary forms of the dominant external culture. By the same token, when once the first stirrings of cultural independence begin, there is a particularly strong incentive for some to approach such forms critically, with a drive to either smash them or at least to fashion them anew. Seen in this light, Dawson's innovative role within his chosen genre and the broader evocation of an anti-imperialist politics in his novel can be understood to be merely two sides of the same coin.[50]

Such observations make clear that MacKenzie Dawson's efforts provide not only a riposte of Pauline Kael and an edifying example of his fellow thriller writers, but also a source of inspiration, more generally, to his fellow Canadian artists. It is for these reasons, as well as for the substance of his political concerns, that a reading of *A Flag for a Shroud* can be seen to launch us on a distinctive adventure in Canadian letters, an adventure which, despite the apparently humble provenance of Dawson's chosen genre, may begin by amusing but end by enlightening us all.[51] His consummate thriller must therefore be greeted with both the frivolousness and the seriousness that it so richly deserves.

MANY YEARS LATER I WAS ASKED, out of the blue, by a senior editor of the Winnipeg-based *Canadian Dimension* magazine, Cy Gonick—who had stayed in my house one summer a number of years before and apparently remembered all the thrillers that clogged my bookshelves—to review a recent mystery novel by Varda Burstyn (a real person and a real book this time!). For Burstyn, herself a well-known Canadian writer of the left, was chancing her arm at crime-story writing, an add-on to her many other impressive accomplishments. Reviewing her work, *Water, Inc.*, was fun—not least because it provided me with another shot at puzzling out the link between progressive politics and thriller writing. This was something that had apparently also intrigued Burstyn herself; moreover, the review, published under the title "Imaginary Toads in Real Gardens" was to move Cy to ask me a few years later to paint a picture of the "political thriller" across an even broader canvas. To this one I will return too, but first the Burstyn review.

PUTTING REAL TOADS IN IMAGINARY GARDENS, that's what Emily Dickinson stated to be her literary task. Varda Burstyn's project is somewhat different: to put imaginary toads—the fictional characters in her new thriller, *Water Inc.* (London and New York; Verso, 2005)—in real gardens.

The real gardens in question are our environment, and all too real as well are the corporate and governmental locusts that swirl around it, scheming to pick it clean for their own profit and aggrandizement. Here water is the name of their game. This is, of course, a growing concern of progressive activists and environmentalists worldwide, including, in our own country, Maude Barlow, Tony Clarke and others: specifically, in this case, the issue is billions of gallons, to be sent, at great cost to the environment and the future, from Quebec in order to service a water-scarce United States, and, not so coincidentally, to fill corporate coffers.

The table is set early: ruthless, believable, (American) corporate magnates, a slippery "sovereigntist" Quebec government (one eager to set its own course independent of Ottawa even at the visible risk of increased subservience to the Americans, and with a wish, as well, to assuage an electorate they apparently expect to be at least as eager for the jobs a huge water export undertaking might provide as alert to the long-term consequences of such a deal). Their opponents: a rag-tag army of enlightened left-environmentalists (in the US, Quebec and elsewhere in Canada) who slowly but surely track down clues about the project and attempt, with mixed success, to get the story into the media and into the court of public opinion.

A rich array of characters appear—although perhaps just one or two too many for absolutely limpid comprehension—from a crude American tycoon (with wayward wife and diverse corporate cronies) to a vigorous American environmentalist and her new ex-US military, now corporate defector, male partner. There's also an intrepid American journalist and a slow to convince but ultimately crucially outspoken Vermont governor as well as various Quebecois figures: suspect politicians, a diverse array of activists and a bright provincial civil servant tipped over the edge to resistance by the willful murder of his wife together with a bold reporter and a young colleague.

There are big questions here, of course: real gardens, indeed. Moreover, some are probably not entirely self-evident to the broader audience Burstyn and Verso, her publisher, apparently seek for such a book. Burstyn therefore feels it necessary—first-novel-itis may also help explain some of this tendency—to have characters give mini-lectures from time to time on the very important issues at stake.

Of course, most good thrillers are somewhat counter-intuitive and need to build in another way of looking at "reality." And a left thriller (if it is to appeal to more than just "the happy few") probably has even more work to do in this respect. This is certainly part of Burstyn's challenge and if occasionally her set pieces of "counter-intelligence" (the early lecture by the aforementioned female environmentalist lead character, the wordy exchange of opinions amongst Quebec activists) seem just a bit creaky, one can only hope that by the time she writes her next thriller the Left will have conquered much more of the terrain of "commonsense," against which to set a progressive argument and/or a progressive novel than is now the case.

Burstyn seems a bit too tightly strapped to the thriller format and to thriller expectations in making her case in another sense too. Thus the willful silencing for so long by the media, in both the US and Canada, of a story that might seem a pretty hot one, does keep her own story going, but is just a little overdrawn. And the ready and slightly unconvincing turn to maximum mayhem by the main corporate protagonists seems somewhat melodramatic too, even with all due deference being paid to normal thriller conventions. But perhaps I'm just being naive about the possible uses and abuses of power. In any case, water certainly does step forward forcefully in this book as one more key to an ever-deepening imperialist puzzle, and an increasingly important one!

For this is a highly (and plausibly) politicized left-thriller, make no mistake about that. Nor is Burstyn's choosing to write a thriller necessarily an impediment: those on the make know how to wield power, and, as she demonstrates, are quite prepared to do so in order to advance their interests: in this case, to get the water they want. And, as Burstyn demonstrates, those on the Left are forced to struggle bravely, imaginatively and, within the framework of a novel, convincingly to keep up (and even, at least for the moment at the end of the book, to get ahead).

Besides, the book is fun. As a thriller devotee (of the Left!) I all too often have to engage in a "willing suspension of disbelief" in order to extract the excitement and the diversion I seek in the format. There can sometimes be, it is true, populist and anti-authoritarian sensibilities at work in such books but rarely anything further to the Left than that. So, if "suspension of disbelief" occasionally seems, with respect to some of the details covered in her pages, like a stretch here, the "gardens" are, as I've said, real. And some of the toads, on both sides, are pretty real too. Enjoy!!

FINALLY, THEN, my thoughts on the "political thriller."[52] (I could perhaps have added some reflections concerning "film noir," a favourite film genre of mine—as I scan my Turner Classic Movies TV playbill or the Saturday afternoon titles on the list of offerings at Cinematheque, one of my favourite Toronto venues, for films by Lang, Siodmak, Fuller and Mann (the latter two also very good for westerns [Mann with Jimmy Stewart: say no more], of course). But that will have to wait for next time (another life?), as will any reflections I might have on Eleanor Powell or Fred Astaire, on Barbara Stanwyck, Robert Mitchum or Robert Ryan (all three, great personal favourites, also good at both noirs and westerns, among other things), on John Ford, Budd Boetticher (with

Randolph Scott!), Max Ophuls or Jean Renoir. For the moment only this "Feature Presentation," entitled "The Political Thriller."

I REMEMBER WHEN I FIRST ARRIVED, almost fifty years ago, at Princeton after five years at the University of Toronto. I felt pretty green, far from home and familiar landmarks, physical and intellectual. And there were some pretty smart guys (it was all guys in those days!) there too, One of the most obviously intelligent of my fellow grad students, simultaneously friendly and intimidating, was Phil Green, a leftie who would go on to be a member of the *Nation*'s board and also to write a number of thoughtfully weighty tomes (including *Deadly Logic*, a classic on the irrationalities of the nuclear balance of terror, and *Retrieving Democracy*) while teaching at Smith.

We had lunch on one of my first days in New Jersey and I was all ears. After talking a bit of baseball (a New York native, Phil actually rooted for the hated Yankees!), he settled into it: you must read, he said, Joel Townsley Rogers' *The Red Right Hand* and John Dickson Carr's *The Burning Court*, and perhaps, also, Manning Coles' *Toast to Yesterday* and his *Drink to Tomorrow*. Odd sounding titles for weighty political tomes, I thought, but I felt game for anything. So I tracked them down and what did I find? Thrillers. Good ones too, especially the first two, although not particularly political ... and certainly not self-evidently "progressive." What was going on here?

Read and find out, I told myself. So I did, beginning a lifelong parallel pursuit to my Marxist political science and Marxist political practice—that of reading thrillers which, alongside listening to jazz and playing basketball, became my principal not so very guilty pleasures in life. Truth to tell, my reading of the philosophies of life of Lew Archer, Martin Beck, Harry Bosch, Kathy Mallory, Guido Brunetti and John Rebus ranks right up there with my exploration, then and now, of Sheldon Wolin, Bob Engler, Roderick Seidenburg, Brough Macpherson, Frantz Fanon, Baran and Sweezy and Marx himself on my personal hit parade.

Now flash forward to the present from the early 60s and along comes my friend Cy Gonick to spoil my fun. Write us an article, he tells me, on "the political thriller." Well, since you put it that way, Cy, let me think.

What is it?

First off, what is a "political thriller"? Let's not make too heavy weather of this. True, debates rage in the "scholarly literature" on the question (no kidding!) while Wikipedia opines that thrillers "are characterized by fast pacing, frequent action and resourceful heroes who must thwart the plans of more powerful and better equipped villains." Me, I treat the category pretty expansively: in order to cover, primarily, the kind of books, frivolous and not quite so frivolous, I like best to read when I'm not working. Mystery stories, running the gamut from private eyes to police procedurals to the entanglement of "mere" private citizens in mayhem, malevolence and derring-do. And I'll throw in a few spy novels too, as well as various riffs on international intrigue and the murky misdeeds of sundry corporations and governments.

This last phrase is obviously a weighted one, however, and here we must add that second descriptor, "political," into the mix: political thrillers. Again, Wikipedia has a suggestion: the "political thriller" is one "in which the hero must ensure the stability of the government that employs him." Surely not. As often as not, and increasingly, the government "that employs him" (even if that were a relevant criterion) is as suspect as any other government or power centre (in the private sector, for example) out there. In fact, my kind of "political thrillers"—that focus on many protagonists who are not so employed but that even include, say, the police procedurals I like—retain a healthy skepticism about power and motivation, even when they don't often name the system that structures many such sordid realities as "capitalism."

True, many "thrillers" are not really so very skeptical about prevailing social conventions and structures at all. They advance their "mysteries" quite comfortably, albeit often quite imaginatively, on unproblematized socioeconomic terrain. But even those of more skeptical provenance can only go so far. After all, in the North Atlantic world, it's one thing to expose the abuses of power, another to fictionally create a vibrant, if contested, counter-hegemonic alternative around which plots and intrigues might swirl. The fact is that there aren't for the moment, too many alternatives out there upon which to peg and to examine a full-blown (socialist?) solution—and spin a mystery too. Instead, for such enlightenment, we're perforce quickly carried into the realm of the essay, the tract and the speculative tome. And, vital and important as these latter exercises might be and as "left" as we might want them to be, they're not quite thrillers.

No, even if we avoid scrupulously thrillers of the right, the William F. Buckleys and the William Haggards, our enjoyment must, quite a bit more often than not, be compromised by political qualms. Me, within limits and when "the game's afoot," I don't let it bother me. Nonetheless it may be worth contemplating here the quantum of "left political thrillerdom" that is actually out there—being fully aware it is likely, inevitably, to be more effective at exploring (more or less subtly) the compromised nature of power than at exemplifying the alternative (other than to cage, or not, the most reprehensible of "villains," that is).

Of course, thriller writers have taken less and less "for granted" as the years have passed: the psychology tends to deepen and there are fewer social "certainties" one can merely assume too. As the great pre-Second World War innovator in the field, Francis Iles (who himself moved in his writing from the [entertaining] likes of *Trial and Error* and *The Poisoned Chocolates Case* to *Malice Aforethought* and *Before the Fact*), saw the crime story developing into a novel with a detective or a crime interest: "The puzzle element will no doubt remain, but it will become a puzzle of character, rather than a puzzle of time, place, motive and opportunity." (Recall, too, Cornell Woolrich and John Franklin Bardin, Fredric Brown and Helen Eustis among others, in this regard.)

The claims made on behalf of "law and order" are also presented as being rather more doubtful than previously by many of the most thoughtful authors too: already, Hammett (*The Glass Key*!) and Chandler, while spinning good yarns with lots of entertaining byplay, had indicated that the broader social order itself didn't smell quite right to them. Indeed, the celebrated Marxist economist Ernest Mandel was probably correct to note, in his *Delightful Murder: A Social History of the Crime Story*, that "the history of the crime story… is intertwined with the history of bourgeois society itself."

For the latter history is inevitably about property and its negation ("in other words, crime"), and about a society that "breeds crime, originates in crime and leads to crime," in short, "a criminal society." Of course, not many thrillers put it quite like that and in any case Mandel, who, on the evidence of his book, must have read (and enjoyed?) quite a few politically "compromised" works in the genre himself, does also acknowledge that those he calls the "efficient detective story, spy novel and thriller authors" pursue "a technical craft that imposes its own rules: keeping attention, creating tension, maintaining suspense." Not small virtues, these latter, for the thriller addict (including myself), needless to say.

To illustrate: one often hears the holy trinity of hard-boiled detection evoked: Spade, Marlow and Archer. And truth to tell, Ross Macdonald, the author of the Archer mysteries, is one of my very favourites (you name it, I've read it). "Best Canadian" for starters—though born in the

States, he grew up and went to university here before returning, via Michigan and the US Navy, to California to there write more than his fair share of "keepers" (*The Galton Case, The Chill, The Goodbye Look*—I could go on). So, make that "best Canadian" with an asterisk: perhaps the accolade itself should go, more appropriately, to his wife and a fellow thriller writer of great quality, Margaret Millar (*Stranger in my Grave, Beast in View, Beyond this Point are Monsters*): actually born, bred and educated right here, although she too settled in sunny Cal.

But in the present world of globalized thriller writing such national chauvinism may not matter so very much. After all, they're coming at us from all sides: Scandinavia, Italy, Japan, Latin America, Spain, South Africa, and many of them very good (exciting, puzzling and revealing by turns) indeed. Much more important here as regards Macdonald is perhaps a different question. For, aside from sheer enjoyment, what are we lefties to make of his brilliant oeuvre. There's the rub. As one commentator, Jeffrey Mahan (in his *A Long Way from Solving That One*, a study that sets itself to examine "Ross Macdonald's Lew Archer tales"), concludes that "an important element in the conservatism of the hard-boiled detective story is its affirmation of individualism... The moral and psychological focus of the tale is on the implications of the choices that the individual makes in living in a less than ideal world. The individualistic ethic makes difficult if not impossible the compromises that might lead to coalitions for significant social change." Got it in one. In short, a certain amount of our enjoyment even of the likes of Ross Macdonald has to be tempered by the curse of our radical consciousness. Macdonald doesn't dig quite deeply enough into the full range of knotted contradictions that hold the US together, it might be argued, but even less is he able to suggest what might be necessary in order to confront them.[53] But, damn it all, I do like his books.

Perhaps it's the Swedes, Maj Sjowall and Per Whaloo, who come closest to what we'd like to see: excellent police procedurals in which even the policemen begin to become disillusioned with the western social order, including one that's inflected (mildly) by social democracy. For their ten books don't let many of Sweden's less than savoury realities pass by unscathed. In fact, by the end of the series one of the most sympathetic of the cops can't hack it any more: Kollberg resigns the force. This in the tenth and last of the books, *The Terrorists*, one that highlights, as it happens, a manhunt in the wake of the sobering assassination of an Olof Palme-type politician.

Flash forward to the final scene. Martin Beck, the series' main protagonist and a senior officer more firmly, if uneasily, anchored than Kollberg in both his job and in the society he chooses to wade through, is spending the evening socializing with his old friend Kollberg. As the book ends Kollberg tells Beck: "The trouble with you, Martin, is just that you've got the wrong job. At the wrong time. In the wrong part of the world. In the wrong system." Then it's back to their board game, and the apparently idle chatter about the letter "X" that accompanies it. "X, as in ex-policeman," Kollberg had "breezily" suggested earlier—"as if they all didn't know how impossible it was to squeeze in one more example out of that hopeless letter." Now, Kollberg offers, as he settles in to play: "My turn to start? Then I say X—X as in Marx."

Globalizing the thriller

The last sentence of the book. The last of the series. You look back at the ten books and you can suddenly see that ending creeping up on you—surreptitiously, subtly and, with all the benefit of hindsight, seemingly inevitably. Of course, nothing in the present dramatic efflorescence of Scandinavian crime fiction (see my appendix for a preliminary listing of such worthies) thinks to go quite so far. Yet, for the most part, they have refreshingly irreverent views on the people and politics shaped by the Nordic societies they know well: that, for me, is a distinct and attractive plus.

For something more overtly political than the current bounty of Nordic talents you may want to move south, to Spain, say, for the late Pablo Vazquez Montalban. Again, not that Montalban's own politics were so very confident as he turned to thriller writing—after his own jail time for anti-Franco activities and his close accompaniment of the less than invigorating denouement that has followed the Falangist nightmare in his country. But the numerous books in the series (including, recall, *Death in the Central Committee*) are refreshing, nonetheless... and his wry PI Pepe Carvalho as revealed in his asides, his references (including his jokes), and his sensibility is clearly a leftie in his formation. Albeit not a particularly hopeful one. Bracing, but bruised, we might conclude of Carvalho... and of Montalban himself.

Elsewhere, at its best, an even more jaundiced sensibility—good vs. evil, of course, and (relatively) good guys and gals vs. bad ones (of underworld, big business and suspect government provenance) together with some lively writing and plotting—is about the most one can hope for politically. Yet, so many books are, to me, excellent reads that, against my decidedly left instincts, I'm loath to quibble. Indeed, so much is that so that to avoid offering what must appear to be a mere checklist is almost unavoidable, while to render it much more than a hopelessly personal and highly selective one is impossible. Rather predictably, perhaps, I'd rate Rebus/Rankin Scottish adventures particularly high—bracingly tough but charged with intelligent wit by turns—not least the late novels (*The Naming of the Dead* and *Exit Lines*, for example) in his series. In these, high politics begin to intrude ever more convincingly and sinisterly into the world of low crime (even as Rebus himself prepares to retire and seems set to cede his central place in the fictions to his worthy colleague, Siobhan Clarke). Here the lineaments of a sociology of Scotland (the dense interplay of "underworld" and "overworld" is the manner in which Rebus explicitly presents it) as a criminal society are firmly in place, if not, perforce, the politics of transcendence of that condition.

But there's also Graham Hurley (and his Joe Faraday) in Portsmouth and Jake Arnott, as well as those Canadian-based expatriates Peter Robinson (think: Yorkshire's Inspector Ian Banks) and, of Matt Minogue fame, John Brady (who should have stuck to Ireland, in my opinion, instead of heading off fictionally to Austria—but then, earlier, Nicholas Freeling was a lot better off with his Van der Valk in Holland than he ever was with his Castang in France!). Add the old reliable Ruth Rendell, P.D. James, Val McDermid, and a host of others in both Ireland and the UK—along with other expatriate authors, this time in Italy, like Donna Leon and her intriguing policeman Inspector Guido Brunetti (and his redoubtable wife, Paola) hanging out in Venice (together with the late Michael Dibdin and, I've no doubt, a raft of Italian literary accomplices like Andrea Camilleri about whom I don't know nearly enough).

Plus, Fred Vargas in France, and Michael Connelly (who keeps getting better, *Echo Park* and *The Overlook* most recently), Robert Crais, Walter Mosley (a definite pinko, to his credit), Carol O'Connell, Sara Paretsky, Lee Child, S. P. Rozen, and the deeply sour James Ellroy, together with a seemingly endless host of additional thriller writers (of varying quality) in the US. Or, in Canada: Eric Wright, Varda Burstyn, Gilles Blunt, Pat Capponi, Rosemary Aubert (with her former Bay Street lawyer now living rough in the Don Valley!). In short, the "dance of death" continues, intriguingly (if, in these cases and thankfully, fictionally). But how, I ask you, am I ever to get any real work—or real politics—done?

One could advance around the globe too, to numerous outposts far outside the North Atlantic realm, led by both expatriate writers and native ones (and guided, in particular, by the remarkable Soho Crime publishing house, on Broadway): Qui Xiaolong take us to China and Akimitsu Talagi and Seicho Matsimoto to Japan, Colin Cotteril to Laos, Gary Disher to Australia, Cheryl Benard to India and Stan Jones' "Native" sleuth to the Chukchi world in Alaska (as Tony Hillerman's Leaphorn and Chee had carried us to the American Southwest before him). Plus a host of Latin Americans: from Jose Carlos Samoza to the Uraguayan Daniel Chavarria as he navigates, in crime fiction, the callous milieu of that continent's sometime military dictatorships. Or in Germany, there's the world of the "new" migrant worker assayed in Jakob Arjouni's *Listen Turk*. But the list could go on. We're entertained, but we learn more than a thing or two from our travels too and much of it must serve, ultimately, to sharpen our sensibilities, to whatever purpose, political or otherwise, we may feel it important, ultimately, to put them.

Global intrigue

Perhaps the spy story offers us, paradoxically, slightly more scope—at least in political terms. In war, cold or hot, or in the contemplation of the fate of regimes per se rather than the fall-out of particular crimes, one can, perhaps, more easily envisage political change and the complexities and mysteries that surround it. In fact, this seemed easier in the run-up to the Second World War—who, after all, would want to write in favour of Hitler and company—than in the Cold War when it was less easy, except for real ideologues, to distinguish clearly the merits of either the Soviets on the one hand or the at least equally imperial West on the other. Of course, some like Le Carré (for all his somewhat prosy prose) managed to ride the ambiguities of that confrontation entertainingly. Yet one feels more at home, politically at least, when, in his most recent novels, he can more tellingly expose the connivance between multi-national corporations and established governments, in stories that also genuinely entertain: *The Constant Gardener* and *The Mission Song* (as well as his celebrated 2003 article, "The United States of America Has Gone Mad"!).

Small wonder that in the 1930s (to take another example), and amidst all the revealing polarizations of that period, strong writers like Eric Ambler—and perhaps Graham Greene, "slumming" in wearing his "Entertainments" hat—could in fact entertain mightily, probing the horrors that loomed, while also envisaging possibilities (especially in Ambler's books from before the war) that cried out, in a world going mad, to actually occur. Small wonder, too, that one of the best of our contemporary thriller writers can still find in the sad world of the 1930s reasons for fictional protagonists to take personal risk and manifest (legitimate, if worldly) righteousness: Alan Furst in a glittering series that runs from *Night Soldiers* to *The Foreign Correspondent*.

That world, too, gives us Phillip Kerr's Bernie Gunther (*Berlin Noir* and *The One from the Other*), reluctant SS man, who later, in the post-war period unveils, as in real life, both the Americans and the Russians scrambling to recruit Nazis and Gestapo operatives for their own nefarious Cold "War-games." A world lately at (an earlier) war and at risk is also the appropriate setting (as it was the real setting) for intriguing reflections on the murder—involving proto-Nazi authoritarianism and anti-semitism in the upper echelons of the then German state (although I personally would have been more inclined to nominate the social democrats of the time has having sanctioned the fatal blow)—of the true-life and exemplary revolutionary Rosa Luxemburg: Jonathan Raban's bracing if rather baroque *Rosa*.

Perhaps espionage, then, is one of the last refuges of a critical thriller of political weight. But not exclusively, and perhaps not forever. For there are other settings where deep-seated political contestation and contradiction can lend edge to "crime fiction"—South Africa, for example. Thus, the cruel apartheid regime itself spawned the revelatory "thrillers" of James McClure and Wessel Ebersohn. But its subsequent transition from white minority rule to democracy brought, in such venues as the Truth and Reconciliation Commission, startling real-life dramas to the fore...while also promising many gripping future fictions of betrayal and intrigue. The first fruits are interesting enough: Jann Turner's *Southern Cross* and Gillian Slovo's *The Betrayal* and *Red Dust*. And can we not expect the grimly anti-climactic nature, full of contradictions, of a highly compromised post-apartheid South Africa to produce, if not, immediately, a "next liberation struggle," at least ever more tantalizing political thriller material?

And there is also, presently, the grim and intersecting worlds of right-wing Islam and paleolithic Bushian Christian fundamentalism (linked to corporate connivance), a world that is ripe for a "fiction" of bracing cynicism—and, just possibly, an intimation of something better. I've mentioned Le Carré. Closer to the belly of the beast, I've found Daniel Fesperman's recent novels involving. Moving beyond the pervading greyness of the Balkans foregrounded in his early thrillers, he has more recently (in *The Warlord's Son*) married the blight of feckless local

Afghani internecine war-mongering to the fishing by selfish corporations in such troubled waters, and, in *The Prisoner of Guantanamo*, a convincing and cruel picture of, as its cover announces, both "life behind the barbed wire of Gitmo," and of "what goes on in the most secret levels of our government." No answers to our troubles are presented, of course, but such troubles are certainly revealed to us from new angles, and revealed as having more than one singularly inhuman face.

In sum, I'm here to tell you—no surprise—that we'd better not rely on thriller writers, by and large, to do our forward-thinking political work for us. But, as hinted, they can help us, those who choose to be so enlightened, to envisage more clearly the realities of the world—inhuman faces and all and even the occasional shaft of political light —and the problems that confront us a bit more clearly than we might otherwise be able to do on our own. Besides, if you manage to take time off from thinking about and/or making the revolution, many of them are pretty neat. Enjoy!

Appendix: Ten Political Thrillers for Beginners

Bear in mind that, as the accompanying article itself made clear, thrillers never easily slide over into effective political tracts nor allow for the ready evocation of revolutionary alternatives. The following are some good ones nonetheless, books that may also, up to a point, keep the flames of resistance smouldering.

1. Dashiell Hammett, *Red Harvest*: A salty leftie and key thriller writer of decades ago (think: *The Maltese Falcon*), this novel (about union-busting, amongst other things) is considered by many his most overtly subversive; me, I also liked *The Glass Key*, American urban politics at the point where mob and old money meet.
2. Eric Ambler, *Epitaph for a Spy*: Particularly in his excellent thrillers of the pre-war period, Ambler evoked the hard reality of wars that sprang from a balance of power shaped by money and, to quote Ambler himself, by those "who, in satisfying their private ends, created the social and economic conditions that breed war."
3. Alan Furst, *The Foreign Correspondent*: Although he's writing currently, all Furst's thrillers also evoke the Europe of the very pre-Second World War period that Ambler himself lived, exploring intelligently and attractively various continental settings fraught with peril and promise.
4. Manuel Vazquez Montalban, *Murder on the Central Committee*: A Spanish leftie who "paid his political dues" in the struggle against

Franco, Vazquez, in the many years before his death, became less assertively progressive while wearing his thriller-writer cap, but his writing nonetheless retained an overtly left sensibility and frame of reference as well as a bracing irreverence and wit.

5. Ross Macdonald, *Sleeping Beauty*: Not necessarily his best Lew Archer thriller but the one that is most revealing of his own activist bent as a convinced environmentalist (a commitment shared with his wife, another Canadian expatriate—Kitchener native and University of Toronto grad—Margaret Millar, author of *How Like an Angel* and many other exemplary thrillers).
6. Maj Sjowall and Per Whaloo, *The Terrorists*: This is the tenth and last of the series, one that highlights a manhunt in the wake of the assassination of an Olof Palme-type politician, but it should really be read as part of one long novel in ten installments, this being the final chapter.
7. Ian Rankin, *The Naming of the Dead*: A striking elaboration on Rankin/Rebus' conviction that the "underworld" and the "overworld" parallel and reinforce each other in contemporary Scotland (although this distinction is itself actually introduced in his most recent novel, *Exit Lines*)
8. Michael Connelly, *Echo Park*: Too good to leave off such a list (as is his latest, *The Overlook*), though Connelly's politics reflect more an intelligent suspicion of authority than evidence of any visible commitment to a progressive alternative.
9. John Le Carre, *The Mission Song*: Moving beyond the Cold War, his recent books bracingly document the interpenetration of multinationals and rancid governments at the expense of various entrapped individuals and societies of both North and South.
10. Daniel Fesperman, *The Prisoner of Guantanamo*: A convincing and cruel picture, as its cover announces, both of "life behind the barbed wire of Gitmo," and of "what goes on in the most secret levels of our government."

Other political thrillers? Not Donna Leon, perhaps, but she's certainly the author of many good Venice-based policiers that are socially astute, as are those of Sara Paretsky, Walter Moseley (both rather more overt than is Leon in their progressive outlooks) and the great Carol O'Donnell, plus Harlan Coben (*No Second Chance*!), Thomas H. Cook and many others, including a large number of reliable Scandinavians: Arnaldur Indridason, Jo Nesbo, Helen Thurston, Karin Fossum, Asa Larsson, Haken Nesser, Kjell Eriksson, Kerstin Ekman, and the redoubtable Henning Mankell. There are also Phillip Kerr's Bernie Gunthers on Nazism both before and after the Second World War and Jonathan Raban's *Rosa,* a speculative thriller evoking the pursuit of the authors of the murder of stalwart real-life revolutionary Luxembourg that establishes the guilt of various proto-Nazi forces of the time (rather than the social-democrats in government who would be my own nominees as perpetrators of the deed).

---

b) On Listening

I listened to a lot of radio when I was kid (I remember when the first TV arrived on our street, at Jack Harmer's place up the street: his father worked at GE or some such TV manufacturer of the day) and my taste was pretty eclectic. I recall Sunday evenings with Jack Benny and Fred Allen, Mondays with Suspense and the Lux Radio Theatre and, scattered throughout the week, "Escape," "The Shadow," "The Green Hornet," "Mr Keen, Tracer of Lost Persons," "Gunsmoke" ("the first man they look for and the last they want to see," as played by the great William Conrad—long before there was a James Arness), "Our Miss Brooks" (with Jeff Chandler as Mr. Boynton, can you believe it), the Wayne and Shuster Show and so many more. There were also music shows (Keith Sandy and his Make Believe Ballroon on CKEY), often with some comedy thrown in (as with Less Lye and his pal Abercrombie, also on CKEY). Every week though, on Saturday morning, I'd be sure to check out the CBC radio "hit parade" programmes: that tired old boy Neil Leroy, "with all those [pop] hits you supposedly thought were just jim dandy during this past week," and Bill Bessy with the country top 10.

I particularly liked the country motif: Webb Pierce, Faron Young, Hank Williams plus, for Canadians, Hank Snow and later Ian Tyson ("Summer Wages" his greatest) and Stan Rogers (on the cusp of categories, but think: "The Song of the Candle," the writer's anthem). Indeed, as a kid, I also used to flit about the dial late at night to keep up with the latest hits, WWVA, Wheeling, West Virginia being a favourite of mine ("Stevens' Work Shirts,

Stevens' Work Pants: Just a Little Bigger, Just a Little Better!"). And I felt the earth move as Elvis Presley shot up the country listings with "I Forgot to Remember to Forget" and, within several weeks, had broken through and off the country chart altogether, taking "Heartbreak Hotel" to the very top of the pop rankings! Elvis' impact was extraordinary quite generally in fact, fracturing the smug little world of North Toronto cataclysmically—as it did a lot of other heretofore closed cultural worlds in the '50s.

My first dates with my soon-to-be wife in college also had musical accompaniment. Our very first outing was to hear the Weavers at Massey Hall, as my wife was to recall to a delighted Ronnie Gilbert herself when she spoke at York many decades later. And we heard Josh White at Eaton's Auditorium and the likes of Jimmy Rushing and Ben Webster at the old George's Spaghetti House on Dundas, too. But, paradoxically, it was in Tanzania, where we spent seven years in the 1960s, that my jazz soul began to stir most markedly. Sol Piciotto of the Law Faculty was a jazz fan with some very good Dizzy Gillespie sides, as I recall, as was Roger Murray, from London and the *New Left Review*, who, when working briefly in Dar es Salaam at TANU headquarters, would become one of my dearest friends and my first real jazz mentor. A man of formidably "big ears" (as they say in the music aficionado business), he knew as much about jazz as he apparently knew about everything else and when he finally left Dar he left behind with me a small and precious stack of records, many (Davis, Rollins, Monk, Coltrane, Coleman) purchased at, of all places, the "Dar es Salaam Music and Sports" store.

I jumped on the jazz train then, a late beginner, but my taste and intelligence would grow, especially when I returned to Toronto in the early '70s and fell under the influence of John Norris and Bill Smith, the definitive Mr. Inside and Mr. Outside of jazz tastes at their mecca, the Jazz and Blues Record Store, on Yonge Street just north of Davenport and later on King near Bathurst. The endless hours (and dollars) I would spend there, just listening to sounds and to the two of them talk jazz with each other, with me and with an endless stream of other jazz junkies! Me, I related most closely (although not exclusively) to the more avant-garde vibe, grooving high as Bill and others brought, in the '70s, a very hip, altogether fabulous, series (including Sun Ra, the Art Ensemble of Chicago, Anthony Braxton, Cecil Taylor and others) both to York University and to St. Paul's United Church on Avenue Road. I was also privileged to sit in the studio to see and hear a range of just such top-notch players (Shepp, Taylor, Bley and Dixon) as Smith and Ron Mann shot their great movie, *Imagine the Sound*. There were other influences too: Winston Smith and his extraordinary radio programme sustained over a number of years and Gord at his Backbeat store, first on Dundas and later up on Yonge Street, and various other jazz-heads around and about, many of whom have now moved on to other venues and other undertakings.

Nonetheless Ajay Heble, for one, keeps the flame of the avant-garde alight, each year, at the Guelph Jazz Festival—as do the extraordinary players he brings in from across North America and around the world each September. And thereby hangs a tale, or at least an essay, one that I've included here. But, first, the tale.

I wrote the article that follows on Buddy Bolden with my daughter, Jo, in the aftermath of my horrific accident in late 2003, and as, in part, a form of occupational therapy. The point of the possible benefits to me of such "occupational therapy" had been quickly grasped by Colin Leys, my good friend, who soon after my accident (that is, by mid-2004) began to work with me on a piece on "Dependency" (eventually to be published in Douglas Johnson's edited volume *The Elgar Companion to Development Studies* [2006]) that we had actually been talking about before the accident. Jo also perceived the exact same point. Thus, knowing my love for jazz, Jo offered me, as I began to resurface in 2004, a challenge of an even more daunting and novel sort. Why didn't she and I do a paper together for the scholarly workshop of jazz discussion and debate that Heble and his colleagues run alongside their various music sessions in Guelph each year?

But what to write about? Jo, while an accomplished writer and student of literature, was not a "jazz-head" and I, of course, was no jazz writer. But I liked the idea so we began to discuss what we might do. Suddenly, it occurred to us: New Orleans, the legendary birthplace of jazz (Louis Armstong, King Oliver, Freddy Keppard, Jelly Roll Morton) was also, post-Katrina, in the news. And I, of course, knew something of Buddy Bolden of New Orleans, the storied "first jazz-man." The only drawback was that absolutely no examples of his actual playing existed (a storied cylinder said to be of his performing had never been found), and the actual stories of his life were themselves befogged by hyperbole and apparent false report! Still, the very mystery of his life and legend had attracted various writers and players to imagine him into life and into sound.

Moreover, one such writer was Canadian novelist and poet, Michael Ondaatje, who, in his *Coming Through Slaughter*, had sought to evoke the life and career of Buddy Bolden. And Ondaatje's literary work was something Jo knew well, having written extensively about him—especially as regards his own family "autobiography," *Running in the Family*. Here, it seemed, was a natural starting point for collaboration and a topic we thought that, even as relative neophytes in the real world of jazz studies, we could really get into. In short, why not seek to combine our talents and to imagine Bolden by bringing the literary evocations of him by Ondaatje and other writers attracted by his mystery together with a consideration of jazz players who had also attempted to fill the silence by seeking to evoke Bolden's very playing. So we did, the result being well received at Guelph when we presented it there later that year and also well received by Heble and his fellow editors when we revised it (with their help) for eventual publication in Guelph's own jazz journal, *Improvisation*. The ultimate publication of the article left me merely to listen to my own extensive jazz record collection—and to retire "undefeated" as a jazz critic! But full of gratitude, for this initiative and much else, to Jo. Meanwhile, here's the article itself:

IT COULD BE SAID THAT ALL ART INVOLVES "IMPROVISATION" if it is to be more than rote repetition of established norms, practices, and procedures.[54] However, jazz can perhaps be deemed the art of improvisation par excellence. In jazz, established norms and historically derived conventions—ranging from notes to styles to pre-written "songs"—have weight and resonance, but "innovation" is welcomed. The skill with which the individual player or free-thinking group bend and break "the rules" is, when imaginatively undertaken, widely praised. Indeed the very "slipperiness, mobility and inventive flexibility" of jazz, its drive to accent "contingency, improvisation, risk, dissonance and play [in order to] buck oppressive systems of culture and knowledge"[55] is one of the music's great strengths. "Innovation" and "improvisation"—the distance between these two words is not great, but, one might argue, of some importance. Improvisation implies something more immediate and spontaneous, although any such "improvisation" is obviously also "structured" by experience, understanding, and foresight. "Innovation," which addresses the idea of rule breaking or opening up new territory, is even more self-conscious (although this notion itself as a marker of distinction between the two concepts is a tricky one) and, at least in some sense, more reflected upon. In other words, both acts require structure, art and imagination, and overlap markedly at the edges of their meaning.

Much human creative endeavour—writing, playing, painting—has this tendency to be innovative and improvisatory, and even "to trouble, to question, to make both problematic and provisional any [...] desire for order or truth through the powers of the human imagination."[56]

This is, of course, something that various postmodernists have been at great pains to emphasize. At the same time, there is also a "real" out there, however fugitive and debatable, that is most self-evident in documented historical, social, and biographical accounts. Behind cultural memory lies a structure, and a lived record of person and event. The creative writer and the conscious artist, as well as the commentator who seek to evoke the past, must live the inevitable tension that exists between the imaginative creation of the person, place or time they wish to invoke and the record of established "facts" that must also claim our attention.

As this essay will establish, this is nowhere more true than in the case of Buddy Bolden, the legendary—and we use the adjective advisedly—cornet player of early New Orleans jazz, said indeed by some to be the first jazz-man (see Shipton). For dealing with Bolden, himself a putative godfather of jazz improvisation, demands an especially strong measure of creative imagination on the part of both writers and players, in order to allow us to invoke his memory. As we will see, with Bolden we must, even beyond the normal requirements of such an exercise, "improvise" the man and even his sound in order to represent him and to position him both within the New Orleans of his time and the broader tradition of jazz to which he is deemed to have made such a singular contribution. We have no aural record of Bolden's actual playing and only fragmentary, often contradictory, accounts of his life. "Improvising the improvisor"—in effect voicing Bolden's silence—is precisely what writers and players have sought to do. Jazzmen like Jerry Granelli and

Malachi Thompson, for example, and perhaps most notably on the printed page, Michael Ondaatje, whose highly regarded "novel" *Coming Through Slaughter* attempts, quite precisely, an imaginative "re-creation" of Buddy Bolden.

Who was Buddy Bolden? What did he sound like? How can improvisations on Bolden's life act as both reconstruction and revelation? Granelli, Thompson, and Ondaatje offer creative answers to these questions. But let us first begin with context and setting. What of jazz and of New Orleans itself—Bolden's stage—in the music's very earliest days?

Jazz and New Orleans: Blending Communities, Expanding Musical Practices

The launching of "jazz" (including whatever role Buddy Bolden played in this endeavour) was a dramatic undertaking in a very broad sense. Indeed, it stood as a crucial means by which the black population in the United States found its voice and encouraged others to listen. This is complex historical terrain, of course, and we will point here merely to certain key dimensions that must form the background for our subsequent discussion. First, what of the centrality of New Orleans itself? Not only was it Buddy Bolden's own hometown, but also the setting for the "birth of jazz" or so it is often argued. Perhaps its importance could be overstated (much also happened elsewhere to hasten "the birth"), but the city's centrality is widely acknowledged. New Orleans also gave birth to an extraordinary number of the early masters, from Bolden himself to Jelly Roll Morton and Sidney Bechet, the Dodds brothers, Johnny, Baby, and Kid Ory, to such remarkable women as Dolly Adams and Emma Barrett, and within the cornet/trumpet lineage, to Freddie Keppard, Joe "King" Oliver and Louis Armstrong (while also including, amongst the more limited white contingent of early players, the Original Dixieland Jazz Band who made the first known phonograph record of "jazz" in 1917).

The roots of this musical centrality of New Orleans are much debated in the literature. Emphasis is placed variously on the interpenetration—owing to a complex colonial history—of French and Spanish sounds and traditions (including a set of somewhat more flexible Catholic practices) with British and, of course, African ones, as well as the entrepot function the port played for multiracial Creoles and black freemen from various parts of the Caribbean from fairly early on. Much has been made of the Creole/freed slave dichotomy in post-Civil War New Orleans. The former community is seen to have spawned a more structured and formally trained musical itinerary for its practitioners and the latter, a more African, spontaneous, and rurally rooted one.[57] Indeed, in New Orleans itself the two groups lived in separate quarters of the town, divided by different cultures. Geographically, it would seem, they were set apart from each other by Canal Street. Such differences did have an impact, although it is also true that as time went on the grim, over-riding logic of black-white divisions was slowly, but surely, qualifying its saliency.[58]

As it is well known, in the broader setting of post-emancipation and post-reconstruction America (beyond, but also including, New Orleans) wider changes were afoot, changes readily apparent as we try to locate Bolden within an even broader politico-sociological framework. On the one hand, as Donald Marquis, a preeminent historian of Bolden's time and place, has argued in writing of Buddy Bolden's presumptive role as "the first man of jazz," certain musical innovations—such as Buddy Bolden's apparently dramatic improvisations within the sound world of established brass band and ragtime music at the turn of the nineteenth century—only became really possible in a post-Civil War context. Bolden belonged to a generation that "didn't know or particularly care what the rules had been [before the Civil War and its immediate aftermath] and saw life as an open challenge instead of a restricted corridor." (Marquis 21) Here was a world where, at least momentarily, "aggrieved communities [could] gain the hope to assert their own rights, to enhance [their] collective ability to see (and to hear) 'life as possibility'."[59]

On the other hand, within Bolden's own lifetime, and thanks to the death of Reconstruction and the spread of segregation that began to penetrate even New Orleans (especially in the 1890s), such possibilities were beginning to close down at least as rapidly as they were continuing to open. Creoles were shoved highhandedly by new white-made laws into much greater social proximity to, and a much closer sharing of fate with, their "Negro" brothers and sisters, already defined (by whites) as being at the bottom of the social hierarchy. Yet, inadvertently, this blending of communities, however ill received by many Creoles "of colour" at the time, would—as some "began to make the trip uptown to sit in with their darker half-brothers"—have favourable musical results, with both groups, as hinted above, bringing significant, if diverse, strengths to the musical table,[60] whatever the obvious social costs of the resurgence of segregation more generally.

What would be the musical consequences—dare one say benefits—of such self-evident "costs"? LeRoi Jones (Amiri Baraka) suggests:

> [T]he Negro could not even become white and that was his strength; at some point, always, he could not participate in the dominant tenor of the white man's culture. It was at this juncture that he had to make use of other resources, whether African, subcultural or hermetic. And it was this boundary, this no man's land, that provided the logic and beauty of his music. (80)

Perhaps the lifting of the veil of oppression, however momentarily, also had other immediately positive results, albeit more for blacks (read: ex-slaves) in the South than for Creoles, giving the former a glimpse of what freedom might ultimately mean for them. Certainly, the voice of Buddy Bolden proved to be no voice "crying in the wilderness."[61] Indeed, to repeat, we can suspect that something profound was beginning to happen in America with the raising of Buddy Bolden's voice and the assertion of his improvisational vocation. For, beyond Bolden, the formal freedoms of America now gave the black community more room, literally, to move both geographically and, to some extent, professionally and socially as new practices—including new musical ways of thinking and playing—spread across the country. (The itinerant vocation of Jelly Roll Morton is a good example.) In these and other ways, the setting was changing, even if the crust of a redefined American racism was also, rather paradoxically, hardening.

The First Jazz-man: Memory and History

These, then, were forces that defined the world of Buddy Bolden, including his "sound world," as these diverse crosscurrents ran through him, both socially and musically. It is here too, however, that our limitations as "listeners" without firsthand sonic references to Bolden's actual playing (see below) betray us. For there is no doubt that history is drawing us forward from the nineteenth-century musical mélange of plantation music, blues and vaudeville, religious motifs (both "traditional" and new world centered), brass band sounds, and even the subtle yet somewhat overly stereotyped syncopations of ragtime, to the more confident and fluid style of jazz. Just where does Bolden stand in this developmental process? Opinions—guesses, really—differ. Some (Alyn Shipton, for example) present the case for Bolden's innovatory role quite forcefully:

> Apparently a powerful lead cornetist, famous for his sheer volume, Bolden played largely by ear and was credited by many of those who heard him as being the first to bring the explicitly African qualities of flattened blue notes, vocalized tones and 'hot' syncopation into the ragtime setting—in other words, he was seen as the progenitor of improvisation in jazz.

In sum, in this reading, "Bolden was apparently a pioneer of jazz before anyone knew what it was,"[62] holder of a proud place amongst those who were beginning, in the jazz way, to "talk back" on behalf of those apparently far too muzzled by the forces of history: "If Bolden had not existed someone would have had to invent him. He is the single figure on whom the transition into jazz can be pegged."[63]

Other observers are more guarded about the probable nature of Bolden's playing. Leroi Jones, for example, suggests that "the Bolden band and other early jazz groups must have sounded even sloppier. The music was a raw mixture of march, dance, blues and early rhythm with all the players improvising simultaneously." Yet, as Jones also acknowledges, the distinctive characteristic of "the Bolden band was the blues quality, the Uptown flavour of all their music [even if] the music still [also] had the flavour of the marching band." It embodied, he writes, "a wonderful concept, taking the unison tradition of European march music, but infesting it with teeming improvisations, catcalls, hollers, and the murky rhythms of the ex-slaves."[64] Similarly, Digby Fairweather begins by asserting that Bolden's "improvisation, if any, would have been primitive, harmonically elementary (probably confined to melody embellishment) and with a rhythmic approach reflecting the current ragtime vogue." Nonetheless, he too must concede that Bolden was undoubtedly "a riveting performer of personal charisma and crowd-pleasing musical power," a man, in short, with the personality, if not yet quite the playing, of a true jazz improvisor.[65]

Locating Bolden with reference to his historical moment, however guardedly this must be done, can still tell us a great deal. In the post-Civil War, "emancipation" context, Buddy Bolden, as putative founder, demands our attention since the very articulation of "jazz" can be understood as being a crucial means by which the black population in the United States "talked back," found its own voice, and encouraged others to listen. We can also follow Paul Berliner's metaphor of a great chain of the jazz tradition:

> In carrying forth the jazz tradition's early voices within their improvisations, engaging their predecessors' ideas and uniting them with their own, contemporary performers sometimes have the sense of escaping the normal experience of time. Such performances can assume a spiritual quality in which improvisers draw strength from a symbolic link to the past, as if becoming joined to a long chain of expressive human history.[66]

If Bolden can be seen as standing at the beginning of the jazz project's "chain," he is progenitor of an art form that has been defined by its continual state of evolution from firm, if inevitably somewhat hazy, beginnings. It is a small wonder that he has attracted attention and been evoked in song and story, both by earlier artists (Jelly Roll Morton and Duke Ellington, for example) and by more recent writers and musicians. The idea of Bolden as the first jazz-man is a virtual truism of jazz history writing, but this is a perspective that remains controversial. After all, the very facts of his life are much debated and clouded by rumour and misinformation.

Thus, as Fairweather has also observed in writing his aforementioned biographical entry on Bolden for *Jazz: The Rough Guide*, much of the colourful flavouring of what we think we know about Buddy Bolden—he was not, in fact, a barber, nor a scandal-sheet editor, and his (or any other) cornet could not "penetrate for more than a quarter of a mile, even on a clear night"—is "standard Bolden folklore, and it seems a pity that most of it is untrue."[67] Drawing, instead, on Marquis' careful research, Fairweather sketches Bolden's route from his birth in 1877 to his childhood home at 2309 1st Street, and to his leaving school in 1890; from his cornet study with Manuel Hall to his apprenticeship with Charlie Galloway's band; and from his bravura playing as King Bolden in the first years of the new century to his dramatic mental breakdown in 1906-7.[68]

Unfortunately, coming as he did so early in the evolution of the recording industry, Bolden made no records whatsoever (the phantom cylinder which is said to present something of his sound has never been found). Moreover, as a result of his mental illness he remained more or less incommunicado until his death in a state mental hospital in 1931 and, therefore, was not able to elaborate upon, let alone burnish, his own story. As celebrated Canadian author Michael Ondaatje has suggested: "Buddy Bolden was famous but no one really knew him very well."[69] In fact, it is this very silence that has served as at least part of the impetus for other writers, artists, and musicians to inscribe their own stories and meanings onto this legendary figure, to, in effect, "improvise the improviser."

Of course, this latter kind of improvisation has a clear musical reference. What is the link between music and musicians to their tradition? According to Ingrid Monson, "music functions in a relational or discursive manner rather than an absolute manner [...]. [T]he musical quotation or allusion [...] embodies the conflict between innovation and tradition in jazz performance as well as the larger question of how instrumental music conveys cultural meaning."[70] In fact, as we suggest below, those musicians who evoke Bolden most directly in their recent music are well aware of this tension (even evidencing such awareness in their own liner notes) and alert listeners to some of the questions to which it gives rise while giving very different answers!

Truth and Fiction

Creative writers have also attempted to imagine Bolden in their literary endeavors, and this kind of literary "improvisation" is arguably less straightforward. It dismantles what has become a virtual truism: words are referential and music is emotional (as Louis Armstrong famously quipped, "man, if you gotta ask, you'll never know"). Nonetheless, a range of authors have challenged this "truism" in their writings on jazz. How can words capture the sense of a musical experience, especially when the experience being evoked is as elusive, as mysterious, as Bolden's cornet playing? While some authors such as Marquis struggle to establish as accurate a "factual" account as possible of the historical "reality" and to set the record straight, others take, literally, a more imaginative approach. According to Ajay Heble, it is perfectly "possible for imaginative writers to reclaim the world of lived experience in ways largely uninventoried in so-called factual representations." Indeed, Heble explicitly cites Ondaatje's novel *Coming Through Slaughter* as a case in point. In this text Ondaatje asserts the "truth of fiction," suggesting, in effect, that his account may well be at least as faithful, and perhaps even more so, to the complexities of Bolden's life, art, and significance as any strict "documentary style" biographical representation could be.[71]

In his essay, "A Great Northward Darkness," George Bowering asks:

> Now how do you write the story of Storyville? How do you tell about jazz in the first place, and how do you tell about a legendary jazz trumpeter who could not write notes and who never went on record or made one? That is a very appealing problem for a postmodernist writer. How can you write a historical novel with no historical documents?[72]

This is an especially provocative question for Ondaatje who is obsessed with what he calls the "problem of history." As Heble has argued, although Ondaatje repeatedly engages with history by rewriting marginal historical characters into his fiction, he does not do so unselfconsciously. According to Heble, "Ondaatje seeks to reconstruct the past while simultaneously providing a commentary on the very process of writing in which he himself participates."[73] Thus, faced with barely enough "facts" about Bolden to fill one page of his book and working with information that Marquis dismisses as false in his account, Ondaatje invents—at the point where history and structure meet artistic "improvisation"—the rest. For Ondaatje, it is less important, less interesting, and arguably impossible to bring to life the mysterious Buddy Bolden than it is to explore the legend surrounding him through an examination of his effect on others. "History" for Ondaatje is less a product and more of a process. The power of Bolden lies in the way in which he has been passed down to us and variously constructed in the form of legend.

Like his version of Bolden who, when playing his cornet, "tore across the plot," Ondaatje jettisons conventional formal and generic expectations and writes a non-linear, multi-voiced account of the legendary first man of jazz in an attempt to foreground the constructed nature of historical accounting. As one of the first "poet-novelists" in Canada, Ondaatje is particularly conscious of generic boundaries and how they can be usefully transgressed. In his early long poems Ondaatje introduces his characteristic formal and generic experimentation by blurring the borders between fact and fiction and by layering various competing voices.[74] In *Coming Through Slaughter*, a text that George Bowering calls "a wild proliferation of genres,"[75] Ondaatje mixes quotations from the book *Jazz Masters* (changing words here and there), numerous testimonials from friends and family (both real and invented), documents and court proceedings from turn of the century Louisiana, the only existing photograph of Bolden and the band, and a healthy dose of imaginative reconstruction, to make use of the "border-blur" between fact and fiction.

By crossing these borders, *Coming Through Slaughter* reminds the reader that any act of constructing a life story is, as Donna Bennett suggests, "already an act of fiction making" because narratives of lives (autobiographies and biographies) "must confront both a surplus of information, which requires filtering, and information gaps, which mean that what has been lost needs filling in or what is untellable must be elided" (p. 203). Ondaatje works with gaps and absences throughout the text, playing off the mystery that was Bolden rather than trying to pin him down. As in many of his works, Ondaatje highlights the mysterious quality of the main character by making one of the central narrative voices in the text a detective or a searcher. Ondaatje uses the character of the detective to self-consciously draw attention to his own narrative act, his own "improvisation" of Buddy Bolden. Like Ondaatje,

"Webb circled, trying to understand not where Buddy was but what he was doing, quite capable of finding him but taking his time, taking almost two years, entering the character of Bolden through every voice he spoke to" (p. 60). Thus, among various voices in the text, shifts occur among the authorial voice (Ondaatje), the searcher (Webb) and Bolden himself.[76] These multiple shifts in the narrating "I" serve to further demonstrate Ondaatje's exploratory take on subjectivity, but also Bolden's own: "Webb had spoken to Bellocq and discovered nothing. Had spoken to Nora, Crawley, to Cornish, had met the children—Bernadine, Charlie. Their stories were like spokes on a rimless wheel ending in air. Buddy had lived a different life with every one of them" (p. 60).

Ondaatje's text repeatedly demonstrates how identity is never fixed, but is, rather, dialogic. As he reminds us, we continuously invent and reinvent ourselves through an improvisational process: our identity is in effect a series of constructions. This instability may be frustrating for a reader looking for some firmer seeming "truth" about Buddy Bolden, the specifics of his music, his significance in terms of a jazz tradition or even an "accurate" portrait of the complex social, historical, and institutional locations out of which New Orleans jazz emerged (in fact, at least one critic has chastised Ondaatje for not even once mentioning the word "race" in his "novel"). Instead, Ondaatje's text tends to reinforce Bolden's mythic status—passed down through gossip, tall tales, and hearsay, in other words, oral culture—undocumented, and thus largely unhistorical.

The text's focus on improvisation also allows Ondaatje to focus on one of his trademark concerns: the thin line between artistic genius and madness. A number of critics have written about Ondaatje's fascination with this tension in his writing and it is a tension, Ondaatje seems to imply, at the heart of Bolden's improvisational art.[77] Indeed, in *Coming Through Slaughter*, the story actually spins around like a great Bolden cornet solo as the book examines artistic creation as a flirtation with chaos, as constantly on the border between order and disorder. In the novel, Ondaatje has Frank Lewis' comment on this tension in Bolden's playing:

> There was no control except the mood of his power [...] and it is for that reason it is good you never heard him play on recording. If you never heard him play some place where the weather for instance could change the series of notes—then you should never have heard him at all. He was never recorded. He stayed even while others moved into history,

> electronic history, those who said later that Bolden broke the path. It was just as important to watch him stretch and wheel around on the last notes or to watch nerves jump under the sweat of his head. But there was discipline. We thought he was formless but I think now he was tormented by order, what was outside it [...] As it was, when he was playing he was lost and hunting for the right accidental notes [...] There was pain and gentleness everything jammed into each number (pp. 32–3)

In this section Ondaatje could just as easily be talking about his own poetic practice. The tension in his book, between facts from the historical record—the so-called "thin sheaf of information" (p. 135) and Ondaatje's leaps of imagination, his "improvisations"—mimics Bolden's own surprising and powerful playing. To further his point, Ondaatje contrasts Bolden's ability to hold in tension chaos and order with John Robichaux's insistence on order and patterns. Bolden asks:

> Did you ever meet Robichaux? I never did. I loathed everything he stood for. He dominated his audiences [...] When I played parades we would be going down Canal Street and at each intersection people would hear just the fragment. I happened to be playing and it would fade as I went further down Canal. They would not be there to hear the end of phrases, Robichaux's arches (p. 92).

Compare this to Ondaatje's description of his own creative process:

> I don't believe stories are told from A to Z anymore; or, if they are, they become very ponderous. I'm used to commercial breaks. We discover stories in a different way. I discover something about you after knowing you X number of years, and then after thirty years I will find out some other changes that occurred five years earlier. That sense of discovery, of memory, and how we reveal ourselves to each other—none of that is chronological.[78]

The fragmentary nature of Ondaatje's text and his rejection of what he has elsewhere referred to as the "steamroller of plot" echoes his evocation of Bolden's own improvisational style.

One of the most arresting moments in the book comes when Ondaatje's authorial voice identifies directly with Bolden: "When he went mad he was the same age as I am now. The photograph moves and becomes a mirror. When I read he stood in front of mirrors and attacked himself, there was the shock of memory. For I had done that" (p. 134). As in many of his other texts, Ondaatje identifies with the often tortured, always mysterious, main character.[79] Ondaatje, like his version of Bolden, recognizes that the need to break through certainties, to find new ways of thinking and being and seeing, is the very essence of creativity (see also, on this point, the Appendix to this essay).

Bolden's Song

What, then, of Buddy Bolden's own song, his voice, his music? We have seen that critics (such as Shipton, Jones, and Fairweather) have, with Ondaatje and other creative writers, all imagined Bolden's sound somewhat differently. As also noted, Bolden has been evoked by great jazz successors in their own works. There is, for example, Jelly Roll Morton's well known piece "I Thought I Heard Buddy Bolden Say" (Morton), and, somewhat later, Nina Simone sang Duke Ellington's song, entitled, "Yes, Buddy Bolden" on one of her early Colpix albums, *Nina Sings Duke Ellington* (Simone).[80] But it is worth turning to more recent musicians to find several who have sought, even more fully and self-consciously, to evoke Bolden in their playing, to most directly improvise the improviser in specifically musical terms (although that musical exercise does provide its own share of distinctive ambiguities and complexities). Thus, both Jerry Granelli, in the album *A Song I Thought I Heard Buddy Sing* (1993)[81] and Malachi Thompson, in his album *Buddy Bolden's Rag* (1995)[82] played, unequivocally, music of the 1990s. But they also affirmed, in their own liner notes and related commentaries, Bolden's centrality to "the tradition." Note, however, that they also "hear" him in quite diverse ways.

For Granelli, who actually reproduces passages from Ondaatje's novel in his liner notes (as he says, it was through reading Ondaatje that he "became possessed with Buddy Bolden and his life"), Bolden's music is to be invoked as being quintessentially "the blues." Indeed, he calls his disk "a 10-song tone poem and reflection about the blues and the life of one very tortured jazz pioneer" (Seligman). He succeeds, says one reviewer, in capturing, through the life of Bolden, the "fantastic spirit and turmoil of the birth of jazz,"[83] which is something he does, not by trying to have someone "double" for Bolden, but by featuring two guitarists (Robben Ford, a celebrated blues player and the estimable Bill Frisell, also an infinitely flexible and soulful player), and also two strong horn-men: Kenny Garrett on alto sax and Julian Priester on trombone.

The album as a whole is anchored by Granelli's bluesy premise, from the laid back loping recitation of Johnny Hodge's "Wanderlust," through a gay, if perhaps overly raucous, version of the "Oyster Dance" (as celebrated in Ondaatje's pages themselves), to an upbeat version, with welcoming guitar, bass and warm swinging drum work of Charlie

Parker's "Billie's Bounce." Then, in a second section ("Buddy's World"), we confront, with Granelli's own tune "Coming through Slaughter," a slow, probing, rather sad, blues-sax plus guitars and, towards the end, an eloquent trombone. Effective numbers like the upbeat "In That Number" (with firm echoes of "How I Want To Be In That Number") lead to a third section ("Memories") and several cuts in which a slower, more moody ambience prevail (including Jay Hawkins' "I Put A Spell On You"). His album's closing number is particularly eloquent: two versions of Ornette Coleman's "Blues Connotation" which segue from a loosely swinging bluesy vein in the first version, to a much slower and statelier, even appropriately funereal, second version, featuring first a most sober saxophone and then, once again, those mournful guitars.

For Thompson, who does feature trumpeters (his own, fellow members of his Brass Ensemble, and also the great Lester Bowie as powerful guest artist), we are given less Bolden the bluesman and more Bolden the muscular and assertive cornetist. For Thompson's "own investigations into the origin of jazz" have led him to see Bolden as primarily a "risk taker," one linked to ragtime but inclined to "buck tradition [...] by breaking away from the marching band and written music" and, as an improvisor, inclined "to embellish popular melodies, jack-up the tempo and rag the rhythm." Bolden found that, "playing with legendary force and power," his instrumental style very soon took "a definite shape," thereby ensuring that "jazz was born": "Thank you, Buddy," Thompson concludes his careful liner notes, "for your amazing gift."

"Jazz" from its origins has inspired in Thompson's mind, "the principles of freedom and equality, [and] a truly democratic art form," with Thompson, as a result, feeling fully justified in encouraging his group, in Buddy Bolden's name, to play late twentieth century avant-garde music, music which he takes to be fully in the liberated spirit, if not precisely in the style, of Bolden himself.[84] Thus, Thompson moves from a loose avant-brass band sound (on "Buddy Bolden's Rag"), several steps further out, to expressive, well-crafted cuts like "World View," "We Bop" and to "Kojo Time" and beyond, to "Harold the Great." Here, the leader himself assays steer horn, sekulu, and conch shells to pull the global referent even wider while underpinning the whole with insistent, imaginative beat and rhythm from diverse percussionists and with additional expressive horn accompaniments. Particularly notable is the manner in which Thompson and Bowie move from their beautiful extended atmospheric playing on "Nubian Call" to reach a high note in complementing each other's strikingly adventurous playing on the remarkably free "The Chaser in America."

Both albums, in what unites them as part of "the jazz project"—both historical and contemporaneous—but also in what distinguishes them from each other, remind us of just how much the language of jazz continues to be available for diverse projects of "talking back," of sustaining innovative efforts to resist racist oversimplification, mere commercialization, and even tiresome quasi-critical rhetoric. Instructively, both contemporary voices also speak, however speculatively, to the reality that was Buddy Bolden: Buddy as a superior instrumental bluesman, one nurtured by his fellow denizens of New Orleans, with their diverse musical experiments and traditions, and notably by the prevailing semi-rural vibe of his own ex-slave community, but also Buddy as a free and untamed instrumentalist, pointing forward, however notionally, to the marvels of Armstrong and the others (whom Thompson actually specifies in his notes). Here, in one sense, was history—oblique and ambiguous—just beginning, with jazz poised dramatically, with Buddy Bolden, on the doorstep of the very first century of its greatness.

The jazz tradition, it can be argued, is about the revising, not the canonizing, of its own "traditions" and even its texts. If so, the examples above, both literary and musical, suggest just how appropriate, and indeed almost inevitable, it is that Bolden himself be subject to the kind of invention and improvisation we have traced. For Bolden's rather shadowy person and performance, make him more available, in both song and story, for just such improvisation of person than many other equally noteworthy figures in the jazz canon. Moreover, it need come as no surprise if Bolden's legacy were also to continue to be reinvented in order, in Heble's words, to "serve the political needs of the moment"[85] and the interests of those authors, who, in their own ways, are attempting to "talk back" to power, to prejudice, and to willful abuse. Amidst the current rebuilding of a New Orleans (especially its Lower Ninth Ward and Lakeview districts) so recently broken by the ravages of Hurricane Katrina, we find a rebuilding that is, in the entirely appropriate phrasing of one of the reviewers of this essay, driven precisely by an attempted "bleaching and reconstruction of the city without those who made its early musical wealth possible." In the ongoing effort to resist any such post-Katrina "killing of New Orleans" (in Mike Davis' chilling phrase[86]) is it fanciful to think that we can hear, amongst many other things, the wail of Buddy Bolden's powerful cornet?

Appendix: A further note on Bolden in prose

If Ondaatje uses the silence around Bolden as a springboard for his "historiographic" and metafictional strategies and concerns, other writers have a less self-consciously artistic approach to the recreation of their subject. In his "faction" E.W. Russell attempts to capture the spirit of Storyville by playing on tired stereotypes of sexual depravity, demented killers, and venereal disease.[87] Following Wynton Marsalis' vision of New Orleans jazz as a kind of "gumbo" (a melting pot of all things musical), Russell suggests that jazz had to be born in New Orleans—with its whores, hot food, booze and general sinfulness—and that it couldn't have happened anywhere else. But, interestingly, his text is also cut through with the politics of "race," tracing the birth of Jazz back to slavery: "without fools [...] there would be no slavery (and, thus, no Buddy Bolden and Jelly Roll Morton and Louis Armstrong and Ma Rainey): which means there would have been no jazz." He implies that Bolden's voice is lost to history because he was black: "If he'd been White: he almost certainly would have been recorded even though he was confined. But Buddy Bolden was only a nigger. All he'd done was to create—help to create the most soulful music ever heard on earth: [...] Jazz is his monument and everyone alive who can hear—everyone with ears—owes him a debt of gratitude that can never be paid" (108).

What Russell's text at least acknowledges (in a way that Ondaatje's arguably does not) is the relationship between jazz and the politics of race, or "talking back" to white power, and reminds the reader, in Heble's words, that "[music's] meanings reside not in some understanding of the music itself, but rather in the broader social and institutional contexts (of production, distribution and reception) in which it takes place" ("Rebel" 236). Ray Bisso's "jazz poem," *Buddy Bolden of New Orleans*, is marked by rhythm and repetition and the sense that the author is trying to mimic in his writing the actual sound or at least the spirit of the sound of early jazz. In fact many of his stanzas sound like song lyrics (and he incorporates the lyrics of "Funky Butt Blues") and the short spare lines of his poetry maintain a rhythm throughout the text. Bisso evokes the music of Congo Square and the brass bands, the dance hall, the church, and Lincoln Park. By charting the growth of Bolden from an unknown to Kid Bolden to King Bolden and his slow, quiet demise, Bisso maps a geography of sound, always interested in how music becomes meaning: "Moving off the melody lead/Ragging new sounds/Taking the blues/And playing them loud/Copying the colors of/The voice blues/

Sliding/Slurring/Bending/Taking out of the horn/Words that were never spoke/Notes that were never wrote."[88]

---

c) On Watching ... and Playing

I grew up with sports, and I still watch and play them. Fairly expertly as a watcher, less so as a player, although it's true that as a kid, when I wasn't reading, I was out in the yard, throwing the basketball towards the net and backboard (built from scratch by my father), tangling on the street in ball hockey, scrimmaging with a football at Lytton Park, playing catch (throwing a ball, of one sort or another, here there and everywhere, including endlessly in summer up against our outdoor back stairs, filling in a scoring system all of my own, and much to the mounting annoyance of disgruntled neighbours).

And board sports too. An infinite variety (for the time!) of dice-driven baseball games, often invented but also, for example, the most old-fashioned of ice hockey games, the players merely bent metal pieces that you manipulated with a fierce pull that drove them all. Except for the goalie, a straight peg manipulated by your other hand. I could figure out ways to elaborately keep track of the scores and scoring statistics of these games too, playing, most often, with my brother, Bill.

There were sports to watch as well. We grew up with the old Toronto Maple Leafs of the International League, with, for example, Archie Wilson, Sam Jethroe, Lew Morton, Mike Goliat, "Little Jumbo" Vince Plumbo, Hector Rodriguez, Loren Babe, Bob Tiefenauer, Jack Crimian, Humberto Robinson and, for one glorious year, Elston Howard, on his way up to the bigs. But I could go on (stop me, somebody!). After all, the Leafs were the home team and they also had JoJo Crysdale and Hal Kelly going for them on CKEY, including those away games imagined in their detail and colour by Crysdale from the ticker-tape. I used to go regularly too, often driven down to Fleet Street by our neighbour, Ed, an ancient, tough looking but basically kind (and reasonably successful) ex-prospector—for gold in the north—who lived next door with his brother Bill (another ex-prospector) and sister. A real ball-fan, he'd leave me for his good seat and I'd head off to the 75 cent bleachers, and then, after sitting for a while near the familiar group who bet amongst themselves on virtually every pitch, I'd swing around the outside wall, high above the pavement, and onto the other side: the much less cheap seats.

And big league baseball games featured too, increasingly on television (when our family finally got one) and especially the World Series—though I could never figure out who I disliked least, the Yankees or the Dodgers (my brother's favourite), a daunting disability as these two often squared off against each other in the late 40s and early 50s—I remember, though, that my Dad and I watched with appropriate awe Don Larsen's perfect game in 1956. Me, I liked Willie Mays and the Giants (and was thrilled, via the radio, by Bobby Thompson's pennant-winning home run against the Dodgers in 1951!) and Nellie Fox and the White Sox. I followed hockey too, on the radio and TV, and went to OHL double-headers on Saturday afternoons featuring both St. Mikes and the Marlies (with the young George Armstong and Danny Lewicki). I even saw Jean Beliveau with the old Quebec Citadels when he and his team invaded the Gardens for a storied step on their way to the Memorial Cup. And I collected dozens of hockey pictures thanks to Bee-Hive Corn Syrup and Quaker Oats to go with all those bubble-gum cards of hockey and baseball players, now probably worth a fortune, that my mother merely tossed out when she moved and I was far away in Africa.

I still follow sports, of course, often heading off to the opening ballgame with my brother, for example. But Raptors basketball is my chief, continuing sports fixation. I saw George Mikan and the Lakers (with Jim Pollard, Vern Mikkelson, Slater Martin, Whitey Skoog and, of all the great names, Frank "Pep" Saul) play at Maple Gardens in my youth and have never been quite the same since. And I still watch a fair bit of basketball, having seen my son grow into a very formidable player indeed, captain of the Toronto Varsity Blues and an OUA all-star. And now one of my grandsons, playing at eight years of age on a team co-coached by my son, is embarking on a "career" of his own. And I have other grandchildren (who may or may not follow his example, of course).

But I myself have doggedly played diverse sports for years—lacrosse, water polo and, especially, basketball at Victoria College at the U of T, for example. And I have continued to play basketball ever after, with love and enjoyment if decreasing skill, as the following short piece will testify. However, this (heretofore unpublished) article has been, to date, my sole attempted foray into sports' reporting—despite decades of reading such reportage (I still turn to the sports' section of the morning paper first, I must confess). It's entitled "On not keeping score" and bears the sub-heading "Growing old on the hardcourt with friends: a lifelong learning experience":

I BEGAN MY BASKETBALL CAREER, about sixty years ago, as a kid in the basement gym at St. George's United Church in North Toronto, then played intermurally in high school and at the University of Toronto and even, occasionally, in grad school at Princeton. However, by now my greatest claim to hardwood fame was to have my carrel in the Firestone Library just a few stalls away from that of the legendary Bill Bradley, the varsity player (later of NBA and US Senate fame) who was Princeton's greatest contender ever for basketball immortality.

But my own career was far from over, as it turned out. I would go off to Tanzania to teach at the University there for seven years. And to become a member, in the late '60s and early '70s, of the faculty basketball team. We did pretty well, too, when, each year at the Annual Sports Day on campus, we tipped off against the university's own first team.

Truth to tell, though, our secret weapon (secret in more ways than one, as time would tell) was our centre, Steve Lucas, a big bull of a player forcefully dominant in the middle and under the boards. Much to the chagrin of the rest of us (although in line with our own rather vague suspicions), he was later revealed to have been a very busy CIA agent during his time in Dar es Salaam (and later elsewhere). One has to hope that our several victories in the annual game in Dar at least bear beside them an asterisk and footnote to this effect in the University records!

Still, it was also in those games, outdoors under the blazing sun, that I first made the acquaintance of an especially good friend, one with whom I still play almost forty years later: Jonathan Barker (himself an academic "Africanist" of note at the University of Toronto). For when we both returned to Toronto in the early 1970s we quickly slotted into a game, at the U of T's Graduate Student Union, comprised of diverse talents and including many members of the then Toronto Committee for the Liberation of Southern Africa (TCLSAC) with which we were both engaged in liberation support and anti-apartheid activity at the time.

It was a good game too, although over the years we evolved a few variations. Most important was our decision to cease to keep a cumulative score. I, for one, found the conventions of games based on formal score-keeping to be quite negative. Certainly, they made me more chippy and aggressive and more centred on the score itself than I liked. But the impact on the game as a whole was also negative in terms of sheer enjoyment.

Previously, for example, there would be a powerful incentive to get the ball to the top player rather than share it and to rely on him (occasionally her: from time to time we had some women in the game too) to snatch victory. Now, to be sure, each point is contested competitively, but only to a joint and combined total of seven baskets, when substitutions—if overall numbers warrant it—take place. Otherwise the game merely rolls on spiritedly.

True, my own high point did come in a more overtly competitive context. For a number of years we had made our way to London during the Christmas break for an exemplary old-timers tournament. But in the course of several tournaments we had never won even one game. All this changed about a decade ago, however. We did lose our first game that year, but it also happened that I myself was undercut while shooting and sustained a broken foot. There was nothing for it but for me to become coach, something we had never had up to that point.

I did the job as officiously as I could, carefully plotting substitutions and the like throughout our second contest. Comes the final moments and we're still in the game, but now, down but a couple of points and with time running out, only a long-range three-pointer could win it for us. It was our ball out on the side. I called a time-out and drew up a play. Pretty simple, really, I said: get it to Steve Price, our best three-point shooter, and let him take one last desperation shot. We ran the play exactly as we had drawn it up. Steve shot and scored...and we won. Jubilation abounded, at least in our OWN elderly ranks. Indeed, we were so elated that we went on the next day to win our final game as well. Me, I retired from coaching with a perfect record: 2-0, lifetime.

Meanwhile, our own game in Toronto has shifted venues and seen a turnover of players, young and old, over the years—though Jonathan and I remain regular participants. Indeed, when several years ago I suffered a near fatal accident (albeit well away from the court!), Jonathan thoughtfully kept up a steady flow of e-mail reports on my evolving condition to our fellow players and to many others besides. And I did eventually make it back to the court, not shooting as consistently as I like to think I had once done, but agile enough, by and large, to keep up with the game.

When I first started back, I was afraid I might destroy the rhythm of the game, with my fellow players behaving far too deferentially towards me and my condition. However, I was pleased to find that the game was sufficiently competitive (despite the absence of score-keeping!) that I need not have worried. My fellow players remained friendly and supportive but, after about five minutes, were as intense and basket-focussed as ever. In short, I had to earn my court-time through hard-work and tough defense.

But I'm just reaching seventy. Time to move on and hang up the sneakers? I'm not quite sure: as you can tell I just might miss the game, and the camaraderie, too much. As for that seventieth birthday: who, after all, is keeping score?

Well, perhaps I myself was, after all. Come the big seven-oh and a birthday celebration attended by, among others, many of these players (and also a gang of old TCLSAC comrades) and very soon, at my son's advice (he's a great b-ball player himself and I had to listen), I did finally hang up my jockstrap and my tee-shirt. As I wrote in e-mailing my b-ball mates to announce my passing from the game: "I'm trying to make do on the walking machine but its not the same: I'm learning, with difficulty, how to play tough 'D' against a treadmill!" Indeed, I'm still struggling with the challenge of a now entirely self-conscious and self-inflicted exercise regimen. Of course, I loved basketball for the comradeship and for the challenge of the game itself, but, I must confess, I also valued the way it encouraged one to sweat and strain more or less by inadvertence. In contrast, exercising in cold blood demands rather more self-willed discomfort! Still, what more could I say—in the words with which I concluded my "retirement" e-mail—but: "I love you guys, and wish all of you health, happiness... and hoops everlasting."

---

1. As noted in chapter 1 above, see, for some reflections on my Atkinson experience, my chapter, entitled "Thanks for the Memory" in Brenda Spotton Visano and Kristen Taylor (eds.), *Room to Grow: Celebrating Atkinson's Living Legacy* (Toronto: York University, 2009).
2. Arrighi was to die in 2009 and I was both to memorialize him and to reflect further on our diverging positions both on Africa and more generally in an

article, "Arrighi and Africa: Farewell Thoughts," published in the *Review of African Political Economy* in December of that year.

3. For my own thoughts on Slovo's passing see my "Joe Slovo: Words and Deeds," *Southern Africa Report,* 10, 3 (March, 1995); see also Ighsaan Schroeder, "The Renegade Slovo," *SAR/WIP,* July, 1994.
4. Colin Leys, "The World, Society and the Individual," *Southern Africa Report,* 11, 3 (April, 1996), p. 17.
5. Jeffrey C. Alexander, "Modern, Anti, Post, Neo," *New Left Review,* #210 (March-April, 1995).
6. See Colin Leys and John S. Saul, "Dependency," being chapter 1 of John S. Saul, *Development After Globalization: Theory and Practice for an Embattled South in a New Imperial Age* (Delhi, London and Durban: Three Essays Collective, Zed Books Limited and the University of KwaZulu/Natal Press, 2006).
7. On "structural reform" see the essays "South Africa: Between Barbarism and Structural Reform," and "Structural Reform: A Model for the Revolutionary Transformation of South Africa?" in my *Recolonization and Resistance: Southern Africa in the 1990s* (Trenton, N.J. and Toronto: Africa World Press and Between the Lines, 1993). As I have noted, this approach was to be found as often as not *outside* and well beyond the far more conservative inner circles of the ANC: in various sectors of the trade union and community-based movements, for example.
8. For a further examination of the imperatives of agency, site and imaginary in both conceiving and mounting successful revolutionary struggle, see the essay "Globalization, Imperialism, Development: False Binaries and Radical Resolutions" in my *Development After Globalization* (*op. cit*).
9. See Jonathan Barker, "Debating Globalization: Critique of Colin Leys" (together with Leys' own reply to Barker), *Southern Africa Report,* 12, 4 (September, 1997), which is a critique of Leys on globalization as quoted above (in this chapter). But see also Veronica Schild's "Their Hegemony or Ours: Schild Replies to Barker," in SAR, 13, 4 (August, 1998), for a (to my mind) convincing critique of Barker's position.
10. Perry Anderson, *Zones of Engagement* (London: Verso, 1992), pp. 366-7.
11. Ralph Miliband, *Socialism for a Sceptical Age* (London: Verso, 1995).
12. See *Development After Globalization (op. cit.)* and *Decolonization and Empire: Contesting the Rhetoric and Practice of Resubordination in Southern Africa and Beyond* (Delhi, London and Johannesburg: Three Essays Collective, Merlin Press, and University of Witwatersrand Press, 2007).
13. Paul Nugent, *Africa since Independence* (Houndmills, UK: Palgrave,2004)
14. Compare Arrighi writing in Arrighi and John S. Saul, "Socialism and Economic Development in Tropical Africa," being the first chapter of Arrighi and Saul, *Essays on the Political Economy of Africa* (New York: Monthly Review Press, 1973) to Arrighi, "The African Crisis," *New Left Review,* 15 (May/June, 2002), pp. 5-36.
15. Thus Arrighi (in his "World Income Inequalities and the Future of Socialism," *New Left Review,* 189 (September-October, 1991), pp. 39-65, pp 57-8) argued that "the standards of wealth enjoyed by the West correspond to what Roy Harrod once defined as 'oligarchic wealth' in opposition to 'democratic wealth,'" these two worlds being separated by an "unbridgeable gulf."

16. G. Arrighi, B.J. Silver and B.D. Brewer, "Industrial Convergence, Globalization and the Persistence of the North-South Divide," *Studies in Comparative Industrial Development*, 38, 1 (Spring, 2003), pp 3-27.
17. Of course, Arrighi and his co-authors Silver and Brewer, acknowledge that China contains "enormous inequalities within" its own borders. But I have also heard Arrighi in seminar-settings evoke—without too much supporting evidence, unfortunately—the "Bandung spirit" of "Third World" solidarity as a possible point of reference for China's present and future global policy!
18. Terminology fails me here, for if China's economic base and social formation represent something pretty close to capitalism it is (unfortunately for Africa) not "capitalism with a human face" but rather capitalism with a Stalinist face—and a formidably imperialist bent. As David Seddon notes in a recent article (Seddon, "China: Africa's New Business Partner" in the *Review of African Political Economy* (December, 2006), pp. 747-749) "China certainly is already making profitable inroad in the subcontinent. One can only hope that Africa's own development potential is not simply swept aside in the process as the Asian giant reached out for new opportunities with positively imperialist ambitions (749)." A pretty faint hope, one fears.
19. Still by far the best and entirely apposite evocation of this reality remains Frantz Fanon's *The Wretched of the Earth* (Harmondsworth: Penguin, 1969) specifically his ch. 3, "The Pitfalls of National Consciousness."
20. Norrie MacQueen, *The Decolonization of Portuguese Africa: Metropolitan Revolution and the Dissolution of Empire* (Harlow: Longman, 1997), pp. 235-6.
21. See Saul, *The Next Liberation Struggle* (*op. cit.*) and Saul, "The Strange Death of Liberated Southern Africa" in Saul, *Decolonization and Empire* (op. cit.)
22. This is, of course, not true of the more proto-revolutionary anti-IMF riots, a more potentially meaningful kind of "chaos" of a kind not much discussed by Nugent and one that has threatened, from time to time, to bring governments down.
23. See, inter alia, Jonathan Barker *et al.* (1999), *Street-Level Democracy: Political Settings at the Margins of Global Power* (Toronto: Between the Lines, 1999); Patrick Bond, *Looting Africa: The Economics of Exploitation* (Pietermaritzburg and London: University of KwaZulu-Natal Press and Zed Books, 2006), especially chapter 7, "Civil Society Resistance: Two Views;" Leo Zeilig (ed.), *Class Struggle and Resistance in Africa* (Cheltenham: New Clarion Press, 2002); and Trevor Ngwane, "Revolt Against the ANC/ Sparks in the Township," *New Left Review* 22 (July-August, 2002), pp 37-56.
24. In addition to the present text, they are: (1) *South Africa: The Present as History* (under contract with James Currey Publishers; (2) *Southern African Liberation: A History* (under contract with Cambridge University Press); and (3) *Anti-Apartheid and Liberation Support: Southern Africa, Canada and the World* (under contract with Arbeiter Ring).
25. As exemplified, most clearly, in two of my most recent books, *Development After Globalization* (*op. cit.*), "Introduction", and *Empire and Decolonization* (*op. cit.*).
26. Here again I would cite my article, co-authored with Colin Leys, and entitled "Dependency." It appears in both D.A. Clark (ed.), *The Elgar Companion to Development Studies* (Cheltenham, U.K.: Edward Elgar, 2006) and my *Development After Globalization* (*op. cit.*). The present essay represents a synthesis of my present thinking on the development question and for that reason I draw on and cite my own most recent work extensively here.

27. See Richard Kozul-Wright and Paul Rayment, *The Resistible Rise of Market Fundamentalism: The Struggle for Economic Development in a Global Economy* (London: Zed Press, forthcoming); I quote from a pre-publication notification sent by the publisher (n.p.).
28. Giovanni Arrighi, "World Income Inequalities and the Future of Socialism," *New Left Review*, 189 (September-October, 1991).
29. See again Giovanni Arrighi, Beverley J. Silver and Benjamin D. Brewer, "Industrial Convergence, Globalization and the Persistence of the North-South Divide," *Studies in Comparative Industrial Development*, 38, 1 (Spring, 2003).
30. In these paragraphs I draw on the formulations first presented by Colin Leys and myself in "Sub-Saharan Africa in Global Capitalism," this now being chapter 1 in John S. Saul, *The Next Liberation Struggle: Capitalism, Socialism and Democracy in Southern Africa* (Toronto, New York, London and Durban: Between the Lines, Monthly Review Press, Merlin Press and University of KwaZulu/Natal Press, 2005), p. 21.
31. Leslie Sklair, *The Transnational Capitalist Class* (Oxford: Blackwell, 2001).
32. In this paragraph and the preceding one I draw on the "Introduction" to my *Empire and Decolonization* (*op. cit.*).
33. See my "'Humanitarian Imperialism': Ferguson, Ignatieff and the Political Science of Good Empire," being ch 3 of *Empire and Decolonization* (*ibid.*).
34. These quotations from Ferguson (along with similarly outrageous ones from many others, including, not least, Canadian politician and much-published author Michael Ignatieff) are to be found in my "Humanitarian Imperialism" (ibid.).
35. As quoted in John S. Saul, "On War and Peace in Africa: the Mozambican Case," being ch. 4 in my *The Next Liberation Struggle* (*op. cit.*).
36. Samir Amin, *A Life Looking Forward* (London: Zed Press, 2006), pp. 179-80.
37. Paul Nugent, *Africa Since Independence* (Houndmills, UK: Palgrave, 2004). [I drew briefly in this paragraph on my own text, the extended review-article on Nugent's book included in the present chapter, above.]
38. Samir Amin, Delinking: *Towards a Polycentric World* (London: Zed Books, 1985), *Maldevelopment: Anatomy of a Global Failure* (Tokyo and London: United Nations University and Zed Press, 1990), and *Re-Reading the Postwar Period: An Intellectual Itinerary* (New York: Monthly Review Press, 1994), pp. 165-8 and 227.
39. Amin, *Re-Reading the Postwar Period* (*ibid.*), pp. 165-8 and 227.
40. Clive Thomas, *Dependence and Transformation: The Economics of the Transition to Socialism* (New York: Monthly Review Press, 1974), p. 250.
41. This formulation regarding the possible structure of a "socialism of expanded reproduction" appears in my "Introduction" to John S. Saul (ed.), *A Difficult Road: The Transition to Socialism in Mozambique* (New York: Monthly Review Press, 1985).
42. Ken Post and P. Wright, *Socialism and Underdevelopment* (London and New York: Routledge, 1989), pp. 151-2.
43. See my "Identifying Class, Classifying Difference," being chapter 3 of my *Development After Globalization* (*op. cit.*).
44. As argued at length in "Identifying Class, Classifying Difference," (ibid.).
45. In this section, and in this paragraph in particular (including my citations of Leys), I have drawn on my essay "Regrounding Resistance to the Empire of Capital," being ch. 4

of my *Decolonization and Empire* (op. cit.) where the possible ramifications of the issues raised here are discussed more extensively.

46. Bertholt Brecht, "To Posterity" (as translated from German by H. R. Hays in *Bertholt Brecht, Selected Poems* [New York: Grove Press, 1959]).
47. From Jan Myrdal, *Confessions of a Disloyal European* (New York: Vintage, 1969), pp. 98-102; as noted, I have also included this entire passage in an appendix to a chapter in my *Decolonization and Empire* (Delhi, London and Johannesburg: Three Essays Collective, Merlin Press and the University of Witwatersrand Press, 2007), pp. 111-113, a chapter in which I am sharply critical of, amongst others, Micheal Ignatieff and of our country's own recent Afghanistan policies.
48. See Carter's essay "Ishmael Reed's Neo-Hoodoo Detection" in Larry L. Landrum, Pat Browne and Ray B. Browne (eds.) *Dimensions of Detective Fiction* (Popular Press, 1976).
49. It's worth noting in passing that Humphrey Bogart himself puts in an appearance in *Hollywood and Levine*!
50. Some readers, unfamiliar with the canons of literary criticism, may need to be reminded that 'anti-imperialism' and 'anti-Americanism' are not the same thing, least of all in the case of MacKenzie Dawson whose reverence for the achievements of Hammett, Chandler, Parker and other American giants in his chosen field is apparent on every page of his novel.
51. A recent Sid Adilman entertainment-column in the *Toronto Star* has revealed the unfortunate fact that the effort of one Canadian playwright of left nationalist persuasion to bring an adaptation of Dawson's novel to the nation's television screens has been sat on, for reasons best known to themselves, by the CBC brass. Back, they would seem to be saying, to Starsky and Hutch!
52. As the editor's note at the beginning of the original publication in *Canadian Dimension* of the piece that follows stated: "John Saul's own best shot at a 'political thriller' was 'A Flag for a Shroud' in *This Magazine*'s March, 1978 issue [see above], a text regarded by his friend Rick Salutin as "a classic.'"
53. Mahan cites Hammett's *Red Harvest* as one book in which "the possibility of real political reform is considered" and certainly agrees that "The hard-boiled detective is often forced to confront the corruption of the society, the fallenness of the world." And yet, "with rare exceptions," he writes, "the result of confrontation is not social change but confirmation, or salvation, of the moral character of the individual."
54. It is worth also noting here that improvisation may be found in science, but we are thinking, beyond jazz, especially of visual art here, and of abstract painting in particular.
55. Ajay Heble, *Landing on the Wrong Note* (New York: Routledge, 2000), p. 91.
56. Linda Hutcheon, as quoted in Heble, Ajay, *Landing on the Wrong Note* (*ibid.*), p. 209.
57. See inter alia, Alyn Shipton, *A New History of Jazz* (New York: Continuum International, 2001), chapter 2.
58. On these and related themes see David Ake, *Jazz Cultures* (Berkeley and LA: U of California Press, 2002), 10-41.
59. These words are taken from the "Call for Papers" of the 2005 Guelph Jazz Festival Colloquium for which this essay was originally written.
60. See Leroi Jones (Amiri Baraka), *Blues People* (New York: William Morrow, 1963), pp. 78-9.
61. *Ibid.*

62. True, as Alyn Shipton notes in his *A New History of Jazz* (*op. cit.*), since Bolden's "career emerges into a hazy light only occasionally from the tangential and patchy [written] records of the period" the assignment to him of "the word 'legendary' is used advisedly"; moreover, as Shipton also states (p. 84) "his life is the first of many examples in jazz history where folklore and the sharing of stories among jazz musicians have become larger than the truth, as the Chinese whispers of time have exaggerated and distorted the original tale."

63. Shipton, (*ibid.*), pp. 82, 84.

64. Jones (*op. cit.*), p. 145

65. Digby Fairweather, "Buddy Bolden," an entry in Ian Carr, Digby Fairweather and Brian Priestley (eds.), *Jazz: The Rough Guide* (London: The Rough Guides, 2000), p. 80

66. Paul Berliner, *Thinking in Jazz: The Infinite Art of Improvisatio*n (Chicago: The University of Chicago Press, 1994), p. 491.

67. Fairweather, p. 80. As an example, Jelly Roll Morton states, probably accurately, that he had the chance to actually hear Bolden play; however he also claims, rather hyperbolically, to have listened to Buddy's cornet playing from a distance of ten or twelve miles away, all the way from Lincoln Park to his own street!

68. In addition to the findings of Don Marquis (op. cit.), see Danny Barker's *Buddy Bolden and the Last Days of Storyville* (New York: Continuum International, 1998) for another carefully researched, if also occasionally itself somewhat fanciful, account.

69. As quoted in Eleanor Wachtel, "An Interview with Michael Ondaatje," in *Essays on Canadian Writing* (Summer 1994), p. 258.

70. Monson, Ingrid, *Saying Something: Jazz Improvisation and Interaction* (Chicago: University of Chicago Press, 1996), p. 97.

71. In his autobiography *Running in the Family* (Toronto: McClelland and Stewart, 1982) Ondaatje defends the "fictional air" of the text by reminding the reader that "in Sri Lanka a well-told lie is worth a thousand facts" (p. 176).

72. Bowering, George, "A Great Northward Darkness" in *Imaginary Hand: Essays by George Bowering* (Edmonton: NeWest, 1988), p. 8.

73. Ajay Heble, "Michael Ondaatje and the Problem of History," in *Clio* 19, 2 (1990), pp. 107 and 96.

74. A number of critics have written about the role of generic experimentation in Ondaatje's works. Manina Jones, for example, calls Ondaatje's work an example of "documentary collage" (in her *The Art of Difference: "Documentary-Collage" and English-Canadian Writing* [Toronto: U of Toronto Press, 1993]), Linda Hutcheon sees his writing as exemplary of "historiographic metafiction" (in her *The Canadian Postmodern* [Toronto: Oxford UP, 1988]), and Joanne Saul sees much of his work as "biotextual" (in her *Writing the Roaming Subject: The Biotext in Canadian Literature* [Toronto: U of Toronto Press, 2006]).

75. George Bowering, "Once Upon a Time in the South: Ondaatje and Genre," in Jean-Michel Lacroix (ed.), *Re-Constructing the Fragments of Michael Ondaatje's Works* (Paris: Presse de la Sorbonne Nouvelle), p. 35.

76. For further analysis of the various narrative viewpoints in *Coming Through Slaughter*, see Monica Turci, *Approaching That Perfect Edge* (Bologna: Patron Editore, 2001).

77. See, in particular, Sam Solecki's article "Making and Destroying: Michael Ondaatje's Coming Through Slaughter and Extremist Art" in *Essays on Canadian Writing* 12 (1978), 24-47.

78. Eleanor Wachtel, *op. cit.*

79. In *The Collected Poems of Billy the Kid* Ondaatje includes a photograph of himself as a young Ceylonese kid in cowboy gear as a way of suggesting a connection between the author and his subject. Of course, Ondaatje's most self-conscious identification with the narrating subject occurs in his autobiography *Running in the Family.*

80. We also have the "New Orleans" music, notably in the 1940s, of Bunk Johnson, although we also know, thanks again to Donald Marquis, that, however good was Johnson's music, his accounts of his own direct contact with Bolden were grossly misstated.

81. Jerry Granelli, *A Song I Thought I Heard Buddy Sing* (ITMP CD 970066, 1993).

82. Malachi Thompson and Africa Brass, *Buddy Bolden's Rag: 100 Years of Jazz,* including Thompson's own powerful liner notes (Chicago: Delmark Records CD, 1995).

83. Barry Kernfeld, "Jerry Granelli: A Song I Heard Buddy Bolden Sing," in Kernfield (ed.), *The Blackwell Guide to Recorded Jazz,* Second Edition. (Oxford: Blackwell Publishers Inc., 1995), pp. 532-4.

84. Of course, the likes of Lester Bowie, specifically recruited by Thompson for the project, needs no special encouragement to do just that, but it is also the spirit in which the group as a whole is encouraged by Thompson to play. As a result, as Alex Henderson has characterized the album in his "5-star" *All Music Guide to Jazz* review (Fourth Edition as edited by Vladimir Bogdanov, Chris Woodstra and Stephen Thomas Erlewine [San Francisco: Backbeat Books, 2002]. pp. 1240-1), Thompson and company "salute Bolden in an unconventional way: instead of playing traditional New Orleans jazz, they provide inside/outside post-bop that acknowledges Crescent City brass bands as well as avant-garde and AACM jazz." As Henderson concludes his commentary, "Thompson looks back on jazz's early history, but does so without being the least bit dogmatic about it, and the result is a very entertaining and unpredictable LP"—much like Bolden's music itself, Thompson would have us believe.

85. Ajay Heble, *Landing on the Wrong Note* (*op. cit.*), p. 116.

86. See Mike Davis, "Who is Killing New Orleans?" in *The Nation,* April 10, 2006 (pp. 11-20); see also two special issues of *Downbeat,* one entitled "We Will Swing Again" (2005) and another "New Orleans Roots" (2006), both of which contain a range of useful and evocative articles and Peter Vacher, "New Orleans Now" (*Coda* 328, 2006) p. 8.

87. E.W. Russell, *Buddy Bolden Says* (Redwood, N.Y.: Cadence Books, 2000).

88. Ray Bisso, *Buddy Bolden of New Orleans: A Jazz Poem* (California: Fithian Press, 2000), p. 38.

CONCLUSION

On Living

More than a written…?

> I don't want to be misunderstood. Intellectuals are not required to be humourless complainers. Nothing less could be true of such celebrated and energetic dissenters as Noam Chomsky and Gore Vidal. Witnessing a sorry state of affairs when one is not in power is by no means a monotonous, monochromatic activity. It involves what Foucault once called "a relentless erudition," scouring alternative sources, exhuming buried documents, reviving forgotten (or abandoned) histories. It involves a sense of the dramatic and the insurgent, making a great deal of one's rare opportunities to speak, catching the audience's attention, being better at wit and debate than one's opponents. And there is something fundamentally unsettling about intellectuals who have neither offices to protect nor territory to consolidate and guard; self irony is therefore more frequent than pomposity, directness more than hemming and hawing. But there is no dodging the inescapable reality that such representations by intellectuals will neither make them friends in high places nor win them official honours. It is a lonely condition, yes, but it is always a better one than a gregarious tolerance for the way things are.[1]
>
> *Edward Said*

There is the point in any writing of a memoir (even a "quasi-memoir"), I suspect, when one fears, more than anywhere else in the manuscript, the distinct risk of pretentiousness creeping in. For me, now is that moment when, at the end of such a text, one is tempted to reflect on life and on loved ones (on those that make a life of "dissent" less lonely than it might otherwise have been) and on the meaning of it all. But fear not, gentle reader, I'll try to spare you too much of a bad thing (at least as it might come from my own all too a-literary, a-philosophical fingers-on-the-computer-keys). In any case, much of the resonance with which I have sought to invest my life will already be apparent in the materials assembled above: an attempt to find meaning in a struggle, with others, to realize a more just and equitable social order, one that strikes against capitalist globalization and white and male arrogance, and stands up for socialist outcomes more open and democratic than any that have been attempted to date. And to find meaning, as well, in a range of other social endeavours (writing, reading, listening, playing) that "elevate the human condition," as they say.

I've certainly stumbled personally, though, when most needed, I have sought with the unfailing help of others to recover my sense of self and to fly straighter and truer than I did before. I have also stumbled physically, as when I fainted, owing to an under-functioning heart, and pitched face first with a resounding crash of my head (so I was later informed) on to a board-hard deck at my home. The result: a month unconscious with a severe brain injury at Western Hospital in Toronto and a long slow comeback to sentience, to a modicum of articulate intelligence, and, even, finally, onto the basketball court. But, of course, the real weight of my misstep fell upon my immediate family as they waited, first, for the news of my death and, later, as they accompanied me—as did my brother, my two sisters-in-law, and a wealth of friends —on the long, slow journey back to health. I learned a lot from it too, while often thinking of Woody Allen's great and entirely appropriate joke about learning that accompanied me throughout the journey. As he and his friend stand contemplating a sea of their fallen Russian comrades, victims of Napoleon's invading army, while preparing themselves to do battle, his friend intones: "God is testing us." Woody's character's immediate, heartfelt reply: "If he's going to test us couldn't he have given us a written?" A good question but, as it happens, I'm not certain I could really have learned the lessons I needed to learn from this and several other of life's missteps any other way.

Life has taught me, then, how I might seek, if the conditions are right and support available, to fight back to physical stability, to self-respect and to a sense of self worth. Not easily, of course, but more than worth the effort, if the opportunity to try for it is there for you. Life can then seem good and, for me, all the better when I listen to Jane Ira Bloom or Marty Ehrlich, Dave Douglas, Myra Melford or David Murray, on my CD player; read a new Richard Ford or Ian Rankin novel; play a vigourous game of basketball; watch my grandson doing the same (or my granddaughter at her swimming class); go up to Stratford for a play or down to the COC for an opera performance. Or enjoy the multiple pleasures of my family.[2]

Less satisfactory have been the outcomes of the various struggles I've aligned myself with over the years, in Canada of course but also in southern Africa—the "strange death" of whose liberation I have alluded to above. If anything, in southern Africa and elsewhere, "the Empire of Capital" seems triumphant—or, if sometimes effectively challenged and stalemated, this is done, more often than not, in the name of the equally noxious brand of self-righteousness driven by certain forms of religious or ethnic bile. No, instead, I will go to my grave with the thought that human beings are capable of imagining and finding ways to realize societies not based on greed and self-interest as capitalist societies are; nor on the arrogant high-handedness that has characterized virtually all "socialist" societies heretofore; nor on the kind of narrow and sectarian hatreds that move the Osama bin Ladens of our time.

Wake up and smell the coffee, some might say. You refuse, stubbornly and stupidly, to face up to that old devil human nature, so I'm told. Perhaps, but we'll just have to see—though, chances are, I won't be around so much longer that I can really hope to experience as big and humane a change in the premises of social order, both global and local, as I would like. So perhaps I'm merely stuck for my own duration with a depressing variant of an old progressive saw: "Dare to struggle, dare to whine." Nonetheless, the various freeze-frames of my life, some of which I've shared in these pages, have given me many a glimpse of something better, something finer, something worth struggling for—and a glimpse too of people, of comrades and friends on various continents, who seek to so struggle and with whom, in addition, it has been a privilege to "travel." Perhaps, then, I'm not wrong to imagine the reinstating of a more positive scanning of the old saw alluded to above. It is a meaning that my grandchildren, if not my children, may live to see realized concretely in ever more resonant and meaningful ways: "Dare to struggle, dare to win." To win: for that outcome—a victory for freedom, equality, justice, and a genuine socialism that is by definition also profoundly democratic—the struggle will surely continue.

---

1. Edward Said, *Representations of the Intellectual* (New York: Pantheon Books, 1994), p. xvii.
2. Let me then, if only in a final footnote, make somewhat more substantive reference to my family: my wife Pat—whom I love, admire and respect so much—and my two kids, a son and a daughter. My daughter Jo I've already brought on stage, as my co-author (and occupational therapist!) in our work together on Buddy Bolden, but she has been a sometime professor at the University of Toronto, an author (of *Writing the Roaming Subject*, a very good book indeed), co-owner of a wonderful bookstore, TYPE, in downtown Toronto and parent, with her husband Dave, of two wonderful grandchildren, Clare and Charlie whom I adore. But no more so than my other two grandchildren, Ben and Quinn, the offspring of my son, Nick and his wife, a published author herself, Andi. Nick I've introduced too, though only as an excellent basketball-player of accomplishments far beyond my own. In fact, he also did his MA in England on a Commonwealth Scholarship and has been the highly effective head of the Stop Community Food Centre that has moved, during his tenure, beyond its original remit as a "Food Bank" to take an increasingly impressive range of community initiatives in West Toronto. He has also most recently been named the winner of the well-named Jane Jacobs Award, one that honours exemplary community activism.

INDEX

D

E

T

T

Y

Z